Making a Living
from Your

Business

Second Edition

Michael Miller

 800 East 96th Street,
Indianapolis, Indiana 46240

Making a Living from Your eBay Business

Copyright © 2007 by Que Publishing

International Standard Book Number: 0-7897-3646-2

Library of Congress Catalog Card Number: 2004116490

Printed in the United States of America

First Printing: October 2006

09   08   07   06   4   3   2

Trademarks

All terms mentioned in this book that are known to be trademarks or service marks have been appropriately capitalized. Que cannot attest to the accuracy of this information. Use of a term in this book should not be regarded as affecting the validity of any trademark or service mark.

Warning and Disclaimer

Every effort has been made to make this book as complete and as accurate as possible, but no warranty or fitness is implied. The information provided is on an "as is" basis. The author and the publisher shall have neither liability nor responsibility to any person or entity with respect to any loss or damages arising from the information contained in this book.

Portions of this book were previously published in *Absolute Beginner's Guide to Launching an eBay Business*.

Bulk Sales

Que Publishing offers excellent discounts on this book when ordered in quantity for bulk purchases or special sales. For more information, please contact

U.S. Corporate and Government Sales
1-800-382-3419
corpsales@pearsontechgroup.com

For sales outside of the U.S., please contact

International Sales
international@pearsoned.com

Safari
BOOKS ONLINE
ENABLED

This Book Is Safari Enabled

The Safari® Enabled icon on the cover of your favorite technology book means the book is available through Safari Bookshelf. When you buy this book, you get free access to the online edition for 45 days.

Safari Bookshelf is an electronic reference library that lets you easily search thousands of technical books, find code samples, download chapters, and access technical information whenever and wherever you need it.

To gain 45-day Safari Enabled access to this book:

- Go to http://www.quepublishing.com/safarienabled
- Complete the brief registration form
- Enter the coupon code WHKT-QHKJ-TEVG-C3JP-ZY5V

If you have difficulty registering on Safari Bookshelf or accessing the online edition, please e-mail customer-service@safaribooksonline.com.

Associate Publisher
Greg Wiegand

Acquisitions Editor
Michelle Newcomb

Development Editor
Kevin Howard

Managing Editor
Patrick Kanouse

Team Coordinator
Cindy Teeters

Project Editor
Seth Kerney

Indexer
Ken Johnson

Technical Editor
Jenna Lloyd

Designer
Ann Jones

Page Layout
Bronkella Publishing LLC

Contents at a Glance

Table of Contents

Part 2:   Choosing a Business Model

About the Author

Michael Miller is a top eBay seller and a successful and prolific author. He has a reputation for practical, real-world advice and an unerring empathy for the needs of his readers.

Mr. Miller has written more than 75 nonfiction books in the past 17 years for Que and other major publishers. His books for Que include *Absolute Beginner's Guide to eBay, Easy eBay, Tricks of the eBay Masters, eBay Auction Templates Starter Kit,* and *Absolute Beginner's Guide to Computer Basics.* He is known for his casual, easy-to-read writing style and his ability to explain a wide variety of complex topics to an everyday audience.

You can email Mr. Miller directly at ebay-business@molehillgroup.com. His website is located at www.molehillgroup.com.

Dedication

This book is dedicated to Sherry, because I want to.

Acknowledgments

Thanks to the usual suspects at Que, including but not limited to Greg Wiegand, Michelle Newcomb, Kevin Howard, and Seth Kerney. Also thanks to the book's technical editor, Jenna Lloyd, a successful eBay businessperson in her own right.

Tell Us What You Think!

As the reader of this book, *you* are our most important critic and commentator. We value your opinion and want to know what we're doing right, what we could do better, what areas you'd like to see us publish in, and any other words of wisdom you're willing to pass our way.

As an associate publisher for Que, I welcome your comments. You can fax, email, or write me directly to let me know what you did or didn't like about this book—as well as what we can do to make our books stronger.

Please note that I cannot help you with technical problems related to the topic of this book, and that due to the high volume of mail I receive, I might not be able to reply to every message.

When you write, please be sure to include this book's title and author as well as your name and phone or fax number. I will carefully review your comments and share them with the author and editors who worked on the book.

Email: feedback@quepublishing.com

Mail: Greg Wiegand
        Associate Publisher
        Que
        800 East 96th Street
        Indianapolis, IN 46240 USA

For more information about this book or another Que title, visit our Web site at www.quepublishing.com. Type the ISBN (excluding hyphens) or the title of a book in the Search field to find the page you're looking for.

Introduction

Many of us dream of running our own businesses. Until recently, being able to achieve that dream meant obtaining some type of outside financing, finding a retail location or office space, and physically opening the doors to new clients or customers. Today, however, there's an easier way to go into business for yourself—from the comfort of your own home.

This new type of dream business is possible thanks to the advent of eBay, the world's largest online trading community. An eBay business makes money by selling items via eBay auctions. You do all the selling from your own personal computer, collect the payments sent to you electronically and through the mail, and then ship the items you sell via the post office. It's simple, it's relatively easy, and it doesn't take a ton of investment.

It's also an increasingly viable way to make a living. According to the *New York Times*, an estimated half-million people make a full- or part-time living from selling merchandise on eBay. On any given day there are close to 36 million items listed for auction at eBay. For the year 2005, that added up to more than $44 billion worth of merchandise sold online—or *$1,400 worth of sales every second.*

You could be making some of that money. Getting started on eBay is as easy as finding something to sell and creating an auction listing. Anybody can do that—as witnessed by eBay's 180+ million registered users. However, to turn that selling into a business will take a little more effort.

What do you need to know to run an eBay business? More than you think, if you want to do it successfully. You need to determine what kind of business you want to run, write an instructive business plan, establish an effective accounting system, set up a home office, arrange any necessary funding, and purchase and warehouse your starting inventory.

And that's before you sell a single item.

Once you start selling, you have the entire auction management process to deal with. You have to list items for sale, manage your inventory, correspond with winning bidders, handle customer payments, deal with deadbeat customers, and pack and ship all those items you sell. To be truly successful, you need to do all this as efficiently as possible; you'll need to automate those repetitive tasks, manage your costs, and find a way to increase the success rates of the auctions you run.

Fortunately, you don't have to reinvent the wheel. You're not the first person to dream about running his or her own eBay business, so you might as well learn from others who've already done it.

Which is where this book comes in.

Making a Living from Your eBay Business presents everything you need to know to launch and run your own business, using eBay auctions to sell your merchandise. Unlike other eBay books on the market (including several that I've authored previously), this book focuses on the business aspects, not the technical details of running an auction. If you need to learn how to create a basic eBay auction listing, turn elsewhere (to my *Absolute Beginner's Guide to eBay*, for example). Once you know the basics, this book will show you how to turn that knowledge into a workable business model.

How This Book Is Organized

This book is organized into five main parts, as follows:

- **Part 1, "Planning and Launching Your eBay Business,"** walks you through the "homework" you need to do *before* you start selling on eBay. You'll learn how to research your business model, create a business plan, evaluate your funding needs, deal with legal and tax issues, set up a recordkeeping system, and put together your eBay back office.

- **Part 2, "Choosing a Business Model,"** introduces you to six common types of eBay businesses—one of which should be just right for you.

- **Part 3, "Managing Your Day-to-Day Business,"** takes you through everything you need to know about running your business. You'll learn where to buy and how to manage your inventory, how to automate the auction listing process, how to manage customer payments, the best ways to pack and ship your merchandise, how to deal with customers (and customer problems), and how to more effectively automate your auction management.

- **Part 4, "Maximizing Your eBay Sales,"** helps you make your auctions more successful—and your business more profitable. You'll learn some tips for improving item sell-through and increasing your selling price, for choosing the most effective listing options, for creating more powerful auction listings, for taking and displaying better product photos, and for promoting your eBay auctions.

- **Part 5, "Growing Your Online Business,"** shows you how to take the next steps toward business success. You'll learn how to become an eBay PowerSeller, expand your sales to eBay Express and Half.com, open an eBay Store, sell at other online sites, launch a full-fledged merchant website, and manage your business's growth.

At the end of the book you'll find two useful appendixes. Appendix A is a brief accounting primer, for those of you who slept through accounting class in school. Appendix B lists some of the most common abbreviations you can use in your eBay listings.

Taken together, the 30 chapters and two appendixes in this book will help you launch and manage a profitable eBay business. By the time you get to the end of the final chapter, you'll know just about everything you need to know to make money on eBay. Now all you have to do is do the work!

Let Me Know What You Think

I always love to hear from readers. If you want to contact me, feel free to email me at ebay-business@molehillgroup.com. I can't promise that I'll answer every message, but I will promise that I'll read each one!

If you want to learn more about me and any new books I have cooking, check out my Molehill Group website at www.molehillgroup.com. Who knows—you might find some other books there that you'd like to read.

Part 1

Planning and Launching Your eBay Business

1

So You Want to Start an eBay Business...

Starting a business of your own is a thrilling thought—especially if you can run that business from the comfort of your own home. You've heard about this eBay thing, maybe even sold a thing or two on the site, and think that selling on eBay might be the key to your personal business success.

Is it true? Can you really make a living with an eBay business? And just what is an eBay business, anyway?

This chapter answers those questions and many more. Read on to learn more about the basics of running a business on eBay.

What, Exactly, Is an eBay Business?

To the question of what an eBay business is, the simple answer is that it's a company that generates profits by selling merchandise on the eBay site. That company, of course, can be a sole proprietorship run by a single individual, as most eBay businesses are, or it can be a legal corporation with multiple employees. The company doesn't have to sell exclusively on eBay; it can sell through any number of channels (including a traditional bricks-and-mortar store), as long as at least some of its revenues are generated via the eBay family of sites.

Contrary to what you might think, eBay businesses do not have formal business relationships with the eBay corporation, nor do they have to be authorized by eBay. To become an eBay business, all you have to do is start selling on the eBay site. Nothing more formal than a standard eBay membership—in the form of a free Seller's Account—is required.

eBay businesses can be of any size, revenue-wise. Some eBay businesses sell only one item a week; some sell millions of dollars worth of merchandise every year. It doesn't even have to be a full-time thing. Many eBay businesses are part-time endeavors run by people who have other full-time jobs.

What distinguishes an eBay business from the average individual selling on eBay is intent. While individuals tend to sell on eBay because they need the money or want to get rid of old junk lying around the house, eBay businesses sell merchandise that they intend to make a profit on. eBay businesses have to purchase or create the items they sell; they also have to ensure a constant flow of merchandise to feed a continuing schedule of auction listings. eBay businesses sell on eBay every week of the year, not just when it's convenient. And they work hard at it.

And, finally, eBay businesses are *businesses*. That means they have to deal with the same issues any business has to deal with—managing inventory, handling customer payments, paying taxes, dealing with complaints, and the like. The people behind these eBay businesses do what they do because they like it, sure, but also because they want to make a profit.

Understanding eBay's Fees

If you're going to run a successful eBay business, you better get used to paying eBay. That's because eBay gets its cut every time you list or sell an item on the eBay site. *Every time.* It may be a few pennies here and a few pennies there, but eBay's fees add up quite rapidly—and become a significant expense if you're selling a lot of items each month.

For that reason, you need to understand the costs involved before you put any items up for auction. eBay charges two main types of fees to sellers:

- **Insertion fees** (I prefer to call them *listing fees*). These fees are what you pay every time you list an item for sale on eBay. They are based on the minimum bid or reserve price of the item listed. These fees are nonrefundable.

- **Final value fees** (I prefer to call them *selling fees* or *commissions*). These fees are what you pay when an item is actually sold to a buyer. They are based on the item's final selling price (the highest bid). If your item doesn't sell, you aren't charged a final value fee.

Table 1.1 lists eBay's current insertion fees (as of fall 2006); Table 1.2 lists the current final value fees.

Table 1.1   eBay Insertion Fees

Starting Bid Price	Insertion Fee
$0.01–$0.99	$0.20
$1.00–$9.99	$0.35
$10.00–$24.99	$0.60
$25.00–$49.99	$1.20
$50.00–$199.99	$2.40
$200.00–$499.99	$3.60
$500.00 or more	$4.80

Table 1.2   eBay Final Value Fees

Final Selling Price	Final Value Fee
Item not sold	No fee
$0.01–$25.00	5.25% of the final price
$25.01–$1,000.00	5.25% of the initial $25.00 ($1.31), plus 3% of the remaining closing value balance
$1,000.01 or more	5.25% of the initial $25.00 ($1.31), plus 3% of the amount from $25.00–$1,000.00 ($29.25), plus 1.5% of the remaining balance

eBay also charges a variety of fees for different types of listing enhancements, such as bold and highlight. And, as you might expect, all manner of fine print is associated with these fees. The most important things to keep in mind are that insertions

note You can view all of eBay's current fees at pages.ebay.com/help/sell/fees.html.

are nonrefundable; you won't be charged a final value fee if the item doesn't sell; and it doesn't matter whether the buyer actually pays you—you still owe eBay the full final value fee, even if you get stiffed.

Invoicing on your account occurs once a month, for the previous month's activity. You'll get an invoice via email detailing your charges for the month. If you've set up your account for automatic credit card billing or checking account withdrawal, your account will be charged at that time. (If you prefer to pay via check or regular credit card, now's the time to do it.)

Know, however, that these aren't the only costs you'll incur in running an eBay auction. Most sellers opt to accept credit cards via eBay's PayPal service, which charges its own fees. For the average small to mid-sized seller, PayPal charges 2.9% of the total payment price, plus a flat $0.30 per transaction. That's right in line with what a traditional retailer would pay to a bank to handle its credit card payments.

As you can see, these fees start to add up. For most eBay businesses, you can estimate paying 12%–15% in fees for every successful sale you make. This doesn't take into account the actual cost of the item you sell, nor any other costs you incur—such as the costs of packing materials, labels, Internet access, and the like. You'll need to factor all these costs into your business model, just as you would factor in rent, credit card fees, and other operating expenses if you were running a bricks-and-mortar business.

Different Ways to Sell on eBay

If you've never sold on eBay before, you should know that there are several different ways to sell your merchandise on the eBay family of sites. Yes, most merchandise sold on eBay is via the online auction format, but not all. Many businesses sell their items on eBay at a fixed price, just as they would in a conventional store. And there are more sites than just the auction site on which to sell.

note Learn more about PayPal (and PayPal's fees) in Chapter 16, "Managing Customer Payments."

Standard Auction Format

Selling an item via an eBay auction is quite a bit different from selling it off a shelf in a traditional retail store. In essence, an eBay auction works pretty much like an old-fashioned real-world auction, with potential buyers driving the price higher every time they place a bid. The only difference is that there's no fast-talking auctioneer online (the bidding process is executed by eBay's special auction software), and all the bidders aren't in the same room; potential buyers can be located anywhere in the world, as long as they have Internet access.

When you're ready to sell an item via eBay auction, you post a listing for that item, like the one shown in Figure 1.1. When you create a listing, you select the product category, length of the auction (1, 3, 5, 7, or 10 days), and the starting bid price. From there the auction process takes over, with interested buyers making increasing bids on the item; bidding starts at the initial price you specified and goes up from there. At the end of the auction, the bidder with the highest bid wins and pays you for the item. When payment is received, you ship the item to the buyer.

FIGURE 1.1

A typical eBay auction listing.

eBay makes the entire process fairly simple for both the seller and the buyer. Just know that while you're using the eBay site to facilitate the sale (by hosting the auction listing), eBay is not a middleman in the transaction. The buyer pays you directly, not the eBay site. You, however, do have to pay fees to eBay for the services it offers—as we've already discussed.

The thing that makes an eBay auction different from a traditional retail transaction is that there is no guarantee the item will actually sell—nor do you know what the final price will be if it does sell. That's part and parcel of being an auction. If no one bids on your item, you don't sell it. And the final sales price is totally market-driven; the price will go as high as potential buyers are willing to pay. That can be both good (you could get a higher price than you anticipated) and bad (you could sell an item for less than you thought—or not sell it at all). That's just the way it goes.

Reserve Price Auction

eBay offers several variations on its main auction format. One of the more common variations is the reserve price auction. In this type of auction, your starting bid price really isn't the minimum price you'll accept. You set a starting bid price as you would in a normal auction, but you also specify a *reserve price* somewhere above the starting price. This reserve price is the actual minimum price you want the item to sell for. Even though bids might exceed the initial bid price, if they don't hit your reserve price, there isn't a sale.

Many buyers—especially those just getting started—don't like reserve price auctions, and shy away from them. They probably feel that way because these auctions appear more complicated than regular auctions (and they are, just a little), and also because the reserve price is never disclosed to bidders. In this case, lack of familiarity definitely breeds contempt, at least from a certain class of bidders.

Why, then, would you opt for a reserve price auction? There are two possible scenarios:

- When you're unsure of the real value of an item—and don't want to appear to be asking too much for an item—you can reserve the right to refuse to sell the item if the market value is below a certain price.

- When you want to use a low initial bid price to get the bidding going more quickly than if the true desired minimum price (now the reserve price) were listed, the reserve price still guarantees that you won't have to sell below a minimum acceptable price. This is most likely the case when you have a higher-priced item to sell but want to attract interest with a more attractive lower price.

Remember, if no one bids the reserve price or higher, no one wins.

Dutch Auction

Dutch auctions are those in which you have more than one of an identical item to sell, and you want to offer all your items via the auction format. (If you have more than one item you want to sell for the same fixed price, there are other nonauction options available.) A Dutch auction is great if you have a dozen waffle irons, 10 copies of *Ocean's 11* on DVD, or a hundred units of white extra-large boxer shorts to sell.

In a Dutch auction, you specify both the minimum bid and the number of items available in the auction. As in a normal auction, bidders bid at or above that minimum bid for the item—although, in a Dutch auction, bidders can also specify a specific quantity that they're interested in purchasing.

Determining who "wins" a Dutch auction is a little different from determining who wins a normal auction. In a Dutch auction, the highest bidders purchase the items, but all buyers pay only the amount that matches the lowest successful bid.

Let's work through an example. Say you're selling 10 identical copies of a particular *Lord of the Rings* T-shirt. You indicate the number of items available (10) and the minimum bid (let's say $5). Potential buyers enter their bids, which must be equal to or higher than the minimum bid of $5; each buyer also indicates the quantity (from 1 to 10) that he or she is interested in purchasing.

If 11 people bid $5 each (for one shirt apiece), the first 10 bidders will win the auction, each paying $5 for their items, and the last bidder will be out of luck. But if the 11th person had placed a higher bid—$6, let's say—then that 11th bidder would be listed as the #1 bidder, and the last $5 bidder (chronologically) would be knocked from the list. All 10 winning bidders, however—including the person who bid $6—would have to pay only $5 for the item. (Highest bidders, lowest bids—get it?)

In a Dutch auction, the minimum price ends up being raised only if enough bidders place bids above the minimum bid. In our example, if 9 bidders bid over the minimum, but the 10th bidder bid $5, all bidders would still pay $5. But if the lowest bid was $6 (and the other bidders bid from $6 to $10), all 10 bidders would pay $6 (the lowest current bid). Posting a higher bid increases a buyer's chances of winning an item at a Dutch auction, but it also increases the risk of raising the price for everybody.

Sound confusing? It is, a little, even though eBay handles all the details automatically. For most sellers with large quantities to sell, going with either an auction with the Buy It Now option or a straight fixed-price listing is a better way to go—which we'll discuss in a moment.

Auction with Best Offer

Here's one that I'm not too hot on, but some sellers swear by. eBay lets you put an item up for sale with the caveat that interested buyers can make you an offer that's below your initial listed price. You set up a fixed-priced listing (discussed in a few pages), but then add the Best Offer option. With Best Offer, a buyer can click a button (like the one shown in Figure 1.2) and suggest the price he's willing to pay. You can then accept or decline the offer.

I'd recommend Best Offer when you're selling collectibles and similar rare, higher-priced items. You should also know that using the Best Offer option is more time-consuming than a normal listing; you have to manage all the correspondence associated with the offer, as well as make the call on whether or not to accept a particular offer.

That said, I know of at least one seller who uses Best Offer on a regular basis for lower-priced, commodity items. If you go this route, you should make sure you set your price high enough so that there's room for buyers to make an offer that is below your price but still financially acceptable to you.

FIGURE 1.2

An item offered for sale for a given price—or the best offer by a potential buyer.

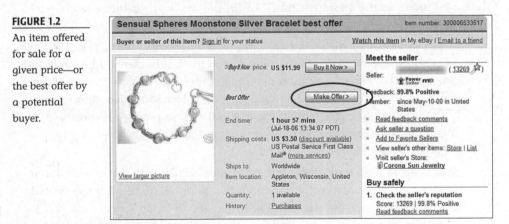

Auction with the Buy It Now Option

eBay's Buy It Now (BIN) option lets you add a fixed-price option to your auction listings. The way BIN works is that you name a fixed price for your item, as shown in Figure 1.3. If a user bids that price, the auction is automatically closed and that user is named the high bidder; bidders can also make a bid lower than the BIN price, via the regular auction process. When you make a BIN sale, it's like selling an item via a traditional retail transaction—but on the eBay site.

FIGURE 1.3
An auction with the Buy It Now option enabled.

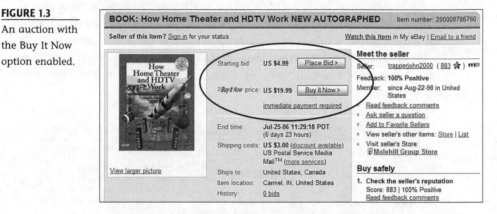

The BIN option is popular among professional eBay sellers with a lot of similar inventory. That is, they're likely to place the same item up for auction week after week. In this scenario, the BIN price becomes the de facto retail price of the item, and you can ship items as soon as you find a willing buyer. You don't have to wait the standard seven days for a normal auction to end.

You might also want to consider the BIN option around the Christmas holiday, when buyers don't always want to wait around seven whole days to see if they've won an item; desperate Christmas shoppers will sometimes pay a premium to get something *now*, which is where a BIN comes in.

Using the Buy It Now option will cost you extra as a seller, however. Table 1.3 details the fees that eBay charges to add a BIN to your auction, over and above the standard listing fees (that we'll discuss in just a few paragraphs).

Table 1.3   eBay Buy It Now Fees

Buy It Now Price	Fee
$0.01–$9.99	$0.05
$10.00–$24.99	$0.10
$25.00–$49.99	$0.20
$50.00+	$0.25

note The BIN price is active only until the first bid is placed (or, in a reserve price auction, until the reserve price is met). If the first bidder places a bid lower than the BIN price, the BIN price is removed and the auction proceeds normally.

Fixed-Price Sales on the eBay Site

Buy It Now isn't the only way to sell items for a fixed price. If you want to avoid the possibility for an item selling for less than the Buy It Now price (which is possible with a BIN-enabled auction), you can simply list an item with a fixed selling price. As you can see in Figure 1.4, eBay's fixed-price listings look just like regular auction listings and have the same duration (1 to 10 days, your choice), they just don't offer the option of placing a bid. When someone wants to buy your item, he clicks the Buy It Now button; there's no way to place a lower bid.

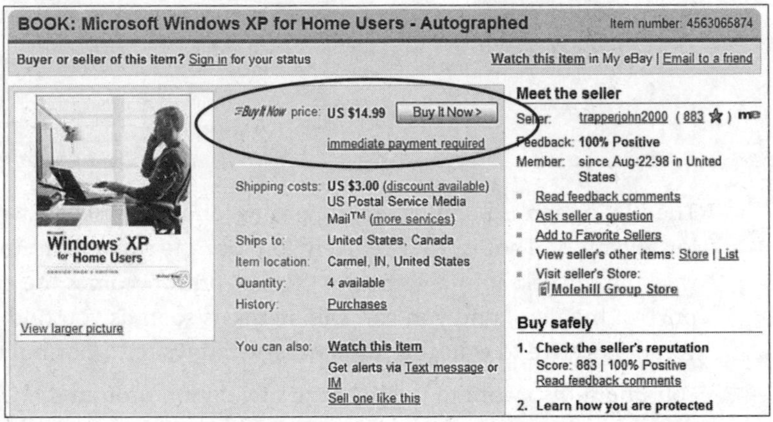

FIGURE 1.4

A fixed-price item listing—no bidding allowed.

Fixed-Price Sales with eBay Express

eBay's auction site isn't the only online marketplace offered by eBay. New to the eBay family of sites is eBay Express, which offers a more traditional retail approach to online shopping. As you can see in Figure 1.5, eBay Express offers a variety of merchandise for a fixed price—no auctions (except for those with a Buy It Now option). For buyers, it's the opportunity to buy merchandise from multiple sellers using a single checkout system. For sellers, it's yet another way to sell your fixed-price items.

eBay Express offers a viable alternative to traditional online auction selling. Learn more in Chapter 26, "Selling Fixed-Price Items on eBay Express and Half.com."

FIGURE 1.5
eBay Express—a
marketplace for
fixed-price
items.

Fixed-Price Sales on Half.com

If you have both new and used merchandise to sell, eBay's Half.com is
another place to make your mark. As you can see in Figure 1.6, Half.com
looks and feels a little like Amazon.com, and offers similar products for sale—
books, CDs, DVDs, and videogames. Half.com lets you items in these categories for a fixed price, with quick and easy listing creation. (All you have to
do is enter the item's UPC or ISBN code, and Half.com fills in all the other
information for you.)

If you sell in these particular categories,
Half.com is worth a look. Learn more in
Chapter 26.

Fixed-Price Sales in eBay Stores

The final way to sell items at a fixed price
on eBay is to open an eBay Store. In this
online storefront, operated in conjunction
with your eBay auctions, you sell multiple
quantities of items at fixed prices. As you

note You can learn more
about these selling
options and a whole lot more in
my companion book, *Absolute
Beginner's Guide to eBay, 4th Edition*
(Que, 2006). This book is also a
good resource if you're just starting
out as a seller; it offers detailed
step-by-step instructions on how to
create an auction listing, how to
manage the auction process, and
so on.

can see in Figure 1.7, an eBay Store is just like a traditional store; you have your items on the virtual shelves, and shoppers can buy what they want for the price listed, at any time.

FIGURE 1.6
Half.com—
another way to
sell fixed-price
items.

FIGURE 1.7
Fixed-price mer-
chandise for
sale in an eBay
Store.

An eBay Store is a good way to sell items that you have in quantity, or items that you haven't yet listed for auction. Learn more in Chapter 27, "Opening an eBay Store."

The Secret to eBay Business Success: Planning

The big difference between the casual eBay seller and the person running a successful eBay business is often nothing more than volume. Whether you're selling one item a month or a hundred, the process is basically the same. It's just that the professional seller has to manage a lot more activity—and do so with the lowest possible expenditure of time and money. Manage this process well, and you'll have a successful eBay business on your hands.

While anyone can become a casual eBay seller, there's a lot more involved if you intend on launching a full-time eBay business. An eBay business is like any other type of business—it requires planning, organization, and a lot of hard work.

I've had a few people read the first edition of this book and comment they thought I spent too much time covering business-related information; in their opinion, you don't need to know all this business stuff to be successful on eBay. Those readers are, of course, mistaken—as they'll no doubt discover for themselves in time.

Yes, it's ridiculously easy for any individual to start selling on eBay. You don't need a business degree to fill out the Sell Your Item form and create a rudimentary auction listing. You don't even need any business savvy to become a relatively successful seller, on a small scale. But when your sales start escalating, you need all the business skills you can muster to manage a large volume of transactions, and to keep the slim profits you generate from turning into losses.

Put another way, it takes planning to launch a successful business, organizational skills to grow the business, and business savvy to stay ahead of the competition and keep your business in the black. While anyone starting out can be lucky, luck alone won't keep you successful over the long term. I know too many former eBay sellers who had a nice ride at the beginning, but didn't have the skills necessary to turn their initial success into a profitable continuing business.

Planning for Success

To that end, I encourage anyone who is considering launching an eBay business to take their time, do their homework, and not rush into things. It's okay to get your feet wet by running a few (or a few dozen) auctions, but make sure you've thoroughly thought through what you're doing before you start buying bulk lots of merchandise for resale. As much as I'd like to tell you how easy it is to get rich quick on eBay, success definitely is not guaranteed.

Success is, however, more likely when you do your planning beforehand. What type of planning am I talking about? Here's a short list:

- Research sales across a variety of product categories to find the right merchandise to sell (covered in Chapter 2)
- Think through your business goals and write a short business plan that outlines what you want to achieve—and how (covered in Chapter 3)
- Evaluate how much money you'll need to get started, and figure out where you can get that money (covered in Chapter 4)
- Determine what type of business entity you want to create—a simple sole proprietorship or a legal corporation (covered in Chapter 5)
- Set up a complete recordkeeping system, including both inventory management and accounting (covered in Chapter 6)
- Determine how much physical space you'll need to manage your eBay sales—including inventory storage, packing and shipping, and your home office (covered in Chapter 7)

As part of this planning, you need to work up a sales projection for your first year of business, along with a budget of your expenses. You should also determine how many hours per week you'll need to put into your business—as well as any employees you might need to hire to help you out.

Choosing a Business Model

As part of the planning process, you have to determine what type of eBay business you want to run. After all, not every eBay business operates exactly the same. With a half-million businesses making a living on eBay, you know that there are a lot of different ways to proceed; there's no one "right" way to run an eBay business.

What kinds of eBay businesses are there? I like to organize the different business models as follows:

- **The Second-Hand Reseller**, who buys a variety of used merchandise and resells it to others (covered in Chapter 8)

- **The Collector/Trader**, who buys and sells on eBay as an extension of a collectible hobby (covered in Chapter 9)

- **The Bulk Reseller**, who purchases large quantities of closeout or liquidated merchandise and resells it one piece at a time (covered in Chapter 10)

- **The Retailer**, who resells new goods purchased direct from the manufacturer, just like a traditional bricks-and-mortar retailer (covered in Chapter 11)

- **The Manufacturer/Craftsperson**, who creates the items he or she sells to eBay buyers (covered in Chapter 12)

- **The Trading Assistant**, who sells items on consignment for other people (covered in Chapter 13)

Each of these models, as different as they are from one another, is equally viable. Which you choose is entirely up to you.

Making It Yours

Now we come to one last point about launching your own eBay business. Most successful eBay sellers aren't in it just for the money. The best business-people sell what they do because they like doing it. There's no point at all in setting up a business in which you have little or no interest. You'll be more successful—and lot happier—when you build your business around something you're familiar with, and something you like. Anyone, after all, can sell paper clips; but only you can create a unique business based on your personal interests and strengths. Researching "hot" categories can only go so far; your final decision needs to be made with your head and your heart.

With that in mind, read on to learn how to research and launch the type of eBay business that's best for you.

Researching Your Business Model

The first step in preparing to launch your eBay business is to do a little research. In particular, you need to find out as much as you can about any and all products you might want to sell. You need to discover how well those products are likely to sell for you, as well as determine the average selling price for each item. Combine what you learn about sales rate and sales price, and you can make a good estimate as to how much revenue you can generate selling that type of item.

The value of this research, then, is that it helps you determine what products to sell. Pick a product category, and research the auction close rate and average selling price. Avoid those categories that don't meet your criteria, and target those categories that do.

esearch Is Important

You should never launch an eBay business—or any business, for that matter—without doing your homework first. You might think you have a great idea for an eBay business, but you won't know for sure until you do some research. When you start poking your nose around the eBay community, you'll get a much better idea of which types of items are good sellers, and which aren't. In short, you use this preliminary research to help you determine your business model—that is, the type of eBay business that you want to run.

To determine your eBay business model, you should research a variety of different product categories on eBay. It's as simple as looking up the historical sales for specific items (by model number) or for entire product categories. There are several questions you want answered, including

- How many items of this type are listed each week, on average?
- What is the sell-through percentage—that is, the percent of all auctions that end with successful bids?
- What is the average final selling price?
- Are sales of this product increasing or decreasing over time?

For example, I discovered that during the month of June, 2006, there were 3,185 listings for Nikon Coolpix digital cameras on eBay. Almost half (44%) of those auctions closed successfully, at an average selling price of $167.97—a fairly hot category.

In contrast, during the same month there were 834 auctions for men's golf jackets. Of these auctions a third (32%) closed successfully, at an average selling price of just $20.16—a less-exciting category, by all measurements. If I had to choose between these two products to sell, I'd be a lot more interested in those digital cameras than I would the golf jackets.

How did I get this information? Read on and discover the many ways to research prior sales on eBay.

Searching Closed eBay Auctions

The cheapest (but not necessarily the easiest) way to research auction pricing is to do it yourself, using eBay's search feature. The downside to this method is that it's labor intensive; you'll have to perform a number of manual searches and then crunch all the numbers yourself. The upside is that the only cost is your time.

Performing the Search

Extracting sales data from eBay is very much a manual process. You have to use eBay's search pages and then comb the results for the information you need. Here's how to do it.

note You can limit your search to specific product categories by making a selection from the Category list.

Start by clicking the Advanced Search link at the top of any eBay page. (You don't want to use the standard Search box; it won't provide the fine-tuned results you need.) When the Find Items page appears, as shown in Figure 2.1, enter one or more keywords into the Enter Keyword or Item Number box. Then—and this is the important part—check the Completed Listings Only option. When you click the Search button at the bottom of the page, eBay will display your results on a separate search results page.

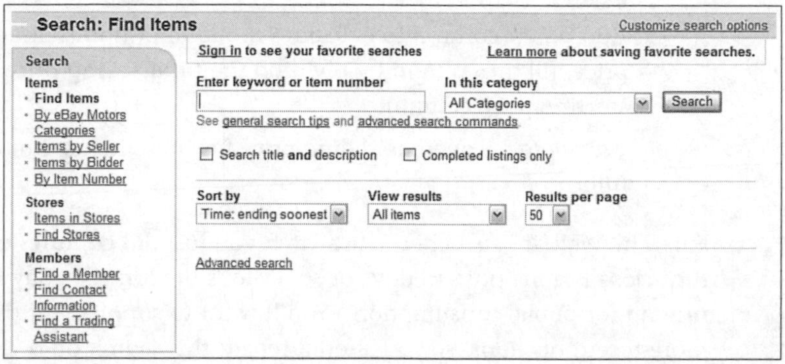

FIGURE 2.1

Use eBay's Find Items page to list auctions of specific merchandise.

The key point here is to search for *completed auctions only*. You don't want to search in-process auctions because you don't know what the final selling prices will be until the auction closes. When you search completed auctions, you'll have all the information you need—including the final selling price.

Extracting the Data

When the search results page appears, it's time to get your fingers dirty. You'll need to click through each of the auctions listed and write down the following:

- Starting price
- Final selling price
- Number of bids

note Make sure you include only those auctions that closely match the type of item you want to sell. For example, if you're selling new merchandise, don't include auctions for used items; if you're selling in lots of 10, don't include single-item auctions.

It's best to enter this information into an Excel spreadsheet, with one row for each completed auction and a column for each of the parameters. If the auction ended without a sale, enter "0" for both the final selling price and number of bids.

Analyzing the Data

Once you've gathered your data, it's time to analyze it. Here are some things to look at:

- Total the number of items listed within the given time period.
- Calculate the percentage of successful auctions by manually counting the number of auctions that had a winning bid and dividing by the total number of auctions.
- Look at the range of prices by sorting the list in order of highest selling price.
- Add a new column to calculate the ratio of final selling to starting price; fill the column by dividing the final selling price column by the starting price column.
- Calculate an average selling price for those items that closed successfully.

Fun, eh? Well, it gets better. The search you just did captures only auctions that closed in the past 15 days or so. (That's the longest eBay keeps this information for public consumption.) You'll want to supplement this data with more recent auctions, so you should repeat this search on a weekly basis. This way you can capture any pricing trends over time.

Using the Data

After you've assembled your analysis of these auction results, you can use your analysis to determine whether a given category is a good one or not. Skip to the "Determining Your Business Model" section, later in this chapter, to learn more.

Using Other Research Tools

Does all that manual number crunching seem like a lot of work? Then let somebody else do it for you! There are a handful of pricing research services and programs available that perform all sorts of analysis on eBay auction trends. The good news is that these services greatly simplify this process and provide highly detailed (and very professional) analysis. The bad news is that you have to pay for what you get.

That said, let's look at the freestanding research tools offered by eBay, as well as some useful third-party tools.

eBay's Hot Categories Report

When you want to find out the best types of merchandise to sell, it helps to know which product categories are hot in terms of sales. Fortunately, eBay makes this relatively easy, with its monthly Hot Categories Report. As you can see in Figure 2.2, this list details the hottest product categories on the eBay site—which are the best categories in which to sell.

FIGURE 2.2

Find out the hottest product categories with eBay's Hot Categories Report.

Crafts

Super Hot

Level 2	Level 3	Level 4
Fabric Embellishments	Fabric Trims	Beaded Trim
Woodworking	Woodworking Lumber	Koa Wood

Very Hot

Level 2	Level 3	Level 4
Scrapbooking	Stickers	Collections, Mixed Lots
Sewing	Sewing Machines & Sergers	Elna

Hot

Level 2	Level 3	Level 4
Cross Stitch	Cross Stitch Fabric	Aida Cloth
Cross Stitch	Cross Stitch Kits	Fantasy, Fairies
Embroidery	Design CDs	Flowers, Gardens
Fabric	Cotton	Fabric Squares
Fabric Embellishments	Fabric Trims	Embroidered Trim
Scrapbooking	Cutters & Trimmers	Corner Cutters
Scrapbooking	Cutters & Trimmers	Personal Cutting Systems
Scrapbooking	Paper Punches	Geometric Shapes
Sewing	Sewing Machines & Sergers	Pfaff

To access the Hot Categories Report, click the Sell link on the eBay Navigation Bar to open the Sell hub, and then click the The Hot List link. eBay updates this report every 30 days, so it's good to check it monthly.

eBay's Market Database

The Hot Categories Report isn't eBay's only research tool. eBay pulls together other essential sales statistics in its Marketplace Research database, which you can search (for a fee). What sort of information are we talking about? Here's a sample, for any given item:

- Average sold price
- Sold price range
- Start price range
- Average BIN price
- BIN price range
- Average shipping cost
- Last sold price
- Last sold date/time
- Number successfully sold
- Average bids per item

Then there are the charts, including trend charts for average sold price, number successfully sold, and average bids per item; and distribution charts for average start price and number successfully sold. You can search the entire database, or filter your results by date, specific sellers, specific stores, country, and so on.

eBay's Marketplace Research can be accessed at pages.ebay.com/ marketplace_research/. Three different packages are available—the Fast Pass provides two days' access for $2.99; the Basic plan costs $9.99 per month; and the more robust Pro plan (which offers more search options) costs $24.99 per month.

I find the Marketplace Research to be a real boon when I need specifics about any given product or product category. It's in-depth data, well worth the money for serious sellers.

Ándale's Research Tools

You can supplement eBay's research tools with those from Ándale (www.andale.com), a popular third-party site. Ándale offers three key research tools—What's Hot, Research, and Sales Analyzer. You can use these various tools to discover hot product categories and determine how to price and when to list your items. We'll look at each of these research tools separately.

What's Hot

Ándale What's Hot is a research tool that provides detailed reports about the hottest selling eBay items, in any category. As you can see in Figure 2.3, the main What's Hot page lets you click through each category to find the hottest products in each category, or search for particular items to see their performance. Ándale also pulls out the hottest products in all categories (for the past four weeks) and lists them on this main page.

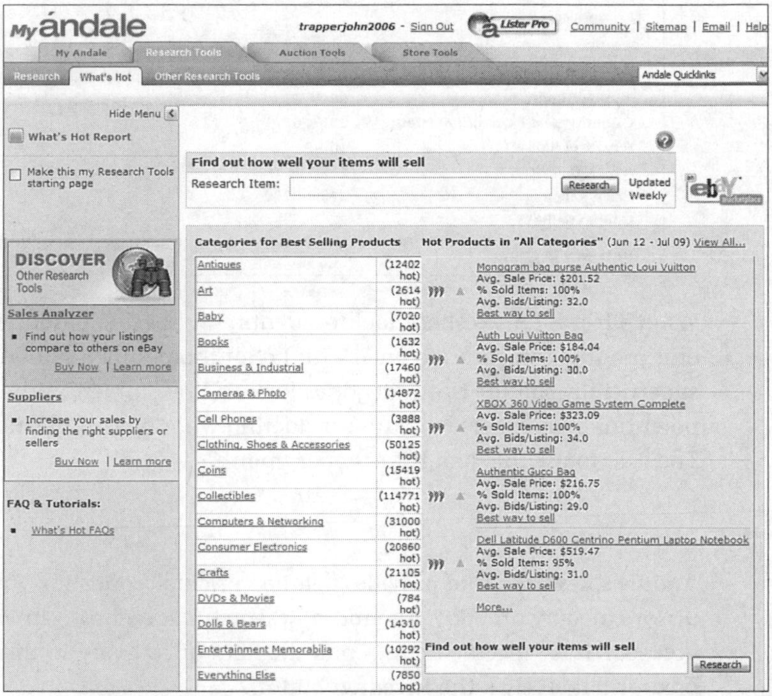

FIGURE 2.3

Discover hot products and categories with the Ándale What's Hot research tool.

When you click through to a specific product, you see the individual product report, as shown in Figure 2.4. Ándale uses a chili pepper icon to denote the relative hotness of any particular product; three peppers means high demand, two peppers means medium demand, and a single pepper indicates just mild demand. You're also presented with the percentage of closed items (the higher, the better), the total quantity listed and sold, the average number of bids per item, the average sale price, the price range, and the number of unique sellers offering this item. If you want to view specifics of each auction, click the See Individual Items link to display a list of auctions monitored over the past month.

FIGURE 2.4

A typical What's Hot product report.

What's Hot on eBay Updated Weekly

Find out how well your items will sell

[   ] [Research]

"NAD Power Amplifier" is burning hot.))))

)))) High Demand))) Medium Demand)) Mild Demand

Find suppliers for this item

▲ Getting hotter ▼ Getting cooler ▶◀ Equal

Product Line Details

Product Line Name:	NAD Power Amplifier See Individual Items
% Sold Items:	88.46%
Quantity Sold / Quantity Listed:	23 / 26
Avg. # of Bids:	10.0
Avg. Sale Price:	$195.92
Price Range:	$90 - $390
Unique Sellers:	22
Best way to sell:	Use Andale Research - Set price, Best start day, Choose features

What's Hot is an excellent tool for identifying specific products to sell or general product categories to enter—and a lot more fully featured than eBay's superficially similar Hot Categories Report. I recommend What's Hot for all potential eBay sellers who are considering what type of business model to use. The cost to use this tool is $3.95 per month.

Research

Ándale's Research tool provides detailed pricing reports for any specific product or category on eBay. The main Research page, shown in Figure 2.5, lets you search for specific items. Enter the item or category in the Research Prices box, and then click the Research button.

FIGURE 2.5

Research products or categories with Ándale Research.

The results of a typical search are shown in Figure 2.6. The Price Summary tab displays some key information and three useful charts. The main information includes the average selling price, number of total listings, number of items listed (there can be multiple items per listing, remember), total number of items sold, and the success rate—the number of items sold divided by the number of items listed.

FIGURE 2.6

Using Ándale Research to track pricing trends over time.

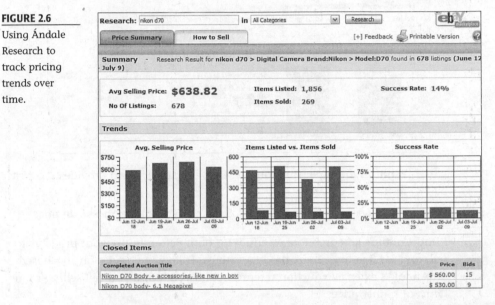

As to the charts, the first one presents the average selling price of the item, for each of the past four weeks. The second chart displays the quantity listed and sold, again for each of the past four weeks. The third chart displays the percentage of successful auctions, again for each of the past four weeks. Below the charts are links to individual auctions, which you can view in more detail.

You can view even more detailed information when you click the How to Sell tab, shown in Figure 2.7. This tab displays a very detailed report about the item or category you selected. A typical How to Sell report includes information on scheduled start day, eBay marketing features, and type of listing.

Most useful is the Summary at the top of the page, which offers advice regarding

- Best category to list your product
- Best day and time to start your auction—and how long an auction to run
- Which listing enhancements (bold, gallery, and so on) are cost effective

FIGURE 2.7

Fine-tune your
auction listings
with Research's
How to Sell tab.

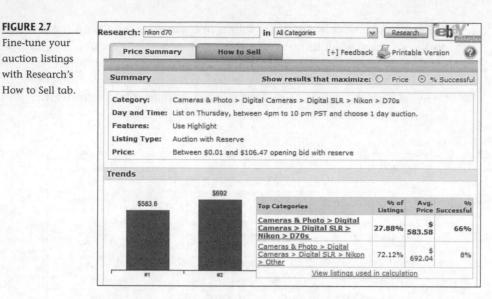

- What listing type (standard, reserve, BIN, and so on) provides the best results
- What opening price generates the most bids and highest sale price

I find Ándale's Research tool essential for both determining what products to sell, and for fine-tuning my product listings. Follow the advice given—based on Ándale's extensive auction research—and you'll find yourself selling more items at higher prices.

The cost to use this tool is $7.95 per month.

Sales Analyzer

Ándale also offers the Sales Analyzer tool ($5.95/month), which is designed to help you better understand your own eBay sales. It provides a detailed analysis of your total sales, sell-through rate, return on investment, and other key metrics. This tool is of more use to established sellers than to new eBay businesses; check it out once you have your business up and running.

Mpire Researcher

Mpire Researcher (www.mpire.com/research/login.page) is a web-based eBay research tool, similar to Ándale Research. Enter a product or category and Mpire returns a report that tells you the average selling price of the top-selling listings and the most effective title keywords, listing enhancements, listing

types, start price, listing duration, ending day and time, and produc...
(Figure 2.8 shows a sample report.)

FIGURE 2.8

Detailed product and category analysis from Mpire Researcher.

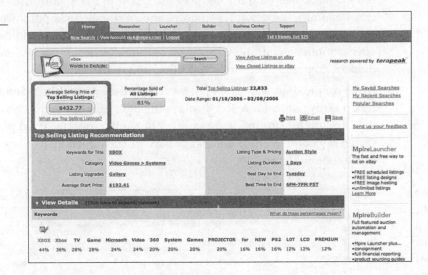

And here's the very best thing about Mpire Researcher—it's free. That's right, unlike Ándale Research and all the other paid research tools and services, there's absolutely no charge to search the Mpire database and generate research reports. You do have to register, but there are no fees associated with that. Just enter your search query and generate your free report.

Terapeak Marketplace Research

Another good web-based research service is Terapeak Marketplace Research (www.terapeak.com). Terapeak searches a three-month running database of eBay listings to provide a variety of detailed research reports. Two plans are available—Research Lite for $9.95/month, or the more fully featured Research Complete for $16.95 per month. The Research Complete plan also includes research on the top sellers in any eBay marketplace, which is a good way to get smarter about the competition.

AuctionIntelligence

AuctionIntelligence (www.certes.net/AuctionIntelligence/) is an auction analysis program available on a subscription basis. Downloading the software is free; you have to pay $14.99 per month to use it.

This program lets you search eBay by category or keyword. After it retrieves all matching auctions, you can generate a wide variety of sophisticated reports just by clicking the name of the report in the Reports list, and then you can customize the report based on your own user-defined parameters. You can generate reports that detail price over time; bidding and pricing trends; the effects of auction duration, premium features, feedback, and PayPal; frequent bidders; common words in listing titles; and more.

For example, Figure 2.9 shows the AuctionIntelligence Search Summary report. This particular report displays the total number of auctions found; the sell-through rate for this item; number of regular, reserve, fixed price, and Dutch auctions; average number of bids for each auction; average price for this item; and more.

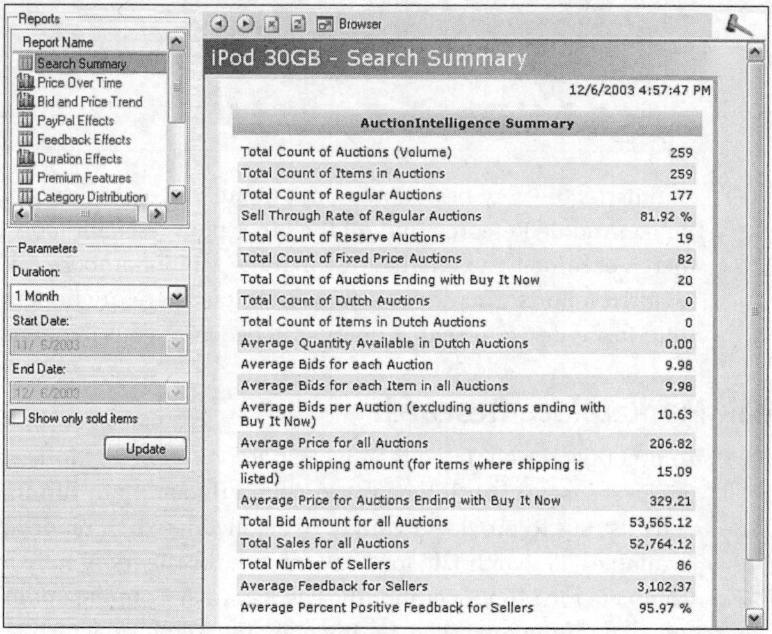

FIGURE 2.9

Basic auction sales analysis from the AuctionIntelligence Search Summary report.

iPod 30GB - Search Summary

12/6/2003 4:57:47 PM

AuctionIntelligence Summary

Total Count of Auctions (Volume)	259
Total Count of Items in Auctions	259
Total Count of Regular Auctions	177
Sell Through Rate of Regular Auctions	81.92 %
Total Count of Reserve Auctions	19
Total Count of Fixed Price Auctions	82
Total Count of Auctions Ending with Buy It Now	20
Total Count of Dutch Auctions	0
Total Count of Items in Dutch Auctions	0
Average Quantity Available in Dutch Auctions	0.00
Average Bids for each Auction	9.98
Average Bids for each Item in all Auctions	9.98
Average Bids per Auction (excluding auctions ending with Buy It Now)	10.63
Average Price for all Auctions	206.82
Average shipping amount (for items where shipping is listed)	15.09
Average Price for Auctions Ending with Buy It Now	329.21
Total Bid Amount for all Auctions	53,565.12
Total Sales for all Auctions	52,764.12
Total Number of Sellers	86
Average Feedback for Sellers	3,102.37
Average Percent Positive Feedback for Sellers	95.97 %

Figure 2.10 shows the Price Over Time report. This report is an excellent way to discover the pricing trends for a particular item, whether the average selling price is going up or down. The results are presented in a highly visual fashion, making it easy to see whether pricing is trending up or down.

FIGURE 2.10

Track pricing trends with the AuctionIntelligence Price Over Time report.

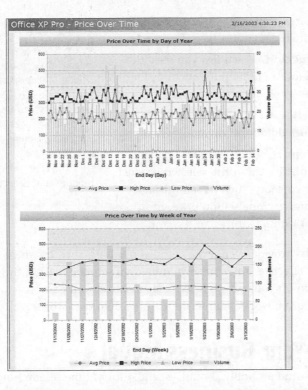

AuctionIntelligence also offers Hot Items and Category Distribution reports. As such, you're looking at an extremely full-featured research program, although it's somewhat technically demanding (it requires the installation of a Microsoft SQL Server 2000 or MSDE 2000 database before it can run) and not the easiest program in the world to use. Given these caveats, AuctionIntelligence can generate some extremely valuable research reports for the serious eBay seller.

HammerTap

HammerTap (www.hammertap.com) is a software program that performs basic auction sales analysis. It's a tad pricey, at $199 for a yearly subscription or $24.95 per month. HammerTap provides fundamental information about any category or specific product, including the number of auctions in the past 30 days, the number of bids for each auction, percentage of items sold, average selling price, and so on.

note The product now known as HammerTap was formerly known as DeepAnalysis—and is still called that in various places in the program and on the company's website. The product formerly known as HammerTap (an auction management program) no longer exists.

HammerTap presents several tabs of information, including

- **Auction**, which lets you view the details of individual auctions for a given product or category
- **Seller**, which provides competitive sales data for individual sellers
- **Report**, which displays relevant statistics about the selected product or category, such as sell-through rate, average selling price, most useful listing features, and so forth

tip Several other companies offer category-specific eBay research tools. These include MiBlueBook.com (www.mibluebook.com) for musical instruments; PriceMiner (www.priceminer.com) for antiques, art, and collectibles; and SmartCollector (www.smartcollector.com) for antiques and collectibles.

Other tabs provide even more detailed analysis, such as which title keywords are most effective. You can save individual searches within the program, as well as export your results to both spreadsheet and database formats. This versatile program works seamlessly with the data available on the eBay site.

Determining Your Business Model

You can—and probably should—spend a lot of time researching a variety of products and product categories. The more information you have, the smarter you'll be about what does and doesn't sell well in the eBay marketplace.

The whole point of doing this research, however, is to help you make a decision regarding what type of merchandise you want to sell in your eBay business. Generating loads of numbers is fine, but it's what you do with these numbers that really matters.

When it comes to determining the model for your potential eBay business, here are some points to consider:

- **Is this a big product category?** You don't want to peg your business hopes on a category that's prohibitively small. How many auctions are listed every week, on average? Is there enough business in this category to generate an acceptable income? (I like to look for categories that have at least 50 listings a week, on average—and more if they're low-priced categories.)
- **Is this a hot product category?** Size isn't everything; you also need to look at the percent of auctions that close successfully. A category with a low close rate is "soft"—that is, customer demand is low, compared to product supply. A category with a high close rate is much

hotter, which means that a larger percentage of customers want the products that other users are selling. Hotter is better. (I like to look for a close rate of at least 60%—and the higher, the better.)

- **How much revenue can you generate?** Is this a high-priced or a low-priced category? The amount of money you make depends not only on the number of auctions you can run (and close successfully), but also on the final selling price of those items. Taking our earlier example of golf jackets versus digital cameras, you have to sell a lot more $20 items than you do $160 items to generate the same amount of revenue—although selling that $160 item may be more difficult than selling a corresponding $20 item. Which pricing strategy do you prefer? When you're just starting out, choosing a higher-priced item might make more sense—you'll have fewer items to list, manage, pack, and ship every week, although you also have to take into account how much profit you make on each of the items. If you make the same $1 profit on each item, you're better off selling the lower-priced one!

- **Is the category growing—or shrinking?** Here's a good reason to track a category over an extended period of time. There's an ebb and flow to the various product categories on eBay. Some categories get hotter, some get colder, and some are fairly constant in their sales. Track a category's sales over time and you can get a sense of whether that category is on the upswing or the downturn. Obviously, getting in on a rising sales curve is better than jumping into a once-trendy category that's nearing the end of its product life cycle.

When you're deciding on a business model, you need to take all these factors into account. But, as you'll soon learn, there is no one right model that suits everyone. Some sellers prefer a constant flow of low-priced products. Others prefer selling the occasional high-priced item. Some prefer selling the same type of item week-in and week-out; others prefer a bit more variety and being able to jump on and off product trends over time. So all this research is just a tool in helping you decide what type of business you want to run. Do your homework to find the model that you're most comfortable with.

tip When you're looking at sales trends over time, remember to factor in any seasonality. Many categories pick up during the holiday shopping season and slow down over the summer. Some categories have different types of seasonality; for example, you'll sell more swim suits in the summer and more ski boots in the winter. Don't mistake normal seasonality for longer-term product life-cycle trends.

CHAPTER

3

Creating a Business Plan

Before you can start your eBay business, you have to determine just what type of business you want to start. Yes, you know that it's going to involve selling (hopefully lots of) stuff on eBay, but what kind of stuff are you going to sell? And where are you going to get that stuff? And just how are you going to manage the selling and shipping of all that stuff? And, if everything goes well, how much money do you expect to make—versus how much money you have to spend?

When—and only when—you can answer all these questions, you're ready to start building your new business. Until then, you're just fooling around. Not that there's anything wrong with fooling around, of course—that describes millions of typical eBay sellers, most of whom do just enough work to make a little money. But if you want to make a *lot* of money—if you want to run a true business on eBay—then you have to do your homework and figure out where you want to go and how you're going to get there.

act of figuring out what kind of business you'll be running is best done
reparing a *business plan*. If that sounds terribly formal and complicated,
't stress out—it doesn't have to be. The plan for your business can be as
ple as some bullet points written out in longhand, or as sophisticated as a
professional-looking desktop-published document. Your plan is simply a formal declaration of what you want to do and how you want to do it. The key
thing is to set down on paper the details about the business you want to create, and then follow the steps in your plan to build that business.

Thinking It Through—Before You Start

The key to planning your eBay business is to sit down and give it some serious
thought. You don't want to rush into this new endeavor without thinking
through all the details. While it is possible to stumble into eBay profitability,
the most successful sellers know what they want to do and how they want to
do it. In other words, they have a plan for success.

If you *don't* plan your business in advance, chances are you'll run into more
than a few surprises. Unpleasant surprises. You don't want to get six months
into your business and then find out that you're losing money on every sale
you make. Far better to think through everything beforehand, so you'll know
what to expect. No surprises—that's my motto.

Can you start selling on eBay without putting together this kind of business
plan? Of course you can. Can you be successful without a business plan?
Maybe—but probably not, at least not in the long term. It's easy to start selling on eBay and even to generate a small profit in the short term. But to
launch a business that generates sustained profits, you need to plan for that
success. If you don't know where you want to go, you'll never get there.

The easiest way to begin this planning process is to ask yourself a series of
questions. When you can comfortably answer these questions, you'll have the
framework of your business plan.

What Type of Business Do You Want to Run?

The first question to ask is the most important: What type of business do you
want to run? Or, put more pointedly, what types of merchandise do you
intend to sell on eBay?

You see, you can't just sell "stuff" on eBay. That's not a real business; that's an
online garage sale. No, you have to determine what *kind* of "stuff" you want
to sell. And you probably want to specialize.

You took a good first step toward determining what to sell when you worked through the preliminary product research in Chapter 2, "Researching Your Business Model." As you learned there, you can easily find out how well any given type of merchandise performs just by searching eBay's closed auctions or using one of the many available research tools. Use this research to help you determine whether selling a certain type of product makes sense. You want to look at sales potential, sell-through rate, and the average final selling price. If the research shows high profit potential, you've made a good choice. If the research shows low sales or low profits, it's time to do some more thinking. You might have your heart set on selling a particular type of product, but if the sales potential isn't there, why bother?

> **note** You can examine six different types of eBay businesses in Part 2 of this book. These general business models include "The Second-Hand Reseller" (Chapter 8), "The Collector/Trader" (Chapter 9), "The Bulk Reseller" (Chapter 10), "The Retailer" (Chapter 11), "The Manufacturer/Craftsperson" (Chapter 12), and "The Trading Assistant" (Chapter 13).

Of course, the answer to this question is easy if you create or produce your own merchandise. For example, if you're a painter, your product is your artwork. If you make hand-sewn quilts, your product is your quilts. Your business is based on your product; your plan is to use eBay to sell your artwork or your quilts. Everything you do from this point forward is designed to accomplish that goal.

If you don't yet have a source of merchandise—if you could, in fact, sell *anything* on eBay—then you have to decide what type of merchandise you want to sell. That involves determining the type of item you want to work with (smaller and lighter is good, for shipping purposes; cheap to acquire but commands a high price from bidders is also good) and then finding a source for those items. You may also want to choose a business model that plays off a personal interest. For example, if you collect comic books, selling comic books on eBay could be interesting and fun.

The point is that you have to know what you're going to sell before you can figure out how to sell it. That's why this step is so crucial to putting together your business plan.

How Much Money Do You Want to Make?

Knowing what you want to sell is one thing. Knowing how much money you want to make is another. And, unfortunately, sometimes they don't match up.

(This is why planning is important—so you'll know what works before you're hip-deep in things.)

Start from the top down. For your business to be successful, you have to generate an income on which you can comfortably live—unless, of course, you're looking for your eBay business to supplement an existing income. In any case, you need to set a monetary goal that you want to achieve. This number will determine how many items you need to sell.

What you *don't* want to do is set up your business first and then ask how much money you'll make on it. Successful businesses start out with a specific goal in mind and then work toward that goal. Unsuccessful businesses open their doors (figuratively speaking, of course) without knowing where they'll end up—and, more often than not, end up going pretty much nowhere at all.

Let's work through an example. You've talked it over with your family and decided that you would be extremely happy if you could quit your current job and generate the same income from your eBay business. You currently earn $30,000 a year, so this becomes the financial goal of your eBay business.

That $30,000 a year translates into $600 a week, on average. (Figure on 50 working weeks a year, giving yourself 2 weeks of vacation; also keep in mind that certain weeks—around the Christmas holiday, especially—will generate more sales than others, which is why that $600/week is an average.) Now you have to determine how you're going to hit that $600/week target.

We'll also assume that you've already decided what types of items you want to sell. For the purposes of this example, let's say that you're selling gift baskets. Based on your research (primarily by looking at sales of similar items on eBay), you've established that you can sell these gift baskets for $20 each, on average. So you do some quick math and determine that you need to sell 30 of these $20 gift baskets every week to reach your $600/week goal. (That's $600 divided by $20.)

Stop right there! There's something wrong with this calculation. Can you figure out what it is?

Here's the problem: This simple calculation fails to take into account any of your expenses! That $20 per item represents your gross revenue, *not* your net profit. So we have to go back and figure out the costs involved with the sale of each item.

The first cost you have to take into account is the actual cost of the merchandise. Let's say that you pay $5 for each gift basket. Subtract that $5 product cost from your $20 selling price, and you have a $15 profit for every item you sell.

But that's not your only expense. You have to pay eBay for every item you list and for every item you sell. If you accept credit card payments, you'll pay a percentage for all purchases made with plastic. And if you avail yourself of an auction management service, you'll pay for that, too.

Altogether, these nonproduct costs can add up to 10–15% of your total revenues. Let's use the top figure—15%—and subtract $3 for each $20 sale.

Now let's do the math. Take your $20 selling price, subtract your $5 product cost and $3 for eBay-related fees, and you have a net profit of $12. To generate $600 a week in profit, you have to sell 50 gift baskets. (That's $600 divided by $12.)

That's not the end of the math, however. Based on additional research, you determine that only about half of the eBay auctions in this category end in a sale. So to sell those 50 items, you have to launch 100 auctions every week, half of which will end with no bidders.

That's a lot of work.

Now you need to start thinking about the options available to you. What if you could find a better-quality gift basket that you could sell for $40 instead of $20? Assuming you could keep the rest of your costs in line, that would cut in half the number of auctions you have to run every week. Or what if you decided you could live on $20,000 a year instead of $30,000? That would reduce your financial nut by a third.

You see where we're going with this. By working through these types of details ahead of time, you can fine-tune the amount of money you expect to make and the amount of effort you have to expend. Want to make more money? Then find a higher-priced (or lower-cost) item to sell, or plan on listing a larger quantity of items every week. It's all related—plan where you want to go; then you can figure out how to get there.

How Much Time Can You—and Do You Want to—Devote to Your Business?

Now you're at a point to ask if all this work seems reasonable. Taking our previous example, can you physically manage 100 item listings a week? Can you pack and ship 50 items a week? And, more importantly, can you realistically *sell* 50 items a week? Are there enough potential customers to support that sort of sales volume?

If you plan on making eBay a full-time activity, you'll have eight hours a day, five (or six) days a week, to devote to managing your auctions. If, on the other hand, your eBay business is only a part-time job, you'll have less time to spend. Think it through carefully. Can you reasonably expect to do what you need to do to reach your desired level of sales?

Of course, if you're selling more expensive items (or, more precisely, items that generate a higher dollar profit), there's less work involved. Let's say you're an artist and think you can generate $200 in profit for each painting you sell (at an average selling price of $250 or so). At these prices, you need to sell only three items a week to hit your $30,000/year target. (That's $600 a week required profit divided by $200 profit per item.) And, since each piece of art-work is unique, you might have a higher close rate than you would on a lower-priced commodity item—so you might have to list only four items a week and ship three, which won't take up too much of your time.

On the other hand, if you're selling less expensive items, you'll have to do a lot more sales volume to hit your desired income level. For example, if you're selling $5 computer cables that generate a $3 net profit, you'll have to sell 200 cables per week to make your nut. (That's $600 a week required profit divided by $3 profit per item.) And that's a *lot* of items to sell.

The point is that you have to realistically estimate the amount of work involved to run your eBay business, and then determine if you have that kind of time—and if it's worth the effort to you. If you have only a few hours per week to spend, you might not be cut out to be a high-volume seller. (Unless, of course, you're selling very high-priced/high-profit items.) If you're willing to put in the hours, however, higher income can result.

Why You Need a Business Plan

Okay. You've thought through what you want to sell and the amount of work involved, and you're convinced that it's doable. Why not just get started now?

There are several good reasons to put your planning down on paper. First, by formally writing down your plan, you're guaranteeing that you'll actually think through what you're going to do; you won't slide by without doing the critical thinking. Second, by committing your plan to paper, you have a real plan—something you can follow in the future and use as a benchmark when evaluating your success. And third, if you need to obtain any funding for your business—to purchase inventory, for example—potential lenders or investors will want to see the plan you've put together.

This last point can't be ignored. Most potential lenders and investors require that you present a detailed business plan before they will even consider giving you money. Since your business plan contains information about your potential market, your business, your strategy, and your planned operation, any investor or lender can read the plan to get a quick snapshot of you and your business.

note Need to borrow money to start your eBay business? Check out Chapter 4, "Evaluating and Arranging Funding."

For that reason, a business plan should not only reflect how you plan to run your eBay business, it should also contain everything a potential lender or investor needs to make an informed decision about whether to give you money. Without a business plan, you won't even get in the door.

How to Create a Business Plan

You may think that a business plan has to be a complex document, full of long sentences, overly technical terms, convoluted legalese, and detailed financial data. Nothing could be further from the truth. If you can talk about your business—and you no doubt can, at length—then you can create an effective business plan.

The best business plans are conversational in tone, are easy to read and understand, avoid as much legalese as possible, and include only enough financial data as necessary to paint an accurate picture of your business's potential. In fact, you could probably dictate the bulk of your business plan in a single sitting, based on your inherent knowledge of what you're trying to accomplish and why.

Imagine you're sitting in a restaurant or a coffeehouse, and someone you know comes up and asks you what you're up to these days. You answer that you're in the process of starting up a new eBay business, and then you start to tell a little story. You tell this person what your business is all about, why you've decided to get into this eBay thing, what kind of opportunity you see, and how you intend to exploit that opportunity. If you're on good terms with the person you're talking to, you might even share the revenues and profits you hope to generate.

Here's the type of story you tell:

> "Let me tell you about what I plan to do. You see, there's a big market out there for gift baskets. They're very popular with women, especially older women, who buy them for gifts. They're so popular, eBay has created a dedicated gift basket category on its site.

"I did a search on eBay and found that the average gift basket sells for about $20, and in a typical week there were more than 500 auctions for these items. I've found a source for gift baskets that are better than what you typically find online, and think I can provide eBay's buyers with a better product than they're currently getting, but for a similar price.

"My source will sell me these gift baskets for $5 apiece. If I sell them for $20, on average, I think I can take 10% of the sales in the category. That means I'll be selling around 50 gift baskets a week. Taking all my costs into account, that should generate about $30,000 in profit a year.

"To handle this volume of sales, I plan to set up kind of an assembly line in my spare bedroom. I'll buy the gift baskets in bulk and store them in my garage. I can purchase shipping boxes from my local box store and ship the baskets via Priority Mail. The buyers will pay all shipping costs, which I'll inflate a little to cover the cost of the box and packing material.

"In addition, I'm going to subscribe to one of those auction management services, which will make it easier to manage all my customer communication and keep track of who's paid and what needs to be shipped. And I'll sign up for PayPal so that I can accept credit card payments.

"At the start, I think I can manage the entire business myself—which is what I'm quitting my job to do. If things really take off, I can hire my cousin Helen to help me out with the packing and shipping. But that's probably a ways down the road; for now, it'll be just me, which is all I'm planning for. If I can hit my numbers, I'll be very happy to take home $30,000 a year for my efforts."

As you can see, this short story (a little more than 300 words) tells your audience everything they need to know about your planned eBay business. They know why you're starting the business, they see the opportunity presented, they understand how you expect to profit from that opportunity, they sense the unique things that you intend to do, and they learn how much money you expect to make. It's all there, presented in a logical order; everything important is included, with nothing extraneous added.

In short, you've just created your business plan—orally. Now all you have to do is put it down on paper.

The Components of a Winning Business Plan

Now that you have the outline of your business plan in your head, let's look at how to translate your story into a written document.

In essence, you take your oral story and write it down, in a logical order. The typical business plan is divided into several

note This chapter presents the type of bare-bones business plan you need for a small eBay business. If you want to create a really serious business plan—or a plan for a larger business opportunity—check out my companion book, *Teach Yourself Business Plans in 24 Hours* (2001, Alpha Books).

distinct sections—each of which maps to a part of your business story. What you have to do is take the story you just told and sort it out into short sections that help the reader understand just what it is your business is about.

Of course, your particular business plan can contain more or fewer or different sections than presented here, but it should contain the same information—because this information will describe and drive your new business. If you were writing a business plan for a big corporation, each section might be several pages long. For the purposes of your eBay business, though, think along the lines of a few sentences or paragraphs instead.

You see, the length of your business plan document depends entirely on your particular circumstances. If your business plan is solely for your own personal use, you don't need to make it any longer or fancier than it needs to be. It's even okay to write in bullets rather than complete sentences. If you expect to present your business plan to others, by all means go a little fancier and use proper grammar and punctuation. The key thing is to include all the information necessary to get your points across.

Mission

The Mission part of the plan, typically just a sentence or so long, describes your dream for your business—why you're doing what you're doing. Although this is the shortest section of your plan, it is sometimes the most difficult section to write. That's because many people find it difficult to articulate the reasons why they do what they do.

Sometimes called a *mission statement*, this section describes the *what*—what your business does and what you're trying to achieve. Someone reading your Mission section should know immediately what your business does—and what you *don't* do.

Using our ongoing example, a relevant mission statement might be something like: "I intend to sell high-quality gift baskets to targeted buyers on the eBay online auction site." It should *not* be "I plan to make a lot of money on eBay." That isn't a very specific mission, and it certainly isn't market-driven.

> **note** A mission is different from a goal in that a mission defines a general direction, while a goal defines a specific target. A business will have but a single mission, but can have many individual goals.

Opportunity

The Opportunity section, sometimes called the *market dynamics* or *market analysis* section, describes the compelling reason for your business to exist; in other words, it presents the market opportunity you've identified. Typically, this section starts out by identifying the target market, sizing it, and then presenting growth opportunities.

The goal of this section is to describe the market opportunity you seek to pursue and to convince potential investors that it's a significant enough opportunity to be worth pursuing. As such, this section will include narrative text (you have to tell a story about the market) and some amount of numerical data. Which data you choose to present, how you choose to present it, and how you weave it into your narrative will determine the effectiveness of this section.

When the Opportunity section is complete, the reader should understand the basic nature of the market you choose to pursue, the size of that market, the market's growth potential, and the types of customers who comprise the market. You can obtain most if not all of this data by searching eBay for similar types of merchandise or by browsing through relevant categories.

Why do you need to present market data in your business plan, anyway? The answer is simple—to help you sell prospective lenders and investors on your specific business strategy. You also need to realistically size the opportunity for your own needs; you don't want to pursue merchandise categories that aren't big or robust enough to achieve your financial goals.

In the case of our ongoing example, you might want to include data on the number of similar auctions during a particular period, the average selling price for these items, and the close rate (number of auctions that result in a sale) for this category.

> **note** Learn more about performing market research in Chapter 2, "Researching Your Business Model."

Strategy

The Strategy section of your plan details how you'll exploit that immense market opportunity described in the Opportunity section and puts forward your potential eBay activities. This section typically includes information about the products you'll be selling, as well as how you plan to obtain and market these products. In essence, you want to describe the business you're in, what you plan to sell, and how you'll make money. You'll probably want to include some sort of timeline that details the major milestones you will likely face in successfully implementing your new business.

For our ongoing example, you'd explain that you're selling gift baskets (and maybe describe what a gift basket is), present where and how you're obtaining your merchandise, describe how you'll be selling the items on eBay, and then detail the selling price, cost, and profits associated with your sales.

Organization and Operations

The Organization and Operations section describes your company structure as well as the back-end operations you use to bring your products and services to market. If your employee base consists of you and no one else, that's okay; if you have plans to hire an assistant or two, throw in that information. The key thing in this section is to describe your "back office," how you plan to get things done. That means describing how you'll create your item listings, how you'll warehouse your inventory, and how you'll pack and ship your merchandise.

In short, this section of your business plan is the place where you detail how your business is structured and how it will work.

Strengths and Weaknesses

The Strengths and Weaknesses section is the last text section of your plan. A lot of businesses don't include this section, but I think it's well worth writing. In essence, this section lays bare your core competencies and the challenges you face—which are good to know *before* you actually go into business.

I like including strengths and weaknesses in a business plan, for several reasons. First, summarizing your competitive advantages serves to highlight those unique aspects of your business strategy. In addition, ending the text part of your plan with a list of your strengths is a great way to wrap things up; in essence, you provide a summary of the key points of your plan. Finally, by detailing potential challenges you might face, you get the chance to reassess the reality of what you're about to attempt—and to proactively address these issues before they become real problems.

Remember, when you answer potential challenges with distinct strategies, you turn your weaknesses into strengths—and present yourself as being both realistic and proactive.

note Although everyone will want to see a few common financial statements, know that different lenders and investors will have different requirements in this regard. You may want to enlist the assistance of a qualified accountant or financial advisor to help you prepare these financial statements—and to prepare for any financial questions that may be asked of you.

Financials

The final section of your business plan document is the Financials section. This is the place where you present the financial status of and projections for your business. Put simply, these are the numbers—at minimum, an income statement and a balance sheet. You'll want to include your current statements (if your business is already up and running) and projections for the next three years.

Whether you're borrowing money or trying to attract investors, your potential business partners will want to know what size of business you're talking about, how profitable that business is likely to be, and how you expect to grow revenues and profits over the years. Your financial statements provide that critical information. In addition, this section helps you come to grips with the financial realities of what you plan to do.

In a way, the Financials section defines the goals you have for your eBay business. The revenues and profits you project for future years *are* your company's financial goals; they're the yardstick with which you'll measure the success of your business strategy over the next several years.

When you're making your projections, you should make sure that the numbers you forecast actually make sense. Is there a logic to the revenue buildup over the period? Do the projected expenses make sense in relation to the projected revenues? Are these numbers realistic? Are they achievable? Are they *comfortable*—to both you and to your investors? Bottom line, do the numbers feel right?

Remember, the numbers you put together quantify your financial goals. Once you accept them, you're committing yourself to running a successful eBay business.

note Don't know an income statement from a balance sheet? Then turn to Appendix A, "Accounting Basics," for a brief financial refresher course.

Writing the Plan

Now that you know what goes into a successful business plan, all you have to do is write it. As daunting as that sounds, it isn't that difficult. The hardest part is just sitting down and getting started. Carve out a few hours of an evening or on the weekend, close the door, turn off the radio, and disconnect the telephone and the Internet. Concentrate on the task at hand, starting with a rough outline and filling in the details as if you were telling them to a friend. Take as much time as you need—a few hours, a few evenings, or a few weeks. Don't overthink it; just start writing and worry about editing later.

Once you have a rough draft down, reread it as if you were a stranger to the story. Even better, give it to someone else to read and see if it tells that person everything he or she needs to know about your business. See what questions they have, and incorporate them into any changes you need in your second draft.

After all the words are right, you can spend a few minutes making your document look pretty. Print it out, give it a final proofreading, and you're done. Then, and only then, you can start *using* the plan—to get your eBay business up and running.

Evaluating and Arranging Funding

Believe it or not, you may be able to start your new eBay business with zero dollars in your pocket. A lot of people do; that's one of the things that makes an eBay business attractive.

It's more likely, however, that you'll have some startup costs involved. If nothing else, you'll need to purchase some initial inventory and shipping supplies. How much money you need depends on the type of business you're setting up and how you plan to handle your day-to-day operations. And if you need more upfront money than you currently have in your pocket, you're going to have to find a source for these additional funds.

This chapter is all about this initial funding—and your ongoing financial needs. You'll need to determine how much money you need, how much money you have, and where (and how) to obtain the difference.

How Much Money Do You Need—and Why?

Before you go seeking funding for your new business, you first have to determine how much money you need. This isn't as easy as it may sound.

First, you need to establish *why* you need this funding. That's because the why will sometimes determine the who (to ask for money).

Assuming that you're starting your business from scratch, you'll need enough cash in the bank to pay for all your *operating expenses* until the time when you start generating real profits—which could be a period of months or even a year or more. You'll also need cash to purchase your opening inventory, as well as any capital expenses you need to make (for computers and similar items).

> **note** Operating expenses are the ongoing, day-to-day costs of doing business—rent, utilities, office supplies, packing supplies, and the like.

Estimating Costs

Let's start on the costs side of things. Just what do you need to purchase to get your business up and running?

Your business costs fall into a handful of major categories, which you should enter into a monthly planning spreadsheet, such as the one here. You can adapt this worksheet for your own particular circumstances, and for the specific items you intend to sell. (If you're spreadsheet savvy, you may even want to plug it into Excel.) You should plan out your costs in each category on a month-by-month basis, for at least 12 months.

Need some details? Here's what these categories should include:

- **Capital expenses**. These are the big one-time purchases you need to make just to get started. Capital expenses are those items that have a high cost and a long life, such as personal computers, printers, digital cameras, scanners, office furniture, and similar expensive pieces of equipment. Lower-cost equipment, such as postal scales, typically doesn't fall into this category, nor do disposable items such as boxes and shipping labels. You should enter the total expense for each item in the month you plan to purchase it.

Cost Estimation Worksheet

Month	1	2	3	4	5	6	7	8	9	10	11	12	TOTAL
Capital Expenses													
Computer													
Printer													
Furniture													
Rent and Utilities													
Office rent													
Warehouse rent													
Utilities													
Internet													
Sales Expenses													
eBay fees													
PayPal fees													
Shipping													
Packing Supplies													
Boxes													
Labels													
Other													
Office Supplies													
Paper													
Toner													
Other													
Inventory													
Item 1													
Item 2													
Item 3													
TOTAL													

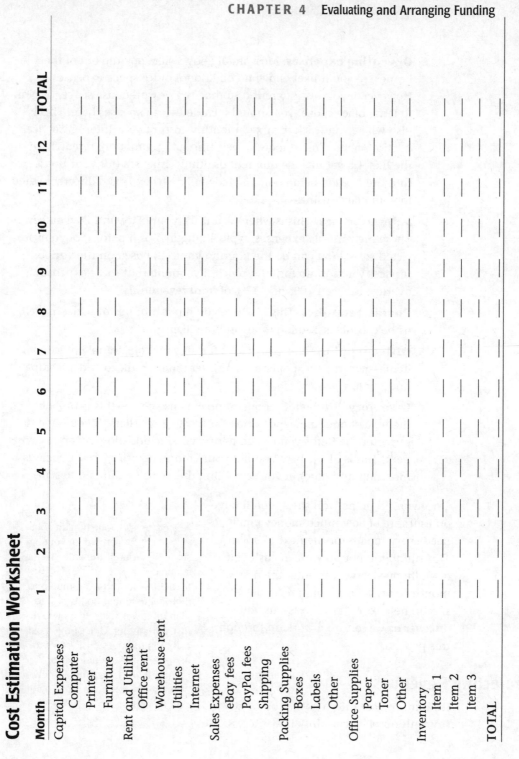

- **Operating expenses**. Most small eBay sellers operate out of their homes, so you'll likely have no additional office space expenses. However, if you need to rent a storage bin or warehouse space, or plan to lease office space, you should include those expenses here. This is also where you track the fixed monthly costs of your Internet service, auction management tools, advertising and promotion, research, and the like. Do *not* include any rent or utility expenses (for your house) that are already being paid; include only new expenses directly related to your eBay business.

- **Sales expenses**. This is where you track your eBay and PayPal fees. These are variable expenses, typically figured as a percent of your projected sales. (You can do the figuring yourself, based on the various services you sign up for; in a pinch, I've found that these expenses average between 10% and 12% of total revenues.)

- **Packing supplies**. This is where you'd put that postal scale, as well as boxes, labels, sealing tape, and the like.

- **Office supplies**. This category is for all your consumable office items—paper, pens, paper clips, printer toner or ink cartridges, staples, and so on.

- **Inventory**. While not an operating expense per se, this is probably the biggest ongoing expenditure for most eBay sellers. If you have to purchase the items you intend to sell, you include those inventory costs here. This is also where you put your "manufacturing" costs, such as materials and labor, if you're making the items you intend to sell.

Once you fill in the worksheet, you'll have an estimate of how much money you'll need every month for the next 12 months. This number is not how much cash you actually need, however. After the first month or so, your ongoing revenues should help cover these costs—as you'll discover as we continue working through this process.

note You shouldn't plan on hitting your stride right out of the gate. It's reasonable to expect your sales to take a few months to ramp up to their full potential, so it's best to plan for lower sales when you're first starting out. One of the most common business mistakes is to underestimate the number of months it will take for your new business to start generating significant revenues.

Projecting Revenues

It's hard to gaze into a crystal ball and say with absolute certainty how successful you're going to be with your eBay sales. All you can do is make a reasonable guess, based on all the planning you did back in Chapter 3, "Creating a Business Plan."

Use the following worksheet to detail your projected sales over a 12-month period.

Sales Projection Worksheet

Month	1	2	3	4	5	6	7	8	9	10	11	12	TOTAL
Sales													
Item 1	__	__	__	__	__	__	__	__	__	__	__	__	__
Item 2	__	__	__	__	__	__	__	__	__	__	__	__	__
Item 3	__	__	__	__	__	__	__	__	__	__	__	__	__
Item 4	__	__	__	__	__	__	__	__	__	__	__	__	__
Item 5	__	__	__	__	__	__	__	__	__	__	__	__	__
Item 6	__	__	__	__	__	__	__	__	__	__	__	__	__
TOTAL	__	__	__	__	__	__	__	__	__	__	__	__	__

Determining Cash Flow

Now that you know how much money you think you'll have going out (costs) and coming in (revenues) every month, you can calculate your monthly cash flow. This isn't your monthly profit, by the way, although it's probably close; it's just a measure of your business's cash position.

You calculate your cash flow by starting with the amount of cash you have on hand (typically the ending cash from the previous month), adding your cash sales for the month, and then subtracting your cash expenses for the month. The resulting number is your *cash position* at the end of the month—which becomes your starting *cash on hand* for the next month.

If your cash position at the end of the month is a negative number, your outflow exceeds your intake and you'll need to come up with additional funds to meet the cash shortfall. If you get a positive number, you've generated extra cash that month—which you can use to pay next month's bills, put in your savings account, or go out and buy something nice for yourself.

Use the following worksheet to calculate your monthly cash flow. Remember that the Cash on Hand number is equal to the Cash Position number from the previous month. If you're profitable, the Cash Position number will keep growing—and the first month it goes positive is the month that your business breaks even.

> **note** The *breakeven point* is that point in time when your expenses and your revenues become equal. Any business conducted before that point was done at a loss; any business after the breakeven point is generating an operating profit.

Cash Flow Worksheet

Month	1	2	3	4	5	6	7	8	9	10	11	12
Cash on Hand	—	—	—	—	—	—	—	—	—	—	—	—
plus Total Sales	—	—	—	—	—	—	—	—	—	—	—	—
minus Total Expenses	—	—	—	—	—	—	—	—	—	—	—	—
Cash Position	—	—	—	—	—	—	—	—	—	—	—	—

Now here's the thing with cash flow: It doesn't matter how much cash you end up with at the end of the year; if you don't have the cash when you need it, you're short. That's why you need to project your cash flow on a monthly basis. (Or, if you want to get really obsessive, you can calculate it weekly; after all, your expenses build up at least that frequently.)

Let's work through a quickie example, as shown in the following worksheet.

If you look to the end of the 12th month, you can see that you're in a very good cash position. You're generating $1,275 in cash each month, and should have a total of $9,200 cash on hand. However, if you look at your very first month, you see that you end that month $2,950 in the hole—and you stay in a negative cash position for the first four months of operation. It takes you until the fifth month to dig yourself out of the hole, when your cash position becomes positive.

All of which means that you need to come up with enough cash to get you through those first four months.

Cash Flow Worksheet: Mike's Gift Baskets

Month	1	2	3	4	5	6	7	8	9	10	11	12
Cash on Hand	$0	(2,950)	(2,600)	(1,950)	(1,000)	$275	$1,550	$2,825	$4,100	$5,375	$6,650	$7,925
Total Sales	$1,000	$1,500	$2000	$2,500	$3,000	$3,000	$3,000	$3,000	$3,000	$3,000	$3,000	$3,000
Capital Expenses	$3,000	$0	$0	$0	$0	$0	$0	$0	$0	$0	$0	$0
Rent & Utilities	$200	$200	$200	$200	$200	$200	$200	$200	$200	$200	$200	$200
Sales Expenses	$100	$150	$200	$250	$300	$300	$300	$300	$300	$300	$300	$300
Packing Supplies	$200	$225	$250	$275	$275	$275	$275	$275	$275	$275	$275	$275
Office Supplies	$200	$200	$200	$200	$200	$200	$200	$200	$200	$200	$200	$200
Inventory	$250	$375	$500	$625	$750	$750	$750	$750	$750	$750	$750	$750
Total Expenses	$3,950	$1,150	$1,350	$1,550	$1,725	$1,725	$1,725	$1,725	$1,725	$1,725	$1,725	$1,725
Cash Position	(2,950)	(2,600)	(1,950)	(1,000)	$275	$1,550	$2,825	$4,100	$5,375	$6,650	$7,925	$9,200

So how much initial cash do you need? All you have to do is look at the biggest monthly loss in the Cash Position line; this number represents the funding requirements for your new initiative. In essence, you want to obtain enough funding to pay for all your expenses until your business becomes self-funding through monthly operating profits. Anything above

note If you have to borrow money just to pay your rent or mortgage, you're in no position to be launching a major eBay business. Make sure that all your basic needs are met *before* you invest more money to become a high-volume eBay seller.

that figure is a safety net; anything less is a disaster waiting to happen.

In our example, the biggest negative cash position comes in the first month. That number—$2,950—is the amount of initial funding you need to get your business up and running.

Now for the tough question: Where do you get the money?

Where to Find Funding

When you need to finance the startup of your business, where you go for funding depends a lot on how much money you need. The less money you need, the easier it will be to find it. If you need really big sums, your options become more limited—and the process more involved.

Let's look at all the places you can find funding for your new eBay business.

Personal Savings

The easiest place to look for money is in your own bank account. If you've been frugal with your money, you might have enough cash on hand to cover the startup costs of your eBay business. Just remember to work through your monthly cash flow to determine when you'll generate enough cash to pay yourself back.

The advantages of going the self-financed route are obvious. You don't have to spend time wooing a multitude of lenders and investors, and you don't have any obligations (legal or financial) to anyone else. The disadvantage, of course, is that it's all your money—and you could lose it all if your new business fails. You also lose whatever interest your money could have been otherwise earning.

It's possible that you don't have enough money to completely fund your eBay business. So self-funding isn't always a viable option. If you have the money, however, it's the fastest and least-complex option available.

Credit Cards

Getting an advance on your credit card is another way of borrowing money from yourself. The big difference between this method and withdrawing funds from your savings account is that you have to pay interest on the funds advanced—which could be a couple of percentage points every month. You may also be charged a fee for making a cash advance to yourself. So when you're calculating your payback schedule, make sure you factor in these additional costs.

Friends and Family

If you don't have the funds, maybe someone you know does. Depending on whom you know (or are related to), you may want to consider borrowing your startup funds from a friend or family member.

The upside of dealing with friends and family is that you're dealing with friends and family. The downside is also that you're dealing with friends and family. Borrowing money from people you know is always a little tricky; even the best of friendships can be tested when the issue of money is involved.

If you decide to hit up someone you know for a loan, my advice is to keep things as professional as possible. That means starting with a well-written business plan and then writing up the entire transaction as a proper loan, complete with an agreed-upon payback schedule and a reasonable rate of interest. Treat your friend just as you would a banker, and make all your payments as scheduled. This way you'll avoid (as much as possible) having this business interfere with your personal relationships.

Loans

If you need more than a few thousand dollars, you may be forced to visit your friendly neighborhood bank or lending company and apply for a small-business loan.

Lenders, of course, require you to give them back the money you borrowed—which means you have to include the loan payback in your financial plans. (This is also the case when you borrow money from friends and family.) You also have to factor in interest payments, which can be significant. This means, of course, that when you're putting together your financial plans, you have to make sure you generate enough profits to cover the loan and interest payments.

Still, if your funding needs are large enough, taking out a loan may be your only option. If this is the case, make sure you borrow no more (or no less) than you really need and that you can realistically pay back on a regular basis. Also be sure to shop around for the best rate possible. When you're talking about the large amounts typical of business loans, a difference of a quarter or an eighth of a point can significantly affect your total payback and your monthly payments.

When you're preparing to approach a banker or a loan official to ask for a loan, remember that lenders aren't expecting some huge payback on their investment; they merely want their principal back along with the designated amount of interest. What they're interested in, then, is your ability to repay the loan. So keep these points in mind when making a presentation to a lender:

- **Show stability**. Show your personal stability. Show the stability of your business model. Show anything you can that says "stable" and "low risk."

- **Concentrate on cash flow**. Lenders are less interested in your profitability (although they *are* interested in that, too) than in your ability to make loan payments. This means you want to stress your cash flow, which hopefully is positive and hopefully is large enough to cover your loan payments.

- **Look professional**. When you deal with professionals, you need to look professional. That means creating a solid business plan and printing it out in a professional fashion. It also means working through your financials so that they're as solid as possible. And remember— when you're dealing with bankers and loan officers, think staid, low-key, and *conservative*.

- **Show a real use for the money**. Bankers won't want to lend you money without a good justification for it. (On the other hand, they also won't want to lend you money if you're so down on your luck that you really need it to survive; you'll have to strike a balance.) Show exactly how the money will be used, and be precise; bankers are nothing if not detail oriented.

note If you have trouble getting a bank to lend you money, you can enlist the services of the Small Business Administration (SBA). The SBA offers a number of different types of loans as well as loan assistance. Learn more at the SBA's website at www.sba.gov.

Most lenders will want to see not only your business plan, but also your current balance sheet and projected P/L. (That's your profit and loss statement projected over the next year or two.) You may also be asked to put up collateral for the amount of the loan. For this reason, many small businesspeople get their startup funding by taking out a second mortgage or line of credit on their houses or other property.

note Large-scale financing—bank loans, investors, and venture capital—might be necessary if you're expanding into the consignment selling, or Trading Assistant, business, especially if you plan to open a retail storefront. Learn more about this business model in Chapter 13, "The Trading Assistant."

Investors

When you need more funds than you can get with a simple loan—when you want to raise really large amounts of money, typically in the tens or hundreds of thousands of dollars—you need to consider equity funding. It's called *equity funding* because you sell equity in your business in return for the funding dollars. The people or companies that buy shares of equity are called *investors*; they're investing their money with the hope that their equity position will be worth more at a later date than it was when they purchased it.

When you take on investors—of any type—you're gaining partners. An investor buys a share of your business and thus has a lasting equity stake. Even though that equity stake can be small, it's still there—which means for every investor you add, the business adds a new co-owner.

The stake of the business that an investor purchases is called a *share*. Each share of your company's stock that you sell is assigned a specific price; this price can vary for different types of investors and will vary over time. As long as your company is private, you set the value of your shares. Once your company goes public (and it doesn't ever have to, of course), the value of the shares is set on the open market of a stock exchange.

There are many types of investors you can pursue for equity funding. In most cases, you'll be going after small investors—sometimes called "friend and family" or "angel" investors, people you know from other business dealings who are willing to

note Although your business plan is a good document to use when looking for a loan, it is just one of the documents you need to prepare when pursuing equity funding. Any time you sell stock in your company, the Security and Exchange Commission (SEC) requires that you prepare and distribute a private placement memorandum (PPM), which must contain some very specific information in a very specific format. Your business plan can accompany your PPM, or you can use your business plan as the cornerstone of your PPM. Ask your lawyer for more information.

invest in the future of your business. If your funding needs are *really* large, you'll be dealing with venture capital (VC) firms, who will demand a major stake in your business in return for their investment—and will expect high growth numbers to make their investment worthwhile.

The ins and outs of equity funding are beyond the scope of this book, and (fortunately) beyond the needs of most eBay sellers. If you think you want to form a business with equity partners, you'll need to bring in expert legal and financial help to put the deal together.

Which Funding Option Is Right for You?

Among these various funding options, which are the best for you and your new business? To find out, you have to get down to work and do some comparisons.

If you have relatively modest goals and funding needs (as most eBay businesses do), you're not large enough to show up on the radar of the big venture capital firms. This is probably for the best, because it's unlikely you'd want the hassle (and control issues) associated with venture capital funding.

Equity placement with small investors is also out of the question for most eBay businesses. Again, this is probably for the best, as you have all sorts of legal issues, not the least of which is developing a dividend-based or profit-sharing payout for your partners.

A more popular source of funding for eBay sellers is your friendly neighborhood banker. It's much easier to get a bank loan than to solicit investments. Borrow enough money to get up and running, make sure you pay it back in time, and then you're free of all obligations.

Even more popular is the self-funding option. If you start modestly (and you should), you probably have enough cash in the bank (or a high enough credit card limit) to handle your minimal startup costs. Just make sure that the costs of launching your business don't keep you from paying your rent or mortgage, and you should be able to pay yourself back in short order.

Establishing a Legal Business Presence

Now that you have a plan for your business and know how to arrange funding to get things started, it's time to work on the nuts and bolts of setting up an official and legal business.

Wait a minute, some of you are probably thinking. There are millions of sellers on eBay who don't go through any of this legal stuff, who sell items out of their garage and do just fine, thank you.

This is true. But those sellers aren't trying to make a business of it; for them, selling on eBay is a hobby or an occasional pursuit. If you want to make serious money on eBay, you have to treat your activity as a serious business—which means setting yourself up as a legitimate business entity.

Choosing a Type of Business

When you're setting up any small business—eBay businesses included—you first need to decide what type of structure you want your business to have. The different types of businesses—sole proprietorship, partnership, and corporation—each have their pros and cons, and you should seriously evaluate which structure is best for your individual situation.

> **note** I am not a lawyer, nor am I an accountant; I just write books. For that reason, you should take the information in this chapter as general in nature, and consult an appropriate professional for more specific legal and tax-related advice.

Sole Proprietorship

Most eBay businesses are set up as sole proprietorships. In this type of structure, you are your business—and vice versa.

A sole proprietorship is the easiest type of business to form, and the easiest to manage on an ongoing basis. You don't have to file any papers of incorporation, nor do you need to withhold and pay monthly payroll taxes and the like. You file income tax for the business under your own name, using your Social Security number as your tax identification number. You'll file and pay this tax in quarterly estimates (described in the "Dealing with Taxes" section, later in this chapter), but the paperwork burden is minimal compared to other forms of businesses.

On the downside, the owner of a sole proprietorship is personally responsible for the debts and legal obligations of the business. That means if the business owes money, you're personally on the hook for it—and if your business gets sued, you end up in court.

Registering as a sole proprietorship is relatively easy and relatively cheap. You can probably handle all the paperwork yourself—although using an accountant or attorney is never a bad idea. Your business can share your name, or you can do business under an assumed name or *dba* (doing business as). To do this legally,

> **note** For more information about the legalities of starting a small business, check out Business.gov (www.business.gov), the U.S. government's guide for businesses; the Business & Human Resources section of the Nolo website (www.nolo.com); and the Entrepreneur's Help Page (www.tannedfeet.com). Another good source of information is your local secretary of state's office (or website), which should have all the forms you need to get started.

you'll need to file a *fictitious name affidavit* in the county in which you do business. If you choose to open a bank account under your business name, you'll need to present this fictitious name affidavit. See the office of your county clerk for specific details.

Partnership

A partnership is like a sole proprietorship, but with more than one owner. The two or more partners have to contractually agree as to who is responsible for what, and how to share the business's profits or losses. You'll definitely want to draw up formal partnership papers, which means bringing in a lawyer. Legal registration is similar to that of a sole proprietorship.

In a partnership, all partners are held personally liable for losses and other obligations. This also means that one partner is liable for the other's actions; if your partner runs up a huge debt or is sued, you can be held responsible.

In addition, breaking up or selling a partnership is often problematic. If one partner wants to quit, the other one(s) has to buy out his or her share—and valuing a business at the breaking point is seldom quick or easy.

A partnership has to file a tax return and must have a Federal Employer Identification Number (EIN), although the business itself pays no income tax. The individual partners report the company's income on their personal tax returns.

A few words of caution, however: If you're thinking of opening an eBay business in partnership with a close friend or family member, know that one of the most effective ways to ruin a good friendship is to go into partnership together. Even the best friendships are tested in the stressful environment of running a day-to-day business. I've seen far too many friendships end up on the rocks because of shared business stresses. It may very well be true that while friends can be partners, partners can never be friends.

Corporation

Almost all large businesses (IBM, Microsoft, Viacom, and so on) are incorporated. Small businesses can also incorporate, although for many, going to the effort is more trouble than it's worth.

One of the main advantages of incorporating your business is that it separates you personally from the business entity. That means your personal liability is reduced if the business falls into debt or gets sued—in theory. In practice, however, lenders will often require the owners of small corporations to sign personal guarantees, which pretty much obviates that purported advantage.

Another advantage of incorporating is that if you eventually have to hire additional workers to help you run your eBay business, you can set up health insurance and retirement plans for your company's employees. In addition, if you ever decide to get out of the business, selling a corporation is easier than selling other forms of businesses. Corporations can also sell stock, so if you have dreams of going big time, this is the way to start. There may also be tax advantages of incorporating. Consult your accountant for details.

And, depending on the amount of revenue your business generates, you may pay fewer taxes as a corporation than you would as an individual. At higher levels, you can shield some of your personal income from employment tax by having the corporation pay you a dividend rather than a salary. (Dividends don't have employment tax attached; salaries do.) Of course, any dividends paid to stockholders (that would be you) are still subject to personal income tax. You'll need to consult your accountant to determine which if any tax benefits accrue in your particular situation.

Potentially offsetting this tax savings is the fact that the corporation itself has to pay taxes on its profits. You minimize this corporate tax burden by taking all the profit out of your corporation, typically in the form of a big year-end bonus or dividend to yourself, so that the business has no net profit. It's a numbers thing.

These benefits come at a cost, however, in the form of increased fees and paperwork. At the very least, a corporation must have a Federal EIN and withhold and pay monthly employment taxes for each of its employees. (That's you again.) You'll probably need an attorney or accountant to handle the details for you.

Thee are several types of corporations you can form, the most popular of which is the *subchapter S corporation*. This type of incorporated business is the simplest to set up, and the profits of such a business aren't subject to corporate taxes. (You're still subject to personal income taxes, of course.) Forming a subchapter S corporation also enables you to offset any business losses against your personal income.

If you have additional investors in your business (besides yourself, that is), you might want to consider filing as a *limited liability corporation (LLC)*. In an LLC, the business's income and losses are shared by all investors, although investors are subject to limited liability (hence the name) for the corporation's debts and obligations.

In addition, several states recognize another form of small business corporation, called a *statutory close corporation (SCC)*. An SCC typically is less formal (and therefore easier to establish) than a typical corporation, with operation similar to an LLC. You should ask your lawyer about the benefits of forming an SCC if you live in Alabama, Arizona, Delaware, Georgia, Illinois, Kansas, Maryland, Missouri, Montana, Nevada, Pennsylvania, South Carolina, Texas, Vermont, Wisconsin, Wyoming, or the District of Columbia.

note While it's always good to work with a local attorney, you can complete your incorporation papers online with LegalZoom (www.legalzoom.com). This website lets you create all manner of simple legal documents—typically for a lower cost than you would otherwise.

All this said, most small eBay sellers opt against forming a corporation for their eBay businesses. I can only speak for myself here, but I've found that whatever slight advantages incorporation might offer to a small business are more than offset by the increased paperwork. For an eBay business just starting out, sole proprietorship is probably the way to go.

Filing and Registering

While it's possible to just go online and start selling on eBay, if you're running a business, you probably have to register with your local government. The rules differ from state to state (and sometimes from county to county!), but a good attorney or accountant can fill you in on what specifically you need to do where you live. You should also check with the staff at your county clerk's office or chamber of commerce, or on your state's official website; they'll tell you what you need to do.

As to what exactly you need to do, many states, counties, and cities require that you register any new business with them. Some locales require you to obtain a permit or license for your activity; you should also check to see if your location is zoned for the type of business you plan to conduct.

As we'll discuss next, you'll also need to collect, report, and pay sales tax on all sales you make to residents of your state. That means obtaining a tax license and number from the state, and possibly a sales permit or reseller license from your local government. Your sales tax number also functions as a *resale certificate*. You

note For a state-by-state list showing where to obtain business licenses, check out the Where to Obtain Business Licenses page on the SBA website (www.sba.gov/hotlist/license.html).

can present this number to any wholesalers you work with, which saves you from paying sales tax on the goods you purchase.

Dealing with Taxes

The only things sure in life are death and taxes. We'll skip the death conversation and focus on the tax side of things, because that's (hopefully!) more relevant to budding eBay sellers.

Collecting Sales Tax

Here's the question nearly everyone asks: Do I need to collect sales taxes on my eBay sales? The answer is a firm "perhaps."

Part of the answer depends on how much business you do on eBay—that is, whether your eBay sales are part of a steady business or more of an occasional hobby. Not that I'm recommending it, but occasional eBay sellers can probably get by without collecting sales tax, just as most individuals running garage sales fly under the tax radar. When you're running a legitimate day-to-day business, however, there's no sliding by this requirement: You *must* collect sales tax, and you must report your collections to your state tax authorities. Failure to do so has legal implications.

Of course, just what sales taxes you collect depends on the state in which you live. If your state has a state sales tax (and all but Alaska, Delaware, Montana, New Hampshire, and Oregon do), you'll need to charge sales tax on all sales made to buyers who live in the same state you do. You do not have to, at this point in time, charge and collect sales tax on sales made to out-of-state or out-of-country buyers.

So, for example, if you live in California, you charge sales tax on all sales made to California residents. If someone from Nevada buys something from you, you don't charge tax.

Of course, when you collect sales tax from a customer, you also have to report and forward that tax to your state government. This procedure varies from state to state, so you'll have to check with your local authorities (or your accountant) to get the appropriate details of how this is done—monthly, quarterly, or whatever. You can also find this information online.

note eBay makes it relatively easy to collect sales tax on your in-state sales. All you have to do is check the appropriate option on the Sell Your Item listing form when you're creating your auction listing. Tax will automatically be added to the final price during the checkout process.

Check out the list compiled by the Multistate Tax Commission (www.mtc.gov/
txpyrsvs/actualpage.htm).

Paying Taxes on Your eBay Income

While we're on the subject of taxes, here's another one you're not going to
like. When you're running a legitimate eBay business, you're going to have to
report all the money you generate from your eBay sales as income. Failure to
report your income is definitely actionable.

Again, if you're just selling a few items a month, the government probably
isn't going to come after you for nickels and dimes. (Although it could if it
wanted to.) But when you become a high-volume professional seller, your
eBay activity is a real business—and real businesses have to pay taxes. That's
all there is to it.

If you're running a sole proprietorship, the income you generate from your
eBay sales, less any expenses related to those sales, is your business income,
which you report on IRS form Schedule C. Your business income then becomes
part of the calculation for your personal income tax, which you report on
your normal form 1040. (It goes without saying that this process is even more
complicated if you're incorporated.)

Unfortunately, keeping track of the taxes you owe is a little more complicated
when you're running your own business than it is when you work for someone else. Since you're working for yourself, there's no employer to withhold
taxes from your paycheck (what paycheck?); instead, you'll need to estimate
and pay these taxes quarterly, using IRS form 1040-ES. (You'll also need to pay
state quarterly estimated taxes, using the appropriate state form.) You might
as well mark the dates on your calendar now—June 15, September 15,
January 15, and April 15 are the four quarterly payment dates.

Fortunately, most everything you spend
money on that's related to your business
can be deducted from your taxes as a
business expense. And I mean *everything*—
Internet service, your computer, automobile trips to the bank or office supply store,
even a fair share of your household utilities (for that portion of your house you use
as a home office) may all be legitimate
deductions. And the more deductions you
have, the lower your reportable income for
tax purposes.

note It's important that
you factor your
quarterly tax payments in your
budget. If you're used to having a
regular job, with your taxes automatically deducted from each paycheck, paying this way will be a
new thing for you. When you run
your own business, you're responsible for estimating your own taxes—
and for making those payments
every three months.

All this accounting sounds complicated, and it is—which is another reason to hire a professional to handle your business accounting and taxes. Your accountant will know just what you can and can't deduct, no guessing involved. Even better, it's likely that your accountant will find things to deduct that you never thought of—which will more than pay for his or her fee. You can also get "official" tax information from the Internal Revenue Service. Check out the IRS's Small Business One Stop Resource website (www.irs. ustreas.gov/businesses/small/).

Withholding Employee Tax

Depending on the size and complexity of your eBay business, you may need to worry about one more type of tax. If you have employees working for you in your eBay business, you'll need to withhold income tax from their paychecks, and then report and pay this tax to the state and federal government. This is actually a fairly complicated process, and not for the numerically challenged—yet another good reason to employ the services of a qualified accountant.

If you have to deal with withholding taxes, the federal form you need to file is the SS-4; more information is available on the IRS website. For state withholding information, check out the state-by-state list compiled by the Federation of Tax Administrators (www.taxadmin.org/fta/link/forms.html).

Setting Up Your Bank Accounts

When you're running a business, your banking needs are likely to be different from your previous personal needs. While you *can* make do by running your eBay payments through your personal savings and checking accounts, it's much cleaner to establish a separate banking identity for your business. This way it's clear which funds are personal and which are business-related.

Merchant Checking Account

The best business practice is to set up a merchant or business checking account separate from your personal accounts. While you're not required to do this, it will make your recordkeeping easier. Having a bank account in your business name should also minimize any potential confusion when it comes to depositing or cashing checks made out to your business name or dba.

To set up a merchant account, you'll need that fictitious name affidavit we talked about earlier. If you're running a partnership, the partnership's bank account should be separate from all the partners and should require more than one name on the checks. (That's to protect against any one partner running off with all the funds.)

note Rather than setting up a specific merchant account, it may be easier (and cheaper) to set up a second personal account—especially if you're a sole proprietorship. The important thing is to set up a separate account; it doesn't have to be a literal merchant-type account.

Dealing with Credit Card Payments

While you're at the bank, you should ask about what's involved in establishing a merchant credit card account. You'll need to accept credit card payments for your eBay auctions, and if you can easily and affordably set up a merchant account with your bank, all the better. Know, however, that most banks make it difficult for small businesses to do this; you're probably better off going with PayPal for your credit card payments.

Obtaining Insurance

If you're truly relying on your eBay sales as your sole source of employment, you'll need to obtain health and disability insurance for yourself and your family (if you don't already have it)—and, if you're incorporated, for your employees. While eBay offers a health insurance plan to PowerSellers, all other sellers are on their own.

Fortunately, while you're on your own, you're not truly alone; there are many health-care insurance providers that offer plans for small businesses and the self-employed. In addition, many business organizations and associations offer group insurance plans to their members. Here are some websites you can use to search for small business health insurance:

note Learn more about PayPal and credit card payments in Chapter 16, "Managing Customer Payments."

You can also shop for health insurance—and find a wealth of other information—when you join the National Association for the Self-Employed (www.nase.org), a great organization for all types of self-employed businesspeople.

- HealthInsurance.com (www.healthinsurance.com)
- Health Insurance Resource Center (www.healthinsurance.org)

■ Insure.com (`www.insure.com`)

■ National Association of Socially Responsible Organizations (`www.nasro-co-op.com`)

You should also consider obtaining insurance on your business itself. This type of business insurance is designed to protect you from specific business liabilities, such as creditors and potential lawsuits. Check with your insurance agent to shape a policy that works for you.

Hiring Professional Help

Now that I've sent your head spinning with all the paperwork required to get your eBay business off the ground, let me tell you how to make most of these details go away:

Hire someone to do it for you.

That's right, when it comes to setting up and managing a small business, there is a definite advantage to hiring professionals to handle all the paperwork and record keeping. Yes, it's an additional cost you'll have to pay, but for most of us it's not only worthwhile—it's a necessity.

What kinds of professionals am I talking about? Just two: an accountant and an attorney. The attorney is necessary to help you get your business registered and legal, and the accountant is necessary to keep track of your taxes and finances on an ongoing basis. While you might be able to do all this work yourself (or not), a professional is more likely to know what's required, and thus keep you out of any potential hot water. Professionals also do this for a living, so they can do it better and faster than you can. Let the professionals handle all this busy work—so you can focus your attention on the important job of running your business!

And remember—all professional fees are tax deductible.

> **note** Learn more about hiring an accountant and managing your business's accounting in Chapter 6, "Setting Up a Recordkeeping System."

Setting Up a Recordkeeping System

When you're running a business, you need to keep track of what you're doing. That means keeping records about what you sell, whom you sell it to, and how much money you make (or don't) from what you sell. These records not only help you manage your business on a day-to-day basis, they also help you prepare your yearly taxes.

This chapter walks you through the records you need to keep and suggests how to set up your own recordkeeping system.

Why You Need to Keep Good Records

How profitable is your business? You'll never know if you're not keeping track—which is reason enough to set up some sort of recordkeeping system.

Keeping records can be both a defensive and an offensive activity. It's defensive in that you have key information about your business in case you ever need it in the future—to answer a query from the IRS, for example, or to investigate a customer complaint or notify customers in the case of a product recall. It's offensive (in a good way) in that you can use this information to generate more sales, by selling additional items to your existing customer base.

And then there's that matter of tracking the progress of your business.

You need to know how much things cost and how much you sell them for in order to gauge the success of your business. If nothing else, you have to report your business income to the Internal Revenue Service at the end of each year, and you can't do that if you don't know what you've sold and for how much. The more detailed and accurate your recordkeeping, the easier it is to put together your yearly tax returns—and to claim all the allowable deductions against your income.

In addition, setting up a simple accounting system lets you generate monthly financials, which tell you on a near-real-time basis just how well your business is (or isn't) doing. After all, you don't want to wait until the end of the year to find out that you're going broke—or getting rich!

Components of a Bare-Bones Recordkeeping System

When we talk about setting up a recordkeeping system for your eBay business, we're talking about assembling and tracking some very bare-bones data. Let's look at each component of the recordkeeping system in detail.

Inventory Records

Setting up an inventory management system sounds like an extremely complex undertaking. It's really not. Just think of it in these simple terms:

You want to track when you got your stuff, how much it cost you, when you sold it, and how much you sold it for.

That's not rocket science.

In the old (pre-PC) days, many businesses tracked their inventory on 3"×5" index cards. (I know; I used to work with a system like this.) Each card typically included the following information:

- Item name
- Item description

- Item model number (if appropriate)
- Item serial number (if appropriate)
- Cost of the item (sometimes called the *cost of goods sold*, or *COGS*)
- Date the item was purchased
- Date the item was sold
- Final sales price of the item

The one bad thing about "the old days" was that we had to enter all this information by hand and then manually add up the numbers on all the cards at the end of each month. Now that we all have personal computers, however, a lot of this manual work is automated.

The simplest way to track your inventory on a PC is to use a database program, such as Microsoft Works Database or Microsoft Access. You can also use a spreadsheet program, such as Microsoft Excel, as a kind of simple database; Excel's database functions are good enough for most small business inventory management.

Just set up your database or spreadsheet with fields for each of the items listed previously. Then create a new record for each item in inventory. Whenever you purchase new inventory, create new records. When you sell an item, mark the record for that item sold, and fill in the date sold and sales price fields.

At the end of each month, have your program run a report that lists the total cost of the entire inventory you currently have in stock. You should also run a report showing all items sold and calculating your total profit (sales price less cost of item) on these items. That should provide the basic inventory and sales information you need for your accounting system (discussed later in this chapter).

Once you get good at it, you can use your inventory management system to help you decide when to order more items for sale. Set a minimum quantity that you want to keep in stock, and program your database to alert you when the number of units on hand drops below this number. This capability is particularly useful when you're selling large quantities of each item and when you have to purchase each item in quantity.

Another option for tracking the inventory of your eBay business is to use one of the advanced auction management tools offered by various third-party sites. These tools are discussed in more detail in Chapter 19, "Automating Auction Management." The best of these tools will track both your inventory and your customer activity, all in a single package.

Customer Records

Just as it's important to track what you sell, it's also important to track who buys it. Establishing a customer management system not only lets you recall which customers you've sold to, it also lets you match up your customers with specific item purchases—and possibly leverage that information for future sales.

You can use Access or Excel to store your customer information. In addition, you can use eBay Selling Manager or most other auction management tools to track your customers and their sales activity.

What customer records should you keep? Here's a short list:

- Customer name
- Customer address (street, city, state, ZIP code)
- Customer email address
- Item number purchased
- Item description
- Price of item purchased
- Date item listed for auction
- Date auction closed
- Date item paid for
- Payment method
- Date item shipped
- Shipping method
- Shipping cost
- Tracking information

You might also find it useful to track all the communications you send to each customer. This way you'll know which customers you've contacted about payment and who might need a reminder email.

Once you have all this customer information stored, what do you do with it? First, it's good to have, *just in case*—just in case a customer claims not to have received an

note You can feed some of this customer information back to your inventory management system—which is why a lot of recordkeeping systems integrate the inventory and customer management functions. The date sold and sales price data, specifically, transfer directly to the same fields in your inventory management database. There's no point in entering the same information twice if you don't have to.

item, or just in case a customer has a complaint and wants his or her money back. In addition, some sellers use their customer lists to solicit additional sales, mailing or emailing them when they have new merchandise available or a sale coming up. It's always wise to know who your good customers are; making additional sales to an existing customer costs less than acquiring a completely new customer.

Financial Records

You can use the information stored in your inventory and customer management systems to help you prepare your ongoing financial records. In particular, you'll want to transfer the data relating to item cost, date sold, and sales price; this information will form the key lines on your monthly income statement.

You'll also need to track additional information relating to the costs of running your eBay business and then use that information to perform your regular business accounting. In particular, you'll need to hold onto certain items for tax purposes—specifically those little pieces of paper that document items you've purchased or sold. Even if your "system" consists of throwing all your receipts in an old shoebox or file folder, you need to hold onto all these items—not only for your monthly accounting and end-of-year tax preparation, but also in case the IRS ever decides to audit you.

How long should you hold onto your original documentation? Some experts say to hold onto all your receipts and invoices for a minimum of three years, but that might not be long enough. For example, the IRS requires that you keep documentation on all your assets for the life of the asset. And if the IRS thinks you've filed a fraudulent return, there's no statute of limitations at all.

This means you might want to hang onto this basic documentation *forever*. Just clear out a corner of your garage or attic where you can store all your shoeboxes, and be done with it.

What kind of hard-copy documentation should you be holding? Here's a short list:

- Bank statements
- Credit card statements
- Receipts for all business-related purchases and expenses (including shipping expenses)
- Invoices for all inventory purchases
- Invoices or sales receipts for all items sold

- Automobile mileage (keep a log for all business-related travel—like all those trips to and from the post office)

note Want to learn more about setting up a small business accounting system? Then check out Accounting for Everyone (www.accountingforeveryone.com) or the Accounting section on the BusinessTown site (www.businesstown.com).

Setting Up an Accounting System

Throwing all your receipts in a shoebox is just a start. To truly track your business's finances, you need to incorporate all the data from those receipts and from your inventory and customer management systems into some sort of an accounting system.

This chapter isn't the place to go into all that's involved in setting up a detailed small business accounting system; lots of other books and online resources are more appropriate to the task. We can, however, take a look at what you need to track to make your accounting system work.

Tracking Your Business Activity

All accounting systems track basic types of activities: revenues and expenses. *Revenues* are the sales you make to your eBay customers. *Expenses* are the costs you incur in the running of your business—the inventory you have to purchase, as well as all those other things you need to buy to make your business run.

In accounting terms, the money you take in creates a *credit* on your books. The money you spend creates a *debit*. When your credits exceed your debits, you're making a profit (or at least generating positive cash flow). When your debits exceed your credits, your business is losing money. Obviously, the former position is preferable.

To make your accounting system work, you have to enter each and every financial activity of your business. Purchase some merchandise for sale, enter it in the books. Make a sale, enter it in the books. Buy some supplies, enter them in the books. You get the idea.

At regular intervals—typically at the end of each month—you add up all the credits and debits (after putting them in the proper slots) and take a snapshot as to how your business is doing. These

note Confused? Brush up on these essential accounting concepts in Appendix A, "Accounting Basics."

snapshots are the financial statements you use to measure the financial condition of your business.

Key Financial Statements

There are two key financial statements that you should prepare at the end of each month. They are the *income statement* (sometimes called a *profit and loss statement*, or *P/L*) and a *balance sheet*. These documents measure the condition of your business from two different angles.

Income Statement

The income statement reflects the revenue your business generates, the expenses you pay, and the profit (or loss) that filters down. This is done by showing your revenues, subtracting the cost of goods sold (which reveals the gross profit), and then subtracting all your operating expenses to show your net profit. And, after all, it's that net profit number that really matters.

The top of the income statement lists all the money your business took in— your business's revenues. The bottom of the statement lists all the money you paid—your business's expenses. Subtract the bottom from the top and the number you get, expressed on the last line of the statement, is your business's profit or loss.

Most businesses will create an income statement for each month in the year and then a comprehensive income statement at the end of the year. Many businesses like to track their progress over the course of the year and create a year-to-date income statement at the end of each month, as well.

Balance Sheet

The other essential financial statement is the balance sheet. The balance sheet looks at your business in a slightly different fashion from an income statement. Instead of looking at pure monetary profit (or loss), the balance sheet measures how much your business is worth. It does this by comparing your assets (the things you own—including your cash on hand) with your liabilities (the money you owe to others).

Assets go on the left side of the balance sheet, and liabilities go on the right. The total number for each column should be equal—hence the "balance" part of the title. You should generate a balance sheet at the end of every month and at the end of the year.

note See Appendix A for a detailed explanation of income statement and balance sheet line items.

Software for Small Business Accounting

How do you put together all your business data and generate these financial statements? You have two practical options: hire an accountant or use an accounting software program. (You could also, I suppose, keep your books by hand, on oversized sheets of ledger paper while wearing a green eyeshade—although hardly anyone except latter-day Bob Cratchets do it that way anymore.)

We'll look at accounting software first.

There are many different programs you can use to keep your business's books. The simplest of these programs are the personal financial management programs, such as Quicken and Microsoft Money. They may be able to do the job if your business is simple enough, but most small businesses will find them somewhat limited in functionality. A better choice for many eBay businesses is QuickBooks, which is a more full-featured small business accounting program. If your business is big or unique enough, however, even QuickBooks might not be powerful enough; in that instance, you can evaluate other more powerful business accounting packages.

Quicken

The most popular financial management program today is Intuit's Quicken (www.quicken.com). Quicken comes in various flavors, only one of which has features of use to the small business. That version, Quicken Premier Home & Business, lets you track your business expenses, record assets and liabilities, generate customer invoices, and create basic financial statements.

Microsoft Money

Microsoft Money (www.microsoft.com/money/) is a direct competitor to Quicken. Like Quicken, Money comes in various flavors; the version of interest to eBay businesses is Microsoft Money Small Business. This version offers similar functionality to Quicken Premier Home & Business, as well as basic payroll management.

QuickBooks

A better option for most small business owners is Intuit's companion package to Quicken, called QuickBooks (www.quickbooks.com). There are a number of versions of QuickBooks—Simple Start, Pro, Premier, and Enterprise Solutions. For most eBay businesses, either the Simple Start or Pro version (shown in Figure 6.1) should be more than good enough.

FIGURE 6.1

One of the most popular small business accounting packages— Intuit's QuickBooks Pro.

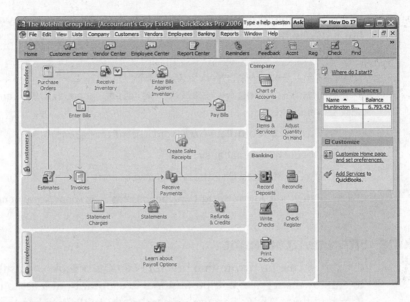

You can use QuickBooks not only to do your monthly accounting and generate regular financial statements, but also to manage your inventory, track your sales, and do your year-end taxes. QuickBooks even integrates with PayPal, so you can download all your PayPal-related transactions into the software program, and manage everything all in one place.

Intuit also offers a web-based version of QuickBooks, called QuickBooks Online Edition, which you can access from the main QuickBooks website. This Online Edition keeps all your records online, so you can do your accounting from any computer, using nothing more than your web browser. QuickBooks Online Edition isn't quite as robust as the standalone version, which makes it best for those eBay businesses with simpler needs. You'll pay $19.95 per month (or more, depending on the plan) for this service.

> **tip** If you use QuickBooks, you want to download eBay's Accounting Assistant program. Accounting Assistant lets you export eBay and PayPal data directly into QuickBooks, and is free to use—although to generate the necessary data you also need a subscription to eBay Stores, Selling Manager (Basic or Pro), or Seller's Assistant (Basic or Pro). Get more details—and download the program—at pages.ebay.com/help/sell/accounting-assistant-ov.html.

Other Small-Business Accounting Packages

If QuickBooks doesn't satisfy your accounting needs, other small business accounting programs are available. Some of these programs are more fully featured than QuickBooks, and more complicated to use. That might not present a problem if you're relatively numbers-savvy, but if accounting doesn't run in your blood, some of these programs might be more than you can handle.

Here are a few of these accounting packages to consider:

- Business Works (www.2020software.com/products/Business_Works.asp)
- Cashbook Complete (www.acclaimsoftware.com)
- DacEasy (www.daceasy.com)
- MYOB BusinessEssentials (www.myob.com)
- Peachtree Accounting (www.peachtree.com/peachtreeaccountingline/)

Working with an Accountant

Even if you use an accounting program like QuickBooks, you still might want to employ the services of a professional accountant—at least to prepare your year-end taxes. That's because an accountant is likely to be more experienced and qualified than you to manage your business's tax obligations.

Many small businesses use QuickBooks to generate their monthly financial statements but then call in an accountant to prepare their quarterly estimated taxes and year-end tax statements. This is a pretty good combination; you can have QuickBooks print out just the right data that your accountant will need to prepare your taxes.

Of course, you can also use an accountant to handle *all* of your financial activities. This is a particularly good idea if (1) your business is generating a high volume of sales, and (2) you aren't particularly interested in or good at handling the books. You'll pay for this service, of course, but if your business is big enough, it's probably worthwhile.

Where do you find a reputable accountant? You should check with your local chamber of commerce or SBA office, as well as other local small business organizations. It wouldn't hurt to ask other small business owners; word-of-mouth is often the best way to find simpatico service providers.

In addition, you can use the Internet to search for small business accountants in your area. Check out these websites:

- 1-800-Accountant (www.1800accountant.com)
- CPA Directory (www.cpadirectory.com)

■ The National Association of Small Business Accountants (www.
smallbizaccountants.com)

However you find an accountant, know up front that he or she will need you
to keep some very specific financial records—like those we discussed earlier in
this chapter. Your accountant can't track your business unless you're tracking
your business, so work with your accountant to set up the best recordkeeping
system for your business needs.

Organizing Your Home Office

Running an eBay business involves a lot of work—and a lot of *different* work. There's a fair share of bookwork involved, especially when it comes to managing your eBay auctions, which means working behind a desk or at a computer. Then there's the physical management of your inventory. And the packing and shipping of all the items you sell.

All of these back office activities have to be done someplace. Assuming that you're running your eBay business out of your home, that means carving out space to run your business—space for your desk and computer, space to store your inventory, and space for your "shipping department." That might mean appropriating a spare bedroom, or setting up shop in your basement, or even portioning off part of your kitchen or living room. Wherever you find the space, it's important to get your back office set up and running smoothly so that you can perform your day-to-day eBay operations with a minimum of fuss and muss.

Setting Up Your Home Office

Let's start with the "white collar" part of your eBay operation—your home office. This is where you'll perform all your online operations and manage all your paperwork.

note All of your business expenses should be tax deductible, so keep track of all your receipts.

Personal Computer

A decent personal computer system is a necessity for any eBay business. After all, you need the computer to get online and manage your eBay auctions!

How fancy a computer do you need? Fortunately, not too fancy. Your computing needs will be fairly modest, so you don't have to spend a lot of money on a state-of-the-art powerhouse PC. In fact, you can probably get by with one of the lowest-priced models available—or just use your existing PC, if you already have one.

What kind of PC are we talking about? Here are the minimum specs I recommend if you're looking to buy a new PC—and more is always better:

- 2.8GHz microprocessor
- 512MB memory (RAM)
- 100GB hard drive
- CD-R/RW drive
- 17" LCD monitor
- Windows XP Home Edition operating system (or Windows Vista, when it's available)

In today's market, you can find a PC that fits these specs for around $500 or so. And if you're an Apple fan, similarly featured Macintoshes are also easy to find.

Naturally, you should also outfit your PC with the right type of modem for your Internet connection, which we'll discuss in a few pages. Ideally, that means a cable or DSL modem for a fast broadband connection, rather than a (slower) dial-up connection.

If you have more than one PC in your home or business, you might want to invest in the appropriate equipment to network your computers together. Your

note Learn more about buying a new PC—or upgrading your old one—in my companion book, *Absolute Beginner's Guide to Computer Basics, 3rd Edition* (Que, 2005).

network can be either wired or wireless; the easiest solution is to buy an all-in-one networking kit that includes all the equipment you need to assemble and configure the network.

You can shop for a new computer in a number of places; just about every type of retailer carries computers these days, from Wal-Mart to CompUSA and everywhere in between. You can even find good buys on brand-new or used PCs from fellow eBay merchants.

Computer Software

You'll use your PC not only to access the eBay website, but also to manage all your auction transactions and your business's recordkeeping. That means you'll need to install the appropriate computer software for your business needs.

What software do you need? Table 7.1 shows what I recommend.

Table 7.1   Recommended Computer Software

Function	Software	Website
Web browser	Internet Explorer *or* Mozilla Firefox	www.microsoft.com www.firefox.com
Email	Microsoft Outlook *or* Outlook Express	www.microsoft.com
Letters, memos	Microsoft Word	www.microsoft.com
Photo editing	Adobe Photoshop Elements *or* PaintShop Pro *or* Picasa	www.adobe.com www.jasc.com picasa.google.com
Number crunching	Microsoft Excel	www.microsoft.com
Customer database	Microsoft Access *or* Microsoft Excel	www.microsoft.com
Accounting	QuickBooks *or* Quicken Premier Home & Business *or* Microsoft Money Small Business	www.quickbooks.com www.quicken.com www.microsoft.com

You should also consider a decent backup system, to create archival copies of all your important customer and accounting records. I recommend investing in a second, external hard drive for this purpose. You can find large backup

drives for well under $200, and most come
with their own automated backup software. Alternatively, you can use an online
backup service, which lets you back up
your files online to a separate Internet
site; this way, if your office burns down,
your key files are safely stored offsite.
Some of the more popular online backup
services include @Backup (www.backup.com), IBackup (www.ibackup.com), and
Xdrive (www.xdrive.com).

> **note** You can get
> Microsoft Word,
> Excel, and Outlook together in the
> all-in-one Microsoft Office suite. See
> www.microsoft.com/office/
> for more information.

Printer

One of the key components of your computer system is your printer. You'll be
printing lots of invoices and labels, so there's no point spending the money on
a color printer. Buy a good black-and-white model that can handle a heavy
printing load.

You'll need to choose between inkjet and laser printers. Inkjets are lower
priced but could end up costing you more in the long run; all those replacement ink cartridges add up over time. Laser printers cost more, but are faster
and better suited to heavy printing loads. If you think your eBay business will
generate a high volume of sales, a laser printer is probably the way to go.

If you think your business will need fax capability—or if you see the need to
make copies of documents—then consider a combo printer/fax/copier/scanner
machine. These units (sometimes called *all-in-one* machines) are very efficient,
both in terms of cost and in desktop footprint. You can find combo units in
both inkjet and laser varieties, starting from $250 or so.

Finally, consider investing in a separate label printer for your packing and
shipping operation. While you can print labels from your main printer, a freestanding label printer (and associated label-printing software) is often more
convenient, especially if you're shipping dozens or hundreds of items each
week.

Scanner and Digital Camera

You might not think of these next items as absolutely necessary—but you'd be
wrong. You need both a computer scanner and a digital camera to capture
images of the items you'll be selling on eBay.

A scanner is good for scanning images from flat items—CDs, books, small packages, and so on. A digital camera is needed to capture three-dimensional items. Both pieces of equipment save their images as digital files, which you download to your computer's hard disk. Once they're stored on your PC, you can edit the pictures with your image editing software, as you'll discover in Chapter 23, "Displaying More Powerful Photographs."

What kind of digital equipment should you buy? The scanner is relatively easy: Go for a decent flatbed scanner, something in the $100 range. Choosing the right digital camera is more complex. You can find models as low as $100 or as high as $1,000 (or more!). Fortunately, your needs are modest. You don't need a camera with lots of megapixel resolution; the pictures you post on eBay will be low-resolution JPGs. Look for a model that's easy to operate and (especially if you plan on selling smallish items) includes a macro or close-up focus capability. You can probably find what you need in the $200 range.

And, while you're at the camera store, spend an extra $20 or so to buy a tripod. This is a small price to ensure rock-steady photographs of the items you intend to sell.

Internet Connection

As you manage your eBay business on a day-to-day basis, you'll find yourself connecting to the Internet *a lot*. For that reason, you may not be happy with a traditional dial-up Internet connection. As you probably already realize, a dial-up connection is slow (56.6 kilobits per second) and cumbersome (you have to make a new connection every time you want to go online). For your new eBay business, something better is in order.

That something better is a high-speed broadband Internet connection. A broadband connection can speed up your Internet access by 10 times or more; plus it's always on, so you don't have to waste time dialing in to connect. Whenever you want to check your eBay auctions, just launch your browser and you'll be connected to eBay almost instantly.

Three primary types of broadband connections are available today. You can choose from

■ **Digital cable**. Digital cable is the most popular form of broadband in the U.S. today. Cable modems easily connect to digital cable lines and typically offer speeds between 1Mbps–2Mbps.

- **DSL (Digital Subscriber Line)**. DSL piggybacks on your existing telephone lines and provides speeds of at least 384Kbps—more typically, 500Kbps–1Mbps.

- **Digital satellite**. If you have a clear view of the southern sky, you can get your Internet via satellite. Download speeds average 400Kbps.

> **note** Learn more about all types of broadband Internet services and find a provider near you at Broadbandreports.com (`www.broadbandreports.com`).

You typically get DSL service from your local telephone company, and cable broadband from your local cable television company. Digital satellite service is available from HughesNet (`www.hughesnet.com`) and StarBand (`www.starband.com`). DSL and cable broadband typically run $40 or less each month; satellite Internet service will run a little more.

Telephone and Fax

Your home office needs its own communication system—and that means more than just email. You'll need a separate phone for your office, even if that phone shares your home line. (You can choose to invest in a separate business phone line, but that's probably not necessary unless you generate a large volume of outgoing or incoming calls.) Consider a phone with a built-in answering machine or access to some sort of voice-mail system, so that you won't miss any calls when you're away.

If you do decide to go with a separate business phone line, invest in a two-line phone. This way you can run both your home and business lines into the same phone, and use either line as necessary. You can find a good two-line cordless phone for less than $200.

Another option is to use your cell phone as your business phone. This is a good way to keep your business calls separate from your personal calls. This is also a good idea if you need to remain in contact with the outside world even when you're not in the office.

Yet another way to go is with an Internet-based phone service. eBay recently purchased Skype (`pages.ebay.com/skype/`), which lets you call anywhere in the world using your Internet connection as your phone line. Skype and similar Internet phone services typically cost less than traditional landline phone service, although you may have to purchase some additional equipment to get your new phone system up and running. In addition, eBay lets you add Skype "click to call" buttons to your eBay profile and certain types of auction listings. It's worth considering.

You may also have need of a fax machine. While a separate fax machine will work (and, with the proper devices, connect to your regular phone line), a better solution for many is the all-in-one printer/fax machine we discussed earlier. If nothing else, an all-in-one machine takes up less desk space than separate printer and fax machines.

> **tip** An option to purchasing a fax machine is to use a web-based fax service, such as eFax (www.efax.com), which lets you send receive faxes via the Internet, using your web browser or email program.

Filing System

In the course of running your eBay business, you're going to generate a lot of records. Many of these records will be electronic, which are easy to deal with by using the appropriate software program. However, you'll also generate a fair amount of paper records, which you'll have to keep on file.

Short-term paperwork probably needs to stay on top of your desk. You can employ the "multiple pile" method of desktop filing, or you can go the more organized route and use a series of desktop baskets and organizers. I recommend the latter.

For your longer-term paper storage, nothing beats a good, old-fashioned filing cabinet. Go for either a two- or a four-drawer model, and keep things organized with the appropriate filing folders. You don't have to buy anything fancy, either; those low-priced metal filing cabinets work just as well as expensive wooden ones.

Furniture

The subject of filing cabinets brings us around to a bigger issue—office furniture.

The biggest and most obvious piece of office furniture you need is a desk. Your desk has to be big enough to hold your computer, printer, scanner, and other equipment, and still provide enough desk space to let you spread things out and do a little paperwork. That probably rules out using a folding card table—although some swear by the old wooden-door-laid-on-top-of-two-filing-cabinets approach. My personal preference is an L-shaped desk with filing-cabinet drawers on either end; I put my computer equipment on one side of the L and use the other side for desk-based paperwork.

Another option is to go with a smaller desk and a separate computer stand. In any case, just be sure you have enough space for all the different kinds of office work you'll be doing.

Of course, you need a place to sit while you're doing all this work. Your office chair may be more important than your desk, in that it directly affects your physical comfort. Choose the wrong chair and you could end up either uncomfortable or in physical pain. And since we come in all different shapes and sizes, it pays to get a chair that adjusts to your own personal preferences—and to test-drive any chair before you buy it.

We already discussed filing cabinets, but you should also consider whether you need a bookshelf or two in your office. If you find yourself frequently referring to printed matter—like this book, for instance!—then by all means include a bookshelf in your office plans. Remember, your bookshelves can hold all types of books, from dictionaries to phone books to software instruction manuals. If you need one, get one.

Your local office supply store should have a good variety of furniture to choose from, at affordable prices. Also good are retailers like Ikea or traditional furniture stores. If you're on a tight budget, consider buying your furniture second-hand. Check out the "previously used" section at your local business furniture rental store, or keep an eye out for companies that are going out of business. (A lot of entrepreneurs were able to snatch up fancier-than-normal furniture when all those dot-com companies went bust!) Naturally, eBay is also a good place to look for these kinds of bargains.

Office Supplies

Don't forget to stock your office with all the odds and ends you need to conduct your daily business. Your personal needs may differ, but here's a starter list of the office supplies you're likely to need:

- Note paper
- Letter paper (plain and letterhead)
- Envelopes (plain and letterhead)
- Labels
- Pens
- Highlighters
- Paperclips
- Stapler and staples

- Rubber bands
- Sticky notes
- Ruler
- Scissors

note eBay has created a special portal specifically for the needs of eBay businesses. Check out the eBay Business Marketplace (www.ebaybusiness.com) for deals on office equipment, computers, and the like.

You should find space in your immediate office for those supplies you'll be using on a regular basis. Additional quantities can be stored somewhere less convenient.

Configuring Your Space

Of course, you have to have enough space to put all this new equipment and furniture—and that space has to be conducive to actually working. It won't do to place your home office in the corner of a busy living room. You need to be able to separate your work life from your personal life. That might mean utilizing a separate room—preferably one with a door you can close.

How much space do you need? Think through all the equipment you'll have; then add an appropriate amount of clean desk space to write checks and spread out a few file folders. Make sure you have enough room to actually roll or walk around comfortably. Then take this total space—*and double it*. That's right, you'll always end up needing more space than you think, so you might as well plan for it from the start. Over the next several months you're bound to buy more computer equipment, add extra filing cabinets, or need to store *something* that you hadn't planned on. Plus, you might actually have visitors—and where will they stand or sit? Your home office has to be comfortable, so don't start out cramped. Whatever space you allocate, you'll end up filling it!

And where, pray tell, should this space be located? This is definitely a personal decision, and one that depends on what space you have available. I definitely don't recommend carving out space from a high-traffic public area. It's better to find a spare bedroom or area of your basement that you can partition off. Worse comes to worst, you can use a corner of your bedroom—assuming, of course, that it's a room that is otherwise vacant during working hours.

Another option, of course, is to rent office space outside your home. While this might sound appealing (especially if you want to get away from the kids while you work), it's expensive and not typically necessary. Still, if you can find affordable space nearby, it's worth considering.

After you stake out your space, make sure it has enough electrical outlets for your needs. Consider everything you'll be plugging in—your computer, monitor, external modem, printer, scanner, telephone, desk lamp, whatever—and make sure there's a plug for everything. And, while you're at it, make sure you have the appropriate phone and cable jacks for your telephone, fax, and Internet connections.

note Remember, your dedicated (not shared) home office space is eligible for the home office tax deduction. Consult with your accountant for more details.

You should design your workspace with you in the center. Put your most important task—your computer—right in front of you, and everything else within reasonable reach. In this aspect, it pays to think *vertically*. That means incorporating a series of shelves above your desk, rather than spreading out sideways from your working area. There are lots of innovative storage options available that let you expand your workspace up instead of out.

Ergonomics is also important. You want everything in your office to be within comfortable reach. You should pay special attention to the relationship between your chair, computer screen, keyboard, and mouse. Consider one of those split ergonomic keyboards, such as the Microsoft Natural keyboard.

You should also pay attention to light. Your office needs to be well-lit—and that means more than a small desk lamp. Natural light is always good, if you have a window nearby, but appropriate artificial lighting is also necessary. Consider a combination of uniform and task lighting—which probably means both a floor or overhead lamp and a desk lamp. And you don't have to make do with flickering fluorescent lighting, either; you can upgrade both desk and floor lamps with full-spectrum bulbs that simulate sunlight.

Setting Up Your Packing and Shipping Center

Your office is the place where you handle all your eBay-related paperwork and online activities. It is *not* where you store the items you have for sale or where you pack them up for shipping. You'll need to set up separate areas for inventory storage and for packing.

We'll discuss inventory storage last. Right now, let's focus on setting up an efficient packing and shipping center for your eBay business.

Finding the Space

The first thing to consider is *where* you'll be doing your packing. The place you choose depends to some degree on what kinds of items you're selling. If you're selling relatively small items, you can get by with less space. If you're selling really large items, you'll need a lot of space. You'll have to do the math.

However much space you need, you'll want this space to be dedicated to the task at hand. If you're shipping out dozens (or hundreds) of items every week, you don't want to have to assemble and disassemble your packing area every time you sell an item. It's best to have everything set up and ready to go, permanently.

What type of space do you need? Well, you'll need a large, flat area—some kind of tabletop or countertop, large enough for you to spread out your boxes or envelopes as you pack. You'll also need space to store your packing supplies, and additional space nearby for your packing boxes and envelopes. Then you'll need some sort of staging area to temporarily store your packed boxes until they're shipped. Again, depending on the size of what you're selling, this could amount to a fair amount of space.

Where should this space be? For most of us, it has to be someplace in the house. Many eBayers carve out a part of their garage for this operation. I use my kitchen. (I'm not much of a cook, so I might as well use my kitchen for something productive!) In any case, the space needs to be large enough but also easily accessible for the task at hand.

Essential Supplies

Your packing center needs to include storage space for the supplies you use for packing your eBay items. You need to keep these basic packing supplies on hand so that you're not constantly running off to the office supply store every time one of your auctions closes. These items should always be available and easily accessed.

What items are we talking about? Consider the following items:

- Packing tape (both clear and brown)
- Bubble wrap
- Styrofoam peanuts *or* old newspapers
- Scissors
- Box cutter or similar kind of knife
- Postal scale

- Black magic marker
- Shipping labels
- Return address labels
- Other necessary labels—Fragile, This End Up, and so on
- Labels or forms provided by your shipping service of choice
- Rate lists from your preferred shipping service(s)

> **note** Another item—not on the list—you may want to keep on hand is a rolling hand cart. This type of small, lightweight cart is particularly useful when transporting multiple items to the post office, or from one end of your house to the other.

Now for some elaboration. I recommend clear tape not just to seal the box but also to tape over the address label and make it somewhat waterproof. Brown tape can be used to tape over labels and logos when you reuse an old box. I prefer Styrofoam peanuts to newspapers because peanuts don't leave ink stains and because of the weight factor; using newspapers as filler can substantially increase your package weight, and thus your shipping costs. (Of course, newspapers are free and peanuts aren't—but peanuts are cheaper than the added shipping costs you'll incur with newspapers.)

The other materials are somewhat self-explanatory—although you might ask why you need a knife when you're packing. I find myself using the knife primarily to slice off old shipping labels from boxes I reuse for my eBay shipping. Although some old labels tear off rather easily, most don't. To remove them, you have to cut (shallowly) around the label and then lift off the outermost layer of the cardboard box.

That's just a start, however. Learn more about packing your items in Chapter 17, "Organizing Your Packing and Shipping."

Boxes and Envelopes

The other items you need to find space for are the boxes and envelopes in which you pack your items. Of course, what types of boxes and envelopes you need depend on what types of items you'll be selling. Chapter 17 will help you determine the kinds of shipping containers to use. Read ahead to learn more.

Once you've determined what sizes and types of shipping containers you'll be using, you're faced with another challenge: Where do you find supplies of these items?

The first thing you need to know is that some boxes are free. That's right, if you're shipping via the U.S. Postal Service, you can get free Priority Mail and

Express Mail boxes, envelopes, and tubes. Some post offices carry these free containers, or you can order in bulk—but still free—from the eBay and the USPS (ebaysupplies.usps.com) and have them delivered directly to your home. (Figure 7.1 shows some of the free co-branded eBay/USPS boxes available for Priority Mail shipping.)

FIGURE 7.1

Free shipping containers for USPS Priority Mail.

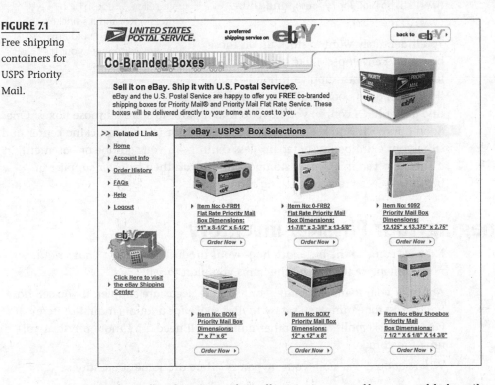

Most post office locations also sell various types of boxes, padded mailers, mailing tubes, and other packing materials, although their prices tend to be a little on the high side. A better choice for high-volume shippers is your local office supply store, such as Office Depot, Office Max, or Staples—or a specialty box/shipping store.

Another good source of shipping supplies is your fellow eBay retailers. Several eBay Store sellers specialize in packing supplies for other eBay sellers. Just go to pages. ebay.com/businessmarketplace/ and click the Shipping & Packing Supplies link.

note Other carriers may or may not offer their own free shipping containers. FedEx, for example, offers certain sizes of envelopes and boxes for your (free) use, as does UPS.

Finally, there are lots of online merchants that offer good deals on packing materials. Check out BubbleFAST (www.bubblefast.com), eSupplyStore.com (www.esupplystore.com), ShippingSupply.com (www.shippingsupply.com), and Uline (www.uline.com).

You'll definitely want to stock up on those boxes and envelopes. I like to keep at least a one-month supply on hand—and if you can get a good deal on a larger quantity, go for it! Of course, you have to find a place to store all those boxes. One good approach is to keep a week's supply in your in-house packing center and store your extra boxes someplace less central—in your garage or basement, in a shed, or even in a rented storage bin. You can then transfer supplies of boxes as needed to your packing center.

> **note** Many eBay sellers recycle old boxes, shipping out their items in boxes that were originally shipped to them. While this works for low-volume sellers, it doesn't look very professional—and it's unlikely that you'll have enough old boxes sitting around to meet your high-volume shipping needs.

Managing Your Physical Inventory

Now we come to the big space hog—your product inventory. That's right, you need someplace to store all the items you plan to sell.

Again, if your items are small, your storage needs are simpler. If you sell baseball cards, for example, it's easy to find space for a lot of small, flat items. If you sell basketballs, on the other hand, you'll need a lot more physical volume for storage.

Where should you store your inventory? Here are some suggestions:

- A spare closet
- Your garage
- Your attic
- Your basement
- A friend's garage (or attic or basement)
- A spare room
- A storage shed
- A rented storage bin
- Rented warehouse space

Naturally, the first few options are less expensive than the last few. If you absolutely positively have to rent storage space, make sure you figure those costs into your business plan. For most eBay businesses, however, you'll want to minimize your storage costs—which means minimizing your space needs, as much as possible. That means either keeping less stock on hand or selling physically smaller items. (In this fashion your storage capacity can help determine the types of items you intend to sell.)

Finding the space is only part of the equation. If you're selling smaller items, you may need to install some sort of shelving to help organize your inventory. Consider

note Here's another option—don't stock anything for sale. That's right, depending on what you sell, you might not have to carry your own inventory. You may be able to employ the services of a fulfillment company. You make the sale (via eBay), but the fulfillment company carries the inventory and ships directly to your customers. A variation on this is to become an authorized dealer for a particular brand or product, and let the manufacturer handle the inventory and shipping. Learn more in Chapter 14, "Purchasing and Managing Your Inventory."

the type of inexpensive plastic or metal shelving that you can find at your local hardware or home store. You might also need some sort of container to hold your really small items. Think about plastic drawers or bins, or even clear plastic bags. Again, home stores and office supply stores should stock what you need.

If you have a variety of items in your inventory, you'll also need some way to identify what you have on hand. That means some sort of labeling system, which can be as simple as handwritten pieces of paper or cards. If you really have a *lot* of different items, consider creating some sort of plan-o-gram or map to help you remember where you put what.

How much inventory should you stock? Not too much—especially if space is at a minimum! I like to have no more than a few weeks' worth of inventory on hand; anything more than that and you're at risk if sales suddenly turn downward. On the other hand, you may need to buy larger quantities to get an attractive discount, or perhaps you may only be able to buy your items in large lots. In any case, the less stock you can keep on hand, the better—and the easier it will be to find space for.

Of course, you don't have to stock all your inventory where it's easy to get to. Just as with your shipping boxes, you can store a certain amount of inventory where it's convenient for immediate shipping and store the rest offsite until you need it. Just make sure you can get your hands on enough items to fulfill the sales you make. The last thing you want to do is sell something that doesn't exist!

Part 2

Choosing a Business Model

8

The Second-Hand Reseller

In the first section of this book, we discussed the planning you need to do before you launch your eBay business. Deciding what type of eBay business you want to run is part of that planning.

So what kind of eBay business should you launch? It all depends, of course—on what type of merchandise you want to sell, how you want to acquire that merchandise, and how you want to price and sell it. This combination of what you sell and how you sell it will define your eBay business model.

If you browse through the various sellers on eBay, you'll discover a lot of different types of businesses. Some eBay businesses sell high-priced goods, some sell low-priced goods; some sell used merchandise, some sell new merchandise; some buy their goods at garage sales and estate sales, some buy direct from manufacturers. It's a real mix.

Interestingly, all these hundreds of thousands of eBay businesses can be divided into a few common business models. There are those businesses that acquire a variety of used merchandise to resell; those that buy bulk lots and closeout merchandise to resell; those that buy and sell collectible items; those that sell products that they themselves create or manufacture; those that sell new in-the-box merchandise; and those that sell items on

> **note** Obviously, not all businesses fall squarely into a single model. Every business is unique: Some sellers fall into multiple categories, and some sellers conform to models not described here. But these half-dozen business models define the majority of eBay businesses, and thus are worth looking at in depth.

consignment from others. When you're deciding what type of business to launch, chances are you'll choose from one of these six business models.

Which leads us to where we are right now. In this and the next five chapters, I'll provide a general overview of these different types of eBay businesses—how they work, their pros and cons, what you can expect from each. I hope these overviews will help you better choose what type of business you want to run.

Easing into Business—By Selling What You Own

Probably the most common type of eBay business is what I'll call the second-hand reseller. This is, as the name suggests, an eBay seller who buys and sells second-hand merchandise. This type of seller doesn't sell new merchandise, he doesn't purchase large lots of closeout items, he doesn't necessarily specialize in a particular category of collectibles. This type of business sells the kind of stuff that people have lying around the house, cluttering the garage or basement. Some people might call it junk, but to a savvy seller, it's a potential goldmine.

If this type of selling sounds familiar, that's because it's the type of selling that most casual—that is, nonbusiness—sellers do. Selling stuff from around the house is how most people get started selling on eBay. You have some old clothes hanging in the spare closet, or some unused utensils in the kitchen, or some discarded tools or electronics sitting in the garage, and you decide to make a quick buck by selling them on eBay. If you do your job well, you sell that first round of leftovers and generate a little spare cash—and get a taste of what selling on eBay is like.

The next thing you know, you're looking for more stuff to sell. You start cleaning out the closets and basement and attic and garage, looking for more junk you can put up for auction. If you have a lot of junk sitting around the house, this can fuel your auction business for several months. But sooner or later you run out of stuff you want to get rid of—and then what do you do?

Well, if you're like some of us, you ask your friends and family if they have any old stuff they'd like to part with. Maybe you start hanging around garage sales and yard sales, looking for bargains that you can resell on eBay. You keep your eye out for anyone getting rid of anything that might be of value—and you keep sorting through your own possessions, opting to sell off unwanted presents, out-of-style clothing, and anything else that isn't nailed down or plugged in.

This is how a lot of big-time eBay sellers got started, and it's actually a great way to learn the ropes. Sell a few dozen items like this, and you'll get a good idea of how eBay selling works. You'll gain valuable experience in preparing items for auction, in creating auction listings, in managing the auction process, and in packing and shipping. You may even get the opportunity to deal with a persnickety buyer or two; unpleasant as this may be, it's great training for when you have to provide customer service on a larger scale.

In fact, the only difference between the occasional junk seller and the full-time second-hand reseller is volume. The more stuff you find to sell, the closer you move toward becoming a real eBay business.

Moving from Pastime to Business

How do you make the move from occasional seller to a full-time business? It's a matter of volume, yes—but that volume is predicated in identifying a constant flow of merchandise to resell, and in selling that merchandise at an acceptable profit.

The business of reselling second-hand merchandise is a real business, as you know from the proliferation of bricks-and-mortar flea markets, second-hand clothing stores, and the like. The only difference between you and them is that you sell your merchandise on eBay, rather than in a traditional storefront. Like the traditional second-hand merchant, you face the big challenge of finding merchandise to resell; it's only the way you sell that's different.

To build a business based on the second-hand reselling model, you have to put together a plan for locating merchandise for resale. You have to lay out a budget for buying second-hand goods, and then feed that merchandise into your eBay sales machine. You can't just hope to stumble over stuff to sell; you have to actively pursue second-hand merchandise to ensure a constant flow of inventory.

And when you obtain that merchandise to resell, you have to put it some-where. Inventory management is a big part of running a full-time reselling business. You have to store all your inventory, as well as (in some cases) clean it up or fix it up for resale. You have to know what you have at any given point in time—where it's located, how much it cost you, and how much you plan to sell it for. The more different types of items you resell, the more com-plicated this all becomes.

Occasional eBay sellers don't have this type of hassle. They don't have to sec-tion off part of their garage or basement to store merchandise that they plan to resell. They don't have to budget funds for purchasing merchandise, nor worry about how high they can mark up an item over the initial purchase price. They're just selling stuff for fun, and the money they generate goes straight into their pockets. You, on the other hand, need to funnel the profits from what you sell back into your business, to help pay for additional mer-chandise that you'll resell next week or next month. For them, it's a one-time thing. For you, it's a continuing business.

Where, then, is the line between reselling as a hobby and reselling as a busi-ness? To me, there are two factors. First, as a business, you're in business to make a profit; hobbyists are often in it for enjoyment, and any profit gener-ated is secondary. Second, as a business, you invest the money you make in additional merchandise to resell; hobbyists simply keep (or spend) any money they happen to make. If you actually generate a profit and then reinvest that profit to buy more merchandise to sell, then you've moved across the line and are running a business.

Sell Everything—or Certain Things?

Some second-hand resellers will sell anything they can make a profit on. Other resellers, however, prefer to specialize in particular types of merchan-dise—children's clothing, for example, or antiques. Each approach necessitates a slightly different business model.

Selling all types of used merchandise makes it somewhat easier to find inven-tory to sell—you're not as picky about what you buy. By not limiting your selection, you also get to play in a lot of different product categories and open yourself up to all manner of pleasant surprises. That said, there's more work involved in researching, storing, packing, and shipping a wide variety of items, since you never buy or sell the same thing twice; every piece you han-dle has new and different requirements.

When you limit your selection to a handful of specific categories, you can more quickly become an expert in those categories. When you buy and sell second-hand clothing, for example, you'll learn all the ins and out of the used clothing market—what sells, what doesn't, what something is worth, how to efficiently pack and ship it. Deal with one type of item long enough and you develop a good eye for bargains and for potential hot sellers. You can also work out an efficient routine for listing, storing, packing, and shipping those similar items.

What kind of specialization are we talking about? There's a lot you can focus on. Some of the most popular categories for second-hand reselling include used books; used men's, women's, and children's clothing; vintage clothing (which is different from "used" clothing); vintage toys, model kits, and other collectibles; records and tapes; jewelry and watches; and antiques. Just about anything that anyone might collect is a good category to specialize in; also good are those categories in which people like to get good bargains on used items (such as clothing).

That said, limiting your selection to a single type of item means you might have to pass over potentially lucrative merchandise outside your category of specialization. In addition, you may have to visit a larger number of garage sales and thrift stores to find enough merchandise to feed your ongoing auction business.

So which should you do—sell anything (within limits) or specialize? That's a personal decision; both models can be profitable. You should choose the business model that best suits your interests, as well as your own strengths and weaknesses. Just know that whichever model you choose requires a slightly different approach, and plan your business accordingly.

Running a Second-Hand Merchandise Business

So what is it like to run a second-hand reselling business? Let's take a quick look at the day-to-day routine of a typical second-hand reseller—from finding stuff to sell to shipping it out after a successful sale.

Finding Merchandise to Resell

The biggest challenge—and a big part of the workload—of a second-hand reseller is finding merchandise to resell. Where does a successful second-hand reseller find items that will sell on eBay—while avoiding pure junk that nobody will want?

There are lots of places where you can find used merchandise for sale. Savvy resellers know to haunt local garage sales, yard sales, tag sales, rummage sales, and the like, to pick up the cream of what's available before it gets picked up by other buyers. Also good are estate sales and auc-

note Learn more about acquiring merchandise of all sorts in Chapter 14, "Purchasing and Managing Your Inventory."

tions, where you can purchase a lot of different merchandise all in one place. Depending on what type of item you want to sell, you can sometimes find merchandise at antique dealers and flea markets—although you might not always find good bargains there. Along the same lines, traditional used, second-hand, or vintage retailers can sometimes be good sources to fill your inventory. You can't forget thrift stores and dollar stores (including the ubiquitous Goodwill Stores), or even pawn shops, although you may need to sort through a lot of merchandise to find the best bargains. And eBay itself can sometimes be a source of goods for resale—if you can score a low-enough price from a seller.

Another approach is to actively solicit merchandise for resale. Some sellers have good luck placing small "wanted" ads in their local newspaper classifieds. If you go this route, offer to pay cash on the spot, and offer to buy in bulk. Make sure, of course, that you're well-versed in the type of items you're buying—so you can buy smartly, without investing in a lot of unsellable merchandise.

Notice the emphasis on finding *used* merchandise. By definition, the second-hand reseller specializes in selling second-hand items. That doesn't preclude you from picking up the occasional new item for resale, especially if you can get it for a bargain price. You want to be on the lookout for closeout and liquidated merchandise, factory seconds, returned items, and the like. Look for closeout sales at traditional retailers, bulk bargains at the wholesale clubs, and the ever-popular going-out-of-business sale.

Of course, one of the challenges of acquiring inventory is buying merchandise at as low a price as possible. Obviously, you want to avoid paying full price for anything, and negotiate as low a price as possible, if negotiating is part of the deal. You're looking for items that cost you a buck but can be resold for $5.00 or more. You don't want to pay $4.50 for that $5.00 item; you have to develop a talent for finding real bargains.

Sometimes you have to buy a bunch of junk to get a few treasures. This is especially the case when haunting estate sales, where you may be forced to bid on piles or boxes of merchandise. You purchase the entire lot in the hopes of finding a few items that have high resale potential. The rest of the stuff might end up in the trash.

As you can probably tell, this whole business of finding low-priced merchandise to resell is a lot of work. It's also a constant chore—you're always on the lookout for items that you can pick up for pennies and resell for dollars. For many second-sellers, this is the most fun of the whole process; it's kind of like an ongoing treasure hunt!

Managing the Auctions

Once you've acquired your inventory, you have to do something with it. For the second-hand reseller, organization is important. When you purchase a group of items, you have to identify and categorize them, clean them up or fix them up as necessary, and then put them someplace where it will be easy to find them when they're sold.

After the merchandise is cleaned up for sale, it's time to start the auction. You'll need to do a little research so that you can intelligently describe the item in the item description and judge an appropriate starting price (and estimate a probable final selling price). Then you'll have to photograph the item, create the item listing, and post it for auction on the eBay site.

Obviously, if you're running a high-volume business, you'll be posting more than one auction at a time. Most second-hand resellers try to have a dozen or more auctions running at any given time. You may want to start and end all your auctions on the same day, or you may want to stagger your auctions so that you have something closing on every day of the week. However you approach it, you'll need to be prepared to spend a lot of time at the computer getting things launched.

The period of time the auction is running is actually a bit of down time for you; there's not much to do over the course of the auction other than watch the bids come in. This time between launch and close is when most second-hand resellers do their inventory hunting. If you don't need to be at the computer, you might as well make good use of your time by finding more stuff to sell!

Packing and Shipping

Once the auction closes, you then have to contact the buyer and collect payment (typically in the form of a credit card payment to your PayPal account).

When the payment is in your hands, it's time to pack the item and ship it out. This is one of the more challenging parts of the process, especially if you sell a wide variety of merchandise. In fact, it's best if you work through the packing before you start the auction so that you know what type of box is required, and what other packing materials are necessary. It's also good to estimate the shipping cost ahead of time (so you can include the cost in your item listing), which means weighing the item (including the packaging) and choosing the appropriate shipping service.

note Learn more about packing supplies and shipping services in Chapter 17, "Organizing Your Packing and Shipping."

Packing done, you now need to ship the item, which probably means a trip to the post office. If you run a lot of auctions, you might not want to make a separate trip for each item you sell; many sellers prefer to "gang" their shipping so that they travel to the post office only two or three days a week. Better to take several boxes at once than make lots of trips for single items.

And remember, you'll probably be dealing with lots of different sizes of boxes—and, perhaps, several different shipping services. One of the things with selling second-hand merchandise is that no two items are alike; every sale you make is a new experience!

Pros and Cons of Second-Hand Reselling

Is second-hand reselling for you? Let's take a quick look at the pros and cons of this particular business model.

Pros

What are the advantages to the second-hand reseller model? Here are a few of the things that many resellers like about this type of business:

- **You won't get bored**. For many eBay sellers, the fact that every sale is different is one of the appeals to second-hand reselling. There's a certain joy of discovery when you search for items to resell; you never really know what you're going to find next. It's hard to get into a rut when every item you buy or every sale you make is different from what you've done before. If you think that selling one type of item day-in and day-out would get boring, the "sell anything" school of second-hand reselling is for you.

■ **Specialization breeds familiarity**. On the other hand, if you choose to specialize in a particular type of second-hand merchandise, you won't have that much variety in what you buy and sell. What you gain, however, is familiarity—which is a good thing. If you build up a high volume of business in a particular type of item, you'll get to know that category very well, which makes it easier to buy smarter and sell more efficiently. If all you do is sell used tools, you can become very good at selling that type of item.

■ **Riding the trends can be profitable**. Successful second-hand resellers become quite adept at identifying and riding category trends. It's a fact that some categories get hot as others cool down; it's quite rewarding to acquire a batch of merchandise just when that category is on the upswing. It requires some skill to predict the trends and identify merchandise that is just on the verge of being hot. Sometimes this requires you to buy merchandise and then sit on it for several months, as you wait for the trends to turn. But if you can learn to buy low and sell high, you can make a lot of money with this business model.

■ **You have insurance against category downturns**. For those second-hand resellers who don't limit themselves to a single category, that variety is one of the great things about second-hand reselling. If one category cools down, simply quit selling those items and move to something else. Sellers who specialize in a particular category can get seriously burned when a category capsizes. By not relying on a single category, you're protected from the vagaries of any given category.

■ **There's a low initial investment**. One of the most appealing things about this type of eBay business for newbies is that it doesn't take an arm and a leg to get started. Since you're not dealing with large minimum inventory purchases, as you are with some other models, you can get started by buying just a few select pieces for resale. You can start with a larger inventory, of course, but you don't have to; you can size your business as big or as small as you're comfortable with.

■ **You can make the occasional big score**. This is what most second-hand resellers live for—finding that item you pay 50 cents for at a garage sale and then reselling it for $50 or more online. Scoring big requires one part luck and one part skill at identifying diamonds in the rough. Most resellers develop a good eye for finding valuable items that others have overlooked. Remember—what's junk to one person is a vintage collectible to another!

In short, second-hand reselling is a good choice if you're fast on your feet, like a lot of variety in your life, and have a good eye for finding bargains and identifying items with high resale value.

Cons

Now that you know what's good about this type of business, let's look at some of the challenges. They include

- **There's a lot of junk**. Let's face it, not every piece of junk you obtain is a diamond in the rough; some of it's just junk. Especially when you're buying large lots at auctions or estate sales, you have to wade through a lot of rubbish to get to the good stuff—and a lot of that rubbish is old and smelly and not very pleasant to handle. Even if you don't mind handling other people's hand-me-downs, what do you do with the stuff you can't sell? Junk is not always fun.

- **Making it saleable takes work**. Even the good stuff you acquire might take a lot of work to become saleable. You may need to wash or dry clean used clothing, patch up some holes and sew on some buttons, polish up the jewelry or silverware, and get out your screwdriver to fix minor electrical problems. You can't sell junk that looks like junk; you have to make your merchandise attractive to potential buyers. The elbow grease you put in is part of the cost of running your business.

- **You have to put it all somewhere**. So you hit the garage sales and flea markets every weekend, stuffing your car full of good deals you can resell for a tidy profit. Where do you put all that stuff until it's sold? I hope you have a big garage or unused basement because if you're a high-volume reseller, you're going to have *lots* of stuff stored away at any given time. And the larger the items you sell, the more space they require. If you get successful enough, you may have to consider renting a storage barn or other warehouse space—which adds to your business costs.

- **It's unpredictable**. Some people like to be able to plan everything out well in advance. If you're one of those people, you should steer well clear of second-hand reselling. Second-hand resellers seldom know what they'll be selling next week, next month, or next year. What your business will be is dependent on what items you can find to resell between now and then. Bargain hunting can be fun, but it's extremely unpredictable.

■ **There's no consistent source of inventory**. While some resellers are able to find steady sources of merchandise, most rely on picking through the bargains at flea markets, thrift stores, and estate auctions. It's not like you're ordering items out of a catalog; you're constantly on the hunt for more stuff to sell. Not only is this manner of acquiring inventory unpredictable, it's also a lot of work. And there's no guarantee that you'll actually find enough viable merchandise to keep your business afloat.

■ **It requires constant research**. Since you're constantly acquiring all manner of items for resale, you are also on a constant quest for information about those items. How do you know what a particular coin or figurine is worth? How do you know what category in which to list that item you picked up at a garage sale last week? How do you adequately describe that batch of used magazines you're ready to list for auction? All this requires research, and lots of it—which can be extremely time-consuming. For some, research is both fun and enlightening; for others, not so much. If you don't like Googling for answers, this part of the business won't be much fun.

■ **There's more effort required to list each item**. Along the same lines, every item you list requires a new and unique description, photographs, and item specifics for the item listing itself. There's no economy of scale, since every item is a new experience. With other business models, you resell similar items over and over, and you can save time by using eBay's "Sell Similar" option. Second-hand resellers don't have this option because they're never selling anything similar to what they sold before.

■ **You get little or no efficiency in packing and shipping**. For many second-hand resellers, no two items they sell are alike. That means every item will take a different sized box, and will need to be packed and shipped differently. There's no economy of scale when you need a limitless variety of boxes and packing material; there's also no learning curve when you're packing a glass vase today and a pair of socks tomorrow. Sellers who specialize in specific types of merchandise can get by with stocking just one or two different types of boxes, and create a bit of an assembly line for packing and shipping those items; second-hand resellers can't.

In other words, all those factors that make second-hand reselling an adventure also help to make it a bit of a challenge. There's little consistency, little predictability, and little efficiency to be gained from selling so many different types of items. Plus, making all those items presentable takes a lot of work—and a lot of space to store them until they're sold. If you opt for this business model, make sure you consider all these issues beforehand and are comfortable with them.

How to Become a Second-Hand Reseller

If second-hand reselling sounds good to you, what are the next steps?

First, I advise you to dip your toes in the water before you make a final decision. This step is particularly easy with this type of business, because you probably have lots of stuff around your house that you can sell on eBay. Take a half-dozen items and put them up for auction. Work through the entire process to get an idea of what's involved. See if you really like it.

If you do, you need to do a little planning. Take another read through the chapters in Part 1 of this book, "Planning and Launching Your eBay Business." Do some research about what types of merchandise are hot and what aren't, put together a short business plan, evaluate your funding needs, start up some sort of recordkeeping system, and have a talk with your accountant. Think about how much space you need to store your inventory, where you'll do the packing, whether your home office is sufficient for all your auction management tasks. In short, get ready to go big time.

Then you need to get into bargain hunting mode. Figure out the best sources of second-hand merchandise in your area. Locate the flea markets and thrift stores. Find out where people advertise their garage sales and yard sales; learn how estate sales work. Get smart about identifying merchandise with high resale potential.

And when you're done with all this preparation, just turn the key. Start buying, start listing, and start selling. This is an easy type of business to start small and then ramp up as you get more experience. You don't have to plan on selling $2,000 worth of merchandise your first month. Go easy until you're comfortable with what you're doing, and then start doing more of the same. That's how little businesses become big ones.

Seller Spotlight: clact

eBay seller **clact** is, in reality, Martin Adamo, a 40-year-old CPA and investment advisor, and his wife, Cheryl, who works as a controller at a mid-size business. Martin owns his own accounting firm and, with Cheryl, runs an eBay business that specializes in reselling second-hand merchandise. Their eBay store, shown in Figure 8.1, is called Once Upon a Bid (`stores.ebay.com/Once-Upon-A-Bid/`).

FIGURE 8.1

Martin and
Cheryl Adamo's
eBay Store,
Once Upon a
Bid.

Martin and Cheryl got started selling on eBay in January of 2004. Under the **clact** ID, they sell a variety of items on eBay—books, collectibles, toys, games, and "Funny Friends," a line of stuffed animals made by Cheryl's employer. They find merchandise to resell at a number of different places, including local flea markets, thrift stores, book sales, and discount stores.

In addition to selling on eBay, Cheryl is an eBay educational specialist. She teaches the "Basics of eBay Selling," "Beyond the Basics," and "Basics of eBay Buying" courses in the Greater Wallingford area, near New Haven, CT. (You can view information about Cheryl's classes at `clact.poweru.net`.)

Martin and Cheryl believe that it's best to have many sources of items across many categories, in order to have maximum flexibility. They've found that by offering a lot of different items, they can get a feel for what people like or are looking for, and if it does well, they tend to do more of that type of item.

The initial cost of the item is also a consideration. Martin says that they get the best return with items that cost very little to acquire. For example, he once acquired a used book for $1 and resold it for $70. As Martin states, "Things acquired for less than two dollars account for much of our profits."

Most months Martin and Cheryl list 350 or so items for auction. Their sell-through rate is typically in the 40%–60% range, although some categories achieve sell-through of 80% or more. They've been averaging close to $2,000 each month in revenues.

I asked Martin about his most memorable sale, and he related this story:

"Back when I first started selling, I would sell to U.S. customers only. I received a very nice email from a fellow in Holland. He was beaming that he just found a book I had in the listings while browsing, titled *Hope for the Flowers*. He had remembered and wanted this book for years, but could never think of the title or author. He saw the gallery picture and was excited and wanted to know if I would ship to him. I did, and he was particularly happy that the book had an inscription from one person to another in high school about love, he thought that made the book special."

The Adamos' advice to other resellers is simple: Read and research. As Martin says:

"I read almost all the new books on eBay selling, I also read a few of the e-books sold on reputable sites. I learn something from almost every book or e-book. These little things add up to success in the eBay world. There are many excellent books out there. Also, I read and research other sources of information as much as possible. I strongly recommend that new sellers buy a few books (which can later be resold on eBay, as they sell well) and make at least a brief business plan before launching their sales."

All that research has certainly paid off for Martin and Cheryl, who are now eBay PowerSellers with a solid red-star feedback rating. You can read more about Martin and Cheryl's eBay experiences on their blog, The Incredible World of eBay (worldofebay.blogspot.com).

The Collector/Trader

For many eBay sellers, their businesses began as an offshoot of a hobby. If you're a collector, chances are whatever you collect is actively bought and sold on eBay. And anywhere there's buying and selling, there's a business opportunity!

What kinds of things do people trade on eBay? Just about anything imaginable, from antiques to vintage clothing to comic books to HO trains to political buttons to sports cards to glass milk bottles to Hummel figurines to plastic model kits to pocket watches to Barbie dolls to…well, you get the picture. Just as there are numerous bricks-and-mortar stores that specialize in various types of collectibles, there are also many eBay businesses that are collectibles-based.

Turning a Hobby into a Business

The step from hobby to business is a matter of setting up yourself to sell the things you collect, and then doing that selling in volume. If you're a serious collector, you're probably already using eBay to purchase items for your collection—it's the world's largest marketplace for collectible items, after all. Well, if you can buy collectibles, you can sell them, too. And there's your business model.

There's a comic book store near my house. The guy who runs it started out as a collector, amassing huge boxes full of old comics in his basement. One day he realized he had enough comics collected to start his own store, and that's what he did. People come into his store to buy vintage comics and also to sell him old comics from their collections. Is he running a business or indulging a hobby? Both, actually. It's as good a reason as any to open a business; his business is buying and selling those things that he loves.

You can apply this same model in the eBay marketplace. If you're a collector, by definition you have a collection of things. That collection can be the starting inventory for an eBay business. Assuming that you keep feeding that inventory by collecting additional items (either on eBay or in the real world), you can set up a continuous stream of auction listings, as well as populate a companion eBay Store. Your customers, of course, will be your fellow collectors and hobbyists.

Naturally, running a collecting/trading business is slightly different from simply collecting as a hobby. You need to feed your sales by buying new collectibles on a consistent basis; you need to set up an assembly line to photograph, list, pack, and ship the items you list for sale; and you need to manage your hobby like a business, keeping track of sales and expenses and worrying about taxes and the like. But all that probably won't take much more work than what you're already expending on your hobby. You're just going pro, is all.

Grading and Authenticating Your Merchandise

When you're selling collectible items on eBay, it helps to know what kind of shape your items are in. Most serious collectors expect the items they buy to be exhaustively photographed and described, in accordance to the conventions of that particular collectible category. For many categories, that means grading the item's condition—according to some very formal rules—or getting the item authenticated.

If you're not familiar with the process, grading is a way of noting the condition of an item, according to a predetermined standard. Collectors use these grading scales to help evaluate and price items within a category. If you know the grade of your item, you can include the grade in the item's title or description, and thus more accurately describe the item to potential bidders.

What kinds of items are typically graded? It's a long list, including stamps, coins, comic books, sports cards, and gems. In addition, anything of a sufficient value that's autographed can and probably should have the signature authenticated. If you play in one of these categories and *don't* grade your auction items, you won't be considered a serious dealer.

Understanding Grading Systems

When it comes to grading, every category does it a little different; there is no such thing as a "universal" grading system for all items. For example, trading cards are graded from A1 to F1; stamps are graded from Poor to Superb. You'll need to learn the specific system for the items you intend to sell.

That said, many collectible categories use a variation of the Mint grading system shown in Table 9.1.

Table 9.1   Mint System Grading

Grade	Abbreviation	Description
Mint	MT, M, 10	An item in perfect condition, without any damage or imperfections.
Very Fine	VF	Similar to mint.
Near Mint	NM, 9	An item with a very minor, hardly noticeable flaw. Sometimes described as "like new."
Near Fine	NF	Similar to near mint.
Excellent	EX, 8	An item considered above average, but with pronounced signs of wear.
Fine	F	Similar to excellent.
Very Good	VG, 7	An item in average condition.
Good	GD, G, 6	An item that has clear indications of age, wear, and use.
Fair	F	An item that is heavily worn.
Poor	P, 5	An item that is damaged or somehow incomplete.

Grading can sometimes be a little confusing. Why is Near Mint below Mint, but Near Fine is above Fine? Beats me, but that's the way it is. In addition, degrees between grade levels are often indicated with a + or –. (For example, an item between Fine and Very Fine would be designated as F+.) Naturally, the definition of a Mint or Fair item differs by item type.

note eBay provides a page of links to "authorized" authentication services at pages.ebay.com/help/community/auth-overview.html.

Getting Graded

If you're not sure what grade an item is, you may want to utilize a professional grading and authentication service. These services will examine your item, authenticate it (confirm that it's the real deal), and give it a professional grade. Some services will even encase your item in a sealed plastic container or bag.

Where can you get your items graded? Table 9.2 lists some popular websites for grading and authenticating collectible items.

Table 9.2   Grading and Authentication Services

Collectible	Site	URL
Autographs	Global Authentication	gacard.net/ebay/cardmain.asp
	James Spence Authentication	www.spenceloa.com
	OnlineAuthentics.com	www.onlineauthentics.com
	PSA/DNA	www.psadna.com
Beanie Babies	Peggy Gallagher Enterprises	www.beaniephenomenon.com
Coins	American Numismatic Association Certification Service	www.anacs.com
	Numismatic Guaranty Corporation of America	www.ngccoin.com
	Professional Coin Grading Service	www.pcgs.com
Comic books	Comics Guaranty	www.cgccomics.com
Jewelry	International Gemological Institute	www.e-igi.com
Native American artifacts	Authentic Artifact Collectors Association	www.theaaca.com
Photos	PSA/DNA	www.psadna.com
Political items	American Political Items Collectors	www.apic.us

Table 9.2   Continued

Collectible	Site	URL
Sports cards	Beckett Grading Services	`www.beckett.com/grading/ebay/`
	Global Authentication	`gacard.net/ebay/cardmain.asp`
	Professional Sports Authenticator	`www.psacard.com`
	Sportscard Guaranty	`www.sgccard.com`
Stamps	American Philatelic Society	`www.stamps.org`
	Professional Stamps Experts	`www.psestamp.com`

The cost of these authentication services varies wildly, depending on what you're authenticating, the age or value of the item, and the extent of the service itself. For example, Professional Sports Authenticator rates range from $5 to $150 per sports card; Professional Stamps Experts rates range from $8 to $500 per stamp, or (in some cases) 4.5% of current catalog value. Make sure that the item you're selling is worth it before you go to this expense—and that you can recoup this expense in your auction.

Running a Collector/Trader Business

Running a collector/trader business isn't a whole lot different from buying and selling items as a hobby. There are a few more details to worry about, and you will probably want to ramp up the volume. That said, let's look at what's involved in running a typical collector/trader business.

Finding Merchandise to Resell

The first stage in the process is collecting items to resell. Obviously, one important source of merchandise is other collectors. You're used to this—you buy some items, you sell some items. That's the way collecting works.

You probably don't want to limit your purchasing to the collector's market, however. Depending on the type of item you intend to trade, you may want to scour garage sales, estate sales, flea markets, pawn shops, conventions, and the like for hidden bargains. The key is to pick up items of value to collectors from sources that don't necessarily have the same level of interest—and that value those items for far less than would a serious collector. You've probably been doing this a little already; it's time to ramp it up and become a serious collectible hunter.

Preparing Items for Auction

Collectors have different—and higher—expectations than the general public. Whatever you collect, you'll need to clean it up and get it into a presentable condition. For some items, that means enclosing the item in an particular type of bag or container. Comic books go in plastic bags, cards go into a penny sleeve or top loader case, stamps go into transparent envelopes, and so on. Take care to make every item a true collectible.

Obviously, this is also the time to get the item graded or authenticated, if necessary.

Managing the Auctions

Providing detailed descriptions of your collectible item listings is important. Include the item's grade, describe the condition, note any flaws, and so on. Also include photos or scans of the item. Antiques require lots of photos to document the item's condition; other items, such as comic books, cards, and stamps, can be handled with a nice clean scan.

Once you list the item, be prepared for lots of questions from potential bidders. This is part and parcel of a collectibles auction; collectors want to know exactly what it is they're bidding on. Some of the questions will be quite detailed and often technical. Make sure you can provide good answers, and that you do so in a timely fashion.

Packing and Shipping

After the auction ends, you'll need to pack and ship the item in an appropriate fashion. Again, different types of items have their own particular packing/shipping needs. Make sure you do what you need to do to get the item to the buyer in pristine condition. Depending on the price or rarity of the item, you may also want to offer shipping insurance—just in case something bad happens in transit. Remember—collectors can be persnickety!

Pros and Cons of Collecting and Trading

A collecting/trading business can be a lot of fun; after all, you're still working with your hobby, even if you're out to make a profit. Let's look at what's good and what's bad about this particular business model.

Pros

What are the good points about basing a business around your hobby? Here are a few of the pros:

- **It's your hobby, so it should be fun**. The theory is that since you like collecting this type of item, you'll also like the business of selling it. If you like collecting soap opera magazines, a business based on selling soap opera magazines should be more fun than working in an office and filing forms. If it's not fun, why do it?

- **You already know a lot about it**. This assumes that you don't start collecting an item the day before you open your eBay business. If you've been collecting for a few years, presumably you've gained some expertise. All that research that typically gets done before launching a business, you don't have to do—or at least, you don't have to do as much. If you know what you're doing (collection-wise, anyway), moving into a business environment won't be that difficult.

- **There are established rules**. Most collectible categories have their own established ways of doing things. If you collect comic books, for example, you know that there's a certain grading system to use, a certain way to store and pack the books, and so on. You don't have to reinvent any wheels—just follow the rules that everyone else follows.

- **You already know your customer base**. One of the key things about selling is to know who your buyers are. If you're a collector, you already know other collectors. You know your customers; you know what they like and dislike, and what they'll pay big money for. That's a big head start over starting any other type of business.

- **There's always the hope of a big score**. The holy grail of any collector is to find that one item sitting in someone's attic or lying on a penny table at a garage sale that you can sell for $10,000 to informed collectors. While you might never find that holy grail, what other business offers the opportunity for that type of score?

The main benefits of running a collecting/trading business, then, accrue from the fact that you're already involved in this category, as a collector. You know what you're doing, and turning your hobby into a business is a relative small step.

Cons

Now that you know what's good about this type of business, let's look at some of the challenges. They include

- **You can only do as well as other collectors**. Collecting is rather predictable, the search for a holy grail aside. Yes, there are ups and downs and some guys are better at it than others, but most collectors are going to do just about as well as other collectors in the business. The opportunity to break out from the pack is small.

- **You're stuck if there's a market downturn**. If you're a collector, you're presumably focusing on a single type of collectible. What do you do when the market goes bust? If you're buying and selling vintage slot cars and the slot car market goes soft, you're pretty much stuck. The lack of diversity can be a big business risk.

- **Do you really want to sell your private collection**? Most collectors get started in business by selling the very items they've been collecting over the past several years. Do you really want to part with your precious collection? You may need to build up an inventory of items less valuable to you, or set aside part of your collection as not for sale, to avoid seller's remorse.

- **Hunting for new items to sell can be challenging**. Collecting can be a lot of fun—until you're literally forced to find more stuff to collect to feed your business. For many collectors/sellers, the hunt for new merchandise takes at least as much time as they spend on managing their eBay auctions. Do you have the right stuff to be on continuous watch for new collectibles to sell?

- **Grading/authentication/packing can be costly**. If you're collecting items that are expected to be graded or authenticated, make sure you factor those expenses into the cost of running your business. Additionally, you may need to purchase specific mounting or packaging supplies to meet the expectations of your customers, and that might be a tad more expensive than sticking a coin into a first-class envelope.

- **If it's a business, it might not be fun anymore**. This is probably the biggest risk of running a collectibles-based business. If you have to do it full time, for money, it's not a hobby anymore—it's work. And work isn't always fun. I've met quite a few former hobbyists who got burned out when they went pro. If you want to keep loving what you do in your spare time, think twice about doing it full time.

Bottom line, running a collectibles-based business has the same risks as running any other type of business—plus a few. The biggest risk is the exclusionary nature of it; many risk-averse businesspeople prefer to have a more diversified product mix, to protect against downturns in any single category. If you can get past that, however, there's a lot to be said for this business model.

How to Become an eBay Collector/Trader

Want to turn your hobby into a business? Then you need to get serious. Make a full inventory of your current collection, and assign individual values (both original purchase value and estimated current market value) to every item you own. Put together a plan for obtaining more items, on a regular basis. Work out all your possible costs, including storage and packing. Research eBay to see if your sales projections are reasonable. Crunch the numbers to see how much profit you're likely to generate.

Do all that, and the next step is easy. Create a few auction listings and get the business off the ground. The move from collector to eBay business is a short one!

Seller Spotlight: bushellcollectibles

Many eBay sellers make a good living selling collectibles—case in point being Jeanette Bushell, who operates under the **bushellcollectibles** ID. Jeanette is 37 years old and lives in northwest New Jersey. Her eBay business is a part-time one; during the day she works as a business professional in Manhattan. (That's four hours of commuting every day!) Jeanette says that "coming home to eBay helps me unwind from that commute and keeps me wishing for the day when eBay is my full-time job—and I don't have to take the train anymore!"

Jeanette started on eBay by buying cross-stitch supplies, but didn't become a seller until about a year later. The first items she sold were cross-stitch books and kits, but then got into selling the kinds of antiques and collectibles that she'd been interested in all her life. Today she specializes mostly in vintage souvenir collectibles—"the more fragile, the better." She sells items from all over the United States, often back to the town or city they came from originally.

Finding collectibles to sell is part of the fun; as Jeanette says, "I live for the thrill of the hunt." She says that the best places to scour for treasures are tag sales, flea markets, thrift stores, auctions, and antique/collectible stores. She loves finding something at an antique store for a bargain price and then reselling it on eBay for a tidy profit.

During her prime selling months (she tends to sit out the summer), Jeanette lists about 40–60 items per month. About 45% of what she lists actually sells. She doesn't consider herself a "big hitter," but still generates between $500 and $800 a month—a good second income.

In addition, Jeanette supplements her eBay sales by selling in a local antiques and collectibles mall. She finds that the two channels complement each other quite well, and what she learns from one place helps her with her sales in the other.

One of the nice things about selling collectibles, Jeanette notes, is that you often help people find those long-lost or broken items from their youth. She recalls the following story:

"I sold to one lovely lady a Singer sewing machine pin dish. She wrote back that she had been looking for this for years, as her mother had this dish but it had been broken. When she won the dish, she was so happy to get back this happy memory from her childhood, as her mother had passed on."

When it comes to selling, Jeannette says that her biggest challenge is storage space at home. All those collectibles have to be stored somewhere! She offers the following advice to prospective sellers:

"Set up an eBay Store and keep a good-sized inventory, so even if you're not able to list in the auctions every week, your customers will see that you're here to stay and will keep you bookmarked to check back often. If you don't sell an item, relist at a lower price or put the item in your store. You cannot expect the person who wants your Napco turkey candle holder to be online 24/7. I have found that if an item doesn't sell the first time, sometimes it will sell a few weeks later from my store." (You can check out the Bushell's Collectibles store, shown in Figure 9.1, at `stores.ebay.com/Bushells-Collectibles`.)

FIGURE 9.1

The Bushell's Collectibles eBay Store.

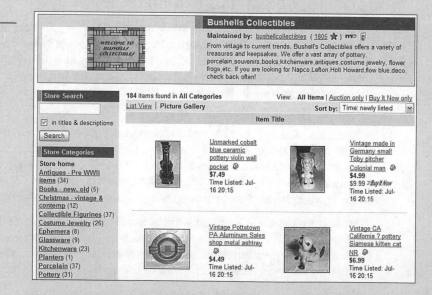

Jeannette also recommends setting up an About Me page and providing some personal information about yourself. "I have received numerous emails on my About Me page alone, people who liked my cats or just the fact that I took the time to create the page and keep it updated."

The Bulk Reseller

In the previous two chapters we examined two types of eBay businesses that resell used merchandise acquired at garage sales, flea markets, collector's shows, and similar places. Reselling lots of onesies and twosies can be profitable, but it's certainly a labor-intensive model. You're always on the search for something new to sell, and you're always reinventing the wheel.

That's why many sellers prefer selling large quantities of a single item to selling small quantities of multiple items. Instead of buying one shirt to resell, you buy 100 or 1,000 shirts—and thus sell 100 or 1,000 units of the same item. In many ways, this is a more efficient business model, as you can build your business around a single type of item. You can take one photograph and reuse it in hundreds of item listings, you have to stock only one type of box, and you'll always know what your shipping costs will be. Being a bulk reseller might lack variety, but it makes up for that variety in consistency.

Selling in Bulk Means Buying in Bulk

When you want to sell large quantities of a single item, you have to buy large quantities of a single item. This requires buying in bulk, so you can have enough inventory to last for several weeks' or months' worth of auctions.

Where, pray tell, do you purchase bulk quantities of merchandise? There are plenty of options, if you know where to look.

First, know that most bulk items offered are not first-run goods. Yes, most of it is new (not used) merchandise, but it's often last year's model, factory seconds, store returns, overstocked inventory, and the like. That's why it's available in bulk and at good prices; it's "leftover" merchandise waiting for someone to take it off the supplier's hands.

This means that you want to shop for bulk merchandise at wholesalers who specialize in closeout and liquidated items, or at thrift stores or dollar stores that offer large lots of items for sale. You can find lots of these closeout suppliers on the Web, including eBay Merchandise.com (www.ebaymerchandise.com), Liquidation.com (www.liquidation.com), SalvageCloseouts (www.salvagecloseouts.com), and Surplus.net (www.surplus.net). What all these suppliers have in common is that they don't sell single items; everything they offer is in bulk quantities.

A recent visit to SalvageCloseouts found such items as a lot of 2,000 girl's summer outfits ($2.95 per outfit, or $5,900 total); five plasma TVs ($1,295 per unit, or $6,475 total); a pallet of high-end linens and bedding ($850 per pallet); 1,000 pieces of costume jewelry ($1.95 apiece, or $1,950 total); and a trailer load of 34 pallets worth of Sears-brand hardware and tools—more than 1,600 items in all (best offer accepted). That's a lot of variety.

Most of the bulk merchandise offered by liquidators consists of brand-name items that were ordered by a given department store but didn't sell; instead, the store returned the items to the supplier. Instead of destroying the returned merchandise, the supplier offers it at fire sale prices in the liquidation market. The only catch, of course, is that you have to take a large quantity, and you have no choice as to what exact items are included in the assortment.

That said, you get what you get at really good prices. It's cheaper for the supplier to sell 1,000 of an item to a single buyer than it is to sell one item each to 1,000 buyers. So you buy your 100 or 1,000 units of a particular item (in various sizes

note Learn more about buying closeout and liquidated merchandise in Chapter 14, "Purchasing and Managing Your Inventory."

and colors, of course) and obtain your inventory at literally pennies to the dollar. Your hope is that you can take this closeout merchandise and sell it for higher prices on eBay—and thus profit handsomely.

The downside of buying in bulk is that you have to buy in bulk. You're not just buying a dozen jeans—you're taking a dozen dozen, or more. Even if you get the merchandise extra-cheap, that's still a large check you have to write. And, even more challenging, you have to find someplace to store all that merchandise until you sell it. That's if you can sell it, of course.

Specialize—or Vary Your Inventory?

When you buy in bulk, you have some choices to make. Obviously, if you buy 1,000 pairs of baby shoes, you're going to be selling baby shoes for some time. But what do you do when your inventory runs out? Do you order more baby shoes or move onto something else? For that matter, do you sell baby shoes exclusively or order additional lots of some other type of merchandise to sell simultaneously? In other words, do you specialize in one type of bulk item, or do you vary your inventory?

Specializing in a given type of item has appeal, in that you can tailor your operation to that product category. There's a downside, however; you're stuck if the category fizzles out. It may be better, in the long run, to move in and out of various types of merchandise—baby shoes this month, sunglasses the next, DVD players the month after. Although, to be fair, every time you change categories, you're essentially starting up a new type of business. You're a shoe seller this month, a sunglasses merchant the next, and an electronics retailer the month following.

Even if you wanted to specialize in a specific category, that might not always be possible. That's because you're limited to buying what bulk inventory is available at any given time. Yes, SalvageCloseouts might have a great deal on girl's summer outfits this week, but when it's gone, it's gone. When you go back to order more, there probably won't be any more left. You're at the mercy of whatever closeout or liquidated merchandise is available at any given time. You may still be able to play within a general category (women's clothing, for example), but you probably won't be able to specialize in a particular type or brand.

Running a Bulk Reseller Business

Let's say that this business model sounds good to you. What's life like when you choose to be a bulk reseller?

Making the Buy

Probably the most important part of bulk reselling is making the initial product purchase. That means scouring the liquidation and closeout websites, looking for the best buys, and then ponying up to place an order. Some eBay sellers watch the sites for weeks on end, waiting for that one load of merchandise that has the best potential. You definitely shouldn't make a buy at the first site you visit. Shop around, like a serious consumer, and be savvy about what you finally buy.

Of course, making the buy means writing a big check—or, more likely, making a big charge to your credit card. Most of these websites accept credit card payments, some accept checks (although business checks are more accepted than personal checks), and some will even let you open an account of credit, providing you meet their business requirements. In any case, you'll probably be laying out $1,000 or more in a single purchase—which you won't get back until you sell all that merchandise.

When you're making your purchase, pay attention to shipping charges. Some liquidation sites offer free or discounted shipping for large orders, but most don't. You'll definitely want to factor in the shipping to your order's total cost.

And that shipping cost could be hefty, since you're receiving a lot of merchandise. Here, size makes a difference. A lot of 1,000 socks isn't that big a shipment, physically, while a lot of just a dozen plasma TVs can cost a ton to ship. Make sure you get an estimate of shipping costs up front, before you finalize the order.

Storing and Managing the Inventory

After you place the order, you wait around for the merchandise to arrive. This is a good time to plan out exactly where you're going to store those 1,000 frying pans or 100 electric motor scooters. That's one of the challenges of buying in bulk— warehousing in bulk. Move the car out of the garage, clean out the basement, talk

note If you want temporary storage space at your own home, consider renting a container from PODS (www.podsusa.com). Different sizes are available, and you need rent it for only as long as you need it.

to Aunt Edna about taking over her spare room. You may even need to rent a storage bin or other warehouse space.

note Learn more about inventory management systems in Chapter 19, "Automating Auction Management."

Receiving the merchandise could also be a challenge. Depending on what you order, you might be surprised to find a huge semi truck pull up outside your front door. The merchandise could be packed in multiple manageable boxes, or it could be loaded into a single large pallet. And that truck may or may not have a lift in the back—which means you could be faced with manhandling a huge crate off a truck platform five feet off the ground. Avoid surprises by finding out how the item will be shipped before you order.

When you finally warehouse the inventory, you'll need to do so in a way that organizes the individual items and makes it relatively easy to pick and pack from the lot. You don't want to store everything in a huge stack. Put the size 32 reds in one place, the size 34 blues in another, and so on. Then make a map or guide to all the bits and pieces of your inventory, so you'll know immediately where to go when you get an order.

Speaking of getting organized, you'll also need to create some sort of inventory management system. You'll want to know at any given time how many small, medium, and large items you have, and in what colors. After all, you don't want to take an order for an item that you've sold out of. Managing your inventory can be as simple as creating a big Excel spreadsheet, or as complex as writing your own database program. Many eBayers strike a middle ground by using an auction management tool that includes an inventory component. However you do it, it's important.

Managing the Auction Process

Once your inventory is stored and cataloged, it's time to start selling. One of the nice things about buying in bulk is that you get to sell the same items over and over again. No need to reinvent the wheel here; you can take one photograph and reuse it in hundreds of auctions, just as you can with your item description and other copy. You can also figure out your shipping costs ahead of time, which makes the item listing process that much easier.

One thing you want to be prepared for is that you probably won't be able to sell the entire quantity of what you ordered. Among those 1,000 Tommy Hilfiger shirts you ordered will be one or two in such an ugly color or unusual size that no eBay buyer will ever be interested. At some point you'll give up on the last of these leftovers, which means writing them off your books—and eating the cost of that unsaleable inventory.

By the way, when you have this much similar inventory to sell, you should definitely consider listing multiple items with either a fixed-price listing or an auction with the Buy It Now option. You should also consider augmenting your eBay auctions with a permanent eBay Store; an eBay Store is a good place to sell bulk merchandise, as well as to "park" those items you haven't put on auction yet. Turn to Chapter 27, "Opening an eBay Store," to learn more.

Packing and Shipping

You'll also want to set up some sort of assembly line for packing and shipping your items. Since you'll be shipping out lots of the same thing, you can get by with a single type of box. And you can save money by buying that box in large quantities. If you know you'll be selling 1,000 items, you might as well order 1,000 boxes.

Ah, but where do you put 1,000 boxes? This presents another storage challenge, but it's probably worthwhile, considering the discount available for buying packing supplies in bulk. Just something else to plan for ahead of time.

Pros and Cons of Bulk Reselling

Are you cut out to be a bulk reseller on eBay? Let's take a quick look at the pros and cons of this particular business model.

Pros

What are the advantages to buying and selling in bulk? Here are a few of the things that resellers like about this particular type of business:

- **You're selling high profit margins**. When you buy in bulk, you buy at a high discount. (Or you should, if you do your job right.) Assuming that you pick the right merchandise, you can still command a fair price when you resell that merchandise on eBay. Buying low and selling high is one of the key ways to make big bucks in business— which is one of the prime appeals of this business model.

- **There's a lot of consistency**. When you're selling the same type of item week-in and week-out, you don't have to reinvent any wheels. You set up your business around the inventory you buy, and then settle back and let things pretty much run themselves. No need to worry about what surprises might come up tomorrow.

- **Item listing is very efficient**. Part of that consistency is the fact that you'll probably be able to create similar auction listings for all the items in your inventory. This depends somewhat on the assortment you purchase, of course, but if you buy 100 model 8520-B DVD players, you don't have to write 100 different descriptions. Create the item listing once; then copy that description for each additional listing you run. The same thing goes for photographs: Take one photo and reuse it in multiple auctions. This is less true if you have 1,000 pairs of shoes in all different colors and styles, but there still will be some similarities.

- **Packing and shipping are also efficient**. The similarities definitely continue over into the packing and shipping process. If you have 500 T-shirts of the same general shape and size, you'll quickly learn the best way to pack and ship those shirts. That means you can customize your packing operation to efficiently pack all those shirts and buy a large quantity of boxes (or envelopes) at as cheap a price as you can find. You don't have to worry about stocking multiple types of boxes for multiple items; one type of box will do it.

- **You can book additional sales through an eBay Store**. Naturally, you're not going to put all 1,000 baby rattles on auction at once; you'll spread out the auctions over a multiple-week (or multiple-month) period. That doesn't mean you can't sell those items that aren't yet up for auction, however. Open an eBay Store and list all your excess inventory; you can generate sales without having to run individual auctions for all the items.

As you can see, the primary benefits of the bulk reseller model are profit and efficiency—which itself translates into profits, in terms of time savings. It's a big operation, with potentially big returns.

Cons

Okay, so if bulk reselling is so great, why doesn't every eBay seller do it? That's because this business model offers some very significant challenges, including

- **It's a big inventory commitment**. This is not the type of business you just dabble in. You can't test the waters by selling a shirt or two. You have to dive in head first and order 100 or 500 or 1,000 units of a single type of item. That's a big commitment—and a big risk. What do you do, after all, if those 1,000 coffee mugs don't sell?

■ **It's a big space commitment**. All that inventory has to go somewhere. Just where are you going to store a pallet of sporting goods, or a container of men's briefs, or a gross of pots and pans? If you live in a small (and already crowded) house or apartment, buying in bulk may be physically impractical. And if you choose to rent additional warehousing space, that's another cost of doing business you need to factor into the equation.

■ **It's a big financial commitment**. Here's the show stopper for a lot of sellers. Buying in bulk requires spending big bucks up front. Do you have the $11,000 it takes to buy a full pallet of closeout electronics, or even the $750 it takes to buy a lot of 50 leather jackets? You have to spend money to make money, but what if you don't have the money to spend? You don't want to get in over your head to buy a few month's worth of inventory. If your funds are limited, bulk reselling may be out of the question.

■ **It's a big financial risk**. Buying in bulk is also out of the question if you can't afford to lose that money. Again, what do you do if all those DVD players don't sell? Once you make the investment, you're stuck with the merchandise, even (and especially) if no one wants to buy it. If you can't afford to lose that $1,000 (or $5,000 or $10,000), you shouldn't spend it in the first place.

■ **It's a challenge to manage**. Even if you can afford to buy in bulk, you might not be up to the management challenge. Do you have the systems (computer or otherwise) set up to track 500 or 1,000 different units of inventory? Can you identify which units have sold and which haven't? Inventory management is a bit of a science, and it requires an organized mind and some technical know-how. If you're not that organized (or don't want to invest in a computerized solution), you'll quickly get buried under the work.

■ **You're tied into a single category for an extended period of time—even if the category cools down**. Here's another risk. When you buy a lot of 1,000 pairs of designer boots, you're going to be selling boots for a good long time. What do you do if the fashion trends change a month into your endeavor—and you still have two months' worth of inventory left? This long-term inventory commitment makes you somewhat of a slow-moving reseller; you won't be able to jump on and off the fast trends and evolving product life cycles. You definitely don't want to invest in a product with a short shelf life—commodity products are safer!

■ **There's no guarantee of future supply**. When you finally run through your supply of 10,000 no-name golf balls, what do you sell next? Chances are your original supplier has no more of what you originally purchased, which means you need to source another product for your next bulk purchase. If you like long-term consistency in your business dealings, bulk reselling is less than ideal.

Okay, you get the picture—bulk reselling requires a big commitment, period. You're taking a big chance when you buy a lot of anything. Not only do you have to manage all that inventory, you're betting that you can actually sell it all before the product trends shift. That may not always be possible. But then, for some resellers, it's the gamble that makes this business fun!

How to Become a Bulk Reseller

If bulk reselling sounds good to you, don't get out your checkbook just yet. First, make sure you have the physical space and systems to cope with an onslaught of not-yet-sold merchandise. If you intend to store all that stuff somewhere in your house, make sure you (and the rest of your family) can really spare the room. If you have to rent additional warehouse space, factor those costs into your business plan. And wherever you decide to put it, make sure you're up to the task of tracking all those individual items.

When you're making this size of upfront commitment, it pays to do a little research beforehand. You need to identify a product category that is robust, that has a high sell-through rate, and that has some legs. That means searching through recent eBay auctions or investing in an online research tool, such as those offered by Ándale (www.andale.com) or Mpire (www.mpire.com). You'll want to track sales trends (by category) over time, close rates (the percentage of auctions that end with a successful bid), and final selling prices. Use that information to guide you toward the types of merchandise to purchase.

Then it's a matter of seeking out the best bargains. Hit all the closeout and liquidation sites, and see what's available. Bide your time; there's no reason to jump at

note Learn more about eBay research in Chapter 2, "Researching Your Business Model."

the first offer you see. Avoid the temptation to shop by price only. The lowest price isn't always the best deal; sometimes you'll have more success selling slightly higher-priced (and more well-known) merchandise. In other words, become a savvy shopper. When it comes to bulk reselling, the better you are as a buyer, the more successful you'll be as a seller.

Seller Spotlight: rosachs

There's money in shoes. Well, not literally inside the shoes, but rather in selling them—as eBay seller **rosachs** knows quite well. Rosachs is Robert O. Sachs, a seller located in Memphis, Tennessee. He sells shoes—and lots of them—in eBay auctions and via his eBay Store, My Discount Shoe Store (`stores.ebay.com/My-Discount-Shoe-Store`), shown in Figure 10.1.

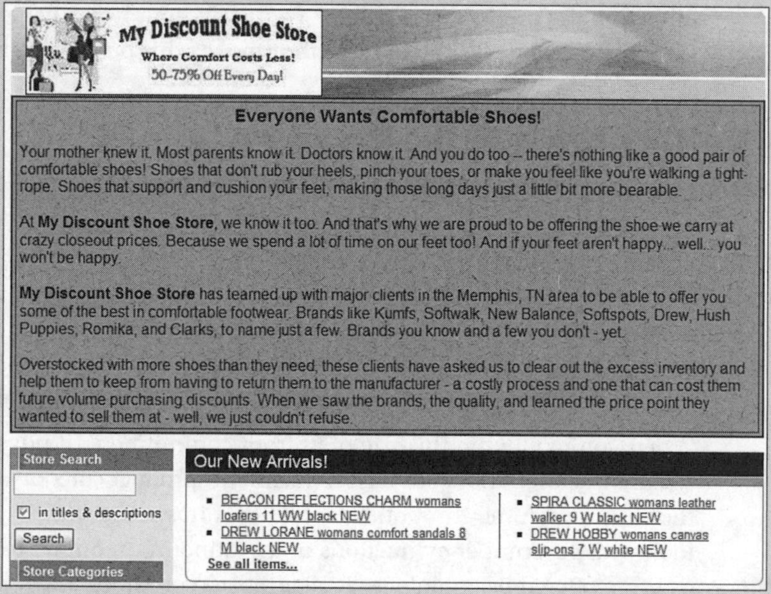

FIGURE 10.1

Items for sale at My Discount Shoe Store.

Bob got started selling on eBay when his wife started complaining about his growing collection of "stuff." Like most of us, Bob's first sales were those items lying around the house that he didn't really need. When he got into collecting (and buying and selling) limited-edition Pepsi bottles, he was hooked.

Today, Bob is a bulk reseller of overstock shoes of all styles and sizes, and as he'll freely tell you, it's a hot category. He reached Bronze PowerSeller status after just two months of selling shoes online, and his sales keep going up month after month. (He's since reached Silver PowerSeller status.)

Bob got into the shoe biz as an offshoot of his ongoing Trading Assistant business. He received a call from a gentleman who wanted him to sell some old personal electronics items, and when he went to pick up the merchandise, Bob discovered that the man worked for a shoe wholesaler. One thing led to another, and before long, Bob had signed an agreement to sell this company's excess stock on eBay. Bob's been at it for over three years, and he's now up to $6,000 in monthly sales.

What's unique about Bob's business is that while he's selling in bulk, he's not always buying in bulk. In most cases, he's actually selling on consignment for the shoe wholesaler. This arrangement relieves Bob of any financial obligation, since he doesn't have to buy the products he sells. It's a good example of how many eBay sellers operate under a blend of different business models.

Bob does buy some merchandise in bulk, however—and passes on some, as well. He told me how he once received an offer to buy 144,000 pairs of new overstock shoes from an overseas manufacturer. (That's a lot of shoes!) Bob had never heard of these particular shoes before, so he did a little research. He found that dozens of these shoes were listed every day on eBay, yet only one or two pairs were selling—and they weren't bringing the best of prices. Bob did a quick estimate of how many of these shoes he could reasonably expect to sell per week, and discovered that it would take him *years* to sell off the entire inventory. He passed on the deal.

Currently, Bob likes to keep about 600 pairs of shoes running on eBay at any given time, with about 500 of them running in his eBay Store as Good 'Til Cancelled listings. He lists about 20 or more items per day for auction, and what doesn't sell is relisted—first as a fixed-price listing, and then in his eBay Store. He used to use the Buy It Now option for all his auctions, but has recently switched to the Best Offer option, instead; about 25% of his sales come from Best Offer transactions, and another 25% from his eBay Store.

What started out as a part-time endeavor is now Bob's full-time job; in December of 2005 he ceased doing part-time contract programming and became a full-time eBay seller. Here's what he says about the business:

"Everyone thinks that selling on eBay is super easy, and it is if you are only selling a few items to clear out a closet or straighten up the attic. But when you get down to serious day-in, day-out selling, shipping 2–3 times a week every week, dealing with returns, answering the same questions from buyers over and over—it's a whole 'nuther ball game! You have to consider how much time you have to work your sales, how much space you have to store your inventory, how to properly price your shipping (boxes, peanuts, and tape aren't free!), and how to make time to find that next client, who is just as important as your current client."

He advises other potential sellers to "play it smart—keep an eye on your true costs and make sure that what you are paying yourself for the work you do is an acceptable wage." As he notes, if you work 60–70 hours a week at selling (and that isn't unheard of) and at the end of the week you have only $50 in profit to show for it, something's not right. Going big-time should mean a big-time payback, or you're not managing your business right.

Given the kind of volume he does, Bob is a big fan of auction automation, eBay Blackthorne Pro in particular. As he says, "you simply cannot grow beyond a hobby status without automation, not anymore. Automation allows you to post with much greater speed, track sales with more accuracy, send emails with more details, and just spend more time doing the things that really need doing, rather than the bookkeeping things that we all know our computers are better at than we are, anyway."

Bob also counsels other sellers to take advantage of all the free resources that eBay offers—the discussion forums, workshops, and the like. I first met Bob on the Seller Central discussion board and can attest to how useful these forums are. And when you visit, say hi to Bob!

The Retailer

Our next eBay business model isn't for everyone. In fact, not everyone can qualify. That's because this type of business is a traditional retailer, more or less, selling authorized products on the eBay site.

This type of online retailer buys merchandise direct from the manufacturer or authorized wholesaler, just as a traditional bricks-and-mortar retailer does. In fact, many of these eBay sellers *are* traditional bricks-and-mortar retailers, who supplement their real-world sales with eBay sales. In any case, this type of business requires the establishment of an official selling relationship with the supplier, which then enables you to sell that supplier's products online.

Becoming an Authorized Dealer

The key part of being an official retailer is finding a supplier who will sell to you as it would any other retailer. That is, you have to become an authorized dealer. This often means signing some sort of dealer agreement, agreeing to meet various terms of sale and distribution, and sometimes

note One thing you'll almost certainly need to buy on a retailer basis is a state tax ID or reseller's license. Learn more in Chapter 5, "Establishing a Legal Business Presence."

agreeing to meet specified sales targets. In other cases, becoming an authorized dealer is no more involved than placing an order. How you become a dealer all depends; every supplier does it a little differently.

If you're already set up as an authorized dealer for a bricks-and-mortar business, you're probably good to go when it comes to eBay sales. Note that I said "probably." That's because some manufacturers set limits as to how and where their products can be sold. I know of some musical instruments companies, for example, that prohibit their dealers from advertising their products online—which means no selling on eBay. Other manufacturers will let you sell online but require you to advertise their goods at a set *minimum advertised price* (MAP). For dealers of these products, that means you can't use the standard auction process (where you'd be listing the items below the MAP); instead, you have to list your items with a Buy It Now price equal to the MAP and set a reserve price also equal to the MAP. When in doubt, check with your supplier as to what is and isn't allowed.

If you're not already set up as a dealer, you have some work to do. First, you need to determine what kinds of products you want to sell. You should do your homework before you make this decision, by finding out which product categories sell best on eBay—which are hot, and which aren't. You probably also want to choose a category with which you're somewhat familiar so that you're not reinventing any wheels. You don't want to go into business selling hang gliders if you've never flown before in your life!

Next, you have to find a supplier for those products—which isn't nearly as easy as it sounds. The first place to start is with the products' manufacturer. For example, if you want to sell Sony electronics products, you need to contact Sony directly. In some cases, the manufacturer sells direct to dealers. In many other cases, however, the manufacturer uses a two-step

note Learn more about researching eBay sales in Chapter 2, "Researching Your Business Model."

distribution process. That is, the manufacturer sells to a distributor who then sells to dealers. If this is the case, you'll need to contact a distributor for the product you're interested in selling.

Where do you find manufacturers and distributors? For manufacturers, the best plan of attack is to do a Google search. This should lead you to the manufacturer's website, where you should be able to find some sort of contact information. Flex your fingers and either send an email or phone the main switchboard and pose your query.

Finding a distributor is often a bit more difficult. I suggest starting with the manufacturer, who will often direct you to the nearest authorized distributor. You can also try Googling, but that's more problematic, as you (a) don't know who you're searching for and (b) often discover that the distributor is a business-to-business operator that doesn't have a traditional consumer-oriented website. This leads you to more detective work, such as contacting other dealers (either online or in your area) and asking them who they buy from. Going through all these steps is a lot of legwork, but it's necessary.

Once you're set up as a dealer, you're in business—you can start ordering products and selling on eBay.

Running a Retail Business on eBay

Running an online retail business is, in many ways, like any other type of eBay business. The big difference is that you're selling pretty much the same items day in and day out, just as a traditional retailer does. This means running dozens (if not hundreds) of identical auctions, which should lead to very efficient operations.

Ordering and Stocking the Product

As with any business, you have to decide which products you want to offer for sale. You can choose a very narrow product mix or offer a wider assortment. You can also vary your mix over time.

Unless your supplier offers drop shipping services, you'll have to order your merchandise before you start selling. While some suppliers let you buy exactly what you need (including onesies and twosies), many have a minimum order requirement (and sometimes a minimum opening order requirement) that forces you to buy in larger quantities. Plan accordingly.

And while you're planning, you better start planning your warehousing. If you have to buy in large quantities, you have to put those large quantities someplace. If you have to rent warehouse space, factor this into your costs ahead of time.

note Learn more about eBay Stores in Chapter 27, "Opening an eBay Store."

Also, you need to find out how you're expected to pay the supplier. Some suppliers let you establish a line of credit, which means you can order merchandise and not have to pay for it for 10 or 20 or 30 days. Other suppliers demand payment up front, others will ship C.O.D. Find out what's required, and plan your finances accordingly.

Managing the Auction Process

The nice thing about retailing a consistent assortment of merchandise is that you're running the same auction listings over and over. Shoot one photograph and use it in hundreds of listings; write one description and use it over and over. (In fact, you may be able to use official manufacturer artwork in your listings, which could save you the trouble of shooting your own product photos.)

Since you have a steady product assortment, this is an ideal time to open your own eBay Store. In this instance, your eBay Store functions just like a traditional storefront, letting you sell your merchandise 24/7, regardless of which and how many auction listings you have running. You may even want to launch a non-eBay merchant website, to supplement your eBay-related sales. It all depends on how big you want to grow.

Packing and Shipping

Selling a lot of the same items also has advantages when it comes to packing and shipping. Since you know you'll be shipping a lot of the same thing, you can order large quantities of boxes and packing supplies and save by buying in bulk. You also should be able to set up a very efficient packing operation, since you'll get lots of experience packing the items you sell.

Pros and Cons of Official Retailing

Becoming an official retailer has its advantages and its drawbacks. Let's look at each.

Pros

If you're thinking of becoming an official retailer, take a look at these good points:

- **If you're already a dealer, you're ready to go**. Augmenting your bricks-and-mortar sales with eBay sales is a good deal. You can increase your sales volume without increasing your rent or advertising expenditures—you just sell more of what you already sell. And since increasing sales means increasing your purchases, you can often buy at lower prices. Assuming your supplier lets you sell online, this is a good deal all around.

- **Some customers prefer to buy from an authorized dealer**. Let's face it; not everyone is comfortable buying merchandise from unknown sellers. Some people like buying brand-new merchandise from authorized dealers. You'll have a better chance selling to these cautious buyers if you have legitimate goods to sell and if you can claim "official" seller status.

- **You may be able to get higher prices**. Since you're selling new goods from an official source, you may be able to command higher prices than unauthorized sellers. Some people will pay more for the real deal.

- **You'll have first-line merchandise to sell—no closeouts or factory seconds**. Selling closeout and liquidated merchandise isn't for everyone. There's something special about selling brand-new items, fresh out of the factory-sealed box. If this rings your bell, there's no other way to go.

- **You can develop a very efficient operation**. Selling a limited assortment of merchandise—and the same merchandise day-in, day-out—leads to a very efficient operation. You can save by bulk-purchasing the necessary boxes, and by getting good at packing and shipping those same items day after day.

- **Your supplier may offer drop shipping services**. Some suppliers don't require you to stock their merchandise; they'll take your order and drop ship directly to your customers. This can be a very good thing, both for cash flow (you don't pay until you make a sale) and for warehousing (there's nothing to store) .

Official status definitely has its benefits, not the least of which is that you're somehow more legitimate than the average eBay seller—at least in some customers' eyes. Being an authorized dealer lets you play with the big boys and (sometimes) command higher prices.

Cons

Official retailing isn't for everyone. Here are a few reasons why you might want to avoid this sort of authorized reselling:

- **Getting set up as an authorized dealer is tough**. If becoming an authorized dealer were easy, more sellers would do it. Fact is, it's not—at least, not always. Many manufacturers have stringent requirements for their dealers (in terms of sales volume, location, advertising, and the like), and you might not meet them. Many manufacturers just don't like dealing with small fry, which is what you are when you're first starting out. You may have better luck working with a distributor, but it's still tough. You'll have to work hard to convince suppliers to accept you as a dealer worth dealing with.

- **You may have to live with minimum purchase requirements**. Even if you can get set up as an authorized dealer, you still may have to work with a supplier's minimum order requirements. Do you really want to buy 100 DVD players or a gross of blue jeans? If you're an authorized dealer, you may have to—which could strain your finances and your storage space. (Plus, are you sure you can sell all those items?)

- **There may be limits on how you can sell your merchandise**. Some suppliers won't let you sell online, or they limit the prices you can advertise. Make sure you know the rules before you sign up and that you can live with them.

- **You have to compete with other authorized dealers**. Now that you're an authorized dealer, you have to compete against other authorized dealers. Depending on what you're selling, your competition might include Best Buy and Wal-Mart. Do you really want to play head-to-head with these big boys? (Remember—not all authorized dealers buy at the same price; chances are Best Buy and Wal-Mart are paying a lot less for their merchandise than you are!)

- **You have to compete with other _unauthorized_ dealers**. If you're an authorized dealer, you're buying off the manufacturer's or distributor's official price list. Unauthorized sellers might be able to buy similar merchandise for less from liquidators and closeout suppliers, which means that your "official" goods might end up being priced significantly higher than these similar items on eBay. This could drive your prices—and your profit margins—lower, or put a big dent in your sales rate. In many categories, eBay is a buyer's market, wherever the merchandise comes from.

In short, becoming an authorized dealer carries its fair share of limitations. You simply may not be big enough to buy direct from the supplier, or you may not be able to work within that supplier's rules and regulations. Even worse, you may find your prices getting undercut by black market or liquidated merchandise—and if this happens, there's little you can do about it. In other words, becoming an authorized dealer doesn't let you write a blank check, especially when it comes to eBay sales.

How to Become an Official Retailer on eBay

As noted earlier in this chapter, the hardest part of the official retailer model is becoming an authorized dealer. When you pursue this model, it's especially important to do your homework ahead of time, and prepare a detailed business plan. This model is most like that of a traditional business, so you should pattern your business on other businesses in the product category you choose.

This advance planning is necessary because this is one business model you can't just ease into. You have to make big commitments up front, in order to achieve authorized status and make the necessary inventory purchases. With this model you start big—which also means you can fail big. Make sure you know what you're doing before you commit.

Seller Spotlight: bobbibopstuff

eBay seller **bobbibopstuff** is a business run by John and Sandi Larson, from Beaverton, Oregon. They're both in their late 50s and think of themselves as semi-retired. The Larsons began their eBay business when they were downsized from their jobs several years ago; they decided to pursue an independent business again, instead of trying to find new jobs.

The Larsons settled on running an eBay business because of the great flexibility in working hours and pace. Today, they use their eBay business and related online store (www. bobbibopstuff.com) to generate income while they work with their church, giving financial advice and training to those in debt. Their online store supplements their eBay Store (stores.ebay.com/BobbiBopStuff), which is shown in Figure 11.1.

FIGURE 11.1

The BobbiBopStuff eBay Store.

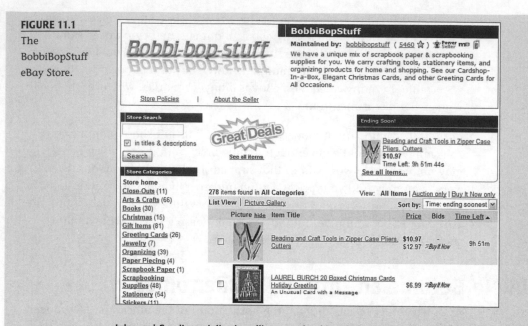

John and Sandi specialize in selling scrapbooking and craft supplies, stationery, greeting cards, and similar items. Sandi had been a regional manager for a chain of gift and stationery stores, and that experience helped the Larsons to build their eBay business.

They do most of their purchasing direct from select manufacturers and distributors. They don't do any selling through drop shippers, preferring to buy and carry their own inventory. (Their garage is their warehouse.) John notes that he wants to be in full control of their fulfillment process, and this is the only way to do that.

The Larsons' purchasing process consists of reviewing various catalogs and analyzing the business's sales history. They then make projections of what their product mix should be. It's a skill John and Sandi learned from their years of owning or managing various retail stores. They tend to place orders of $500 or more, and try to work deals with shipping whenever they can.

The Larsons augment their normal inventory by purchasing from several closeout distributors. These contacts are made at the various gift industry trade shows they attend each year. John says he particularly likes the Associated Surplus Dealers/Associated Merchandise Dealers show, held in Las Vegas every August. (You can find out more about the ASD/ASM trade show at www.merchandisegroup.com.)

John and Sandi achieved PowerSeller status in the spring of 2004. Today, the Larsons average $2,000 per month in sales over much of the year, with sales increasing to $4,000 per month over the holiday season. Their average sale is in the $8 range, which means they have to work hard to clear a small profit. On the other hand, their sales are consistent and predictable.

John offers quite a bit of useful advice to potential sellers:

"First, treat your eBay business like a real business. Be serious about making it a success. If you don't have any business background, check out some books from the library and learn about marketing, customer service, keeping books, and organization. Answer all your mail. Be professional.

"Second, buy your products for a great price. Be a frugal shopper. Don't load up with inventory before testing to see if it will sell.

"Third, list, list, list. Customers can't view or buy anything if the products are not present when they are browsing. Experiment with timing, pricing, wording, and products.

"Fourth, do all you can to make your customers happy. Remember that they are the customer and, though not always right, always the customer. Stay in touch with them through frequent email updates. Pack products well and ship them quickly.

"Fifth, go the extra mile with your customers. We include an inexpensive free gift with every order. It isn't much, but we get enough comments that we keep doing it. When you make a mistake (and you will), fess up and tuck in a little something extra for the customer's trouble.

"Sixth, keep track of your inventory. One of my most embarrassing moments is to tell a buyer that I didn't really have the item in stock that they bought. Don't run out of best-sellers. Don't load up on slow sellers.

"Finally, work out standard processes for your business. Make an auction template and keep it up-to-date. Decide how many listings you'll do each day, and do them. Make email templates or get an auction management program to help you stay on top of your communications and shipping. Be organized in your approach to getting things done. Make checklists, use tickler files, and pre-print your forms. Have your shipping materials on hand and organized."

Lots of advice, and all of it good. It's what's propelled **bobbibopstuff** to PowerSeller status, and made John and Sandi successful eBay businesspeople.

The Manufacturer/ Craftsperson

Figuring out what kind of eBay business to run is easy if you're a product manufacturer, or if you make your own art or crafts. Your business revolves around the things you create; you sell what you make.

Many artists and craftspeople have found eBay to be an essential channel for selling their works. Before eBay, you were limited to local arts and crafts fairs and the occasional gallery showing. With eBay, you can sell your work 365 days a year and help generate a more steady and consistent income. Plus, your work gets exposure across the entire country (and around the world, if you like), which dramatically broadens your audience. And the more people who see your work, the better.

Small manufacturers of all types have also found eBay to be a boon to their business. It's relatively easy to augment your traditional sales with direct-to-consumer sales on the eBay family of sites.

Whether you choose to run traditional auctions or list fixed-price product in an eBay Store, as long as you're equipped to ship directly to consumers, it costs very little to generate supplemental sales. The marginal cost is small to reach a whole new market for your products.

eBay for Manufacturers

Calloway Golf. Dell Computers. HP. JBL, Harmon Kardon, and Infinity.

What these manufacturers have in common is that they all sell merchandise on eBay, direct to consumers. And they're just a few of many; hundreds and thousands of smaller specialty manufacturers have developed eBay businesses that function as supplemental sales channels to their main businesses.

If you choose to sell your products on eBay, you have some distribution questions to answer. The chief question, of course, is what kind of products you want to sell on eBay—that is, do you want to sell your entire product line, selected products, or do you want to use eBay as a outlet for your overstock and distressed merchandise? The latter option is one that many of the big boys take; they find eBay a great way to move product that had no outlet previously. In addition, using eBay for closeout product helps to minimize channel conflict, as you're selling products online that aren't available (or even wanted by) your traditional retail channels.

For example, Dell Financial Services (stores.ebay.com/Dell-Financial-Services) operates an eBay Store that sells refurbished computers that have come off-lease from their corporate clients. As you can see in Figure 12.1, this is a great way for Dell to move these recycled products that it might otherwise have no way to offer to the public.

Back to the issue of channel conflict: This is definitely something that most businesses need to address. It's nice to establish a new stream of sales, but not if it ticks off your established retail partners. The last thing a bricks-and-mortar retailer wants to see is the same product he's buying from you offered for sale directly from you to the general public; retailers don't really like competing with their suppliers for business. It's best if you can find some way to distinguish your eBay sales from the sales you make otherwise.

In addition, if you're going to sell on eBay, you better be set up to ship directly to consumers. Some companies are, some aren't; don't assume that the distribution operation you have fine-tuned to service bulk orders to distributors and retailers can also handle one-off orders direct to individuals. Servicing individual consumers isn't nearly as easy as you might think; not only could you screw up the individual's orders, shoehorning direct-to-consumer shipments into your warehouse could cause stress to your existing operation. I'm not kidding here; think carefully before you add B2C sales to what was exclusively a B2B operation.

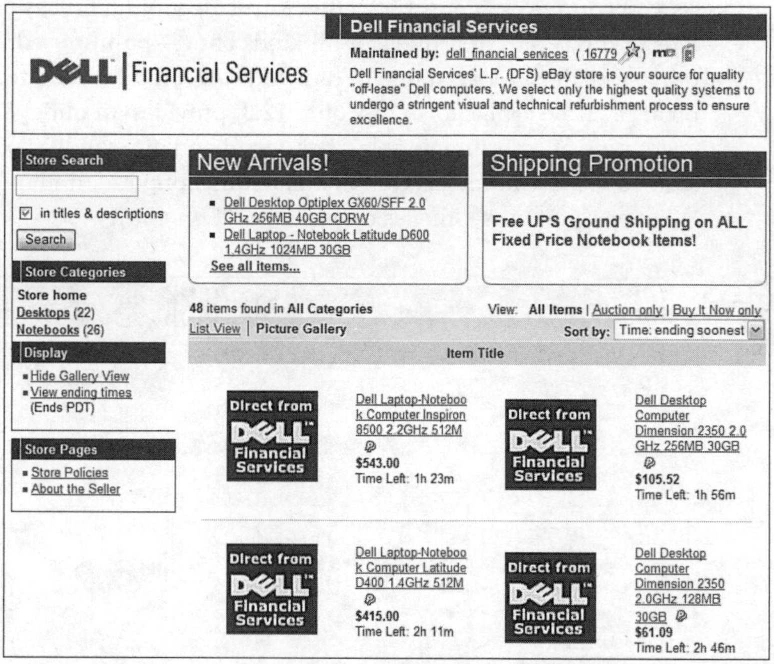

FIGURE 12.1

The eBay Store of Dell Financial Services, which sells refurbished computer systems.

That said, selling on eBay has helped many manufacturers, both small and large, move overstock and clearance merchandise and add a nice supplemental revenue stream to their existing businesses. And, of course, if you're just starting out, there's no reason not to consider eBay as your primary sales channel.

If you do decide to sell on eBay, it's a good idea to open an eBay Store. Yes, you can use the traditional auction process (perhaps supplemented with Buy It Now listings) to move a lot of merchandise, but you probably have a lot more items in the warehouse than you can list for auction at any given time. Make sure you route a fresh supply of merchandise into your weekly auctions, but then supplement those listings with stock merchandise in your eBay Store. This combination works well for manufacturers in all product categories.

eBay for Artists and Craftspeople

If you're an artist or if you make your own crafts, you're also a manufacturer of sorts. Fortunately for you, eBay hosts a thriving arts and crafts community. As you can see in Figure 12.2, eBay's Art category (art.ebay.com) includes tens of thousands of listings for all kinds of art—paintings, drawings, photographs, sculptures, even digital drawings. And the Crafts category (crafts.ebay.com), shown in Figure 12.3, provides an outlet for just about every type of craft imaginable—basketry, bead art, candles, pottery, crochet, stained glass, embroidery, pillows, macramé, origami, quilting, and more. Whatever you make, there's a market for it on eBay.

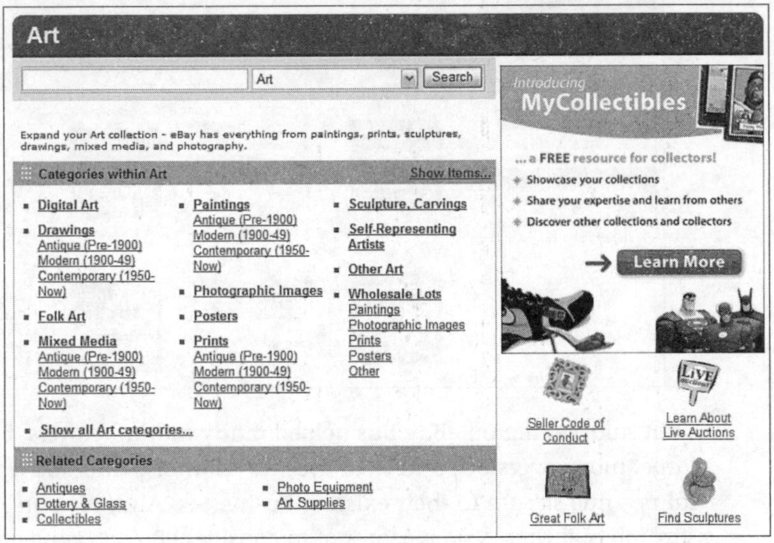

FIGURE 12.2

eBay's main Art page.

Naturally, before you can sell anything on eBay, you have to make it first. (Unless you're selling commissioned work, of course.) Finish a painting or a piece of pottery, list it for auction, and see what happens. The more art you create, the more listings you can make. And eBay is a true marketplace; your art will sell for whatever the market will bear.

That said, selling original items is somewhat different from selling other types of items on eBay. For one thing, eBay isn't really an art gallery, which is what makes the process a tad difficult. That difficulty is eased somewhat when you know the ins and outs of selling artwork online.

FIGURE 12.3

eBay's main Crafts page.

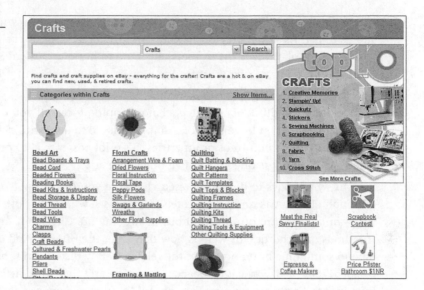

Know, however, that you shouldn't get your hopes up for selling every item you create—at least in its initial listing. While some artists achieve high sell-through rates, others sell only about 20% of what they list. It's important to relist your unsold items and perhaps establish an eBay Store to "park" your previously listed artwork. In this instance, your eBay Store becomes a virtual gallery for your work.

An eBay Store is also a good idea if you have some lower-priced items to sell in addition to your larger pieces. Sometimes a buyer will like your work but not want to splurge for a high-priced piece; having some smaller (and lower-priced) alternatives available in the store might salvage a sale.

You can also show your other work on your eBay About Me page. While you can't sell from the About Me page, you can display additional pieces to give potential buyers a feel for your style. And if you have a separate website for your work, you can link to it from your About Me page.

Deciding What to Make

The business of selling your arts and crafts on eBay probably isn't that different from your current working process. You still have to create your pieces, after all. After that, it's a matter of listing those items for sale on eBay and then following through during the entire auction process.

> **note** Learn more about eBay Stores in Chapter 27, "Opening an eBay Store."

The first step in selling arts and crafts on eBay is determining which of your items to list. As stated previously, eBay isn't the best forum for selling high-priced original art; true art connoisseurs tend to hang out at galleries, not online. eBay is more about art for the masses, which means that lower-priced, more accessible artwork tends to do better.

You should also think about the packing/shipping factor. If you create two-ton iron sculptures, you have a bit of a shipping issue to deal with. Same thing with overly large paintings or tapestries. It's a lot easier to ship an 8-by-10-inch piece than it is one four or five times that size.

This is why it pays to do a little research before you sell. Browse around through eBay's Arts and Crafts categories and see what other artists are offering—and, more important, what buyers are buying. Check out their shipping methods and charges, as well as how they offer their items. And definitely spend some time hanging out at the relevant eBay discussion forums (pages.ebay.com/community/boards/), particularly the Art & Artists and Hobbies & Crafts boards. You can learn a lot from the experienced sellers who post there.

Managing the Auction Process

Listing artwork and crafts is pretty much like listing any other item on eBay, with a few caveats. First, a high-quality picture is important. If you're selling a painting or photograph, consider making a full scan, instead, which will often show more detail than a photograph. In any case, make sure you show potential buyers just what you have to offer.

It's also important to list your item using the Gallery option. This option places a thumbnail picture of your item, like the ones in Figure 12.4, next to your item title on item listing pages. Pictures are particularly important when you're selling paintings and other artwork, whether the potential buyer is browsing or searching. Adding the Gallery option costs $0.35, but it's pretty much a necessity in these categories.

note Unscrupulous sorts can sometimes appropriate your images to use in their own auctions, or to pass off their work as yours. The solution to this problem is to use an image editing program to place some sort of watermark text or image ("This image property of Jane Smith") over the top of your picture. Picture thieves won't steal an image with somebody else's name plastered across the front.

FIGURE 12.4

Gallery photos on a typical art listing page.

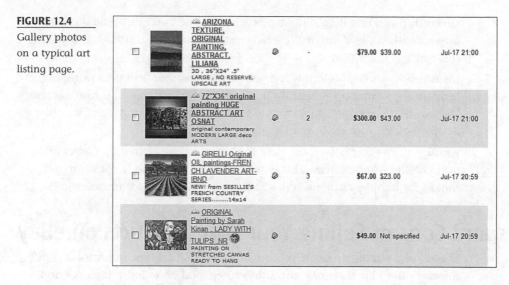

If you're selling higher-priced artwork—or if you think what you're selling is worth a higher price—then consider using the reserve price option. This way you can start the bidding at a lower price (always good for attracting bidders) but reserve the right not to sell unless the bidding reaches a higher level.

Once the bidding is underway, the rest of the auction process is pretty straight-forward. Remember to contact the winning bidder when the auction ends; then get ready to pack and ship.

Packing and Shipping

As most artists know, shipping large paintings and artwork is particularly troublesome—and often expensive. That's because this type of item is charged by size, not by weight. You also have to work with very large boxes and lots of wrapping and padding.

Making your own boxes might be necessary if you can't find large-enough standard boxes to house large pieces of artwork, paintings in particular. It's even hard to find the right-sized box for some smaller pieces; you need some-thing big but flat, and that's hard to come by. Fortunately, you can make your own "custom" boxes out of existing packaging, by sandwiching your artwork between a flattened (unopened, unassembled) Priority Mail box. Then insert that first box into a larger flat Priority Mail box and tape the ends. The pack-age may not be pretty, but it gets the job done.

You'll probably want to offer insurance on everything you ship—and maybe include the cost of insurance in your standard shipping/handling charges.

Given that you're selling unique pieces of art, you can't just send out the buyer another one if the first one gets lost or damaged in transit; that's why insurance is important.

Insurance is also important when you're shipping smaller crafts work, particularly glass, ceramic, or other fragile items. Careful packaging is also necessary. Use lots of tissue paper, bubble wrap, and Styrofoam peanuts, and consider double-boxing your most breakable pieces.

Finally, when you pack up the item to ship, consider including a letter of authenticity with the item. This letter actually adds value to the item and makes for happier customers. (It's also good advertising for future work!)

Pros and Cons of Selling Your Own Products on eBay

Should you sell the products you make on eBay? This type of business is not for every manufacturer or artist, that's true. Read on to learn the pros and cons.

Pros for Manufacturers

There are some significant potential benefits for manufacturers selling their products direct to consumers via eBay. These include

- **It's a new—not a replacement—sales channel**. The bit about eBay supplementing your existing sales also applies if you're a manufacturer. eBay sales should augment your traditional sales channels, not replace them.

- **You're already in the business of selling your products**. If you're a manufacturer, you already sell your stuff. True, you probably due it with a force of salespeople, but still. Who knows better than you the benefits of the products you sell—and who better to sell them?

- **It's a way to move merchandise you might not sell otherwise**. Manufacturers love eBay as a way to move overstocked, closeout, returned, and damaged merchandise. Think of eBay as the ultimate online outlet store. It's better than throwing all that old merchandise away!

In short, the biggest plus for any manufacturer selling on eBay is that it's an addition to your current business—if you do it right.

Cons for Manufacturers

That said, product manufacturers should think twice before establishing eBay as a new sales channel. In particular, consider the following:

■ **Your products might not be conducive to online consumer sales**. Some products sell well online, direct to consumers; some don't. What you produce might not be a good fit with the eBay marketplace.

■ **Your business might not be set up for direct-to-consumer sales**. If you currently ship large orders to a few accounts, you may not be equipped to handle small orders from a lot of accounts. Do you have the staff on hand to process all these onesie and twosie orders? Is your warehouse equipped to ship small boxes? Do you have arrangements with shipping companies to ship items to residential addresses? Don't take any of these operations for granted; if you haven't done it before, it won't be easy.

■ **You may generate channel conflict**. Retailers don't want to compete with their suppliers. If you start selling the same products direct to consumers that you formerly sold via two- or three-step distribution, you're not going to win a lot of friends. You may end up losing more business from your established distribution/retailer partners than you gain from selling direct via eBay.

You have to realize that selling direct to consumers is a much different process than selling to consumers via distributors and retailers. The extra revenue may be enticing, but the costs involved—monetary and otherwise—may be too steep. And don't minimize the issue of channel conflict; you don't want to damage your existing business by opening a new sales channel on eBay. Make sure you think this one completely through before you take the leap.

Pros for Artists and Craftspeople

If you create your own artwork or crafts, what benefits do you get by selling your work on eBay? Here are a few of the things that artists like about this particular type of business:

■ **You get to sell what you know and love**. If you're an artist, what's better than getting paid to do what you love? You create your work, you sell it; not a lot of research involved. It's a nice way to make a living.

- **It's not truly competitive**. Unlike most other types of eBay businesses, when you're selling original artwork and crafts, you're selling unique items—so unique that buyers can't price-shop between you and another artist. Your work is one-of-a-kind, so there's no direct competition with other artists.

- **It increases your exposure—and potential future sales**. When an artist lists her work on eBay, she's showing it to millions of potential buyers all across the country. Even if these folks don't buy anything today, they may buy something tomorrow—including higher-priced commission work.

- **It's an adjunct to the traditional ways of selling**. If you're already a successful artist, selling on eBay is gravy. It's a year-round business that sits on top of your existing sales.

In short, if you've never sold your products or artwork on eBay, what's the harm in trying?

Cons for Artists and Craftspeople

Then again, selling your own artwork and crafts on eBay isn't all milk and honey. Let's take a quick look at the challenges involved:

- **You may be disappointed in the selling prices**. Know that artwork doesn't always command high prices at auction. Original art goes for higher prices than prints, but it's still a buyer's market. eBay tends to be more for bargain hunters than art lovers, so reaching a sufficient volume of work will be important.

- **eBay is a mass market—not an art gallery**. eBay is not for hoi polloi. Highly stylized, "arty" work doesn't always sell that well; paintings of cute cats and dogs do. Depending on your style and sensibility, this may not be the best venue for you.

- **You may not create enough work to feed your business**. If you're an artist, don't count on a lot of five-figure sales on eBay. Most eBay artists sell a lot of lower-priced works. If you're not that fast a worker, you may not be able to create enough pieces to feed a full-time eBay business.

- **Packing and shipping artwork is a pain**. I mentioned this before, but it bears repeating: Large paintings and heavy crafts pieces do not ship all that easily or cheaply. You may need to get creative on your packing, and make sure you charge enough to cover what could be expensive shipping charges.

For artists and craftspeople, there are some realities you have to face up to. Selling a piece at a local arts fair, where the buyer walks away with it in his hands, is one thing; packing and shipping that same item clear across the country is another. And when you're selling on eBay, you have to deal with the packing and shipping. If you can't handle the hassle, it's not for you.

Selling on eBay also isn't for you if you think you're going to get rich quick. While you *could* (anything is possible…), you are more likely to end up selling a lot of lower-priced items. That isn't necessarily bad, as long as you didn't have your expectations set otherwise.

Seller Spotlight: artchick48

Lee Smith is a 53-year-old self-taught artist who lives in Greensboro, North Carolina. After 23 years of working for large corporations, she quit the corporate world in 1995 to focus on her painting. Since 2001, one of the primary outlets for her paintings is eBay.

Lee offers both original paintings and prints on eBay, via normal auctions (using the ID **artchick48**) and through her eBay Store (`stores.ebay.com/Lee-Smith-Art`), shown in Figure 12.5. When she's able to work without interruption, she can produce up to 10 original paintings in as many days; realism takes more time, she says, so she may be able to paint two or three realistic works over the same 10-day period. To date she's sold almost 300 original paintings through eBay, with close to 100% sell-through. Her monthly sales range from $300 (when she's busy with other projects) to $1,000. Her highest-priced eBay sale was a painting that went for $460.

On eBay, one sale can often lead to multiple sales. Lee recalls one lady who won a small cat painting for $39 and then turned around and purchased another painting from her store for $250. Another customer, a gentleman in assisted living, won a small work for $31, and then shortly after ordered a commission oil portrait of his granddaughter. Another collector of her cat paintings went on to commission a total of eight paintings, one of each of her cats.

eBay isn't the only venue for Lee's paintings. She has her own website (`www.LeeSmithArt.com`) and also participates in several local gallery exhibits and weekend shows each year. She has a long-term contract with a North Carolina gallery for designer and corporate works and a consignment contract with a South Carolina gallery that represents her folk art at various art festivals in the Atlanta and Charlotte areas.

Lee notes that artist sellers are unique because they create the items they sell; time to produce ample inventory is the number one challenge. "Life gets in the way, sometimes," she notes. And one can't ignore the many hours of photography, marketing, packing, and shipping necessary to complete the auction process.

FIGURE 12.5

Lee Smith's eBay Store.

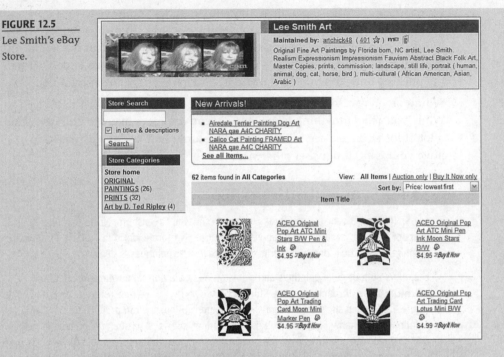

She offers the following advice to other artists on eBay:

"Research eBay to see if there's a market for your style of work. Have reasonable expectations according to your circumstances: family obligations, style, medium, and preferred method of working. Some artists may use 'formula' or assembly-line methods to produce high volume, or paint 16 hours a day to list 10 to 25 originals per week. Others who have just a few hours a day to create or spend weeks on one work may want to offer prints. As your sales increase, hire out the tedious tasks, the paperwork, accounting, photos, listings, packing, and shipping. The main thing is to be flexible, have patience, and most of all, continue to market your work in other venues."

The Trading Assistant

Over the past few years, a new type of eBay business has emerged. This type of business exists to sell merchandise for other people—folks who are otherwise too busy or too intimidated to run their own eBay auctions. The clients agree to let the business sell their items on eBay on a consignment basis; when the item sells, the business takes a cut of the selling price.

You've probably seen some of these consignment resellers on eBay or even in your own town. eBay calls these resellers *Trading Assistants* (TAs); they're also commonly known as *drop-off stores*, and they're becoming a big business.

Selling Other People's Stuff

The part and parcel of consignment selling is that you're selling someone else's merchandise. The owner contracts with you to manage the entire auction process, which you proceed to do. You take possession of the merchandise, research it, photograph it, write up an item description, and create and launch the auction listing. You manage the auction and collect the buyer's payment when it sells; then you pack it and ship it out to the buyer. You also pay all applicable eBay fees (although you pass them on to the client as part of your fees to him or her). Your client, the owner of the merchandise, doesn't have to do a thing.

Of course, you get compensated for all this work. Many consignment resellers receive some sort of flat fee up front (in case the item doesn't sell), as well as a percentage of the final selling price. Most sellers also pass through all the eBay and PayPal fees to the client.

All in all, it's a nice business model. Particularly nice is that you don't have any financial outlay to acquire merchandise to resell. You don't have to buy a thing, other than packing supplies. The result is a business that generates strong cash flow with minimal initial investment. And you're doing a service for those folks who don't want to or can't be troubled by running their own auctions on eBay.

Setting Up Shop—and Setting Prices

Setting up a consignment business is as simple as establishing a selling procedure, writing up a contract, and then going out and finding clients. And, as you can imagine, it's the finding clients bit that's most difficult.

Create a Consignment Contract

All legitimate consignment resellers should create a contract for their clients to sign. This contract spells out exactly what it is you are and are not responsible for, and clarifies your legal position in terms of ownership of the product.

Your contract should include the following items:

- The names and contact information for both parties (you and your client)
- The purpose of the contract—that you will offer the items owned by the client for sale on eBay
- A detailed listing of the merchandise to be consigned

note It goes without saying that you should be familiar with selling on eBay before you dive headfirst into consignment selling. Clients expect you to be the expert—so you better have enough experience under your belt before you start charging for your services. This is not a business model for the eBay newbie. (In fact, the higher your feedback rating when you start out, the easier it will be to attract clients.)

- The services you, the reseller, will offer—writing the listing, taking photos, listing the item, managing the auction, handling payment, packing the item, shipping the item, and so on

- Who takes possession of the merchandise during the transaction (typically you) and who retains ownership of the merchandise (typically the client)

- How and when the client can cancel the transaction

- What happens if the item doesn't sell (relist, return the merchandise to the client, whatever)

- Who handles customer complaints and returns (probably you, but not necessarily)

- Fees

Obviously, both you and your client need to sign this contract before you can begin the selling process.

Set Your Fee Schedule

As a consignment reseller, you make your money from the fees you charge for your services. There are no set guidelines for these fees; you can charge pretty much whatever you want, or whatever the market will bear.

First, consider establishing a flat fee of $5 or $10 for every transaction, in addition to a selling commission. This fee, typically paid up front, ensures that you get paid something whether the item sells or not. It also helps to weed out the riff-raff; if clients have to pay a little up front to get in the game, they might think twice about the salability of what they bring to the table.

If you don't use a flat fee, consider only selling higher-priced items—say, items with a minimum bid of $10 or higher. Again, the goal here is to avoid selling lower-priced items, in favor of more-profitable higher-priced merchandise.

As to the selling commission, you'll find sellers charging anywhere from 10% to 50% of the final selling price. For example, if you charge a 25% commission, your fee is $25 if the item sells for $100.

You might also want to consider offering a sliding fee schedule, with varying percentages for different price points. For example, you might charge a 40% fee for items that sell for less than $50, a 30% fee for items that sell over $500, and a 20% fee for items that sell over $5,000. The goal here is to maximize the dollar amount of your commission; you charge a higher percentage on lower-priced items (which generates a higher dollar fee), and a lower percentage on higher-priced items.

Then you have all the various eBay and PayPal fees to consider. Most consignment sellers pass on these fees to the client, in the form of additional charges. This means that you'll charge back the client for eBay's listing and final value fees, plus the PayPal or merchant credit card fees (if any)—in addition to your regular commission on the final sales price.

Consider Opening a Drop-Off Location

Many consignment resellers work out of their home. If you go this route, you'll either have to pick up items from your clients' homes or have your clients drop off items at your home. While some clients might like this homey touch, others might be a little nervous about dealing with a business that doesn't look like a business.

A more professional (and more expensive) option is to rent your own retail storefront for merchandise drop-offs. Chances are you'll attract more clients with a drop-off location, and not only because your signage will provide added visibility; many people will be more comfortable leaving their merchandise at a retail location than at some stranger's house or apartment. You also get lots of added space to store the consigned merchandise and conduct your business.

The downside of this, of course, is you have additional costs—the rent and utilities for your store, plus signage and the like. And you'll pay those bills every month, no matter how much auction business you do. But you don't need a *big* store, and it doesn't have to be in a high-rent location. Any type of storefront or office space will do.

Go the Franchise Route

Another option for the consignment reseller, one not available for any other type of eBay business, is to buy into one of the several auction drop-off franchise operations that are starting to bloom. With a franchise you get lots of help getting started; the main office will help you choose a retail site and negotiate your lease, plan your store layout, and market your operation. You'll also get training

note eBay calls a Trading Assistant with a drop-off location a *Trading Post*. To qualify for official Trading Post status, you must offer a staffed drop-off location with regular hours, have a feedback rating of 500 or higher (with at least 98% positive), and have achieved Platinum PowerSeller status (monthly sales of at least $25,000).

and ongoing operations support, plus the value of the franchise name. For all this, you pay a large upfront fee and a percentage of your monthly revenues.

Is a franchise a good idea? Maybe, especially if you're new to this or generally inexperienced in running a business. Maybe not, if you're an experienced seller, know how to run a business, and prefer to work for yourself (and keep all the profits yourself). If you're interested in doing the franchise thing, definitely check out several different franchises, visit a few of the stores, and talk to some of the franchise owners. Know what you're getting into before you sign that first check.

Some of the more popular eBay drop-off franchises include

- Auction It TODAY (www.auctionittoday.com)
- e-Powersellers (www.e-powersellers.com)
- eAuction Traders (www.eauctiontraders.biz)
- FoundValue (www.foundvalue.com)
- iSold It (www.i-soldit.com)
- NuMarkets (www.numarkets.com), shown in Figure 13.1
- OrbitDrop (www.orbitdrop.com)
- The Online Outpost (www.theonlineoutpost.com)
- QuikDrop (www.quikdropfranchise.com)
- QuickSELLit (www.quicksellit.com)

FIGURE 13.1

The home page for the NuMarkets franchise.

Remember, before you enter into any franchise agreement, do your homework: check out the franchisor's finances and history, talk with other franchisees, and compare franchise fees with other franchises. And it's worth noting that the franchise route doesn't come with any guarantees. Of the seven franchises I listed in the first edition of this book, three are no longer in operation—and six new ones have sprung up to take their place.

Running a Consignment Business on eBay

Running an eBay consignment business is just like running your own auctions—with the additional responsibility of finding clients who have merchandise they want you to sell. Let's take a look at what a typical consignment business involves.

Finding Clients

To sell items on consignment, you first have to find some clients. Now, if you have a drop-off location, you can sit behind your counter and wait for your clients to come to you. (Although a little advertising and promotion probably wouldn't hurt, of course.) If you're running your consignment business out of your home, however, how do you obtain new clients?

First, you should make your business known to other members of your community. Get some business cards made and pass them out—and don't forget to tack them up on any bulletin board you find. Consider advertising in local newspapers, if the rates are affordable. And remember to talk yourself up to everyone you meet—word-of-mouth is often the best promotion.

You'll probably need to do some targeted hunting for business. Make up some flyers and hand them out to anyone running a garage sale or yard sale; there's always something left at the end of the sale that you could sell on eBay. Another good source of consignment business is small businesses and manufacturers in your area. Almost every local manufacturer or business has liquidated, refurbished, or returned products it needs to somehow dispose of—and you can help with this problem. You'd be surprised how eager these

note Many consignment sellers try to avoid reselling low-priced items, for the simple reason that there's not enough money in these transactions to make them worth their while. eBay recommends using a Trading Assistant for items over $50 only; other TAs set their lower limit at $100. Whatever limit you set, you don't want to waste your time selling a lot of $5 and $10 items—when you could be reselling items for $100 or more.

companies are to get rid of old merchandise just taking up space in their warehouses.

Finally, make sure you're a registered member of the Trading Assistant program so that you're listed in eBay's Trading Assistant Directory. This directory is the way a large number of customers find a Trading Assistant near them.

Advertising Your Business Online

You should advertise your consignment business in all your regular eBay auctions. You can do this by adding eBay's Trading Assistant button, as shown in Figure 13.2, and linking it back to your eBay Trading Assistant page. To do this, you'll need to know your Trading Assistant number (found at the end of the URL for your TA listing) and a little bit of HTML. Here's the code:

```
<a href="http://contact.ebay.com/ws1/
➥eBayISAPI.dll?TradingAssistant&page=profile&profileId =XXXXX">
<img src="http://pics.ebaystatic.com/aw/pics/trading_assistant2_
➥88x33.gif"
➥vspace="5" border="0" height="33" width="88">
</a>
```

FIGURE 13.2

Add a Trading
Assistant button
to all your eBay
auction listings.

Replace *XXXXX* with your Trading Assistant number, and the button will be added. Anyone clicking on the button will be taken directly to your eBay TA page.

You can also advertise your TA business on any web page you might have, using eBay's Trading Assistant logo, shown in Figure 13.3. Just add this code to your web page:

```
<a href="http://contact.ebay.com/ws1/eBayISAPI.
➥dll?ShowMemberToMemberDetails&member=XXXXX">
<img src="http://pics.ebay.com/aw/pics/tradingAssistant/
➥taLogo_100x100.gif">
</a>
```

Again, replace *XXXXX* with your Trading Assistant number, so anyone clicking on the logo can go directly to your eBay TA page.

Taking Possession of the Merchandise

When you agree to sell an item for a client, you need to take that item into your possession. You're in the consignment business, after all; you need to have the item in your possession in order to sell it. Plus, if you don't have it, you don't know for sure that it exists—or that your client hasn't disposed of it elsewhere. Remember, it's your name on the eBay auction; you'll be held responsible if the item isn't actually available for sale.

If you're running your consignment business out of your home, you'll probably make your initial contact with a client over the phone. One phone call is all it takes to get a feel for the client, find out what he or she wants to sell, and determine whether it's worth your time. You should also take this opportunity to tell your prospective client about you and your business, discuss fees, and work out any other details. Then, if all goes well on the phone, you can arrange for the client to drop off the merchandise—or for you to pick it up.

While you can try to get all your clients to drop off their items at your home, chances are you'll have to do some merchandise pickup yourself. Going to a stranger's home can get a little dicey, so you'll want to play it as safe as you can. If you have a relative who happens to play football, take him along with you. Otherwise, judge the location carefully, and if you're at all nervous, arrange to meet the client at a neutral (and safer) location, like a local coffeehouse or fast-food joint.

Managing the Auction Process

Once you have the merchandise in your possession, selling it is just like running any auction. You'll need to do a little research to learn more about the item and determine the appropriate starting price. You'll also need to photograph the item and write the item listing. There's nothing special you need to do at this point.

note You don't have to accept everything that your clients want you to sell. It's okay to turn away goods that you think you'll have a hard time selling or that you think are worth considerably less than the client does—or that you think may have been obtained illegally.

Packing and Shipping—and Settling with the Client

At the end of the auction, you receive payment just as you would with any other auction. (The payment comes to you, not to your client!) Then you pack and ship the item, and get ready to settle things up with your client.

Once you've received payment from the buyer, you need to figure your fees and create an invoice for the client. Start with the final selling price, subtract your commission, subtract all the eBay and PayPal fees, and the balance is what you pay the client. If it's an occasional client, cut a check right then (or within the time frame specified in your contract). If you have an ongoing relationship, you may want to arrange payment for all that client's auctions at the end of each month.

Pros and Cons of Consignment Selling

eBay consignment selling has become a big business. Why is that, and what possible pitfalls are there?

Pros

The benefits of selling other people's stuff are numerous. They include

- **It's a big market**. As big as eBay is, it could be bigger. Just ask around; lots of people out there would like to sell some of their old junk on eBay, but either don't know how, are afraid of dealing online, or don't have the time. All those people are potential customers for a consignment business.

- **No upfront costs to buy merchandise**. Unlike other business models, you don't have to buy what you end up selling on eBay. There are *zero* costs for merchandise acquisition—which means you don't need a lot of cash to get started.

- **Big profits for minimal effort**. Assuming you charge an average commission of 25% or more on each sale, that's good money for creating an item listing, packing a box, and driving to the post office. If you can limit your business to higher-priced merchandise (say, $100 or more), that's at least $25 or so in your pocket for every successful auction you broker, pretty much free and clear. That's not chump change.

- **You're providing a real service to people**. Here's the part that many consignment sellers really like. You're helping people who otherwise wouldn't know what to do with their old stuff. Not only do you help them move their merchandise, you help them generate some cash that they also wouldn't otherwise have. It's a real service.

■ **You won't get bored**. Another thing that many sellers like is the variety of merchandise that comes across the consignment doorstep. There's always something new and interesting to sell, and since you're selling across many categories, you're insulated from potential category downturns.

Sounds like easy money, doesn't it? Well, it is—after you find your clients, anyway. It's a true service business, as opposed to an inventory-based or resale business, which all other eBay businesses are.

Cons

Consignment selling, of course, does have its challenges. They include

■ **There's plenty of competition**. Remember that list of drop-off franchises earlier in the chapter? They're all potential competition to your consignment business—as are all the other Trading Assistants in your neighborhood, as well as company-owned chains like AuctionDrop (www.auctiondrop.com). And there's always the chance that even bigger players will get into the market. Circuit City actually tested eBay drop-off services in some of its stores but ultimately decided against it. When something looks like a sure-fire moneymaker, expect lots of folks to jump in.

■ **It's a never-ending search for new clients**. Part and parcel with increasing competition is the constant search for new clients. You can't just launch a website and expect potential clients to stumble over it; you'll need to put in a lot of footwork to build your client base.

■ **There's little or no consistency or efficiency**. Since you have little control over what your clients will want you to sell, you won't be able to generate any long-term efficiency in selling or shipping. One client might bring you a Hummel figurine, another might bring you a farm tractor. You need to be prepared to sell anything.

■ **There may be conflicts between you, the client, and the buyer**. When you're selling someone else's stuff to a buyer on eBay, you now have a three-way transaction—you, your client, and the buyer. If the buyer has a complaint, it's easy to see how a lot of finger-pointing could result. You'll need to spell out who's responsible for what ahead of time, but even the best of contracts break down when one of the parties is unhappy. You'll have to figure out a way to deal with such disputes.

- **You may need to open a retail storefront**. With increased competition, potential clients will tend to gravitate toward those resellers that offer the best services—which, for all practical purposes, means the convenience of dropping off their merchandise for resale. You may be able to operate out of your house for a while, but expect pressure to build for opening a drop-off location.

- **You'll need a lot of storage space**. The more business you do, the more client merchandise you'll need to store. Even if it's just storing something for a week or two, it's still space. Where will it all go?

In other words, as good as consignment selling sounds, there's a lot of work involved—and a lot of things that can go wrong. Before you dive in, make sure you're prepared for all that's involved in running what is a very real business.

How to Become an eBay Trading Assistant

All eBay Trading Assistants are consignment sellers, but not all consignment sellers are Trading Assistants. That is, you don't have to be an official TA to consignment sell on eBay. Nothing in eBay's rules and regulations prohibits a regular member from reselling merchandise for other people. In fact, if you're just testing the waters, there's no real reason to bother with joining the TA program. Test the waters with a few "unofficial" consignment auctions before you decide to launch your own boat.

Once you decide to become a full-blown consignment seller, there's no reason not to join the TA program. It doesn't cost you anything, and you get the benefit of being listed in eBay's Trading Assistants Directory—which is how many users find TAs to sell their items for them.

Joining the TA program doesn't have any really stringent requirements. Here's all that eBay requires:

- You've sold at least ten items in the past three months.
- You have a feedback rating of at least 100.
- You have a positive feedback percentage of at least 97%.
- Your eBay account is in good standing.

That's it. To join up, just go to the Trading Assistant Program hub (pages. ebay.com/tahub/), shown in Figure 13.4, and click the Become a Trading Assistant link. Follow the onscreen instructions and you'll be ready to go.

FIGURE 13.4

The home base for all eBay Trading Assistants.

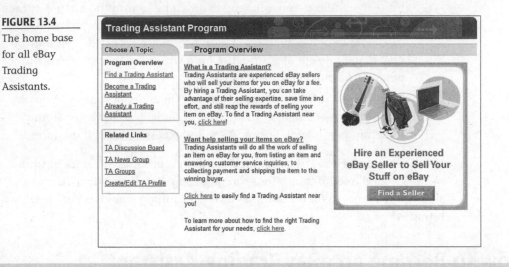

Seller Spotlight: GOing1nceAMC

Sally Milo is a 52-year-old eBay Trading Assistant doing business under the **GOing1nceAMC** ID. She makes her living on eBay selling items on consignment for other individuals and businesses.

Originally from Detroit, Sally now lives in Tucson, Arizona. A graphics designer/illustrator by training, she started selling on eBay in 1999, when a coin-collector friend asked her to manage his eBay auctions; Sally had the computer and graphic skills that would be useful in such an endeavor. (She continues to manage her friend's coin auctions today, under the **AzBCC** ID.) In March of 2003 Sally and her partner Kyle Bennett set themselves up as eBay Trading Assistant resellers; their eBay Store (stores.ebay.com/GOing1nceAMC) is shown in Figure 13.5.

To attract clients, Sally and Kyle started out by going door-to-door to businesses they thought might be potential clients. Of the 18 companies they visited during their first day of cold calling, 8 of them became clients. Sally continues to attract new clients by telling everyone she runs into about her eBay business, and by handing out lots of business cards. She also says that her listing in eBay's Trading Assistant directory has provided her with several clients.

FIGURE 13.5

The About Me page for GOing1nceAMC.

Today, **GOing1nceAMC** resells a wide variety of items for their consignment customers. They've sold things as small as a single fava bean (previously owned by a late Mafia godfather) to as large as a several-ton manufacturing furnace. They have no restrictions on what they'll accept on consignment, as long as it's not prohibited by eBay.

Like many Trading Assistants, Sally launched her business out of her home—although by the time you read this, she should have her brand-new drop-off location open. Before she decided to go the storefront route, everything about her business was home-based; her living room was her shipping room and photo studio, a former bedroom was her warehouse, and a former den was her packing materials room. Obviously, having a retail storefront will change all that.

Sally and Kyle don't charge a set-up fee for regular items; bidding begins at $9.99 for a 7-day auction. They also offer a premium plan for higher-priced items, which does have a set-up fee ($19.99) and begins bidding at a higher price for a 10-day auction. The bulk of their revenues come from their selling commissions, which start at 40% of the final selling price and operate on a sliding scale from there.

In a typical week, **GOing1nceAMC** will have at least 20 items listed for auction on eBay. They have a very high sell-through rate, selling more than 95% of the items they list—although some of those items sell upon relisting, rather than during the initial auction period. During the whole of 2005 their sales averaged from $2,000 to $4,000 per month, with sales climbing closer to $10,000 per month toward the end of the year.

Sally says that their most memorable sale started when a long-time client asked them to list 11 old decks of playing cards. They priced each deck from $5 to $20. One of the $20 decks was quite nice, she remembers, but they couldn't dig up any information about them. This particular item ended up in a bidding war among a few bidders, and ultimately sold for $2,575. Needless to say, both Sally and the client were amazed by—and quite happy with—the final price. The buyer, a Norwegian card collector, told them that particular deck had not been offered anywhere in nearly 30 years.

Sally has the following advice for anyone wanting to start an eBay consignment business:

"First, get a good amount of experience selling your own stuff—collectibles you have around your home and nifty items you picked up at the flea market. And buy some stuff from your fellow eBayers to get an idea how sales are handled from the customer's point of view, and to build up your feedback. Of course, to be a registered eBay TA, you must meet the requirements. Know and act as a professional businessperson!"

You can learn more about Sally and Kyle's consignment business at the GOing 1nce website (www.going1nce.com).

Part 3

Managing Your Day-to-Day Business

Purchasing and Managing Your Inventory

While occasional eBay sellers get by selling a few items from time to time, running a successful eBay business involves the selling of large quantities of merchandise, week-in and week-out. To sell that merchandise, you first have to obtain the merchandise, which means finding a steady supply of items to sell. These items become your business's inventory.

Managing your inventory sounds simple on paper. You identify items you want to resell, purchase those items (at as favorable a price as you can negotiate), store those items until they're sold, and then sell and ship them to your customers. When you run low on inventory, you order more. Hopefully, you don't order more merchandise than you can actually sell. And hopefully, you can sell your inventory for a higher price than what you paid for it—and high enough that you can pay all your other expenses (and make a little profit) from the difference.

Sounds simple, but it's a lot of work. Finding the best supplier is a big challenge, and handling all that inventory takes space and elbow grease. It's a process that never ends; as soon as you sell some, you have to order more. And the bigger your business gets, the more involved the whole process becomes.

This chapter looks at the entire inventory issue—how you find items to sell and how you manage that inventory in the day-to-day running of your business.

Where to Find Merchandise to Resell

When you put together your business plan, you indicated the type of business that you wanted to conduct. If you planned your eBay business around merchandise that you currently own or create yourself, you can skip this section. But if you planned your business around the resale of new or used merchandise, you have to find a source for the items you want to sell.

Sourcing your inventory is one of the toughest tasks for high-volume eBay sellers. While the average eBay seller typically finds items in his or her own home or in garage sales, high-volume sellers have to find a constant supply of new merchandise. In essence, high-volume sellers are *resellers* because they purchase merchandise from wholesalers or other sources and then resell that merchandise to their customers via eBay auctions.

Where can an individual find a source for merchandise to resell on eBay? There are several options, all of which involve buying items in bulk. That means laying down the cash up front to buy large quantities of items, and then making your money back later, one sale at a time. This is one reason why a budding eBay business needs a source of funding; purchasing your starting inventory can tie up a lot of cash.

Whatever type of merchandise you choose to resell, you should always make sure you're buying from a reputable supplier. That means passing up those companies that have a website but no published phone number, or a post office box but no physical address. Even better, research the business on the Better Business Bureau website (www.bbb.org), or check the company's ratings at Dun & Bradstreet Small Business Solutions (smallbusiness.dnb.com) or Hoover's (www.hoovers.com). You can also pick up

note Learn more about obtaining funding for your business in Chapter 4, "Evaluating and Arranging Funding."

the phone and give the company a call; you can tell a lot from a simple conversation.

Another strategy is to go direct to the manufacturer for information (and, sometimes, products). ThomasNet (www.thomasnet.com), the only home of the venerable Thomas Register, is the definitive directory for finding products and companies in the U.S.

Read on to learn about the many different sources of resalable merchandise.

Wholesale Distributors

The way traditional retailers do business is to purchase merchandise from a wholesale distributor. The distributor purchases merchandise direct from the manufacturer, who in many cases doesn't deal directly with retailers. The distributor, then, is a middleman who provides a variety of services to the retailer, not the least of which is warehousing the large quantities received from the manufacturer.

If you want to be an "official" reseller of many types of products, you'll have to deal with the products' authorized distributors. There are thousands of wholesalers out there, most specializing in specific types of merchandise. Most wholesalers are set up to sell in quantity to legitimate retailers, but many also handle smaller orders and smaller buyers, making them ideal for eBay sellers. Many of these distributors operate over the Internet, which makes the process even easier for you.

How do you locate a wholesaler? One way is to attend an industry trade show or conference. Most distributors attend or exhibit at these shows; you can also find out about new products and (sometimes) get special tradeshow pricing. You can also contact the manufacturer directly; most will be glad to direct you to the distributor in your region.

If you live in a major metropolitan area, it may have a trade or merchandising mart where multiple wholesalers may be found. For example, Atlanta's AmericasMart is home to hundreds of specialized distributors, as is Chicago's Merchandise Mart. Check with your local chamber of commerce to see what's available in your area.

In addition, you shouldn't be afraid to ask other retailers (online or local) for the names of wholesalers they buy from. Most merchants are quite helpful, as long as they don't perceive you as a direct competitor.

note You can search for trade shows of interest at the *Tradeshow Week* magazine website (www.tradeshowweek.com).

And here's one advantage of dealing with an official wholesaler: If you do enough business (and your credit rating is strong enough), you may be able to establish credit terms for your purchases. Instead of paying cash on the barrelhead, you may not have to pay until 15, 30, or even 60 days after you receive your merchandise. Check with your wholesaler to see what terms are offered.

> **note** Learn more about buying and selling merchandise direct from the manufacturer in Chapter 11, "The Retailer."

You'll have to conduct your own search for a wholesaler that specializes in the particular type of merchandise you're interested in selling. I'll list a few sites that function as directories or search services of wholesale distributors, but it's hard to beat a targeted Google search. Just make sure you put the words "wholesale" or "distributor" in your query.

Wholesale411

Wholesale411 (www.wholesale411.com) is one of the best search directories for wholesale and closeout merchandise, period. Wholesalers and liquidators list their merchandise and services on the Wholesale411 site, which then organizes the available merchandise into a variety of product categories, as shown in Figure 14.1. You can also search the site for suppliers of specific types of merchandise.

goWholesale

The goWholesale site (www.gowholesale.com) helps you find wholesale suppliers of all manner of merchandise, from custom T-shirts to computer parts. You can browse or search for suppliers, and the site contains a lot of links to suppliers who specialize in selling to eBay businesses. (Interestingly, goWholesale provides the search engine behind the Wholesale411 site.)

Buylink

Another place to find vendors of different products is the Buylink site (www.buylink.com). You have to register as a retailer to search the Buylink marketplace (registration is free), but then you can search for specific products or vendors.

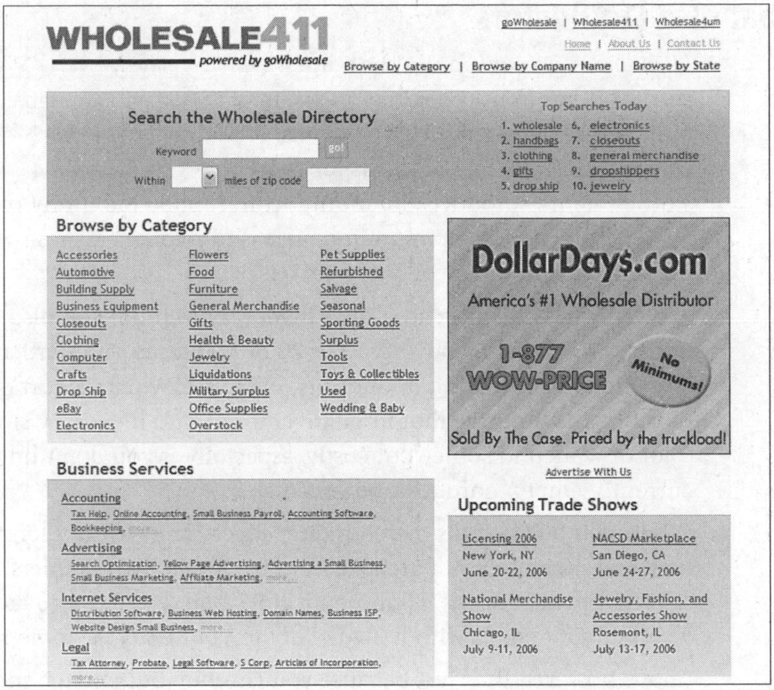

FIGURE 14.1

Browse through the categories or search for specific types of wholesalers at Wholesale411.

Top Wholesale Suppliers.com

When you're looking for wholesalers, you should also check out Top Wholesaler Suppliers.com (www.topwholesalesuppliers.com). This is a free online wholesalers directory, organized by product category.

Wholesale Central

Wholesale Central (www.wholesalecentral.com) is another leading directory of merchandise wholesalers. You can browse for vendors by category or search for vendors of specific products.

WholesaleQuest

Yet another wholesale marketplaces for eBay resellers is WholesaleQuest (www.wholesalequest.com). You can browse through suppliers by product category or search for suppliers of specific types of merchandise.

caution

With so many legitimate wholesaler directories on the web, you want to avoid those scam artists that offer to sell you a "guaranteed" directory (in a book or on CD) of wholesalers or dropshippers. More often than not, you'll pay your money and receive a several-years-old listing of sites—not all of them reputable, and many of whom have since gone out of business. You shouldn't have to pay for information that's available for free on the Web in a much more current form.

Merchandise Liquidators

Liquidators are companies that purchase surplus items from other businesses, in bulk. These items might be closeouts, factory seconds, customer returns, or over-

note Learn more about buying and selling closeout merchandise in Chapter 10, "The Bulk Reseller."

stocked items—products the manufacturer made too many of and needs to get rid of. Liquidators help manufacturers and retailers dispose of this unwanted merchandise to the secondary market.

Just as liquidators purchase their inventory in bulk, you also buy from them in bulk. That means buying 10 or 20 or 100 units of a particular item. You get a good price for buying in quantity, of course, which is part of the appeal. You also have to manage that large inventory—and inventory storage can be both a lot of work and somewhat costly, especially if you don't have a large (and currently empty) garage or basement.

When you buy surplus merchandise, check the warranty terms. Unlike the new merchandise you purchase from traditional wholesalers, most liquidators sell their goods "as is." That means if it's bad, you have to eat it—unless you also sell your goods with no warranty to your eBay customers.

Know, however, that just because you can buy bulk merchandise cheap doesn't make it a good deal. Remember, there's probably a reason why an item is being liquidated. It may be last year's model, it may be factory seconds, it may be used or returned, or it may just be something that no one wanted to buy. If it didn't sell well originally, there's no guarantee that it will sell well (at a lower price, of course) in an eBay auction.

That said, here's a short list of liquidators that can supply you with merchandise for your eBay auctions.

Liquidation.com

Liquidation.com (www.liquidation.com) is one of the largest and most reputable online liquidation services. The Liquidation.com website, shown in Figure 14.2, offers a steady stream of surplus, closeout, and returned merchandise in a variety of categories, from clothing and consumer electronics to construction supplies and vehicles.

FIGURE 14.2

Buy surplus items in bulk at Liquidation.com.

What kind of merchandise are we talking about? How about a lot of 11,000 socks, or 45 radar detectors, or 100 20GB hard drives, or 2,000 belly rings—just for a start. Pricing is pretty good, if you can take the quantities. For example, those hard drives went for just $14.25 apiece at a total lot price of $1,425. Assuming you can resell them on eBay for $30 or more, that's a pretty good deal. The key is to pick an item that you know you can move in bulk over a period of weeks or months.

Note that Liquidation.com actually serves as a middleman between sellers (the original manufacturer or retailer) and buyers (you). Goods are sold in an online auction format, so you'll find yourself bidding on items just as you would in an eBay auction. All auctions start at $100, with no reserve. You can even pay for your merchandise with PayPal.

#1 Accessory.com

The #1 Accesory.com site (www. 1accessory.com) specializes in wholesale jewelry and fashion accessories. You can find both individual items and larger lots.

> **note** Unlike eBay auctions, Liquidation.com doesn't allow sniping. If there's a last-minute bid, the auction is extended by three minutes to enable all interested bidders to respond.

America's Best Closeouts

What you find at America's Best Closeouts (www.abcloseouts.com) is bulk quantities of used, second-hand, and recycled clothing. They're an especially good source of jeans in large lots.

American Merchandise Liquidators

American Merchandise Liquidators (www.amlinc.com) handles closeouts, over-stocks, customer returns, and salvaged merchandise in a variety of categories, including clothing, furniture, toys, tools, and other general merchandise.

AmeriSurplus

AmeriSurplus (www.amerisurplus.com) sells salvage merchandise by the pallet from a warehouse in South Carolina. Products offered include automotive supplies, groceries, small appliances and electronics, sporting goods, and toys.

Apparel Overstock.com

Apparel Overstock.com (www.appareloverstock.com) specializes in wholesale brand name and designer clothing for men, women, and children. You can find quantities of similar merchandise from the same manufacturer, or mixed lots containing a variety of sizes, colors, and styles.

Bid4Assets

Bid4Assets (www.bid4assets.com) is an online auction site offering merchandise obtained from bankruptcies, private companies, and the government. This site offers primarily high-ticket items, including artwork, computer equipment, jewelry, vehicles, and even real estate. The items offered are typically single quantity, not bulk.

Bookliquidator.com

Bookliquidator.com (www.bookliquidator.com) is an excellent source for used and vintage books. The site also offers dropshipping services for its customers.

eBay Merchandise.com

eBay Merchandise (www.ebaymerchandise.com), while not affiliated in any way with the eBay site, offers closeouts, overstocks, returned merchandise, and similar items for sale to eBay sellers. Items can be purchased by the piece, the pallet, the lot, or the truckload; products in a variety of categories are available, from automotive goods to toys.

Luxury Brands

Luxury Brands (www.luxurybrandsllc.com) offers higher-end surplus merchandise than you find at other sites. Items include luxury branded European clothing, accessories, and gift items. Even though this is surplus merchandise, you might recognize some of the brands—including Giorgio Armani, Ralph Lauren Polo, Givenchy, Gucci, and Burberry. The company purchases large mixed parcels of European merchandise, typically end-of-season merchandise, and then imports it for sale in the U.S. You can purchase products in lots of 10, 25, 50, 100, and so on.

Overstock.com

Overstock.com (www.overstock.com) offers surplus merchandise from a variety of manufacturers. The company sells single quantities of closeout merchandise through its normal website but offers larger discounts (and discounted shipping costs) when you buy multiple quantities through the Club O section of its site.

Salvage Closeouts

Salvage Closeouts (www.salvagecloseouts.com) offers liquidated merchandise and department store closeouts in a wide variety of categories, from Apparel and Appliances to Tools and Toys. It also offers a variety of pallet and truckload specials, and has a special eBay Specials category.

Surplus.net

Surplus.net (www.surplus.net) aggregates merchandise from hundreds of different liquidators. It's also one of the portal sites for the Internet Marketing Association of Surplus Dealers (IMASD), an organization of closeout suppliers.

TDW Closeouts

TDW Closeouts (www.tdwcloseouts.com) is another distributor of department store returns and closeout merchandise. It offers liquidated, salvage, overstock, and surplus items in a variety of categories, from Apparel to Toys.

Other Sources of Merchandise

If you're less interested in bulk and more interested in variety, there are a few other sources that can supply you with merchandise for your eBay auctions. I'll list some of the more popular ones next.

> **note** Learn more about buying and selling used merchandise from garage sales and flea markets in Chapter 8, "The Second-Hand Reseller."

Garage Sales

Many eBay sellers got their start by reselling merchandise they picked up at local garage/yard/tag/rummage sales. While this can certainly be a source of merchandise, it may not be a consistently reliable source for all high-volume sellers, for a number of reasons. First, the merchandise you buy isn't limited to a specific category, and it's tough to deal with such a large variety of items. Second, it's not a guaranteed supply; you might stumble across a great deal one week but then go dry the next. Finally, this source looks to be getting tapped in some areas, as more people choose to sell their old stuff on eBay rather than putting it out in their front yards. Take a gander, but don't be disappointed if this source doesn't pan out.

Flea Markets

Flea markets offer similar merchandise to what you find in garage sales, although you can sometimes find surplus items in bulk. If you keep your eyes peeled, you might find the occasional bargain that can supply your eBay auctions for an extended period of time.

Estate Sales/Auctions

Not to be insensitive, but dead people provide some of the best deals you can find. Estate sales and auctions are the equivalent of raiding somebody else's garage or attic for old stuff to sell. Check out the weekly estate sales and auctions in your area, be prepared to buy in quantity, and see what turns up.

Traditional Auctions

Real-world auctions (not the eBay kind) remain a good source of inventory for many eBay sellers. Many auctions feature large lots or bulk quantities, which are perfect for ongoing eBay sales. Make sure you inspect the merchandise before the auction, and don't get caught in a bidding frenzy. Set your maximum price beforehand, and don't exceed it. The Internet Auction List Auction

Calendar keeps a list of ongoing auction events by date and location. Check out the website at www.internetauctionlist.com.

Vintage and Used Retailers

You can often pick up some decent collectible merchandise at your local "vintage" or used merchandise retailer—although you may have to haggle a little to get down to a decent price. The big drawback is that you're typically buying onesies and twosies; this isn't a good source for large lots.

Thrift Stores

Think Goodwill, Salvation Army, and similar stores here. You can sometimes find decent merchandise at low cost—and help out a nonprofit organization, to boot. This approach has the same drawback as buying from a vintage retailer, however; large lots are rare. And many eBay sellers report that the major thrift stores have raised their pries to more closely match the going rate on eBay, so finding a good deal could become more difficult over time.

Pawn Shops

You can't overlook the traditional pawn shop. There are always interesting items to be found, often at a bargain price. Ask about merchandise that's been sitting on their shelves for awhile, and then offer a bulk buyout or perhaps even a consignment deal.

Dollar Stores

Dollar stores or "big lot" retailers are surprisingly good sources of eBay-ready merchandise. Most of these retailers carry overruns and closeouts at attractive prices. You can often pick up items here quite cheap—and enough of them to feed your auction activity for a while. Some of the larger dollar-store chains include 99¢ Only (www.99only.com) and Family Dollar Stores (www.familydollar.com). The Big Lots chain even has a special website for wholesale buyers, located at www.biglotswholesale.com; it's worth checking out.

Warehouse Clubs

You'd be surprised what deals you can find at your local Sam's Club (www.samsclub.com) or Costco (www.costco.com). Buy something cheap enough here, and it's not too hard to resell that item at a decent markup on eBay. (Plus, Sam's Club holds its own online auctions that sometimes offer good bargains for the savvy eBay seller.) Just remember that the clubs' product mix is continually changing, so you'll need to visit often to find the latest deals.

Closeout Sales

You don't have to shop at a cheap retailer to find a good deal. Many mainline merchants offer terrific deals at the end of a season or when it's time to get in next year's merchandise. If you can get enough good stuff at a closeout price, you have a good starting inventory for your eBay sales.

Going-Out-of-Business Sales

Even better, look for a merchant flying the white flag of surrender. When a retailer is going out of business and says "everything must go," that means bargains are yours to be had—and don't be afraid to make a lower-priced deal, if you can.

Ándale Suppliers

If you're not sure where to find specific types of merchandise, you're in luck. Ándale Suppliers (www.andale.com) is a free service that helps you find suppliers of various types of merchandise for resale. It does a good job of matching resellers with suppliers, by keeping a big database of both.

When you sign up for Ándale Suppliers (it's free, remember), you start by filling out a buyer profile. Select the categories of merchandise in which you're interested, and Ándale Suppliers will automatically match you with suppliers who match your criteria. You can choose to receive your leads by email or on the Ándale site itself. Each lead listing includes the supplier's location and eBay feedback rating, so you can judge its trustworthiness.

> **note** You can find Ándale Suppliers on the Ándale site under the Research Tools tab.

eBay

This leads us to the final place to look for items to sell on eBay—eBay itself! Yes, it's possible to make money buying something on eBay and then turning around and selling it to someone else on eBay at a later date. The key is timing. Remember, you have to buy low and sell high, which means getting in at the start of a trend. Being successful at this approach is possible—although it takes a lot of hard work, and not a little skill.

One way to find goods for resale is to use eBay's search feature. Make sure you include the words "case," "closeout," "lot," or "surplus" in your query.

Another option is to go directly to eBay's Wholesale Lots category (pages. ebay.com/catindex/catwholesale.html). As you can see in Figure 14.3, this page lists eBay auctions of surplus merchandise in almost all of eBay's major categories. Just click through to bid on merchandise ideally suited for resale.

FIGURE 14.3

Sourcing surplus merchandise on eBay's Wholesale Lots page.

Managing Your Inventory Levels

Once you find a source for merchandise, you now have the challenge of managing your newfound inventory. That means determining how much to buy and when to reorder.

Ordering the Right Quantity

Establishing how much merchandise to order is tough, especially when you're first starting out. The problem is amplified when a supplier requires you to order large quantities of an item, or if you need to order a large quantity to qualify for a larger discount. It's tempting to shoot the moon to get the best possible price, but that's sometimes a dangerous strategy. It's also problematic if your storage space is at a premium; you certainly don't want to order more stuff than you have room for!

The best strategy is to research similar auctions on eBay, as discussed in Chapter 2, "Researching Your Business Model," and make an educated guess as to how

note When you're dealing with a commodity product for resale, it's better to order too few than too many. If your business is an overnight success, you can always order more.

many items you can sell in a typical week. Multiply that number by four and round off a little to come up with a *conservative* estimate of your first month's sales. That's because when you're first starting out, keeping a month's worth of inventory on hand is a safe way to go. If your guess is off by 50% either way, you're still okay; you'll either have two weeks' or two months' worth of inventory on hand, either of which you can comfortably handle. If, on the other hand, you order two months' worth of inventory and you're off by 50%, you're either out of stock in a week or stuck with four months' worth of stuff— neither of which is terribly desirable.

In addition, when you place an order for a large quantity of merchandise, you need to make sure that there is a sufficient long-term demand for that product. Fads and fashions change over time. Don't order six months' worth of inventory if the current fad looks to burn itself out in three. It may be more prudent to pay a higher per-item price for a lower quantity than risk not selling a substantial portion of a larger-quantity order. (And remember—you have to store all those items somewhere.)

And it's worth repeating that when it comes to ordering inventory, you shouldn't bite off more than you can chew. Paying a higher price for a smaller quantity is better than getting stuck with a garage full of unsold merchandise!

Managing Your Reorders

Once you start selling, you need to keep track of how much inventory you have on hand. That's where your inventory management system (see Chapter 6, "Setting Up a Recordkeeping System") comes into play. You have to subtract every item you sell from the quantity you initially had on hand. When your inventory drops to a specified level, it's time to reorder more.

note Don't wait until your inventory drops to zero to reorder—you'll be stuck with nothing to sell, and no income coming in. Better to reorder before you run out so that your auctions can continue uninterrupted.

Of course, this situation poses two questions: At what level should you set your reorder point, and what quantity should you reorder?

To the first question, your reorder point should be based on how long it takes you to receive any order you place from your supplier. For example, if your supplier ships within a week of your order, you can safely set your reorder point at a week's worth of inventory. Let's say you're selling 20 units per week, and your supplier reliably ships within a week of your order. Set your system to alert you when your inventory drops to 20 units. Place your reorder immediately, and you'll have your new stock arrive just as the last of your old stock runs out.

> **note** When you're factoring the cost of your merchandise, don't forget to include warehousing costs. This might be zero if everything fits in your garage (and you don't mind parking outside) but could add up if you have to rent a storage bin or warehouse. You might think that large-quantity discount is worthwhile—until you have to pay through the nose to store all those boxes somewhere.

Naturally, if your supplier ships more slowly, you should set your reorder point higher. Let's say your supplier takes two weeks to fill an order. If you're selling 20 units a week, you should set your reorder point at 40 units—two weeks' worth of inventory.

As to how much you should reorder, the answer depends on how many units you're selling per week, how long you expect sales to stay at this rate, how much inventory you feel comfortable with, and what discounts are available for larger orders. If you're fairly confident that sales will continue at current levels for the next two months, and you get an extra discount for larger quantities, go ahead and order two months' worth. (Assuming you have the space to store it, of course.) On the other hand, if you think sales will slow (because of changing fashions, or seasonal trends, or whatever), don't go out on a limb—order another few weeks' or at most a month's supply. Order the quantity you feel comfortable with—you're the one who has to assume the risk.

Deciding to Drop Ship

This is as good a place as any to discuss the issue of *drop shipping*. This is the practice of selling an item that you don't physically have in stock. You make the sale (via eBay) and then notify your supplier of the purchase. Your supplier then drop ships the merchandise directly to your customer, billing you in the process.

While not all distributors offer drop ship services, many do. Check with your wholesaler to see what services are available, or check out this short list of popular drop shippers and drop ship directories:

- 123DropShip.com (www.123dropship.com)
- Doba (www.doba.com)
- MegaGoods.com (www.megagoods.com)
- The Shipper (www.theshipper.com)
- Worldwide Brands, Inc. (www.worldwidebrands.com)

In addition, Wholesale411, eBay Merchandise, and the other wholesaler directories listed previously often note whether a particular wholesaler drop ships or not.

While drop shipping might sound attractive from an inventory management standpoint (you have none to manage), it might not always be the best deal for your customers—especially if your supplier isn't always a speedy shipper. Remember, your customers hold you responsible for shipping the products they purchase, and if a drop shipment isn't prompt, you are the one who'll get the complaints (and the negative feedback). If, for whatever reason (like being temporarily out of stock), your supplier drops the ball and never ships the merchandise, you're on the hook. If this happens too often, you could get the boot from eBay.

So when you're researching drop shipping services, keep a few things in mind. Make sure you understand all the charges you'll have to pay over and above the cost of the item. Some drop shippers charge a larger shipping fee to cover the actual costs of drop shipping, while others charge a separate handling fee for the same reason. Some charge a flat, often excessive amount for shipping, while others calculate shipping based on the delivery ZIP code. (While a variable shipping fee might sound best, you won't know how much you'll be charged for shipping until after the fact—which makes it difficult to pass on this charge to your buyers.)

Finally, make sure you have access to accurate inventory levels (necessary before you decide to post an eBay listing) and that you're provided with tracking information for all items shipped. Given that you have no real control over the fulfillment of a drop-shipped sale, it's important to at least have as much information as possible about the shipment.

CHAPTER

15

Automating Item Listing

Occasional eBay sellers get by using eBay's standard Sell Your Item listing process, which you access by clicking the Sell link at the top of any eBay page. For the high-volume seller, however, this is an extremely time-consuming way to post your auction items. Going through that cumbersome procedure for a dozen or more items at a time isn't very appealing; trust me.

A better solution for high-volume sellers is to use a bulk listing program or service. These tools let you create a large number of item listings in advance and even reuse saved listings—great if you run multiple auctions for similar items. You then schedule your auctions to launch at the time of your choosing, and you're done with it.

A number of these bulk listing tools are available; I'll discuss some of the most popular ones next. Which ones should you choose? That's entirely up to you, of course; they all offer many of the same functions. One of the big differences is price; they range in cost from free (eBay Turbo Lister) to 25 cents or more per

ing—and some even charge a final
ue fee on top of that! Fortunately, most
of these services provide free trials, so you
can try them out before you commit. Pick
the tool that works best for you, with a
cost you can live with. Remember—all
these individual fees can really take a cut
out of your profits, so make sure you factor the costs into your overall financial
plan.

note If you prefer to create your listings one
at a time, eBay's standard Sell Your
Item pages will probably do the
job, no additional tools necessary. I
cover standard listing creation in
my companion book, *Absolute
Beginner's Guide to eBay, 4th Edition*
(Que, 2006). Turn there for step-by-
step instructions for creating basic
auction listings.

eBay Turbo Lister

eBay offers its own bulk listing software, called eBay Turbo Lister. To download
the Turbo Lister software, go to pages.ebay.com/turbo_lister/. The program
is free, and there are no monthly subscription fees—which makes it the program of choice for cost-conscious sellers.

Turbo Lister lets you create your item listings offline, at your leisure. (It also
offers HTML-based templates you can use to spruce up your item listings—
although they are pretty much the same templates found in the Listing
Designer section of the Sell Your Item page.) Then, when you're ready, it
uploads all your listings at once, with the click of a button. Creating multiple
auctions couldn't be easier.

Creating a Listing

The Turbo Lister software is quite easy to use. It uses a series of forms to
request information about your listings, as well as a WYSIWYG editor for creating great-looking listings.

You start out not by creating a listing, but rather by creating a new inventory
item, complete with item listing, as shown in Figure 15.1. Turbo Lister lets you
utilize the templates in eBay's Listing Designer—for a 10-cent fee, of course.

Once you've completed this process, the item is added to your item inventory.
To view the items you've added to your inventory, click the Item Inventory
tab. This screen lists all the items you've created; from here you can edit,
delete, and create duplicate items—as well as choose which individual listings
you want to upload to the eBay site.

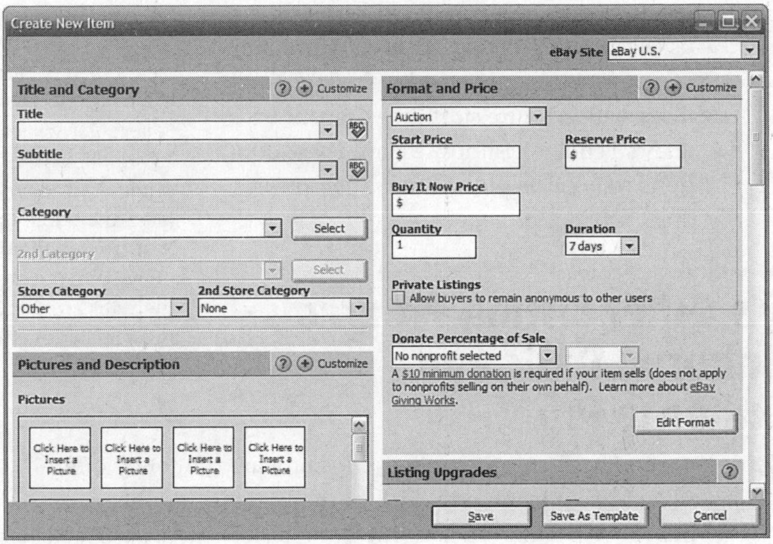

FIGURE 15.1

Designing a new item listing with Turbo Lister.

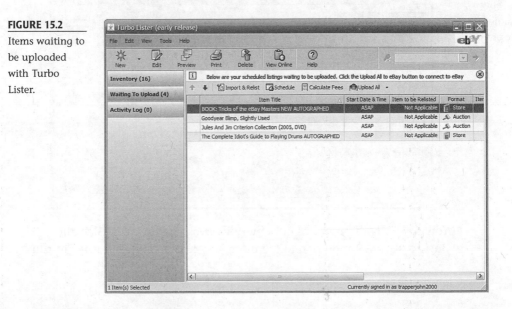

Uploading Your Listings

When you have an item that you want to list on eBay, select the item on the Item Inventory tab and click the Add to Upload button. You can see all the items in your upload queue by clicking the Listings Waiting to Upload tab. As you can see in Figure 15.2, this page shows all items waiting to be uploaded. While they're waiting, you can calculate listing fees and change the start time for any specific auction.

FIGURE 15.2

Items waiting to be uploaded with Turbo Lister.

Uploading your pending auctions is as easy as clicking the Upload All to eBay button. Listings set to start immediately do so, and items with a future start time are sent to eBay's Pending Listings section. These auctions will go live at the time(s) you previously scheduled.

> **note** The Blackthorne Basic and Pro programs used to be called eBay Seller's Assistant Basic and Pro. Although, before that, they were originally known as Blackthorne (after the name of the company that created the programs, which eBay subsequently acquired)—so the return to the Blackthorne name is a familiar one to long-time users.

eBay's Other Listing Programs— Blackthorne Basic and Blackthorne Pro

Turbo Lister isn't the only listing software that eBay offers. Many experienced sellers swear by eBay's Blackthorne Basic (pages.ebay.com/blackthorne/basic.html) and Blackthorne Pro (pages.ebay.com/blackthorne/pro.html) programs. Both programs let you create listings offline and then upload them in bulk to the eBay site. You also get fancy listing templates and a variety of post-auction management tools—including customer email templates. (Figure 15.3 shows the main Blackthorne Basic screen.)

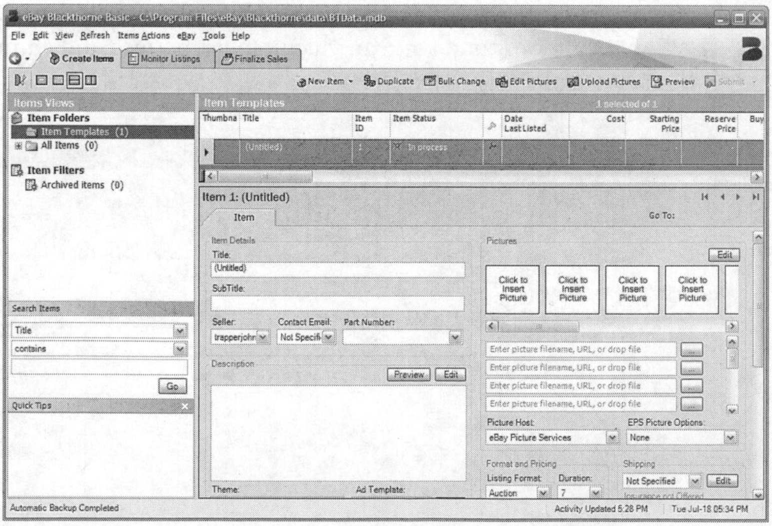

FIGURE 15.3

Another official bulk listing solution—eBay's Blackthorne Basic program.

You pay for both programs on a monthly subscription basis. Blackthorne Basic costs $9.99/month, and the more fully featured Blackthorne Pro runs

$24.99/month. For that higher price, Blackthorne Pro provides a variety of business reports, automated email and feedback, the ability to print invoices and labels, and all manner of inventory management features.

> **tip** When you're choosing among Turbo Lister and Blackthorne Basic or Pro, remember that Turbo Lister is free—but the Blackthorne programs offer inventory management features that Turbo Lister lacks.

Ándale Lister

If you've read this far in this book, you already know that I'm a fan of Ándale's various auction tools. Ándale Lister is the company's primary bulk listing tool, and I like it too.

Ándale Lister, shown in Figure 15.4, lets you create good-looking listings, using a variety of professionally created ad templates. You create your ads in bulk and then upload them according to your designated timetable. (You can even program a series of listings to launch on a regularly occurring schedule—or until your inventory runs out.)

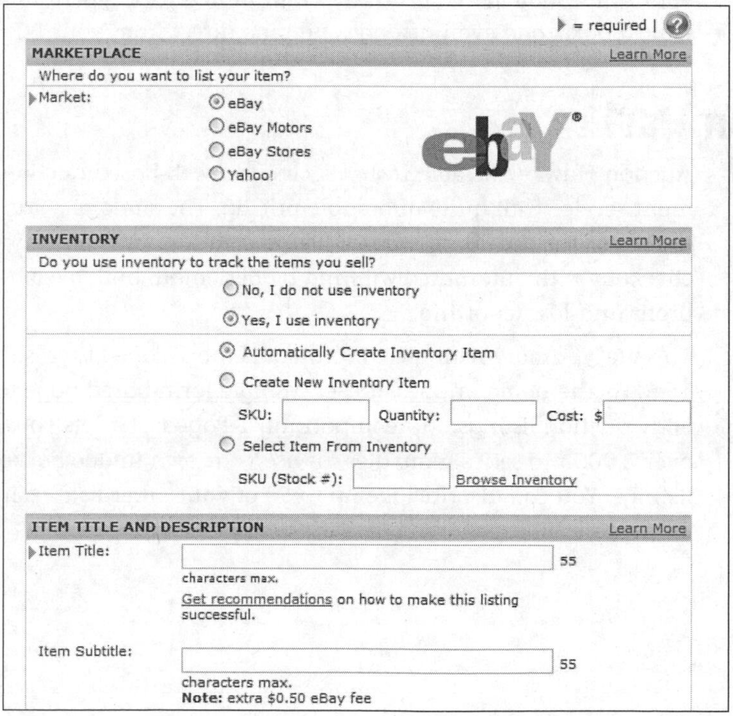

FIGURE 15.4

The Ándale Lister bulk listing service.

Like most of the other third-party bulk listing tools (but unlike eBay Turbo Lister), Ándale Lister isn't free. Table 15.1 details Ándale's rather complex fee schedule for this service.

Table 15.1   Ándale Lister Fees

Monthly Fee	Listings Included	Each Additional Listing
$7.50	40	$0.30
$16.95	110	$0.20
$33.95	275	$0.18
$56.95	550	$0.15
$89.95	1,100	$0.12
$149.95	2,750	$0.10
$224.95	5,600	$0.08

Ándale also offers its Ádale Lister Pro program for sellers that do larger volumes. This service provides complete business management, so you can track your sales, manage your inventory, print invoices, synchronize your data with QuickBooks, and even arrange shipping direct from your PC.

Auction Hawk

Auction Hawk (www.auctionhawk.com) is a web-based auction listing/management service with quite affordable pricing. The site offers various tools in its main service, including built-in listing creation, image hosting, end-of-auction checkout with automated winning-bidder email, bulk feedback posting, and profit-and-loss reporting.

The site's primary listing-creation tool is the 1-Page Lister, shown in Figure 15.5. As the name implies, it uses a single form-based page to create your eBay auction listings. More important, 1-Page Lister lets you use choose from over 2,000 pro-series templates, or use your own image backgrounds for your listings. You can also include up to 50 of your other listings in a scrolling cross-promotion gallery.

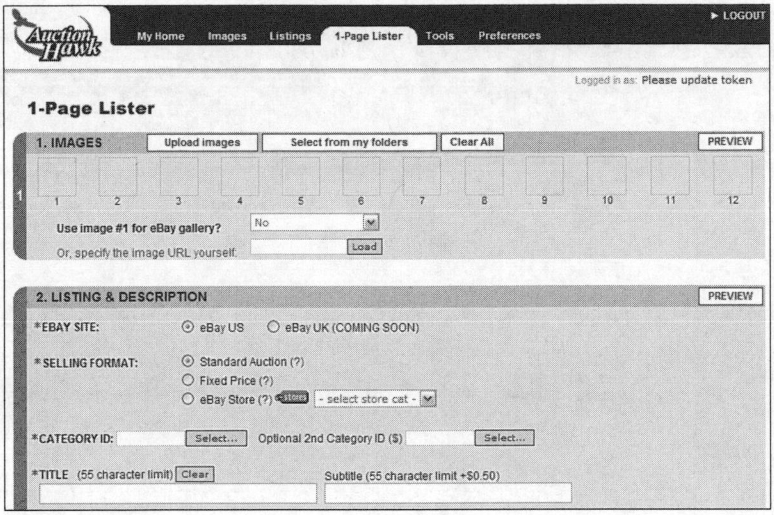

FIGURE 15.5

Bulk listing with Auction Hawk's 1-Page Lister.

Auction Hawk offers a five-level flat pricing scheme, as detailed in Table 15.2.

Table 15.2 Auction Hawk Fees

Level	Monthly Fee	Number of Listings Included
Basic	$12.99	110
Power	$21.99	250
Preferred	$29.99	550
Professional	$44.99	1,100
Unlimited	$89.99	Unlimited

Auctiva

Auctiva (www.auctiva.com) offers a variety of different auction listing/ management services, all of which are completely free of charge. Free is good, which explains Auctiva's newfound popularity among eBay sellers.

Auctiva's One-Page Listing Tool, shown in Figure 15.6, lets you choose from hundreds of pre-designed templates. The templates are pretty basic, similar to what you get with eBay's Listing Designer, but they're free.

FIGURE 15.6

Auctiva's free
One-Page
Listing Tool.

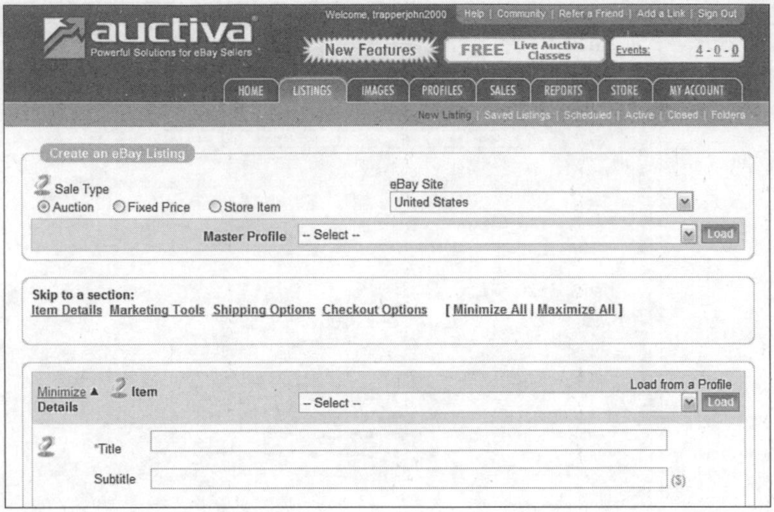

ChannelAdvisor

ChannelAdvisor (www.channeladvisor.com) offers a variety of auction and
retail management tools—most of which are targeted at larger online merchants. The service you want to look at is ChannelAdvisor Pro, which is a surprisingly easy-to-use collection of auction management tools. The package is
quite reasonably priced at a flat fee of just $29.95 per month.

With ChannelAdvisor Pro you can choose from a variety of pre-designed templates or write your own HTML. You also get delayed scheduling, image hosting, and the other expected listing-creation features.

inkFrog

inkFrog (www.inkfrog.com) is a cute name for some heavy-duty web-based
auction management services. The one we're interested in is the Lister and
Scheduler, shown in Figure 15.7, which lets you create your own custom-built
auction listings, based on a variety of pre-
designed templates. You also get bulk listing, delayed auction launching, free
image hosting, and a cross-promotion
tool. Pricing for everything is just $9.95
per month, no matter how many listings
you create.

> **note** inkFrog recently
> merged with the for-
> mer SpareDollar site. All of
> SpareDollar's services are now part
> of the inkFrog service.

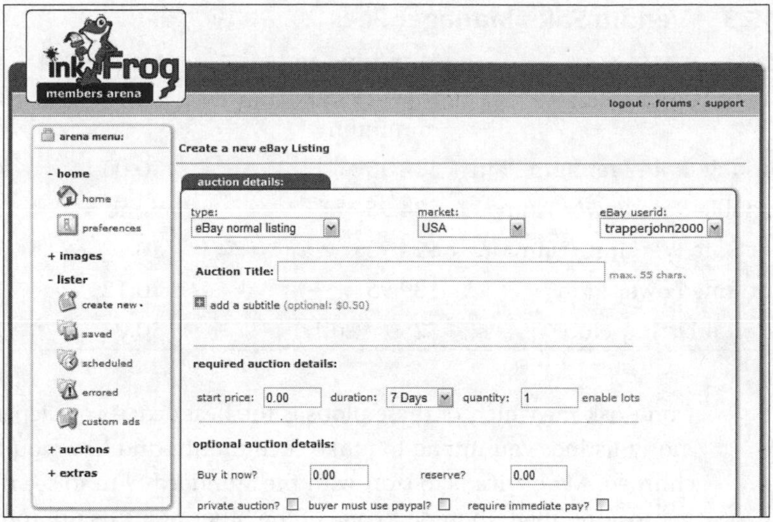

FIGURE 15.7
The i-Lister list-
ing tool from
inkFrog.

Vendio Sales Manager

Vendio Sales Manager (www.vendio.com) is one of the top two third-party auction creation services, with more than 125,000 current users. Vendio offers a
variety of auction management tools on its site; Sales Manager lets you create
sophisticated eBay listings in advance and then upload them in bulk.

You can actually choose from two versions of Sales Manager. Sales Manager
Merchandising Edition is designed for sellers who sell a lot of unique items;
Sales Manager Inventory Edition is designed for sellers who sell multiple
quantities of similar items. Both versions let you create listings based on pre-
designed templates (and customized with your own HTML).

Whichever version you choose, the pricing is the same, using a combination
of monthly fee, per-item listing fee, and per-item final value fee. It's all a little
complicated, especially when you consider that Vendio offers both variable
rate and flat rate plans. Table 15.3 details Vendio's pricing.

Table 15.3   Vendio Sales Manager Fees

Plan	Monthly Fee	Listing Fee	Final Value Fee
Pay as You Go Plan	None ($2.95 monthly minimum)	$0.12	1.25%
Variable Rate Premium Plan	$14.95	$0.06	1%
Variable Rate Power Plan	$34.95	none	1.25%
Flat Rate Premium Plan	$14.95	$0.22	None
Flat Rate Power Plan	$39.95	$0.12	None
Annual Listing Plan	$250 (yearly)	$0.06	None

Don't ask me which of these plans is the best deal. It all depends on how many listings you intend to make each month and how you like to be charged. My advice is to start with the Standard Plan to see if you like the service and then upgrade to one of the other plans as appropriate.

Other Bulk Listing Options

I've covered the major bulk listing programs and services—but they're just the tip of the iceberg. Lots of other companies offer bulk listing tools; you can see a larger list on the Listing Management page of eBay's Solutions Directory (solutions.ebay.com).

As you can see, you have lots of choices when it comes to choosing a bulk listing tool. Don't assume that the most expensive tools are the best—or that the most affordable ones lack features. Most of these tools are offered with some sort of preview plan, so take advantage of the offer and give 'em a trial run!

Managing Customer Payments

How do you like to get paid? That's an important question when it comes to your eBay business, and you have a variety of options.

When you're selling on eBay, you can choose to accept any of a number of different types of payment from your customers. This may seem like an easy decision, but each type of payment needs to be handled differently on your end. You need to choose those payment options that work best for your eBay business.

Evaluating Different Payment Options

As any businessperson will tell you, not all dollars are the same. A dollar paid by one method might actually cost you more (or be more risky) than a dollar by another method. And you definitely want to minimize your costs, especially when they're taken directly from what you're paid.

Fortunately, eBay doesn't force you to use any one payment method. For example, you can limit your payments to credit cards only; there's no law that says you have to accept cash or checks. So you can pick and choose which payment methods you'll accept—just as long as you specify this up front in your item listings.

Of course, the more payment options you offer, the more potential buyers you'll attract. Still, some methods are better than others for different types of sellers. What are the pros and cons of the various types of payment? Take a look at Table 16.1.

Table 16.1   Pros and Cons of Common Methods of Payment

Payment Method	Pros	Cons
Cash	Fast payment, no hassles	Unattractive to buyers; hard to track
C.O.D.	Cash payment	High noncompletion rate; lots of paperwork; not sanctioned by eBay
Personal check	Convenient for buyers	Slow; have to wait to clear
Money order/ cashier's check	Faster than personal checks, almost like cash	Hassle for buyers
Credit cards/PayPal	Fast payment, buyers like it	Fees involved

For what it's worth, most buyers today accept money orders, cashier's checks, and credit cards (via PayPal). Some buyers also accept personal checks, just as some buyers don't accept credit cards (they don't like the fees). I find that 80% or more of all my sales are paid for via credit card (using PayPal), making this method far and away the most popular among buyers. If you don't accept credit cards, you run the risk of significantly limiting your business.

Let's look at each of these payment methods separately.

Cash

As a seller, you certainly won't object to opening up an envelope and finding a few crisp new bills inside. Unfortunately, sending cash through the mail is not one of the

note What do you do when a nearby buyer wants to come by and pick up the item personally, rather than shipping via normal means? There's nothing wrong with this, as long as you get a verifiable payment. That means asking the buyer to bring cash, money order, or cashier's check—or to pay via PayPal before he or she arrives. Definitely do *not* let someone pick up an item and pay via personal check!

smartest things a buyer can do; cash is too easily ripped off and virtually untraceable. You can ask for cash payment (not that you should, of course), but unless the selling price is extremely low (under $5), don't expect buyers to comply.

One other thing: Cash is hard to keep track of—even for extremely organized sellers. There's no paper trail, and it's tempting to take any cash you receive and just stuff it in your wallet. If you do receive a cash payment, try your best to treat it like a money order or cashier's check, at least in terms of how you track it.

The bottom line: If it's bad for your customers, it's bad for you too. You should probably discourage payment by cash.

C.O.D.

Cash on delivery (C.O.D.) sounds good on paper. You ship the item, with the stipulation that the deliveryman (or woman) collect payment when the item is delivered.

There are problems with this method, however. What happens if the buyer isn't home when the delivery is made? What if the buyer is at home but doesn't have the cash? What if the buyer refuses to pay—and rejects the shipment? I've heard stories of up to 25% of all C.O.D. orders being refused, for one reason or another.

Even worse, C.O.D. service often comes with a high fee from the carrier—and it's a fee that you, the seller, have to pay. The additional fee alone rules out C.O.D. for many sellers.

Then there's the fact that you don't get your money until after the item is delivered. The delay in your getting your cash reduces the appeal considerably.

All things considered, it's easy to see why few eBay sellers offer C.O.D. payment—and why eBay has quit offering it as a default payment option. The problems with this payment method tend to outweigh the benefits, and I can't recommend it.

Personal Checks

One of the most common forms of payment is the personal check. Many buyers like paying by check because it's convenient, and because checks can be tracked (or even cancelled) if problems arise with the seller.

As a seller, you should like personal checks a little less because they're not instant money. When you deposit a check in your bank, you're not depositing cash. That $100 check doesn't turn into $100 cash until it tracks back through the financial system, from your bank back to the buyer's bank, and the funds are both verified and transferred. That can take some time, typically 10 business days or so.

note If you accept personal checks, it's a good business practice to state in your eBay listing how long you'll wait before shipping an item paid for by personal check. Better to warn the buyer up front than receive a complaining email afterward.

Because some buyers prefer paying by check, you should probably be prepared to handle this payment method. When you receive a check, deposit it as soon as possible—but do *not* ship the merchandise. Wait until the check clears the bank (two weeks if you want to be safe—longer for checks on non-U.S. banks) before you ship the item. If, after that period of time, the check hasn't bounced, it's okay to proceed with shipment.

If you are on the bad end of a bounced check, all hope is not lost. The first thing to do is get in touch with your bank and ask it to resubmit the check in question. Maybe the buyer was just temporarily out of funds. Maybe the bank made a mistake. Whatever. In at least half the cases, bounced checks unbounce when they're resubmitted.

Whether you resubmit the check or not, you should definitely email the buyer and let him or her know what happened. At the very least, you'll want the buyer to reimburse you for any bad check fees your bank charged you. The buyer might also be able to provide another form of payment to get things moving again. (Credit cards are nice—as are money orders.)

Money Orders and Cashier's Checks

Money orders and cashier's checks are, to sellers, almost as good as cash. You can cash a money order immediately, without waiting for funds to clear, and have cash in your hand. When you receive a money order or cashier's check, deposit it and then ship the auction item. There's no need to hold the item.

The only bad thing about money orders and cashier's checks is that you have to

note If a check bounces, the depositor (you) will likely be assessed a fee from your bank. (Of course, the writer of the bad check will also have a fee to pay—but that's not your problem.) If the buyer who wrote the check offers to make good on the payment, make sure he or she reimburses you for your bad check fee, over and above the final auction price—preferably via a different form of payment.

wait for them to arrive. Even if the buyer puts payment in the mail the very next day, you'll still wait anywhere from three to five days after the auction to receive payment. Still, there's not a lot to dislike about this method of payment—it's hard to get burned with either a money order or cashier's check.

note Beware a common scam where a buyer sends you a money order or cashier's check for an amount larger than the purchase price and then asks you to send funds for the difference. Don't fall for this. Accept payment for the amount of the purchase only!

There's also the (extremely slight) possibility that you can receive a bad cashier's check. To be precise, a cashier's check or money order isn't *exactly* the same as cash; your bank still needs to be reimbursed by the issuing institution, and if this doesn't happen, the cashier's check/money order will bounce—although this is highly unlikely. Be particularly careful of money orders or cashier's checks drawn on foreign banks or issued by unfamiliar institutions. When in doubt, hold the merchandise and ask your bank to verify that the payment is good.

Credit Cards

Until just a few years ago, if you wanted to accept credit card payment for your auction items, you had to be a big-time retailer, complete with merchant account and bank-supplied charge card terminal. This limited the number of sellers who could accept credit card payment, which probably cut down on potential bidders because many buyers like the convenience and relative safety of paying by credit card.

Today, however, there are options available that enable you to accept credit card payments for your auction items. First, several financial institutions provide merchant credit card accounts for smaller retailers, as we'll discuss later in this chapter. Second, you have PayPal—an online payment service that lets any auction seller easily accept credit card payments, with little or no setup hassle. PayPal works by accepting credit card payments from your customers and then sending you a check or depositing funds directly in your bank account for that amount—minus PayPal's fee, of course.

Any time you accept a credit card, with either a merchant account or PayPal, you are charged a fee—typically several percentage points of however much the buyer pays. When you consider that you have to pay eBay's listing fee and final value fee, paying another few points for the convenience of accepting credit cards can really sock it to a small seller—or anyone selling a low-priced item. You should definitely research the payment service's fees before you sign up.

We'll look at credit cards in more detail in the "Accepting Credit Card Payments via PayPal" section, later in this chapter.

Escrow Services

A final payment option, used primarily in higher-priced auctions, is the use of an escrow service. An *escrow service* is a company that acts as a neutral third party between you and the buyer, holding the buyer's money until the buyer receives the purchased merchandise. You get paid only when the buyer is satisfied, which is good protection for the buyer—but delays you receiving your money.

Here's how a typical escrow transaction works. Either during or just after the end of an auction, you and the buyer contact each other and agree to use an escrow service. The buyer sends payment (by check, money order, cashier's check, or credit card) to the escrow service; then—after the payment is approved—the escrow service notifies you and instructs you to ship the item. After the buyer receives the item, verifies its acceptability, and notifies the escrow service that all is hunky-dory, the escrow service pays you.

The escrow service's fees can be split between the two parties, but are more typically paid by the buyer. Fees differ widely from service to service.

For what it's worth, eBay recommends that customers use an escrow service when the transaction is over $500 and the seller doesn't accept credit card or PayPal payments. So, if you accept credit card payments (via PayPal or otherwise), you shouldn't have to bother with escrow.

If you do find yourself in a situation that calls for an escrow service, eBay recommends Escrow.com (www.escrow.com). If you choose to use another escrow company, make sure that it's bonded and legitimate; there are some phony escrow companies operating on the Internet that you need to watch out for.

Accepting Credit Card Payments via PayPal

As you might expect, there's no big preparation necessary to accept payment by cash, check, or money order. Accepting credit cards is another issue. Fortunately, you have a couple of options available to you—the most popular being the PayPal service, which can handle all your credit card transactions.

> **note**   PayPal also lets buyers pay via electronic check and funds withdrawn from their checking or savings accounts—although most buyers use it to pay via credit card.

Setting Up a PayPal Account

PayPal (www.paypal.com), shown in Figure 16.1, serves as the middleman for your credit card transactions. The buyer pays PayPal via credit card, PayPal handles all the credit card paperwork, and then PayPal sends a check to you (or deposits funds in your checking account). PayPal service accepts payments by American Express, Discover, MasterCard, and Visa—and, although it's primarily a U.S.-based service, it also accepts payments to or from more than 55 countries.

FIGURE 16.1
Use PayPal to accept credit card payments from your customers.

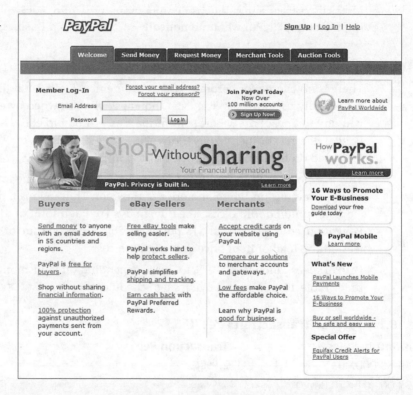

Before you can use PayPal as a seller, you must sign up for PayPal membership. You do this by going to the PayPal website, clicking the Sign Up link, and then following the onscreen instructions to complete your registration.

You can choose from three different types of PayPal accounts:

■ A **Personal** account is for eBay buyers only, not for sellers. You can send payments via credit card and electronic withdrawal and receive payments via "electronic cash," but you can't receive payments made via credit card.

■ A **Premier** account is a type of personal account that works better for small business owners and individual sellers. With a Premier account, you can accept both credit card and non–credit card payments (for a fee). You sign up for Premier status by checking the appropriate option on the Personal Account Sign Up page.

■ A **Business** account is necessary if you're receiving a high volume of payments. With this type of account, you can do business under a corporate or group name and use multiple logins.

Most eBay sellers sign up for a Premier account. If your sales volume rises high enough, PayPal will automatically switch you to a Business membership.

Paying for PayPal

There is no charge for becoming a PayPal member—although there are fees for actually using the service. Even though PayPal is owned by eBay, the fees you pay to PayPal are separate from the fees you pay to eBay. Note that PayPal doesn't charge the buyer any fees; instead, it charges you, the seller, a fee based on the *amount of money transferred.*

This last point is important. PayPal charges fees based on the total amount of money paid, *not* on the selling price of the item. That means if a $10 item has a $5 shipping/handling cost, the buyer pays PayPal a total of $15—and PayPal bases its fee on that $15 payment. So you need to factor your PayPal fees on the total of item price plus shipping costs.

PayPal's fees range from 1.9% to 2.9%, depending on your monthly sales volume. Table 16.1 presents PayPal's fee schedule as of August 2006.

Table 16.1   PayPal Transaction Fees (U.S.)

Monthly Sales	Transaction Fee
$0-$3,000.00	2.9%
$3,000.01-$10,000.00	2.5%
$10,000.01-$100,000.00	2.2%
>$100,000.00	1.9%

You're also charged a flat $0.30 per transaction, regardless of your sales volume. All fees are deducted from your account with every transaction.

Activating PayPal in Your Auction Listings

The easiest way to accept PayPal payments in your eBay auctions is to choose the PayPal option when you're creating an item listing. This is as simple as checking the PayPal box and entering your PayPal ID on the Sell Your Item page.

When you choose this option, a PayPal payments section is added to your item listing, as shown in Figure 16.2. PayPal will also appear as a payment option on your post-auction item listing page and in eBay's end-of-auction email to the winning bidder. Most third-party checkout tools will also recognize and accept PayPal payments.

FIGURE 16.2
This seller accepts PayPal payments.

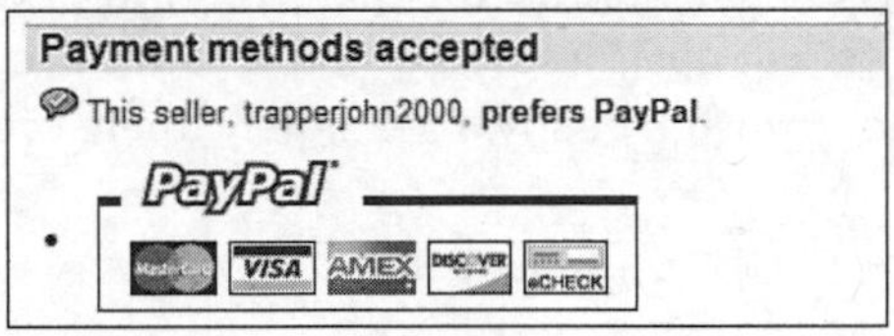

Collecting PayPal Payments

A buyer can make a PayPal payment in a number of ways. He or she can respond to the PayPal link embedded in the end-of-auction email received from eBay, click the PayPal button in the closed item listing, select the PayPal option when accessing the eBay checkout page, or pay directly from the PayPal website.

When a buyer makes a PayPal payment, those funds are immediately transferred to your PayPal account, and you receive an email notification of the payment. This email will include all the information you need to link it to a specific auction and ship the item to the buyer.

In most cases, the buyer's payments come into your account free and clear, ready to be withdrawn from your checking account. The primary exception to this are payments made via eCheck, where a buyer pays PayPal from his or her personal checking account. Because PayPal has to wait until the "electronic check" clears to receive its funds, you can't be paid until then, either. PayPal will send you an email when an electronic payment clears.

Withdrawing PayPal Funds

You have to manually withdraw the funds due to you from PayPal; no automatic payment option is available. You can let your funds build up in your PayPal account, or you can choose (at any time) to withdraw all or part of your funds.

You have the option of okaying an electronic withdrawal directly to your checking account (no charge; takes three to four business days) or requesting a check for the requested amount ($1.50 charge; takes one to two weeks). Just click the Withdraw tab (from the Overview tab) and click the appropriate text link.

> **note** PayPal also offers a variety of auction management tools, including the ability to generate invoices and print mailing labels with prepaid postage. See the PayPal site for more information.

Alternatives to PayPal

Not all sellers like PayPal. Some dislike the (perceived) high transaction fees; some dislike the way PayPal operates; some simply don't like being locked into yet another service owned by eBay. Fortunately, there are alternatives.

BidPay

Many sellers now accept payments by BidPay (www.bidpay.com). BidPay shown in Figure 16.3, is an alternative to PayPal that also lets buyers pay via credit card. In fact, BidPay operates a lot like PayPal, with a slightly lower 2.5% transaction rate—plus a slightly higher 50-cent per-transaction fee.

FIGURE 16.3

An alternative to PayPal— BidPay, by Western Union.

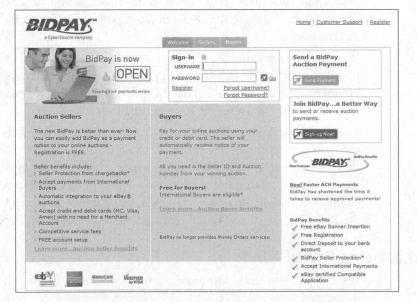

Google Checkout

Here's a PayPal alternative that isn't really an alternative. Google Checkout is an online payment service that lets retailers accept credit card payment for their sales, just like PayPal does. It's even lower priced than PayPal, with a transaction fee of 2.0% (versus PayPal's 2.9%) and a per-transaction fee of 20 cents (versus PayPal's 30 cents).

note BidPay was formerly known as Western Union Auction Payments. You shouldn't confuse this service with a Western Union wire transfer, a method of payment that is frequently (mis)used by scam sellers, particularly those selling outside the U.S.

Given these substantially lower rates, you'd think that Google Checkout would be a great alternative for eBay sellers. Alas, eBay won't let you accept Google Checkout for your auction payment. (eBay owns PayPal, remember, and may not be inclined to endorse a competitor.) While this situation may change in the future, right now Google Checkout simply isn't an option for your eBay listings.

Merchant Credit Card Account

If you're a high-volume seller, you may be able to get a lower per-transaction rate than that offered by PayPal by signing up for a merchant credit card account from a traditional banking or financial institution.

However, there are a few issues around establishing this type of traditional merchant credit card account. First, it's more hassle than signing up for PayPal; you may have to submit various business documentation and possibly have your own credit checked. Second, getting everything up and running may also be more involved than simply plugging into the PayPal system. And finally, upfront or monthly fees may be involved.

note Setup fees for a merchant account can range from $25 to $400 or more, and there's probably some sort of minimum transaction amount that you must maintain each month. Some services also make you purchase expensive software or credit card terminals. Since these fees vary so much, make sure you shop around before you commit.

That said, if you can save half a point or more on every credit card transaction, it may be worthwhile—if your credit card volume is high enough. Most merchant credit card services have rates in the 2% to 2.5% range, which beats PayPal's standard 2.9% rate—but is no better than PayPal's rates for high-volume sellers. Still, many eBay sellers prefer to handle their credit card processing directly, without having to rely on the PayPal service.

If you're interested in establishing a merchant credit card account, here are some services that specialize in providing credit card services to online merchants:

- Cardservice International (www.expandyourbusiness.com)
- Chase Paymentech Solutions (www.paymentech.com)
- Charge.com (www.charge.com)
- CreditCardProcessor.com (www.creditcardprocessor.com)
- Fast Merchant Account (www.fast-merchant-account.com)
- Merchant Accounts Express (www.merchantexpress.com)
- Monster Merchant Account (www.monstermerchantaccount.com)
- ProPay (www.propay.com)
- Total Merchant Services (www.merchant-account-4u.com)

And here's another place to check out—your local wholesale club. That's right, both Costco and Sam's Club offer merchant credit card processing to their business members, at affordable rates.

For example, Costco offers credit card accounts to its Executive members through Nova Information Systems. Costco waives the $25 setup fee and offers a discount rate of just under 2%. (Of course, the Executive membership itself costs $100, so you'll need to factor that in, as well.) See the Costco website (www.costco.com) or call 888-474-0500 for more details.

Oh, and when you inquire, ask about *all* applicable fees. In particular, check on software integration fees, monthly virtual terminal fees, and the like. You may also have to hit monthly minimums or pay an additional fee. Bottom line—sounds like a good deal, but check the fine print before you sign up!

Organizing Your Packing and Shipping

One of the most labor-intensive parts of the entire eBay business process is packing the merchandise you've sold and getting it ready to ship. This is where smart eBay businesspeople really shine, by learning how to streamline their packing/shipping operations.

We discussed packing supplies back in Chapter 7, "Organizing Your Home Office"; you should review the advice in that chapter about setting up your in-home packing center. Assuming you have your packing center set up and ready to go, this chapter focuses on the mechanics of packing and shipping—and how you can become as efficient as possible at both.

Choosing a Shipping Method

You have a number of choices when it comes to shipping your package. You can use the various services offered by the U.S. Postal Service (First Class mail, Priority Mail, Express Mail, Media Mail, and so on) or any of the services offered by competing carriers, such as UPS or FedEx. You can deal directly with any shipping service, or you can use a local shipping store to handle the shipping—and even the packing—for you. (Know, however, that having another company do your work for you will cost you—which means it's preferable to deal directly with your shipping service of choice.)

Which service should you use? That's a good question, but not always an easy one to answer. Ultimately, you have to strike a compromise between cost, convenience, and speed. Pick the cheapest method possible, and customers will gripe when they don't receive their merchandise in a timely manner. Pick the fastest method possible, and customers will gripe that they're paying too much for shipping/handling. (You also may turn away potential buyers with your high shipping/handling fees.) As I said, you need to strike a balance—and also choose a shipper that is easy for you to deal with.

And here's what makes the decision particularly difficult. Once you start checking around, you'll find that shipping rates vary wildly from one service to another—and I mean *wildly*. For example, the costs for shipping a two-pound box from New York to Los Angeles range from around $2 (USPS Media Mail) to more than $45 (UPS Next Day Air and FedEx Priority Overnight). That's a *big* difference.

This variation in shipping costs is yet another good reason to standardize the type of merchandise you sell in your eBay auctions. If you sell only one or two types of items, you can easily calculate your shipping fees ahead of time—and know that they'll stay constant from auction to auction. If you're selling a wide variety of items, calculating shipping for all those different items becomes extremely time-consuming. (Standardizing the merchandise you sell also helps when buying your packing boxes; you have to buy only one or two types of boxes, instead of having to keep a wide variety of packaging on hand.)

Of course, cost isn't the only factor you want to consider. You also want to compare how long it takes the package to arrive, what kind of track record the shipping service has, and how convenient it is

note To compare shipping costs for a variety of services on a single web page, check out iShip (www.iship.com). This site not only lets you compare shipping costs, but also provides tracking services for all major carriers.

for you to use. If you have to drive 20 miles to get to a UPS office but you have a post office just down the street, that might offset a slightly higher cost for Priority Mail.

> **note** You may need to factor weather conditions into which type of shipping you choose. If it's summertime and you're shipping something that might melt in extreme heat (like an old vinyl LP), pick the fastest shipping method possible.

The main thing to keep in mind is that you want to, as much as possible, settle on a single shipper and method of shipping for your eBay auctions. The last thing you want to do is to make trips to multiple shipping stations each day, and deal with a myriad number of packing boxes and shipping instructions. Standardize on a single shipper and method, and you'll make your shipping "department" much more efficient. Don't, and you'll waste a lot of time unnecessarily.

We'll look at each of the major shipping services separately, but with a decided emphasis on the U.S. Postal Service—which is the shipper of choice for a majority of eBay businesses.

U.S. Postal Service

The United States Postal Service (USPS) is used by almost all eBay sellers, for at least some of their shipping needs. Dealing with the Postal Service is convenient, as most sellers have a post office within a short driving distance, and it is set up to easily handle the shipping of small items from individuals.

The Postal Service offers several different shipping options:

■ **Priority Mail**. This is the preferred shipping method for a majority of eBay sellers, big and small. Pricing is generally quite reasonable, and if you're shipping out a small item that can fit in one of the flat-rate envelopes, you can quote a simple rate of $4.05 (as of August 2006), anywhere in the nation. Service is typically in the one-to-three day range, and—as you learned in Chapter 7—the postal service has lots of free

> **note** The cost to ship a particular package is based on a combination of weight, size, and distance. The heavier an item is and the farther it has to go (and the faster you need to get it to where it's going), the more it costs. And when you're factoring package size, you'll need to measure the length of the package and add it to the girth. (*Length* is the longest side of the package; *girth* is the distance all the way around the package at its widest point perpendicular to the length.)

Priority Mail shipping boxes you can use. You can also print out your own Priority Mail shipping labels and postage, direct from either eBay or the USPS website—which we'll discuss in the "Printing Labels with Prepaid Postage" section, later in this chapter.

- **Express Mail**. This is a less-used option, primarily because of its high cost—considerably more expensive than Priority Mail. Express Mail is the Postal Service's fastest service, offering guaranteed next-day delivery 365 days a year, including weekends and holidays. Merchandise is automatically insured up to $100.

- **First Class Mail**. This is an option if your item fits into a standard-sized envelope or small box. It also provides the benefit of shipping directly from your mailbox, without necessitating a trip to the post office—assuming you can figure out the correct postage yourself. Delivery is similar to Priority Mail—typically three days or less. If your item is relatively small, First Class can cost somewhat less than Priority Mail.

- **Parcel Post**. This used to be known as the "slow" USPS service for larger packages, but it's gotten faster of late—and it's priced much lower than Priority Mail. Still, shipping something Parcel Post from coast to coast might take seven to nine days, as opposed to Priority Mail's two (or three) days.

- **Media Mail**. This is a hidden treasure. Media Mail is what USPS used to call "book rate," and can be used to ship books, DVDs, videotapes, compact discs, and other printed and prerecorded "media." The rates are much cheaper than Priority Mail, especially when you're shipping heavy items, and delivery times are somewhere between First Class and Parcel Post—typically less than a week. This is a good, low-cost way to ship many popular items; it's especially good for heavier media items, such as books and CD/DVD boxed sets.

You can find out more about USPS shipping at the USPS website, located at www.usps.com. You can also access the USPS Domestic Calculator (postcalc.usps.gov) to calculate postage for all levels of service.

note You can't use Media Mail to ship every type of printed material. The service is reserved for publications without advertising—so you can't use it to ship magazines, newspapers, or comic books.

FedEx

FedEx is probably the fastest shipping service, but it can also be the most costly. FedEx tends to target the business market (which can afford its higher rates), so it isn't widely used for auction or retail shipping—with one significant exception: FedEx Ground.

FedEx Ground is a terrific choice when you're shipping out larger items. It's designed for bigger and/or heavier packages, and its rates are well below similar services offered by the Postal Service and UPS. I use FedEx Ground to ship DVD players and various audio equipment, and it's extremely cost effective. For example, FedEx charges almost $5 less than Priority Mail to ship a five-pound item from coast to coast. That's a big savings!

FedEx is also a convenient choice for many sellers, especially since you can now ship from any Kinkos location. (The stores are now called FedEx Kinkos, by the way.) You can find out more about FedEx shipping at its website, located at www.fedex.com, and can access the company's rate finder directly at www.fedex.com/us/rates/.

UPS

While UPS is a little pricey for small, lightweight items, it's a good option for shipping larger or heavier packages. UPS offers a variety of shipping options, including standard UPS Ground, Next Day Air, Next Day Air Saver, and 2nd Day Air.

You can find out more about UPS shipping—and access a rate calculator—at the UPS website, located at www.ups.com.

Other Shipping Companies

USPS, UPS, and FedEx are the three most popular shipping services in the U.S.; they're not the only services available, however. Among the other services available are DHL (www.dhl.com) and Purolator Courier (www.purolator.com).

note Less-experienced or occasional sellers might choose to do their packing and shipping through a professional shipping store, such as The UPS Store (www.theupsstore.com) or FedEx Kinkos (www.fedexkinkos.com). Because of the high fees these stores charge, this really isn't a good option for high-volume sellers. Still, you might want to go this route if you have the occasional large or overly fragile item to ship.

Calculating Shipping and Handling Fees

One of my earlier pieces of advice was that you should include all the details about shipping and handling (how much and who pays) up front in your item listing. While this is a good idea, how do you figure shipping costs before you know where the item is going?

Working with Flat Fees

The solution is easy if you're shipping something small and light. Figure the shipping costs from your location to either coast, and either use the highest cost or an average of the two costs. When the shipping is low to begin with, if you're off a dollar one way or another, it's not a big thing.

Flat fees are also easy if you're using one of the postal service's flat-rate Priority Mail packages. You can choose from three now: the long-established $4.05 flat-rate envelope and two different sizes of $8.10 flat-rate boxes. With these flat-rate packages, anything you can fit inside—no matter what the weight—ships anywhere in the U.S. for that flat rate. This option certainly makes it easy to calculate your shipping charges.

If you're shipping a larger or heavier item, however, charging a flat rate is less feasible. That's because the rates vary significantly by distance. A ten-pound item might cost under $10 to ship in-state, but cost twice that to ship coast-to-coast. It's hard to come up with an average that doesn't either hit you hard in the pocketbook or dramatically overcharge your customer.

Working with Variable Fees via eBay's Shipping Calculator

When you're shipping larger and heavier items, your best option is to state that buyers will pay the actual shipping cost based on location, which will be calculated at the conclusion of the auction. You can make this work by using eBay's Shipping Calculator.

The Shipping Calculator, shown in Figure 17.1, is a great tool; it lets buyers enter their ZIP code on the auction listing page and then calculates the actual shipping cost, based on the shipping service you selected. (You can also choose to have the Shipping Calculator add a predetermined handling charge for each shipment, which we'll discuss in a minute.) When a buyer checks out at the end of the auction (or chooses to pay via PayPal), he or she also uses the Shipping Calculator to automatically add shipping/handling fees to the total.

FIGURE 17.1

Add eBay's
Shipping Calcu-
lator to your item
listings so buyers
can automati-
cally determine
shipping and
handling fees.

Calculate shipping

Enter your US
ZIP Code:

Calculate

Learn more about how calculated
shipping works.

You activate the Shipping Calculator when you create a new item listing, by
selecting Calculated from the pull-down list in the Shipping section (shown in
Figure 17.2). Select or enter a package size, the estimated weight, your preferred shipping service(s), and other necessary information, and you're ready
to go.

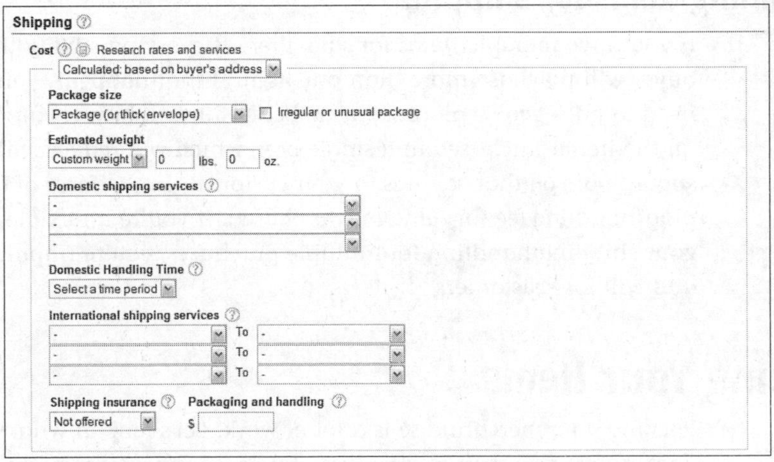

FIGURE 17.2

Activating
eBay's Shipping
Calculator from
the Create Your
Listing page.

Shipping ⑦

Cost ⑦ 🖼 Research rates and services
Calculated: based on buyer's address ⌄

Package size
Package (or thick envelope) ⌄ ☐ Irregular or unusual package

Estimated weight
Custom weight ⌄ 0 lbs. 0 oz.

Domestic shipping services ⑦
- ⌄
- ⌄
- ⌄

Domestic Handling Time ⑦
Select a time period ⌄

International shipping services ⑦
- ⌄ To - ⌄
- ⌄ To - ⌄
- ⌄ To - ⌄

Shipping insurance ⑦ **Packaging and handling** ⑦
Not offered ⌄ $

Since the Shipping Calculator can be added to your item listings free of
charge, there's no reason not to use it—especially because it greatly simplifies
the task of calculating exact shipping charges to your customers.

Determining the Handling Charge

Aside from the pure shipping costs, you should consider adding a handling
charge to the shipping fees your customers pay. After all, you need to be sure
that you're compensated for any special materials you have to purchase to
package the item—labels, boxes, Styrofoam peanuts, and so forth. That
doesn't mean you charge one buyer for an entire roll of tape, but maybe you

add a few pennies to your shipping charge for these sorts of packaging consumables. And if you have to purchase a special box or envelope to ship an item, you should definitely include that cost in your shipping charge. (This argues for planning your shipping before placing your item listing—which is always a good idea.)

> **note** Some end-of-auction checkout tools automatically combine multiple auctions for a single shipping fee. Others don't, which means you might have to manually manipulate these fees to your customers.

So you should have no compunction against "padding" your shipping fees with an additional handling charge. In fact, eBay's Shipping Calculator lets you add a separate handling charge to its calculations. It's an accepted part of doing business online.

Combining Items for Shipping

If you have multiple items for sale, there is every possibility that a single buyer will purchase more than one item. If that happens, you don't always need to pack two or more separate boxes for that buyer; you can often pack all the items purchased in a single box, which will reduce shipping costs. You should pass on that savings to your customer, in the form of a combined shipping/handling fee for all items purchased. If you're inflexible in adjusting your shipping/handling for multiple purchases, you're ripping people off—and will lose customers for it.

Packing Your Items

Packing your merchandise is a lot of work. Let's look at what's involved in packing an item so that it arrives at its destination intact—but doesn't cost you an arm and a leg to get there.

Picking the Right Shipping Container

It's important to choose the right type of shipping container for a particular item. First, you have to decide whether to use a box or an envelope. If you have a very large item to ship, the choice is easy. But what if you have something smaller and flatter, such as a baseball card or a coin? Your choice should be determined by the fragility of your item. If the item can bend or break, choose a box; if not, an envelope is probably a safe choice.

Whichever you choose, pick a container that's large enough to hold your item without the need to force it in or bend it in an inappropriate fashion. Also, make sure that the box has enough extra room to insert cushioning material.

On the other hand, the container shouldn't be so big as to leave room for the item to bounce around. Also, you pay for size and for weight; you don't want to pay to ship anything bigger or heavier than it needs to be.

If you're shipping a breakable or bendable item in an envelope, consider using a bubble-pack envelope or reinforcing the envelope with pieces of cardboard. This is especially vital if your item shouldn't be bent or folded.

If you're shipping in a box, make sure it's made of heavy, corrugated cardboard and has its flaps intact. Thinner boxes—such as shoe boxes or gift boxes—simply aren't strong enough for shipping. When packing a box, never exceed the maximum gross weight for the box, which is usually printed on the bottom flap.

Although there are bunches of different-sized boxes available, sometimes you need something somewhere inbetween this size and that size box. When you face this situation, you have two choices.

First, you can take a larger box and cut it down. That means cutting through each corner of the box to make it shorter and then cutting off the ends of the flaps accordingly. Sometimes it's difficult to fold unscored flaps, so you may want to make your own scores by slicing a knife (shallowly) where you want to bend the box closed. (Also, many mailing centers have their own folding machines that you can use to create custom-sized boxes—at a cost.)

Second, you can combine two smaller boxes. If your box is 16" long and your item is 20", just take two boxes and insert the open end of one inside the open end of the other. You'll need to use sufficient packing tape to keep the boxes from sliding apart, but you'll have created a box custom-sized for the item you're shipping.

How to Pack

How do you pack your box?

Don't just drop your item in an empty box. You need to position the item toward the center of the box, away from the bottom, sides, and top, and surround it with cushioning material. Professional shippers use Styrofoam peanuts, and lots of them;

note Use the combination box technique judiciously; it can significantly increase the weight of the package—and thus your shipping costs.

another option is to use crumpled-up old newspapers. Know, however, that peanuts are *much* lighter than newspaper. Since weight is a factor in how much you'll pay for shipping, anything you can do to lighten the weight of your package is important. Because peanuts cost—well, *peanuts*, they're the cushioning material of choice.

If you're shipping several items in the same box, be sure to wrap each one separately (in separate smaller boxes, if you can) and provide enough cushioning to prevent movement and to keep the items from rubbing against each other. Not only should items be separated from each other in the box, but they should also be separated from the corners and sides of the box to prevent damage if the box is bumped or dropped.

The previous point argues for another technique—double boxing especially fragile items such as glass or ceramic items. That means packing the item tightly in a smaller, form-fitting box and then placing that box inside a slightly larger, shock-absorbing box—with at least 3" of cushioning material between the boxes.

If your item has any protruding parts, cover them with extra padding or cardboard. And be careful with the bubble wrap. Although it's great to wrap around objects with flat sides, this kind of wrap can actually damage more fragile figurines or items with lots of little pieces and parts sticking out. If the bubble wrap is too tight, it can snap off any appendages during rough handling.

When you're packing an item, watch the weight. Have a postal scale at your packing counter, and weigh the item—shipping container and all—during the packing process. With Priority Mail, the difference between shipping a one-pound package and a one-pound, one-ounce package is as much as $1.90, depending on where it's going. Finding some way to cut that extra ounce of packing material can save almost two bucks in shipping costs!

note Make sure you include the weight of the box and the cushioning material when you weigh your item for shipment. A big box with lots of crumpled paper can easily add a half-pound or more to your item's weight—excess weight you'll have to pay for.

After you think you're done packing, gently shake the box. If nothing moves, it's ready to be sealed. If you can hear or feel things rattling around inside, however, it's time to add more cushioning material. (If you can shake it, they can break it!)

How to Seal the Package

After your box is packed, it's time to seal it. A strong seal is essential, so always use tape that is designed for shipping. Make sure you securely seal the center seams at

note Don't use wrapping paper, string, masking tape, or cellophane tape to seal your package.

both the top and the bottom of the box. Cover all other seams with tape, and be sure not to leave any loose tape or open areas that could snag on machinery.

You should use sealing tape designed for shipping, such as pressure-sensitive tape, nylon-reinforced Kraft paper tape, glass-reinforced pressure-sensitive tape, or water-activated paper tape. Whichever tape you use, the wider and heavier, the better. Reinforced is always better than non-reinforced.

One last thing: If you plan to insure your package, leave an untaped area on the cardboard where your postal clerk can stamp "Insured." (Ink doesn't adhere well to tape.)

How to Create the Perfect Label

You've packed the box. You've sealed the box. Now it's time for the label.

Addressing the Label

The best-packed box won't go anywhere if you get the label wrong. For fast and efficient delivery, you need to create a label that can be both clearly read and clearly understood. And it goes without saying that the address information needs to be accurate and complete—partial addresses just don't cut it.

To create the perfect label, you need to write, type, or use your computer to print the address as neatly as possible. You should also use complete address information, including all street suffixes—Dr., Ave., St., Blvd., and so on. And make sure to include the recipient's apartment or suite number (if applicable). Naturally, you should use the proper two-letter state abbreviation, and the correct ZIP code—and, when possible, the four-digit ZIP+4 add-on.

Choosing the Right Label

For most purposes, you can't beat the standard 4"×6" blank white label. There's a reason it's such a great workhorse: Anything smaller is tough to work with, and anything larger just leaves a lot of

note Don't know the ZIP code for the address you're shipping to? Then look it up at the U.S. Postal Service's ZIP Code Finder at www.usps.com/zip4/.

wasted space. You can purchase these labels at any office supply store, on eBay, or even get free versions (for Priority Mail shipping) at your local post office. And if you want to splurge, you can have labels preprinted with your business name and return address.

If you use computer-generated labels, you can program your label-making program (or Microsoft Word) to include your return address when it prints the label. This is a good (and lower-cost) alternative to using preprinted labels. There are several dedicated label-printing programs on the market. These programs work with just about any standard-issue major-manufacturer blank labels.

note You can also purchase or create your own return address labels, to use in conjunction with your main shipping labels. It's easy enough to print out a full page of smallish labels in Microsoft Word; most printing firms (such as Kinkos) can also do up a roll of addresses labels for a nominal charge. If you don't use a preprinted label, you'll want to hand-print your return address on the shipping container or use some sort of return address label.

The most popular label-making programs include

- Avery Wizard and DesignPro (www.avery.com)
- PrimaSoft Label Printer (www.primasoft.com/lb.htm)
- Visual Labels (www.rkssoftware.com/visuallabels/overview.html)

Many eBay sellers prefer to use a separate label printer, as opposed to their standard computer printer. A label printer does just what you think it does; it prints labels (one at a time), and nothing but labels. Most label printers come with their own label-creation software, so all you have to do is purchase the proper rolls of labels.

Attaching the Label

After you've created the delivery label, place it on the top (not the side) of the box. To avoid confusion, place only one address label on the box. If using a packing slip, place it on the same surface of the box as the address label. Do not place the label over a seam or closure or on top of sealing tape.

To avoid ink smudges and rain smears, place a strip of clear packing tape over the address label. (Except if your label includes a bar code—*never* tape over a bar code!) And if you're reusing a box for shipping, remove or cross out all old address labels or markings on the box.

note Some auction management tools also have label printing functions—although many of these services print extremely generic labels that might not suit your tastes.

And here's one last tip: Make a duplicate of your shipping label and stick it *inside* the box, before you seal it. This way if the original shipping label gets torn off or destroyed, anyone opening the box can read the duplicate label and figure out where the box is supposed to go.

note You can also print prepaid postage labels using the USPS' Click-N-Ship service (www.usps.com/shipping/label.htm). This is a good choice if you're printing labels for non-eBay items.

Printing Labels with Prepaid Postage

If you're shipping via the U.S. Postal Service, you can print labels on your home printer directly from eBay/PayPal. You can choose to print plain labels or labels with prepaid postage. Print the latter, and you can save yourself a trip to the post office!

You can access eBay's label-printing function from your closed auction page. Click the Print Shipping Label button, and (after a quick logon page) you're taken to a Print Your Label page on the PayPal site. As you can see in Figure 17.3, you can choose to ship via Priority Mail, Express Mail, Parcel Post, Media Mail, or First Class Mail; you can even choose to purchase insurance with your order. Fill in the appropriate information, and click the Continue button to view a confirmation page. From there you can authorize payment (from your PayPal account) and print the label on your own printer. Just affix the label to your package and drop it in the mail; no need to visit the post office. (And if you do visit the post office, there's no need to stand in line; just drop off your prepaid packages in the handy drop box, or leave them on the nearest counter.)

There are several advantages for printing your own postage via eBay—in addition to the no-standing-in-line thing. When you print a prepaid label, your buyer is automatically notified (via email) that the package has shipped. Even better, you get Delivery Confirmation included at no extra charge. Plus, if you use eBay Selling Manager, your shipping/tracking information is integrated into your transaction listing and the status is automatically updated. Finally, if you're making international shipments via the USPS, the custom forms are combined with the shipping label; you don't have to hand-write them or re-enter the information at the USPS site to print the custom forms separately.

FIGURE 17.3

Printing prepaid postage labels from PayPal.

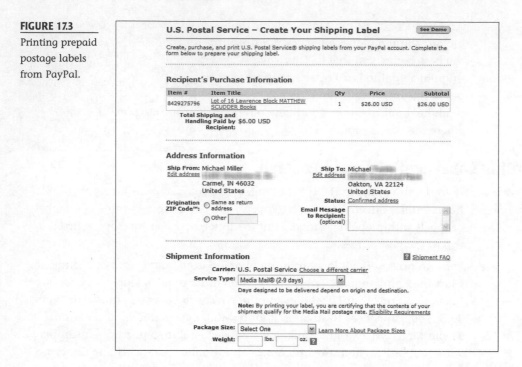

The only issue I have with eBay's prepaid postage labels is that you have to enter the information and print the labels one at a time. This is fine if you only have a few packages to ship, but very time-consuming if you're a high-volume shipper. For higher-volume applications, better options are the services offered by Stamps.com (www.stamps.com) and Endicia Internet Postage (www.endicia.com). Both these sites let you print sheets of prepaid postage labels from your desktop printer, without having to go to the post office. Check them out for more details.

Shipping Insurance

If you're shipping a moderately expensive item (over $50, let's say), it might be worth the trouble to offer insurance to the buyer. It's relatively easy (on the Sell Your Item page) to give the buyer the option of buying insurance—or just do it yourself and include the costs in your normal shipping/handling fee.

The U.S. Postal Service charges $1.35 to insure items up to $50, or $2.30 for items between $50 and $100. UPS includes $100 worth of insurance in its basic rates; additional insurance can be purchased for additional cost.

You can also arrange shipping insurance via a third-party firm. Universal Parcel Insurance Coverage (www.u-pic.com) provides insurance for packages shipped via the USPS, UPS, FedEx, and other carriers. There are two advantages to using U-PIC for your shipping insurance: It's cheaper than carrier-provided insurance, and you can do it all from your home computer. (The big disadvantage is that it doesn't integrate into your auction checkout or automated end-of-auction emails.)

As to pricing, U-PIC charges $1.00 per $100 of insurance for domestic USPS orders (including delivery confirmation), considerably less than what the Postal Service charges. (U-PIC's rates vary by carrier.) If you insure a lot of items, it's worth checking out.

Tracking and Confirmation

If you think the package might be lost in transit, you can always avail yourself of the tracking services provided by UPS, FedEx, and other major carriers. These services typically provide tracking numbers for all packages shipped. In most cases, you can track your package by entering the package's tracking number into the carrier's website.

The one major shipping service that doesn't offer tracking (by default) is the U.S. Postal Service. What you can get from the Postal Service (at a cost of from $0.50 to $0.60, depending on the type of mail) is its Delivery Confirmation service. USPS confirmation, however, does not confirm that an actual person received the package; it only confirms that the mail carrier delivered the package. (Stuck it in the mailbox, that is—or in many instances, left it on the porch.)

You can opt for Delivery Confirmation when you ship your item from your local post office, or have it included free if you print your own labels from eBay/PayPal or with the Click-N-Save service. You can also purchase USPS delivery confirmation forms in bulk from ShipperTools.com (www. shippertools.com). ShipperTools.com uses the official USPS delivery confirmation system and lets you print an unlimited number of confirmation forms for just $6.95 a month.

If you want a signature confirmation on a USPS shipment, you need to send your item with the certified mail option. Certified mail requires the recipient to sign on delivery and costs $2.40. This is a preferred option if you're shipping something extremely valuable.

Streamlining the Packing and Shipping Process

One of the most important things you can do to make your eBay business more efficient is to streamline the entire process of packing and shipping your merchandise. If you find yourself in the routine of schlepping down to the post office every day, loaded down with armfuls of packages, you're not doing it right. Read on to learn how to be a more efficient shipper.

Setting a Packing/Shipping Schedule

The first thing you want to do is get yourself out of the "do everything right now" syndrome. Novice eBay sellers hover over their computer screens or mail boxes, waiting for payments to come in. As soon as that payment arrives, they rush to send out a confirmation email, print an invoice, and pack the merchandise. Then they hop in the car and drive as fast as possible to the post office, stand in line, and ship the thing out.

Wrong, wrong, wrong.

You should not put yourself at the mercy of your customers. Instead, you should work your customer sales into *your* routine.

That means, of course, that you have to establish a routine—a schedule that you follow for all your packing and shipping. If your sales volume is low and your time free, it's okay to pack and ship once a day. But do it at the same time each day, on an appropriate schedule. If your mail arrives around noon, for example, set 2:00 p.m. as your packing/shipping time; that gives you time to process all payments received in that day's mail. When 2:00 p.m. rolls around, gather all the orders that are ready to go and start packing. When you're done—around 3:00 p.m., let's say—you head down to the post office with your daily delivery.

You don't have to ship every day, however. Many high-volume eBay sellers ship only a few days out of the week so that they're not wasting time traveling to the post office every day. You may choose to ship all your packages on Monday, Wednesday, and Friday, for example—or maybe just Tuesday and Friday. Whatever days you choose, you let your paid orders build up until your scheduled shipping day and then get your shipping done all at once.

Creating a Packing Assembly Line

When it comes to packing your items, it pays to have the process down to a science. Have all your boxes and packing material lined up and ready to go so that you can run each item through the "assembly line." Wrap, pack, cushion, seal, and label—that's the routine. And the more uniform the items you sell, the more automated this procedure can become.

What you don't want is to have your routine interrupted. That means not running out of tape or peanuts or having to rush out and purchase a special box just for that one special item. (Which is yet another reason, of course, to standardize the items you sell.) The smoother the process (and the fewer interruptions), the faster you can get everything packed and ready to ship.

Getting It There

When it comes to shipping your items, be prepared. If you use the U.S. Postal Service for shipping, try to time your visits so that you don't have to stand in long lines. That means avoiding lunch hour and the last half hour or so before closing; avoiding Mondays and Saturdays; and avoiding peak shipping periods around major holidays, such as Christmas and Valentine's Day. Early morning and mid-afternoon are typically low-volume times at the post office window.

If you have a lot of packages to ship, don't go to the post office by yourself—take a helper. If large shipments are common, invest in a small hand truck to help you cart all those boxes to the counter.

And if you avail yourself of eBay's prepaid shipping label option, you don't have to stand in line at the post office at all. You can have your packages picked up by your local postal delivery person, or—if you still have to make the trip to the post office—drop off your prepaid packages without having to wait in line. This is where the prepaid shipping option becomes a real time-saver.

Arranging Regular Pickups

The more items you sell, the more you ship. The larger and more successful your eBay business gets, the more burdensome the whole shipping process gets—and all those trips to the post office become especially time-consuming.

As you become a heavy shipper, consider setting up an account with a single shipper and arranging daily pickups from your home. This is easy enough to do if you print your own prepaid postage labels because you can have your mail person pick up all your packages when he or she makes normal rounds.

If your volume is high enough, you can also arrange regular pickup service from UPS and FedEx. (You may even get discounted shipping rates, if your pickup volume is high enough.) These carriers can also pick up single items if you arrange so in advance—but at a much higher fee.

> **note** eBay offers a Freight Resource Center (ebay.freightquote.com) for shipping large items. You can obtain freight quotes and initiate shipping directly from this page, or you can contact Freightquote.com via phone at 888-875-7822.

Shipping Larger Items

Some items are just too big to ship via conventional means. Suppose you just sold an old pinball machine, or a roll-top desk, or a waterbed. How do you deal with items that big?

Assuming that the item is too big even for FedEx Ground or UPS, you have to turn to traditional trucking services. Some of these services will pack or crate the item for you (for a fee); others require you to do all the crating. In addition, some of these firms require you to deliver the item to their shipping terminal and for the buyer to pick it up from their dock. (Other firms offer door-to-door service—again, sometimes for a higher fee.) In any case, it helps to make a few calls and ask for specifics before you decide on a shipper.

When you have an oversized item to ship, here are some of the trucking services that other eBay sellers have used. Check with each firm individually as to its fees and shipping policies.

- AAA Cooper Transportation (www.aaacooper.com)
- Forward Air (www.forwardair.com)
- Vintage Transport Services (www.vintagetransport.com)
- Yellow Freight (www.yellowfreight.com)

Another option is to use Greyhound PackageXPRESS (www.shipgreyhound.com), which lets you ship large (and small) packages via Greyhound bus. You and the buyer have to live relatively close to a Greyhound bus station, and the item will have to be delivered to and picked up from the station—but costs are substantially less than with traditional trucking services.

Shipping Internationally

Packing for international customers shouldn't be any different than for domestic customers—as long as you do it right. Foreign shipments are likely to get even rougher treatment than usual, so make sure the package is packed as

securely as possible—with more than
enough cushioning to survive the trip to
Japan or Europe or wherever it happens to
be going.

What *is* different about shipping internationally is the paperwork—and the shipping costs.

note Given the increased chances of loss or damage when shipping great distances, you should purchase insurance for all items shipping outside North America.

Chances are your normal method of shipping won't work for your international shipments. For example, you can't use Priority Mail to ship outside the
U.S.—not even to Canada or Mexico. This means you'll need to evaluate new
shipping methods and possibly new shipping services.

If you want to stick with the U.S. Postal Service, check out Global Priority Mail
(reasonably fast and reasonably priced), Global Express Mail (fast but expensive), Airmail (almost as fast, not quite as expensive), or Surface/Parcel Post
(slow but less expensive). In addition, UPS offers its Worldwide Express service,
FedEx offers FedEx Express service internationally, and DHL is always a good
option for shipping outside the U.S. Make sure you check out your options
beforehand, and charge the buyer the actual costs incurred.

You'll also have to deal with a bit of paperwork while you're preparing your
shipment. All packages shipping outside U.S. borders must clear customs to
enter the destination country—and require the completion of specific customs
forms to make the trip. Depending on the type of item you're shipping and
the weight of your package, you'll need either Form 2976 (green) or Form
2976-A (white). Both of these forms should be available at your local post
office.

In addition, you can't ship certain items to foreign countries: firearms, live
animals and animal products, and so on. (There are also some technology
items you can't ship, for security reasons.) You need to check the government's
list of import and export restrictions to see
what items you're prohibited from shipping outside U.S. borders. Check with your
shipping service for more detailed information.

note eBay offers several pages of advice for international trading at `pages.ebay.com/globaltrade/`.

Dealing with Customers— and Customer Problems

Customers. They're either one of the joys or one of the major annoyances of running your own business. And when you're running a business with your eBay auctions, you definitely have customers to deal with. Lots of them. So you'd better get used to it.

Some customers will contact you during the course of an auction, asking questions about the items you're selling. Other times you'll have contact only when the auction is over, when you send an invoice or accept payment. And then you have the kinds of customers no one likes—the ones with problems.

How do you deal with all these customers—and these potential problems? Read on and find out.

Answering Bidder Questions

The more auctions you run, the more likely you'll run into potential bidders who have questions about what you're selling. eBay lets bidders email sellers during the course of an auction, so don't be surprised if you get a few emails from strangers asking unusual questions. And, as a responsible eBay seller, you need to answer these queries.

When you receive a question from a potential bidder, you should answer the question promptly, courteously, and accurately. It's in your best interest to make the questioner happy; after all, that person could turn out to be your high bidder. Remember, you are running a business, and all good businesses go to great lengths to respond appropriately to customer queries.

Potential bidders ask questions because they don't understand something about your listing or have some qualms about placing a bid. You need to not only answer the stated question—as thoroughly as possible—but also anticipate any additional questions that customer might have. Your goal, after all, is to sell the item you have listed, so anything you can do to better present the item to buyers will help you make the sale.

When you respond to a buyer's question, you have the option of displaying the question and answer as part of the item listing. This is a good option to check, especially if you think other potential bidders might have the same question. You should opt out of displaying the Q&A if the question is more idiosyncratic, or not necessarily applicable to a larger number of potential bidders.

What happens if you get a *lot* of questions from potential bidders? I have no great advice for you here. There is no secret auction tool that can respond automatically to specific customer questions. You have to craft each response individually, answering the questions as posed. You may want to batch all the query emails into a bunch, however, and answer them once a day. (Although this might not be prompt enough for bidders asking questions in the waning minutes of a live auction.) But you shouldn't worry too much about this; for most sellers, the volume of customer queries will be small and easily manageable.

note If you're getting a lot of questions about a particular auction, it's a sign that you're not including enough information in your item listing. Consider revising the description to be more descriptive, and definitely keep this issue in mind when you launch future auctions.

Managing End-of-Auction Correspondence

As your eBay business grows, you face a major challenge in managing all the customer correspondence that happens after the auction is over. In order, here are the emails that might flow between you and the winning bidder—after you both receive your end-of-auction confirmations from eBay:

- **From you to the winning bidder**: Notification of winning bid; request for street address so you can finalize shipping/handling costs. (You can skip this one—and the next two—if the buyer pays immediately from eBay's end-of-auction email.)

- **From winning bidder to you**: Full shipping information, including street address and ZIP code.

- **From you to the winning bidder**: Total amount due, including shipping and handling.

- **From you to the winning bidder** (after payment is made): Notification that payment was received.

- **From you to the winning bidder** (after the item is shipped): Notification that the item was shipped.

That's three, possibly four, outgoing emails on your part, and at least one incoming email from the buyer. (And you may have to repeat any of these messages as a reminder if the customer doesn't reply promptly.) Multiply this by the total number of auctions you're running, and you can see that email management is a major issue for high-volume sellers.

Know, however, that this tradition of seller-to-buyer correspondence has changed considerably over the past year or so, thanks to eBay's increasingly useful automated end-of-auction notifications. In the old days, you had to contact the buyer personally because there really weren't any other options for determining the final price and arranging payment. Today, however, eBay lets sellers send fairly useful invoices at the end of an auction, which to many obviates the need for separate email correspondence. It's also quite likely that the buyer will never send an email directly to you; many buyers click the Pay Now button in the end-of-auction email that eBay sends, a payment automatically shows up in your PayPal account, and you never have a one-on-one relationship with your customer. This isn't necessarily a bad thing; it certainly reduces your workload as a seller!

Communicating Manually

If your sales volume is low, there's no reason you can't handle your necessary correspondence manually, using your normal email program. Just fire up Outlook or Outlook Express, type in the text of your message, and click the Send button.

You can automate this process, to some degree, by creating your own form letters. That means creating boilerplate text you use for each of your different customer emails, loading that text into a new message, and then customizing the message with the details of that particular auction. This is a better option than starting from scratch with every sale you make.

Sending an Invoice at the End of the Auction

If you don't want to bother with composing your own messages, eBay lets you send an automated invoice to your buyers at auction's end. This invoice, like the one shown in Figure 18.1, tallies the total amount due, including all necessary shipping/handling charges. There's even a place where you can add your own personalized message to the buyer.

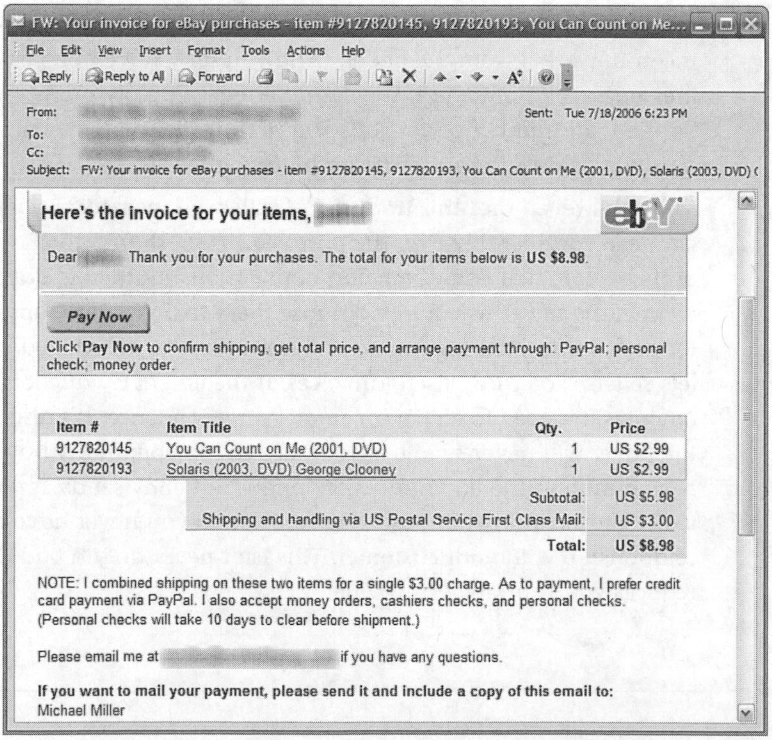

FIGURE 18.1

A typical end-of-auction invoice sent through the eBay system.

To send an end-of-auction invoice, just navigate to the closed auction listing page or to your My eBay page and click the Send Invoice button for that auction. When the invoice form appears onscreen, edit any information as necessary and send it on its way. You can opt to receive a copy of the invoice, if you like. eBay takes care of sending the invoice to the customer—nothing more for you to do.

> **note** One advantage to sending an eBay-generated invoice is that you don't run the risk of the message getting stopped by the buyer's spam filter. Sometimes an individual message from a stranger—like a manual invoice sent from your own email program—might be flagged as spam, and thus never be seen by the buyer.

eBay even lets you combine multiple auctions into a single invoice, for those occasions when one buyer has made multiple purchases. The auctions are grouped by buyer on your My eBay page, so all you have to do is select all the auctions from a single buyer to create a combined invoice. You can even manipulate the shipping/handling costs for the combined auctions, in order to offer a discount for multiple orders.

Communicating with eBay Selling Manager

If you want to send more than the standard end-of-auction invoice but want to automate the procedure, check out the eBay Selling Manager tool. For many sellers, the customer email features of eBay Selling Manager (pages.ebay.com/selling_manager/) make it the program of choice for end-of-auction communication.

While Selling Manager isn't quite as automated as some of the other programs available, you can't beat the low $4.99 per month price. In addition to keeping track of all your open and closed auctions, Selling Manager also lets you send prewritten email end-of-auction messages to all your winning bidders. Selling Manager includes six different boilerplate messages, including

- Winning buyer notification
- Payment reminder
- Request shipping address
- Payment received
- Shipping notification
- Feedback reminder

> **note** Learn more about eBay Selling Manager in Chapter 19, "Automating Auction Management."

As you can see in Figure 18.2, you can easily customize any of these messages. Just edit the boilerplate text and click the Send button.

FIGURE 18.2

Customizing a boilerplate email message in eBay Selling Manager.

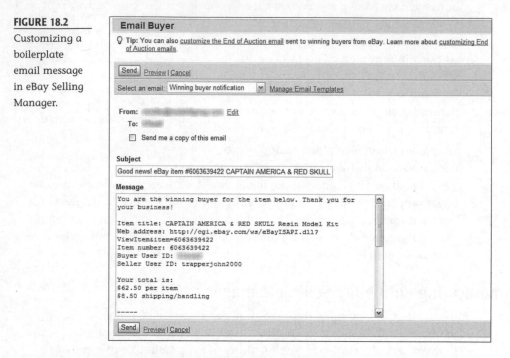

Emailing in Bulk with Selling Manager Pro

There are two major drawbacks to eBay Selling Manager's email management tool. First, you have to manually send email messages; the messages are not sent automatically at the end of an auction. Second, you have to send one message at a time; there's no provision for sending bulk messages to multiple customers.

If you want your messages sent automatically, you'll need to switch to another auction management tool, such as those discussed in the next section. If you want to send messages in bulk, however, all you have to do is upgrade from eBay Selling Manager to eBay Selling Manager Pro.

That's right, one of the big differences between Selling Manager and Selling Manager Pro is the capability of sending bulk email messages. You'll pay more for this feature, of course—$15.99 per month versus regular Selling Manager's $4.99 per month. But for many high-volume sellers, it's worth the expense.

Sending a batch of emails in Selling Manager Pro is relatively simple. All you have to do is go to a Sold Listings page, check the boxes next to those customers to whom you wish to send emails, and then click the Email button. When the Preview Email page appears, select the template you wish to send from the Template list; then click the Send Emails button to send the selected message on its way.

Communicating with Other Auction Management Tools

Other auction management tools also offer email features. Some of these tools totally automate the end-of-auction communication process, automatically sending the proper emails when your auction ends (and when the customer pays via PayPal). In most cases, the email management features are included as part of the overall price of the tool.

Ándale Checkout

Ándale's (www.andale.com) end-of-auction emails are integrated into its Ándale Checkout tool. Ándale Checkout is similar to eBay's Checkout feature, in that it provides a web page that customers use to enter their shipping and payment information. When you activate Ándale Checkout for a particular auction, Ándale will automatically send a winning buyer notification email at the end of the auction. Other emails included with Ándale Checkout include checkout reminder, shipping address request, invoice, payment request, payment receipt, and item shipped notice.

The cost for Ándale Checkout is based on volume, and starts at $7.50 per month (for 40 checkouts).

inkFrog

inkFrog's Sales Manager feature (www.inkfrog.com) manages all manner of post-auction activity, including email correspondence. You can send automatic end-of-auction notices and generate payment requests, payment reminders, shipping notification, feedback reminders, and other customized messages. You get all this plus inkFrog's other item listing and auction management tools for just $9.95 per month, unlimited usage.

Vendio Sales Manager

Vendio Sales Manager (www.vendio.com) includes a variety of customer correspondence features as part of its advanced auction management services. You can configure Vendio Sales Manager to automatically send winning bidder notifications at the end of your auctions, and use it to send payment and shipping notifications. Vendio's fees, unfortunately, are rather complex; you'll pay at least $14.95 per month, unless you opt for the Pay as You Go Plan, which costs $0.12 per listing and a 1.25% final value fee—with a $2.95 monthly minimum.

Handling Buyer Complaints

Not all auctions go smoothly. Maybe the item arrived damaged. Maybe it didn't arrive at all. Maybe it wasn't exactly what the buyer envisioned. Maybe the buyer is a loud, complaining, major-league son of a rutabaga.

In any case, if you have a complaining customer, you need to do something about it. Unfortunately, there are really no hard and fast rules for handling post-auction problems. You have to play it by ear and resolve each complaint to the best of your ability.

On the plus side, most eBay users are easy to deal with and just want to be treated fairly. Others won't be satisfied no matter what you offer them. You have to use your own best judgment on how to handle each individual situation.

What are your options when you have complaining customers? Well, you could just ignore them—not that I recommend this. If you specified that the merchandise was sold "as-is" or that "all sales are final," you're technically in the clear and don't have to respond to customer complaints. That's not a good way to run a business, however, because dissatisfied customers don't generate good word of mouth—and are prone to leave negative feedback on eBay.

Better to try to work something out. If the item never arrived, you can contact the shipping service to put a trace on the shipment. If the item was insured, you can initiate a claim for the lost or damaged item. And if the item doesn't work or isn't what the customer thought he or she was buying, you can work out some sort of refund. Even if you're not disposed to offer a full refund, you can perhaps negotiate a lower price or discount with the customer, and then refund the difference—which may be preferable to taking the thing back and losing the entire sale.

Listing Your Terms of Service

One way to reduce the number of customer complaints is to state very clearly what you do and do not do, right up front in your auction listings. These details are called your *terms of service* (TOS), and they are the rules that you apply to your auctions, the do's and don'ts of how you do business. Think of the TOS as the "fine print" that you want potential buyers to be aware of before they make a bid.

Here is a short list of some of the items you might want to include in your TOS:

- Bidding restrictions, such as "No bidders with negative feedback," "Bidders with positive feedback of at least 10 only," or "U.S. buyers only."

- Payment restrictions, such as "U.S. funds only," "No personal checks," or "Personal checks take two weeks from date of receipt to clear."

- Shipping/handling charges (if you know them) and restrictions, such as "Buyer pays shipping/handling" or "Shipping via USPS Priority Mail only."

Put a short but clear TOS, like the one in Figure 18.3, at the bottom of the item description in every auction you run. It may not eliminate *all* customer complaints, but at least you'll make your position known to all potential buyers.

FIGURE 18.3
An example of detailed terms of service—the way one user approaches his eBay business.

Payment	Shipping	Returns
I accept credit cards via PayPal, money orders, cashier's checks, and personal checks. Personal checks will delay shipment for ten business days.	I ship via USPS Priority Mail. Shipping/handling charge to any location in the continental United States is $6.00. Email me for shipping/handling outside the U.S.	All sales are guaranteed for 30 days after receipt. Please contact me if not satisfied. Buyer is responsible for return postage.

Guaranteeing Your Merchandise

You can head off some customer complaints by guaranteeing the merchandise you sell. (Alternatively, you can sell all items "as-is"—as long as you clearly indicate this in your item listings.)

Some novice eBay sellers might worry that the costs of guaranteeing their merchandise might be prohibitive. This is not the case—if for no other reason than the vast majority of merchandise arrives intact and in good working condition. The number of customers who will actually take you up on a "money back guarantee" will likely be extremely small.

When a customer is dissatisfied with his or her purchase and takes you up on your guarantee, you have a couple of options. First, you can offer to refund the purchase price if the item is returned to you. This approach prevents unsavory customers from taking advantage of you, either by claiming something is bad when it's not or by doing the old switcheroo and shipping you a defective unit while they keep the good unit you sent them; you get to inspect the returned merchandise before you send the refund.

note You can choose to refund (1) just the purchase price; (2) both the purchase price and the original shipping/handling charge; or (3) the purchase price, the shipping/handling charge, and the customer's costs to ship the item back to you. Make it clear which it is before you ask the customer to return the item.

Second, you can offer a full refund on the item, no questions asked, no further action necessary. With this option, the buyer doesn't have to bother with shipping it back to you; this is the way high-class merchants handle their returns. The upside of this method is the extra measure of customer satisfaction; the downside is that you could get taken advantage of, if the customer is so inclined.

You also have to determine just *what* it is that you're guaranteeing. Do you guarantee that the item is in good working condition? Or that it is completely free of defects? Or simply that it's as described in your item listing? Whatever your guarantee, you're likely to come across the occasional buyer who feels that the item he or she received is not as it was described. (Which is another good reason to include a detailed description of the item—and a photograph—in all your item listings.) This situation can quickly deteriorate into an exercise in who said what. It might be best to defuse the situation early by offering some sort of compensatory partial refund, whatever your policy states.

How long your guarantee lasts is another question. Certainly, most retailers guarantee their merchandise to arrive intact and in good working condition—or at least as described in the auction listing. Should you respond to customer complaints if the item stops working after 30 days, or 90 days, or even a year after the auction? While a manufacturer might offer an unconditional one-year guarantee, you probably don't have the same obligation. I'd say that any problems that crop up after the first 30 days shouldn't be your obligation. Most customers will understand and agree.

Whatever guarantee you offer, state it up front in your item listing. eBay includes a Return Policy section in its standard auction listings; just fill out the blanks in this section of the Create Your Listing form (shown in Figure 18.4), and you'll let your customers know that you stand behind what you sell.

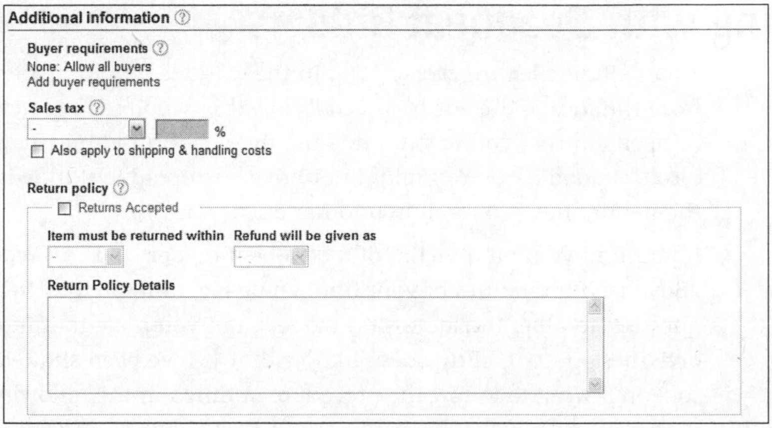

FIGURE 18.4

Adding your
return policy
to your item
listing.

Additional information ?

Buyer requirements ?
None: Allow all buyers
Add buyer requirements

Sales tax ?
[▾]   [   ] %
☐ Also apply to shipping & handling costs

Return policy ?
☐ Returns Accepted

Item must be returned within **Refund will be given as**
[- ▾]   [- ▾]

Return Policy Details
[   ]

Resolving Complaints with a Mediation Service

Of course, you still might run into that rare customer who just can't be satisfied. This person wants a full refund, and you don't see that it's justified. When a transaction devolves into a shouting match, it's time to bring in a mediator—a neutral third party who will look at all the facts and then make a (supposedly) fair and balanced judgment.

eBay offers mediation services through SquareTrade (www.squaretrade.com). This site settles disputes through a possible two-part process. You start out with what SquareTrade calls Online Dispute Resolution. This free service uses an automated negotiation tool to try to get you and your customer to neutral ground. Communication is via email; the process helps to cool down both parties and let you work out a solution between the two of you.

If the two of you can't work out the problem in this manner, you have the option of engaging a SquareTrade mediator to examine the case and come to an impartial decision. This will cost the party who filed the case $29.95. Both parties agree to abide with the results. If the SquareTrade mediator says you owe the customer a refund, you have to arrange the refund. If the representative says you're in the clear, the customer has to stop complaining. (At least to you.)

Given the relatively low cost, there's no reason *not* to use SquareTrade in a disputed transaction—especially if the customer files the claim and pays the cost.

ith Deadbeat Bidders

an eBay seller, the worst thing in the world is a high bidder who disappears from the face of the earth—a *deadbeat bidder* who bids but never pays. If this happens to you, you're stuck holding the now-unsold merchandise. (This is also the good news. You might not have been paid, but at least you still have the merchandise to resell in another auction.)

If you find yourself a victim of a deadbeat bidder, you can report your case to eBay, ask for a refund of your final value fee, and maybe offer the item in question to other (unsuccessful) bidders. But you have to initiate all of these activities yourself; eBay doesn't know that you've been shafted until you say so. You'll want to follow the procedure outlined in the following sections.

Step One: Contact the Unresponsive Bidder

It's on your shoulders to go to whatever lengths possible to contact the high bidder in your eBay auctions. This contact should start with the standard post-auction email, of course. If the buyer hasn't responded within three days, resend your original email with an "URGENT" added to the subject line. You should also amend the message to give the buyer a specific deadline (two days from the date of the message is good) for responding.

If another two days go by without a response, send a new message informing the buyer that if you don't receive a response within two days, you'll be forced to cancel his or her high bid and report the buyer to eBay as a deadbeat bidder.

Step Two: Go Through the Unpaid Item Dispute Process

You can't be expected to wait forever to be paid. If you haven't heard from the buyer in 7 to 10 days, or haven't received payment in two weeks or so, it's fair to write off the buyer and move on. Give the buyer one last chance (with a 24-hour time limit); then notify him or her that you're canceling the auction transaction and contacting eBay about the nonpayment.

Now comes the extra work. The way you notify eBay about a deadbeat bidder is to file an Unpaid Item Dispute. You have to file this form (and wait the requisite amount of time) before you can request a final value fee credit on the auction in question.

An Unpaid Item Dispute must be filed between 7 and 45 days after your auction ends. You file the dispute by going to eBay's Security & Resolution Center (pages.ebay.com/securitycenter/), shown in Figure 18.5. Check the Unpaid

Item option, and then click the Report Problem button. When the Report an Unpaid Item Dispute page appears, enter the auction's item number, click the Continue button, and follow the onscreen instructions.

Step Three: Ask eBay to Refund Your Fees

After an Unpaid Item Dispute has been filed, eBay sends a message to the bidder requesting that the two of you work things out. (It's not a very strong message, in my humble opinion, but it's what it is.) You then have to wait 7 days before you can request a refund of your final value fee. You have to make the request no later than 60 days after the end of your auction, and your claim has to meet one of the following criteria:

- The high bidder did not respond to your emails or backed out and did not buy the item.
- The high bidder's check bounced or a stop payment was placed on it.
- The high bidder returned the item and you issued a refund.
- The high bidder backed out, but you sold the item to another bidder at a lower price.
- One or more of the bidders in a Dutch auction backed out of the sale.

If your situation fits, you're entitled to a full refund of eBay's final value fee—but you must request it. To request a refund, go to your My eBay page and click the Dispute Console link. When the Dispute Console page appears, click through to the item in dispute and select the I No Longer Wish to Communicate With or Wait For the Buyer option. eBay then issues a final value fee credit, and your item is eligible for relisting.

Step Four: Leave Negative Feedback

Naturally, you want to alert other eBay members to the weasel among them. You do this by leaving negative feedback, along with a description of just what went wrong (no contact, no payment, whatever). Limit your comments to the facts—avoid the temptation to leave personally disparaging remarks—but make sure that other sellers know that this buyer was a deadbeat.

note Know that if you leave negative feedback about a nonpaying bidder, that bidder might retaliate by leaving negative feedback about you. There's nothing you can do about this; it's a risk of doing business and shouldn't deter you from warning other users away from this particular deadbeat. The only way you can avoid retaliatory negatives is to never leave negative feedback—which abrogates your responsibility to other sellers via the feedback system.

Step Five: Block the Bidder from Future Sales

Next, you want to make sure that this deadbeat doesn't bid in any of your future auctions. You do this by adding him or her to your blocked bidders list. You can do this by going to eBay's Site Map page and clicking the Blocked Bidder/Buyer List link. Follow the onscreen instructions to add this buyer's ID to your blocked list.

Step Six: Give Other Bidders a Second Chance

Now all that's left to do is deal with the merchandise that you thought you had sold. Assuming you still want to sell the item, what do you do?

You can, of course, relist the item for sale—which we'll describe in step six. However, you may be able to save yourself this hassle by offering the item to other bidders in your failed auction. eBay's Second Chance Offer feature lets you try to sell your item to someone else who was definitely interested in what you had to sell.

You can make a Second Chance Offer to any of the under-bidders in your original auction. The offer can be made immediately at the end of the auction and up to 60 days afterward.

note When a bidder accepts your Second Chance Offer, eBay charges you a final value fee. You are not charged a listing fee. Buyers accepting Second Chance Offers are eligible for eBay's normal fraud protection services.

To make a Second Chance Offer, return to your original item listing page and click the Second Chance Offer link. When the Second Chance Offer page appears, as shown in Figure 18.6, select which buyer(s) you want to make the offer to, select a duration for the offer, and then click the Continue button to make the offer.

note Second Chance Offers can also be used, in a successful auction, to offer duplicate items to non-winning bidders.

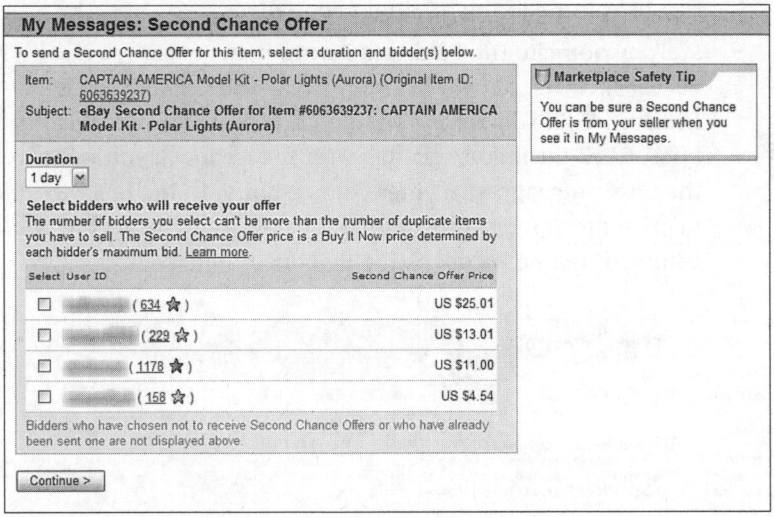

FIGURE 18.6

Making a second chance offer to non-winning bidders.

My Messages: Second Chance Offer

To send a Second Chance Offer for this item, select a duration and bidder(s) below.

Item: CAPTAIN AMERICA Model Kit - Polar Lights (Aurora) (Original Item ID: 6063639237)
Subject: **eBay Second Chance Offer for Item #6063639237: CAPTAIN AMERICA Model Kit - Polar Lights (Aurora)**

Duration
1 day

Select bidders who will receive your offer
The number of bidders you select can't be more than the number of duplicate items you have to sell. The Second Chance Offer price is a Buy It Now price determined by each bidder's maximum bid. Learn more.

Select	User ID	Second Chance Offer Price
☐	(634 ★)	US $25.01
☐	(229 ★)	US $13.01
☐	(1178 ★)	US $11.00
☐	(158 ★)	US $4.54

Bidders who have chosen not to receive Second Chance Offers or who have already been sent one are not displayed above.

Continue >

Marketplace Safety Tip

You can be sure a Second Chance Offer is from your seller when you see it in My Messages.

Step Seven: Relist Your Item

If you don't have any takers on your Second Chance Offer, you can always try to sell the item again by relisting it. The nice thing about relisting an unsold item is that eBay will refund the second listing fee—essentially giving you the relist free. (Obviously, you still pay a final value fee if the item sells.)

Coping with Complaints About *You*

Of course, it's always possible that a disgruntled customer will accuse you of various types of wrongdoing. What do you do when you've been (presumably unjustly) accused?

Responding to Negative Feedback

Probably the most common form of customer complaint on eBay takes the form of negative feedback. Since maintaining a high feedback rating is important to the long-term success of your eBay business, you need to respond appropriately to any negative feedback you receive.

Unfortunately, there's not much you can do if you receive negative feedback; feedback comments cannot be retracted, except in the most extreme instances. What you can do is respond to the negative comments, thus providing some sort of balance to the original negativity.

Start by going to the Feedback Forum page (`pages.ebay.com/services/forum/feedback.html`), shown in Figure 18.7, and clicking the Reply to Feedback Received link. This takes you to a page that displays a listing of all your feedback. Click the link associated with the feedback you want to address; when the next page appears, enter your response in the text box and click the Leave Reply button. Your new comment is now listed below the original feedback comment on the Feedback Profile page.

FIGURE 18.7

Use eBay's Feedback Forum to respond to negative feedback.

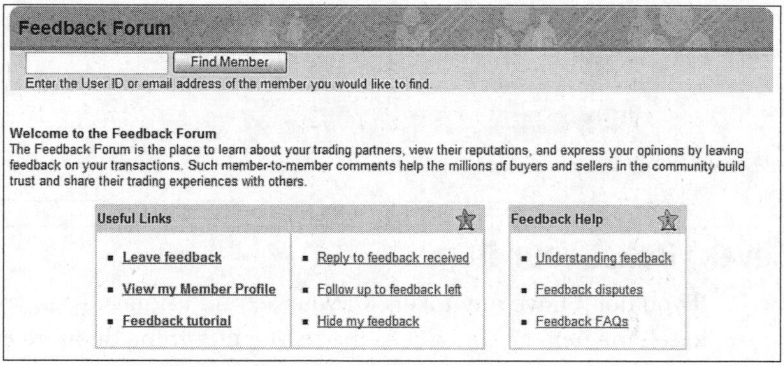

Feedback Forum

[Find Member]

Enter the User ID or email address of the member you would like to find.

Welcome to the Feedback Forum
The Feedback Forum is the place to learn about your trading partners, view their reputations, and express your opinions by leaving feedback on your transactions. Such member-to-member comments help the millions of buyers and sellers in the community build trust and share their trading experiences with others.

Useful Links
- Leave feedback
- View my Member Profile
- Feedback tutorial
- Reply to feedback received
- Follow up to feedback left
- Hide my feedback

Feedback Help
- Understanding feedback
- Feedback disputes
- Feedback FAQs

Getting Negative Feedback Removed

If you feel that negative feedback has been left maliciously, you can petition eBay to remove the feedback. It won't often do so, except in extreme cases—but there's no harm in asking.

You can learn more about feedback removal at `pages.ebay.com/help/policies/feedback-removal.html`. Scroll through the text until you find the Contact Us link near the bottom of the page; click this link to display the web form for feedback removal. Enter the appropriate information and click the

Submit button. If eBay agrees with your arguments, you'll be notified that the feedback in question has been removed. If not, you won't.

note eBay also offers a Mutual Feedback Withdrawal process, for those instances when both you and the seller agree to remove the negative feedback. Use the form located at `feedback.ebay.com/ws/ eBayISAPI.dll?MFWRequest`.

Responding to Item Not Received Complaints

In its quest to assuage the fears of new or reluctant buyers, eBay has instituted a new complaint process for those buyers who do not receive their items within a reasonable period of time. This Item Not Received or Significantly Not as Described process started out with good intentions, but quickly fell victim to the law of unintended consequences. The problem with the process is that buyers can file a complaint if they haven't received an item within 10 days of the end of the auction. Do your math, and you can easily see that many transactions will fall outside this arbitrary waiting period.

Take, for example, the buyer who pays by personal check. Even if the buyer sends the check the day after the auction (and many don't), you won't receive it until 3 days or so after the auction. You then hold the check for 10 business days, to make sure it clears, and then ship the item—which takes another 3 days to get to the buyer. Add in a weekend or two, and it might take 18–20 days for the buyer to receive the merchandise—well outside eBay's 10-day period.

The 10-day period is also problematic when a buyer pays by cashier's check or money order and doesn't mail the payment promptly. Or if the transaction period falls over a holiday or 3-day weekend. Or if you ship via Parcel Post or Media Mail. Or...well, you see the problem. It's no surprise that the Item Not Received process has not been well received by eBay's selling community.

So it's quite possible that you might sell an item to a newbie buyer who starts panicking when 10 days pass and the item doesn't show up on his or her doorstep. Fortunately, nothing major happens if the buyer files a claim at the 10-day mark. Once the buyer files a claim, eBay notifies you (the seller) of the claim and asks for a response; no formal action is taken until 30 days after the end of the listing. If, at that time, the buyer hasn't received the item (or the two of you haven't communicated and worked something out), the buyer has the option of escalating the complaint into eBay's Standard Purchase Protection Program.

At that point eBay can get involved and refund the buyer's money (up to $200) and take action against you as a seller. That action could result in a formal warning, a temporary suspension, or an indefinite suspension. Of course, it's also possible that eBay could evaluate the situation and take no action against you. The outcome depends on the situation.

Obviously, if you're doing your job right, no complaint should escalate into the Standard Purchase Protection Program. If you do get an Item Not Received complaint, make sure you respond and inform the buyer why he or she hasn't received the item yet. The key here is communication—especially when you're dealing with inexperienced buyers.

19

Automating Auction Management

As you no doubt realize, there's plenty of work to do over the course of an eBay auction, and even more after the auction ends. Not only do you have to keep track of the current bids, but you might also have to answer questions from bidders, update your item listing, cancel bids from questionable bidders, and—on rare occasions—cancel the entire auction. Then, when the auction is over, you need to contact the winning bidder, handle payment, pack and ship the item, leave feedback for the buyer, and add all the auction details to your ongoing records.

That's a lot of work!

If you run only a few auctions at a time, there's no reason why you can't handle all your auction management manually. But if you're a high-volume seller, trying to manage each and every auction individually gets real tedious real fast. Many high-volume sellers choose to outsource their auction management to an outside service or utilize dedicated software programs to do the management for them. These programs and services not only track the progress of in-process auctions, but also manage all manner of post-auction activity.

Should You Use an Auction Management Tool?

Here's the thing. Auction management tools cost money to use. (You can't get good help for free!) So when you decide to utilize a particular auction management service, you automatically increase your business's costs.

Before you decide to use a third-party auction tool, you have to ask yourself if it's worth the cost. Can you afford to spend another 25 or 50 cents per item, just to make your life a little easier? That might sound like peanuts—until you start adding up all your other selling costs. Remember, you have to pay eBay to list each item and then pay another fee when the item is sold. If you accept credit card payment via PayPal, you'll pay another fee when a customer pays via that method. Add all these fees together, and you can easily be out a buck or more on each item you sell—and that comes right out of your profit.

On the other hand, if you're doing a large volume of eBay business, can you afford *not* to use an auction management tool? Add up all the time you spend creating item listings, sending emails, and handling end-of-auction transactions. Is it worth 25 or 50 cents per transaction to cut that workload in half?

An important factor, obviously, is just what operations you can automate with these auction tools. While each site offers a different selection of tools, here are some of the tools you can expect to find at the major third-party auction sites:

- **Inventory management**. Enter and track all the items in your inventory, and automatically delete items from inventory as they're sold at auction.
- **Image hosting**. Host photos for your auctions on the service's website, and manage those photos in your item listings.
- **Gallery**. Create a separate photo page of all the items you have for sale so that potential buyers can link to your item listings and browse through all the merchandise you offer.
- **Bulk listing creation**. Create attractive item listings with pre-designed templates, and then list multiple items in bulk.
- **End-of-auction email**. Automatically send notifications to winning bidders, and notify customers when payment is received and items are shipped.

- **End-of-auction checkout**.
Provide a dedicated page that customers can use to verify their purchases, and provide shipping and
payment information.

- **Bulk feedback posting**.
Automatically post customer feedback in bulk.

- **Sales analysis**. Generate reports and graphs to help you analyze your
auction sales over time.

- **Storefront**. Provide other nonauction items for sale on the Web.

> **note** A few of these sites also offer eBay research and inventory sourcing services, although these aren't normally part of the typical auction management package.

Not all sites offer all these services. In addition, the level of services offered
will also vary; some sites are more automated than others. Read on to learn
more about what's available.

Evaluating Auction Management Tools

When it comes to auction management tools, there's a lot to choose from.
And, while it might be tempting to mix and match different tools from different providers (use this site's lister and that site's checkout), the better bet is to
settle on a single service for all your auction needs. While mixing tools and
providers is not impossible, at best it's awkward and at worst it's extremely
impractical. For example, while you could use Ándale Lister to create your listings and Vendio Sales Manager for your post-auction management, these
tools don't work well together. A much tighter integration is possible when
you use tools from the same service—using both Ándale Lister and Ándale
Checkout, for example, or employing Vendio Sales for the entire process.

Comparing these different services is a little like comparing apples and jelly
beans. That's because some services offer their tools in a single package at a
single price, while others offer a menu of different choices, with a la carte pricing. In addition, some services offer a flat monthly price, while others offer different tiers of pricing—and still others offer variable rate pricing based on the
number of transactions you make or the final selling price.

That said, let's give this comparison thing a crack. Table 19.1 lists the different
tools offered by some of the major auction services and offers a glance at rep-
resentative fees (as of August 2006).

Table 19.1 Major Auction Management Services

Service	URL	Research	Inventory Sourcing	Inventory Management	Image Hosting	Gallery
Ándale	www.andale.com	X	X	X	X	X
Auction Hawk	www.auctionhawk.com			X	X	X
Auctiva	www.auctiva.com			X	X	X
ChannelAdvisor	www.channeladvisor.com			X	X	
eBay Blackthorne Basic	pages.ebay.com/ blackthorne/basic.html					
eBay Blackthorne Pro	pages.ebay.com/ blackthorne/pro.html			X		
eBay Selling Manager	pages.ebay.com/ selling_manager/					
eBay Selling Manager Pro	pages.ebay.com/ selling_manager_pro/			X		
inkFrog	www.inkfrog.com			X	X	X
Vendio	www.vendio.com			X	X	X

Now let's try a head-to-head pricing comparison, as much as that's possible. Table 19.2 compares plans from each service for sellers doing 50, 100, and 250 transactions per month. For purposes of this comparison, we'll say that each transaction averages $10 apiece, and we want a package that includes image hosting, listing creation, checkout, end-of-auction

Bulk Listing Creation	End-of-Auction Email	Checkout	Bulk Feedback Posting	Sales Analysis	Storefront	Pricing
X	X	X	X	X	X	"Quick Packs" from $10.95/ month (40 listings); individual services priced separately
X	X	X	X	X		From $12.99/month
X	X	X	X	X	X	Free
X	X	X	X		X	From $29.95/month
X	X	X (via eBay)	X			$9.99/month
X	X	X (via eBay)	X	X		$24.99/month
	X	X (via eBay)	X			$4.99/month
X	X	X (via eBay)	X	X		$15.99/month
X	X		X	X		$9.95/month
X	X	X	X	X	X	Various plans from 14.95/month plus combination of listing and final value fees

emails, and automatic feedback posting. Note that I've tried to manually piece together the best possible deal at each site (with August 2006 pricing), which sometimes means choosing a combination of different services and other times means going with a prepared package. Your mileage may vary.

Table 19.2   Auction Service Pricing Comparison

Service	50 Auctions/ Month	100 Auctions/ Month	250 Auctions/ Month
Ándale	$24.95	$51.90	$87.90
Auction Hawk	$12.99	$12.99	$24.99
Auctiva	$0	$0	$0
ChannelAdvisor	$29.95	$29.95	$29.95
eBay Blackthorne Basic	$9.99	$9.99	$9.99
eBay Blackthorne Pro	$24.99	$24.99	$24.99
eBay Selling Manager	$4.99	$4.99	$4.99
eBay Selling Manager Pro	$15.99	$15.99	$15.99
inkFrog	$9.95	$9.95	$9.95
Vendio	$25.95	$36.95	$69.95

As you can see, the price you pay varies wildly from one site to another. Which service is best depends on the services you need, your expected volume, and the average price of the items you sell. In general, a flat-fee service such as ChannelAdvisor or inkFrog is best if you have a high volume of sales, while a variable-rate site like Ándale or Vendio is best if you have a lower sales volume or if your sales tend to vary from month to month. Watch out for those sites, such as Ándale, that price each of their tools separately; a few dollars here and a few dollars there add up fast.

Of course, you don't necessarily get the same level of service at each site, even if pricing is similar. Some sites are simply better than others, especially when it comes to handling large volumes of transactions. For example, while Auctiva is completely free and inkFrog is just $9.95 per month, their levels of service are somewhat Spartan when compared to a ChannelAdvisor or Vendio; it may not be up for the task if you pump through a lot of transactions.

For that reason alone, it pays to look at each service in depth—and to use any free trial provided to get a feel for how each site works. I'll do my bit by detailing the top auction management sites separately, in the following sections.

Popular Auction Management Tools

To give you an idea of the various auction management tools available, we'll take a look at what's available from eBay and major third-party providers. Remember, all prices and services are subject to change.

Ándale

Ándale (www.andale.com), shown in Figure 19.1, probably offers the most variety when it comes to auction-related services. It's the only site that offers the full range of tools from pre-auction research to post-auction management.

FIGURE 19.1

The Ándale website.

Ándale Checkout (www.andale.com) provides a post-sale checkout option similar to eBay's checkout feature, as well as automated post-auction tools similar to those of Selling Manager Pro. At the close of an auction, Ándale automatically sends the high bidder an email with a link to an Ándale Checkout page. (Buyers can also check out by responding to the end-of-auction email.) You can view the entire post-auction process for all your auctions from Ándale's sales console; you can also use this page to generate invoices and shipping labels.

The charge for Ándale Checkout depends on the number of customers who use the service. Table 19.3 details the various fee plans.

note In case you're wondering (or even if you're not), Ándale is pronounced *on-de-lay*, not *an-dale*.

Table 19.3   Ándale Checkout Fees

Monthly Fee	Checkouts Included	Each Additional Checkout
$7.50	40	$0.30
$16.95	110	$0.20
$33.95	275	$0.18
$56.95	550	$0.15
$89.95	1,100	$0.12
$149.95	2,750	$0.10
$224.95	5,600	$0.08

The nice thing about Ándale Checkout is that its fees are scalable based on the number of auctions you run in a given month. If you run only a handful of auctions, you pay a low fee—20 cents an auction, roughly. You're not forced into a high fixed monthly cost, which can translate into high per-auction costs. It's a good choice for low-volume sellers or sellers whose volume varies from month to month.

Auction Hawk

Auction Hawk (www.auctionhawk.com), shown in Figure 19.2, is an up-and-coming auction management service with affordable pricing. Auction Hawk offers a variety of tools in its main service, including image hosting, bulk listing creation, end-of-auction checkout with automated winning bidder email, bulk feedback posting, and profit-and-loss reporting.

One nice aspect of Auction Hawk's services is that you are not charged any per-transaction or final value fees. In addition, all the services are included in a single price, so you're not nickel-and-dimed to death with a la carte pricing. The full-service monthly plans range in price from $12.99 (for 110 listings) to $89.99 (unlimited listings). At these prices, Auction Hawk is worth checking out.

Auctiva

Auctiva (www.auctiva.com), shown in Figure 19.3, used to offer a variety of different plans at various prices, but now offers just a single plan—and it's completely free. You get listing creation, image hosting, listing tracking, hit counters, automated feedback posting, and all the rest, all at no charge. As you can imagine, Auctiva's popularity has increased substantially since the site removed its fees.

FIGURE 19.2

The Auction Hawk website.

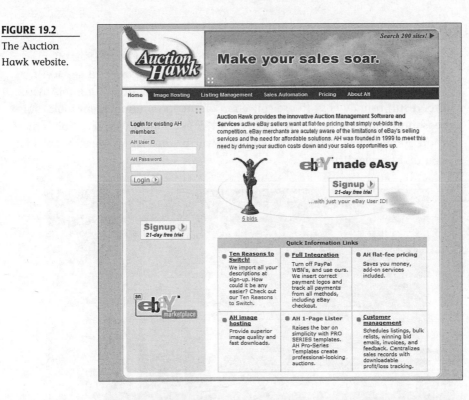

FIGURE 19.3

The Auctiva website.

ChannelAdvisor

ChannelAdvisor (www.channeladvisor.com), shown in Figure 19.4, offers a fairly affordable suite of auction management tools—as well as services for bigger online merchants. The service you want to look at is ChannelAdvisor Pro, a surprisingly easy-to-use collection of auction management tools, quite reasonably priced at a flat fee of just $29.95 per month. If you're doing more than 50 auctions a month, it's definitely worth considering—even more so if you're a heavier lister.

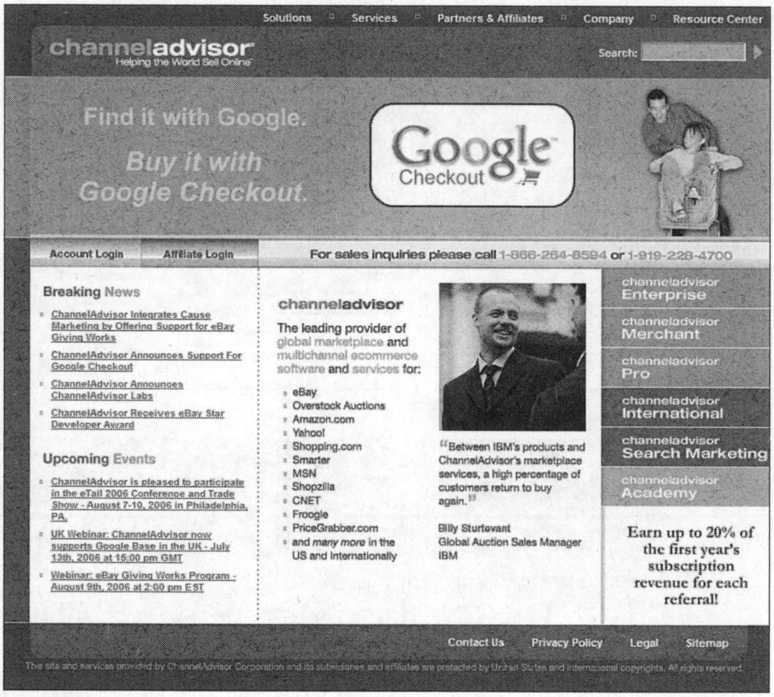

FIGURE 19.4

The ChannelAdvisor website.

eBay Blackthorne Basic

eBay Blackthorne Basic is the latest incarnation of what used to be called Seller's Assistant Basic—and before that was, surprisingly, called Blackthorne. (What goes around comes around.) Blackthorne Basic, shown in Figure 19.5, is a software-based tool offered by eBay that essentially functions as a bulk listing tool with some degree of post-auction management—in particular, auction tracking and email and feedback management. It's a pretty good tool, although it might not be ideal for heavy-duty sellers. That said, since it costs only $9.99 per month (with no per-transaction charges), it's definitely worth considering. Check it out at pages.ebay.com/blackthorne/basic.html.

FIGURE 19.5

eBay
Blackthorne
Basic software.

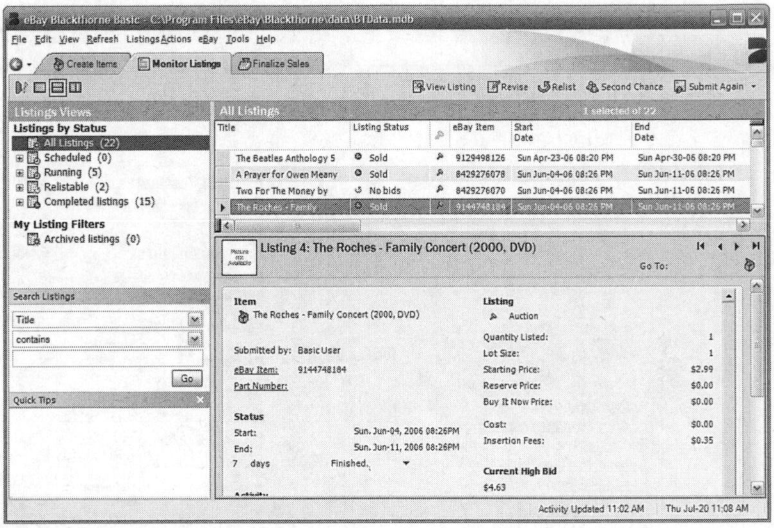

eBay Blackthorne Pro

A more powerful software-based tool for high-volume sellers is eBay Blackthorne Pro (pages.ebay.com/blackthorne/pro.html). This program is essentially Blackthorne Basic on steroids, with many more pre- and post-auction management features. In particular, you get inventory management, sales management and reporting, bulk feedback posting, and the ability to manage consignment sales and suppliers—in addition to the standard bulk listing creation and end-of-auction emails. The program, which has a high adoption rate among eBay PowerSellers, costs $24.99 per month.

eBay Selling Manager

eBay Selling Manager (pages.ebay.com/selling_manager/) is another official eBay auction management tool—this one web-based, not a separate software program. When you subscribe to Selling Manager, the Selling tab of your My eBay page is transformed into a Selling Manager tab, where you can manage all your auction and post-auction activity—including sending customer emails and leaving feedback. Cost is $4.99 per month.

As you can see in Figure 19.6, the main Selling Manager page provides an overview of your active and closed auctions. You can click on any link to see a finer cut of your activity—to view only your active listings, for example, or only those listings that are paid and ready to ship.

The My eBay Selling page turned into eBay Selling Manager.

Selling Manager Summary	Print	Help	Customize Summary

Select a view..... ▾ - ▾ [   ] [Search]

At a Glance			**Sold‡**		Customize	✕
	Sales			Sales	# of Listings	
		$10.00	**All**	$10.00	1	
$10			**Awaiting Payment**	$0.00	0	
$5			Buyers eligible for combined purchases		0	
$0			**Awaiting Shipment**	$0.00	0	
Last 24 hours Last 7 days Last 30 days			Paid and waiting to give Feedback		0	
			Paid and Shipped	$10.00	1	
Listing Activity		Customize ✕	Shipped and waiting to give Feedback		0	
	Sales	# of Listings	**Dispute Console**	$0.00	0	
Active Listings	$74.48	15	Eligible for Unpaid Item reminder		0	
Ending within the next hour		0	Disputes awaiting your response		0	
Ending today		0	Eligible for Final Value Fee credit		0	
Listings with questions		0	‡Includes data for the last 90 days			
Listing with bids		5				
Scheduled Listings		0	**Cross-Promotions**		Customize ✕	
Starting within the next hour		0			# of Listings	
Starting today		0	Items with updated cross-promotions		1	
Ended Listings †		57	Items with manual cross-promotions		0	
Sold		43				
Unsold		14				
Eligible for Relist Fee credit		2				

I don't recommend Selling Manager for high-volume sellers because it isn't very automated; all the transactions have to be handled manually. You also don't get any listing creation features, which is why eBay recommends using Selling Manager in conjunction with the free Turbo Lister program. Together, they're not a bad combination for low-volume sellers.

eBay Selling Manager Pro

As you just read, eBay Selling Manager isn't perfect. One of its biggest problems is that you pretty much have to manage one auction at a time; it lacks features that let you manage multiple auctions in bulk. If you're a high-volume seller, a better solution is eBay's higher-end Selling Manager Pro, which does offer bulk management features (including bulk listing). For $15.99 per month, Selling Manager Pro does everything the basic Selling Manager does, plus

note Learn more about eBay's Turbo Lister in Chapter 15, "Automating Item Listing."

more. It sends email messages in bulk, leaves feedback in bulk, manages inventory items and issues restock alerts, and generates a monthly profit and loss report—including all eBay fees and cost of goods sold. It's obviously meant to compete directly with the offerings from Ándale, Vendio, and other third parties.

inkFrog

inkFrog (`www.inkfrog.com`), shown in Figure 19.7, is kind of a bargain-basement auction service. All of its services are available for a flat $9.95 per month, which makes it extremely popular among cost-conscious sellers.

FIGURE 19.7
The inkFrog website.

The current inkFrog is actually quite a bit different from the inkFrog of just a year ago; that's because inkFrog recently aquired SpareDollar, and integrated many of SpareDollar's services into its own feature set. inkFrog's auction tools include image hosting, listing creation/scheduling, post-auction emails and management, inventory management, page counters, consignment tracking/management, and more.

Note, however, that while inkFrog is attractively priced, its services might prove too limited for some high-volume sellers. That said, many high-volume sellers do use inkFrog, and are quite happy with the results. Give it a try to see if it fits your particular eBay business.

Vendio

Vendio (www.vendio.com), shown in Figure 19.8, is another long-established full-service auction management site. (The company was formerly known as Auctionwatch, back in the old days.)

FIGURE 19.8

The Vendio website.

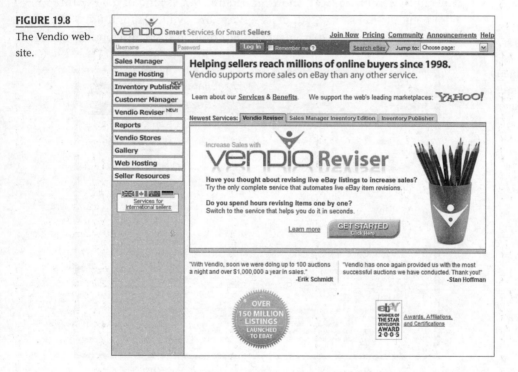

Vendio Sales Manager is a powerful set of listing creation and auction management tools. You can use Sales Manager not only to create new item listings, but also to manage all of your current and post-auction activity. Sales Manager will automatically generate end-of-auction emails, print invoices and packing slips, and upload customer feedback to eBay.

Vendio offers Sales Manager in both Inventory and Merchandising Editions; the mix of features is a little different between the two, but the pricing is the same. The company tries to appeal to different types of sellers by offering a mix of fixed- and variable-priced monthly subscriptions, as shown in Table 19.4.

Table 19.4   Vendio Sales Manager Fees

Plan	Monthly Fee	Listing Fee	Final Value Fee
Pay As You Go Plan	None	$0.12	1.25%
Variable Rate Premium Plan	$14.95	$0.06	1%
Variable Rate Power Plan	$34.95	None	1.25%
Flat Rate Premium Plan	$14.95	$0.22	None
Flat Rate Power Plan	$39.95	$0.12	None

The problem with this type of fee schedule is that you're never really sure which is the lowest-cost plan. I suppose the Pay As You Go Plan makes sense if you're a low-volume seller, or one whose sales volume tends to vary from month to month. If you know you're going to achieve a high sales level, one of the other plans might be in order—and if you're committed to a really high sales level, the Power plans might be cost-effective. But choosing which plan you'll need in advance is often difficult—especially if you're just starting out.

Another Option: Software Tools

Many eBay sellers prefer to manage their auctions offline, on their own time—without being tied to a single service. If you're more of a do-it-yourself kind of seller, you might want to check out some of the software programs designed to help you manage the eBay auction process. Here's a short list of programs for your consideration:

- **All My Auctions** (www.rajeware.com/auction/), $39.95. This is a basic auction management software program; it includes template-based listing creation, live auction management (including the ability to track competitors' auctions), end-of-auction email notification, and report generation.

note The sites listed here are just the most popular of the many auction management services available today. There are also higher-end sites, such as Marketworks (www.marketworks.com) and Zoovy (www.zoovy.com), that help integrate eBay auctions with larger e-commerce sites; there are also several less-expensive sites, such as ManageAuctions (www.manageauctions.com) and Trak Auctions (www.jwcinc.net) that offer a more limited set of services. You should visit the eBay Solutions Directory (solutions.ebay.com) to see all the third-party companies offering eBay auction management services.

■ **Auction Wizard 2000** (www.auctionwizard2000.com), $75/year, $50 annual renewal. This full-featured software offers many of the same tools you find at the large auction management sites, including inventory management, bulk listing creation, end-of-auction emails, bulk feedback posting, and the like.

■ **AuctionSage** (www.auctionsagesoftware.com), $29.95/3 months, $49.95/6 months, $79.95/year. This is software for posting and managing eBay auction transactions, including sending buyer emails and leaving bulk feedback.

■ **AuctionTamer** (www.auctiontamer.com), $22.95/month, $149.95/year. AuctionTamer is an all-in-one auction management software program for both sellers and bidders. For sellers, it lets you create auction listings, schedule delayed auction listings, manage your live auctions, send post-auction emails, and print shipping labels.

■ **Shooting Star** (www.foodogsoftware.com), $60. Shooting Star is a program designed to manage the end-of-auction process. It uses what it calls a "workflow system" to move you through various post-auction operations, including email notification. (Note that a new version 3 of Shooting Star is in the works, which will have more features—and a $120 price.)

As with the web-based auction management tools, make sure you try out any of these programs before you buy.

Part 4

Maximizing Your eBay Sales

20

Increasing Sell-Through

In theory, eBay is a perfect capitalistic marketplace, where the price of an item is driven by the interplay of supply and demand. Experienced eBay sellers, however, know that there are things they can do to improve chances of selling any particular item and to drive the final selling price to higher levels.

Improving your success rate on eBay isn't as simple as it might be with a traditional business, in which advertising and promotion tend to do the job. On eBay there's really no equivalent of traditional promotion; instead, you can affect your results by manipulating your initial bid price, the day and time that your auction ends, and various other listing enhancements. The process is subtle, but with noticeable results.

Setting a Pricing Strategy

The first thing you can do to affect the results of your auctions is to set an initial bid price that attracts the maximum number of bidders. It's a tricky process, though. Set your price too high or too low, and you could end up with disastrous results.

Think about it. If you set your minimum price too high, you might scare off potential buyers. If you set your minimum price too low, you'll probably get more interested bidders, but you might end up selling your item for less than you want or than what it's worth. You have to determine the starting price that attracts the maximum number of bidders while ensuring that you eventually cover your product costs and generate the highest selling price.

So what's the right starting price? It all depends on your pricing strategy, which we'll examine next.

Set It Low Enough to Be Attractive...

To a customer, a lower price is more desirable than a higher one. Think about it. If you see two similar items and one is priced a dollar lower than the other, you're going to be attracted to the lower-priced item.

For that reason, I like setting a price that's low enough to get some interested initial bidding going. That could be as low as 99 cents, or at the very least competitive with the lowest starting bids on similar merchandise also for auction on eBay.

On the other hand, you shouldn't set the initial price so low that it won't eventually rise to the final price you think the item can really sell for. If you think the final selling price will be $100, setting the initial bid at a penny might leave too large a gap to be bridged.

So how do you know what the final selling price will be? Well, you don't for sure, although the research tools discussed in Chapter 2, "Researching Your Business Model," can help you get a pretty good idea of what to expect.

At the very least, you want to be sure you're not setting the starting bid higher than the final selling price for similar items. If you do a search for completed auctions and find that *Star Wars* DVDs have been selling between $10 and $12, don't put a $15 starting price on the similar discs you want to sell. Ignore precedence, and you won't get any bids. Instead, gauge the previous final selling prices and place your starting price at about a quarter of that level. (That would be two or three bucks for our *Star Wars* example.)

note If you want the best of all possible worlds—a low initial price and a high selling floor—consider using a reserve price auction. Learn more about reserve pricing in Chapter 1, "So You Want to Start an eBay Business..."

...But Don't Set It So Low That It's Not Believable

A low initial price is good, but it's possible to actually set the starting price for an item *too* low. That's because if you set too low a minimum bid, some potential bidders might think that something is wrong with the item. (It's the old "if it's too good to be true, it probably is.") Although you might assume that bidding will take the price up into reasonable levels, too low a starting price can make your item look too cheap or otherwise flawed. If you start getting a lot of emails asking why you've set the price so low, you should have set a higher price.

With an ultra-low starting price, you also run the risk of the final selling price not making it up to the level you'd like to hit. Sometimes the difference between here and there is just too great for your bidders to distance.

Make Sure You Recover Your Costs...

Another factor in setting the starting price is what the item actually cost you. Now, if you're just selling some junk you found in the attic, this isn't a big concern. But since you're running a real eBay business and selling a large volume of items for profit, you don't want to sell too many items below what you paid for them. Many sellers like to set their starting price at their item cost—so if the item cost you $5, you set the minimum bid (or reserve price) at $5, and see what happens from there.

...But Not So High You Pay Too High a Listing Fee

Of course (and there's always another "of course"), if you set a higher starting price, you'll pay a higher insertion fee. Here's where it helps to know the breaks—in eBay's fee schedule, that is. Table 20.1 shows the fee breaks as of August 2006.

Table 20.1   eBay's Insertion Fee Breaks

Price Point	Fee
$0–$0.99	$0.20
$1.00–$9.99	$0.35
$10.00–$24.99	$0.60
$25.00–$49.99	$1.20
$50.00–$199.99	$2.40
$200.00–$499.99	$3.60
$500.00 and up	$4.80

Let's think about what this means. At the very least, you want to come in just below the fee break; coming in *above* the fee break will cost you an unnecessarily higher fee. For example, you probably want to list at $9.99 (which incurs a 35-cent fee) and not at $10.00 (which incurs a 60-cent fee). That extra penny could cost you 25 cents!

Obviously, it's in your best interest to minimize any and all fees you have to pay. If you're almost positive (based on completed auction activity) that your item will sell in the $20 range no matter what you price it at, price it as low as is reasonable. And remember—if you set the starting price for anything under a buck, you pay only a 25-cent listing fee!

Make Sure You Can Live with a Single Bid

What happens if you set the starting price at $5 and you get only one bid—at $5? Even if you thought the item was worth twice that, you can't back out now; you have to honor all bids in your auction, even if there's only one of them. You can't email the bidder and say, "Sorry, I really can't afford to sell it for this price." If you listed it, you agreed to sell it for any price at or above your minimum. It's a binding contract. So if the bidding is low, you better get comfortable with it—it's too late to change your mind now!

Go with a Fixed Price

The closer your eBay business is to a traditional bricks-and-mortar retail business, the less comfortable you're going to be with the whole online auction thing. If you sell large quantities of a single SKU, and if you're used to selling each item for a specific price, consider forgoing the auction process completely and listing your items on eBay for a fixed price. Alternately, you can run all your auctions with the Buy It Now option to spur quicker sales. More and more eBay sellers are using eBay as a fixed-priced marketplace; you can go strictly fixed price too, if you want.

So What's the Right Price?

As you can see, there's no one set "best" pricing model. Some sellers set a start price equal to their desired selling price; others like to start much lower and let the price work its way up over the course of an auction. Some swear by 99-cent initial pricing; others would never set their prices that low.

Myself, I typically set the initial item pricing at 25–50% of what I think the final selling price will be. (That's higher than how I used to set it; as more sales are moving to the fixed-price model, the gap between listing price and selling price is narrowing.) But you should come up with your own pricing strategy, based on sales over time. You're the best judge of your own eBay prices!

Determining the Best Days and Times to List

Another big factor in how successful your auction will be is when your auction *starts*—because that affects when your auction *ends*. If you start a seven-day auction at 6:00 p.m. on a Saturday, it will end exactly seven days later, at 6:00 p.m. the following Saturday. As you'll soon find out, some days and times are more effective than others.

Best Time of Day to List

Why is the time your auction ends important? Because some of the most intense bidding takes place in the final few minutes of your auction, from snipers trying to steal the high bid at the last possible moment. To take advantage of last-minute bidders, your auction needs to end when the most possible bidders are online.

For example, if you end your auction at 3:00 in the morning, most of your potential bidders will be asleep, and you'll lose out on any last-minute bids. End your auction in the middle of the day, and you'll miss those bidders who are stuck at work or in school.

Better, then, to end your auction during early evening hours. That's when the most number of users are online, and when you're likely to receive the most number of last-minute bids.

Remember, though, that you're dealing with a three-hour time-zone gap between the East and West coasts. So if you time your auction to end at 7:00 p.m. EST, you're ending at 4:00 p.m. PST—when many potential bidders are still at work. Conversely, if you choose to end at 9:00 p.m. PST, you just hit midnight in New York—and many potential bidders are already fast asleep.

The best times to end—and thus to *start*— your auction are between 9:00 p.m. and 11:00 p.m. EST, or between 6:00 p.m. and 8:00 p.m. PST. That way you'll catch the most potential bidders online—on both coasts—for the final minutes of your auction.

note eBay operates on Pacific (West coast) time. If you're in another time zone, be sure to do the math to determine the proper time for your area.

Note, however, that the best time to end an auction can be influenced by the type of item you're selling. For example, if you're selling an item that appeals to grade school or high school kids, try ending your auction in the late afternoon, after the kids get home from school and before they head off for dinner. Items with appeal to housewives do well with a late morning or early afternoon end time. And business items sell best when they end during normal business hours.

Best—and Worst—Days to List

Just as the time of day your auction ends affects your results, so does the day of the week. While different types of items perform better on different days, the general consensus is that Sunday is the default "best day" to end most auction items.

Here's why.

When you end your auction on a Sunday, you get one full Saturday and *two* Sundays (the starting Sunday and the ending one) for a seven-day item listing. Sunday is a great day to end auctions because almost everybody's home—no one's out partying or stuck at work or in school. End your auction on a Sunday evening, and you're likely to get more bids—and higher prices.

There are exceptions, however.

As with the time you end your auction, your ending day might also be influenced by the type of item you're selling. If you're selling an item of interest to college students, for example, you might be better ending on a night during the week because a lot of students travel home for the weekend; you're more likely to catch them in the dorms on a Wednesday or Thursday night. Items targeted at churchgoers might also be better ending during the week, so you don't catch bidders when they're at Sunday evening church services. (Which makes this one big exception to the Sunday evening rule!)

So if Sunday is normally the best night of the week to end your auction, what's the worst night?

Friday and Saturday are probably the worst nights to end most auctions, because a lot of eBay users are out partying on these non-school nights. End an auction for any item (especially youth-oriented items) on a Friday or Saturday night, and you eliminate a large number of potential buyers.

You should also try not to end your auction right in the middle of a hit television series or major sporting event; some potential bidders might find it difficult to tear themselves away from the old boob tube. That means avoiding

"Must See TV" Thursdays and any block-buster sporting events or award shows. And never—repeat, *never*—end your auction on a holiday!

Seasonal Variations

When you're planning your projected eBay sales and revenue, you need to take into account the fact that sales rates vary

throughout the year. It's no surprise that sales go up in November and December, due to the Christmas buying season. But did you know that sales go down—way down—in the summertime? That's right, eBay traffic in general drops significantly during June, July, and August. Lots of potential buyers are on vacation, and even more are outside enjoying the sunshine.

Keep these seasonal trends in mind when planning your business. That might mean putting fewer items up for auction during the summer months, or holding your highest-potential items for the fall or winter. Just don't assume you'll keep a steady sales rate throughout all 12 months of the year—because you won't.

Other Tricks for Improving Item Sell-Through

Starting price and end time aren't the only factors in determining auction success. Let's look at a few other tricks you can use to juice up your close rate and selling price.

Offer a Discount for Multiple Purchases

When you want buyers to buy more stuff from you, make it worth their while. One popular incentive is to offer a discount on multiple purchases. This approach is particularly popular among sellers who run their own eBay Stores, but any seller can do it, by manipulating payment-due amounts at the end of an auction to override eBay's automatically generated invoices. Incent the buyer to make multiple purchases!

Offer Free or Discounted Shipping

Offering free or discounted shipping is another popular way to close more sales. Confronted with one seller charging whatever to ship the item or another seller offering free shipping, which would you choose? There are even variations on this technique, such as offering free shipping when a customer purchases multiple items on the same order. (Just don't inflate your starting price to compensate for the lower shipping—which could price your item higher than the competition and cost you sales!)

Make Changes Mid-Auction

If several days have passed and an item hasn't received any bids, you might want to make changes to the auction listing to attract more customer attention. There are many changes you can make, including

- Extend the length of the auction
- Rewrite the item title or description
- Add more pictures
- Add the Buy It Now option
- Lower the initial bid price

You can make any of these changes up until the final 12 hours of any auction, as long as there aren't any bidders. Once someone makes a bid, the listing is locked in; you can add to the description, but you can't make changes.

Selling Internationally

Even though most U.S. sellers sell to U.S. buyers (and most Irish sellers sell to Irish buyers, and most Japanese sellers sell to Japanese buyers, and so on), eBay is a global marketplace. This is a good thing because it significantly broadens the market for whatever it is you're selling. The more potential bidders you have, wherever they live, the more likely you'll be to sell your item—and command a higher price. Besides, it can be a lot of fun to deal with people in different countries and cultures.

Pros and Cons of International Selling

That said, not every seller opts to offer goods outside the U.S. That's because international selling is somewhat more complex than selling domestically. You have to balance the pros and cons to determine if you want to limit your sales to U.S. buyers only or take advantage of eBay's global marketplace.

The pros of opening your auctions to non-U.S. bidders include:

- You might be able to attract additional bidders—and thus sell the items at (presumably) higher prices.
- You can offset some of the seasonality of the U.S. market; when it's winter here, you can still be selling swimsuits to the summer market in Australia.
- It's fun (sometimes) to interact with people from different countries and cultures.

The cons of selling outside the U.S. include the following:

- You might run into language difficulties communicating with bidders from outside the United States.
- You might have to deal with payment in non-U.S. funds, on non-U.S. banks.
- Unless the buyer pays via PayPal, you'll have to wait longer to receive payment from another country.
- You'll have to put extra effort into the packing of an item to be shipped over great distances.
- You probably won't be able to use your standard shipping services— which means investigating new shipping services and options, and upsetting your normal well-oiled shipping routine.
- You'll need to deal with the appropriate paperwork for shipping outside the U.S.—including those pesky customs forms.
- If there are any problems or disputes with the item shipped, you have an international-sized incident on your hands.

You'll have to determine for yourself whether the pros (increased sales and higher prices) outweigh the cons (more work and increased complexity).

Accepting Foreign Payments

One of the key issues with selling outside the U.S. is in dealing with foreign currency. First, you have to convert it to U.S. dollars. (How many lira to the dollar today?) Then you have to receive it in a form that is both secure and trusted. (Do

note When you need to convert foreign funds, use the Universal Currency Converter (www.xe.net/ucc/).

you trust a personal check drawn on a small Spanish bank?) Then you have to find a way to deposit those funds—and convert them to U.S. dollars. (Does your bank handle foreign deposits?)

note Issues related to shipping internationally are discussed in Chapter 17, "Organizing Your Packing and Shipping."

The currency issue is simplified somewhat when you specify bidding and payment in U.S. funds only. This puts the onus of currency conversion on the buyer, which is a plus.

The payment process can be further simplified when the buyer pays by credit card, using PayPal or BidPay. For example, PayPal is now active in more than 55 countries and can handle all the payment, conversion, and deposit functions for you.

Payment via international money order is also a good option. Be sure to specify that you need funds in U.S. dollars, and most U.S. banks (as well as your local post office) should be able to cash one of these money orders with little or no hassle.

Choosing the Most Effective Listing Options

In the preceding chapter we discussed things you can do to increase your auctions' success rates. Well, eBay offers you several other ways to draw attention to your auctions—although not all of them are terribly cost effective.

We'll examine each of eBay's listing enhancements (bold, highlight, gallery, and so on), as well as a few more basic listing strategies—such as how to determine the right auction length and category. You can select any of these options when you're creating your auction listing.

Be careful when selecting these options, however; each enhancement you select increases your costs, and you can't run a profitable business if your costs are too high!

Selecting the Right Auction Length

note A 3- or 5-day auction is also a good option if you have to start your auction mid-week but still want it to end on the weekend.

The first option we'll examine is one that, in most configurations, doesn't cost you a thing. eBay lets you choose from five different lengths for your auctions: 1, 3, 5, 7, and 10 days. The first four options come at the standard listing price; 10-day auctions cost you an additional 40 cents.

The default—and most common—auction length is seven days. Choose anything shorter, and you miss any potential buyers who check in only one day a week. Choose the longer option, and it's probably overkill. (Plus, you have to wait an extra three days to collect your money.)

Know, however, that some sellers like a 10-day auction that starts on a Friday or Saturday so that they get two weekends in their bidding schedule. Others prefer a shorter auction (as long as it runs over a weekend), recognizing that most bidding happens during the last few hours, anyway.

My recommendation is to go with the standard seven-day auction, with some exceptions. If you really need your money quickly, go with a three- or five-day auction, but try to time the listing so that you get in a bidding weekend. Also know that some buyers expect and plan on seven-day auctions, so you might not get as much last-minute sniping if you opt for the shorter length.

Choosing a Different Start Time

eBay also lets you choose a specific start time for your auction—which, of course, also becomes your auction's end time. By default, an eBay auction starts as soon as the item listing is placed, so if you place your listing at 10:00 a.m., that's when the auction starts and ends. However, you can pay an extra $0.10 (what eBay calls a "scheduled listings fee") and schedule your auction to start (and stop) at a specified time different from when you created the item listing.

This is a good option if you have to create your auction listings at what would otherwise be a bad time to end an auction—in the morning or early afternoon, for example. It's better to end an auction during the evening, when more users are at home. So if you can't launch your auctions in the evening, spend the extra $0.10 so that eBay can automatically schedule the start of your auction for you. (Alternately, you can subscribe to an auction management service—or use listing creation software—that handles the scheduling of your auctions for you, at no extra charge.)

note Learn more about the most effective auction end times in Chapter 20, "Increasing Sell-Through."

Picking the Right Category

Picking the right category sounds simple, and it used to be a bigger deal than it is today. When eBay was a lot smaller, potential buyers used to browse through the various categories to see what was available. Today, however, there are so many listings in every category that browsing is no longer practical; most items today are found via searching.

That said, the category you choose for an item can be used by potential buyers to help narrow their search. Unfortunately, not every product fits neatly within a single category. Maybe you're selling a model of an American Airlines jet airplane. Does it fit better in **Collectibles: Transportation: Aviation: Airlines: American**, or in **Toys & Hobbies: Models, Kits: Air**?

Where you put your item should be dictated by where the highest number of potential bidders will look for it. In the model airplane example, if there are more bidders traipsing through the Collectibles category, put it there; if there are more potential buyers who think of this as a toy or model kit, put it in the Toys & Hobbies category. Think like your potential buyers, and put the item where you would look for it if you were them.

You can also use various third-party research tools (such as those offered by Ándale and Mpire) to provide data on where other sellers placed similar items. Most of these research tools will tell you which category provided the best results, in terms of success rate and highest selling price.

If you determine that you can improve your results by listing your item in more than one category, take advantage of eBay's offer to list your item in two separate categories. It doubles your listing fees, of course, but it also potentially doubles your exposure. (You make this choice when you create your item listing, right at the start.)

note Learn more about third-party research tools in Chapter 2, "Researching Your Business Model."

...sting Enhancements

...you're creating an item listing, eBay provides all sorts of listing ...ncements" you can use to make your listing stand out from the millions of others currently running. All of these listing options cost extra, above and beyond the normal listing fee, whether they actually improve your success rate or not. Let's look at each option in more detail.

Subtitle

eBay lets you supplement your main title with a subtitle, which appears below the title on your item listing page and on all search results pages, as shown in Figure 21.1. It's on the search results pages that a subtitle has the most value, as it essentially provides another 55 characters for you to describe your item to potential bidders. Of course, you pay for this option, in the form of a $0.50 fee. Is it worth the cost? It depends.

FIGURE 21.1

A listing with subtitle.

In some categories a majority of sellers have adopted the use of subtitles, so if you don't choose this option, your listings will look naked and somehow inferior. Other categories have less frequent use of subtitles, which might make a subtitled listing stand out in the search results. Or not.

In addition, it's worth noting that adding a subtitle doesn't help potential buyers find your item. The text in a subtitle is not included in eBay's standard title search; it comes into play only if a user has expanded his or her search criteria to include the item description.

So, all things considered, I'm not a big fan of the subtitle option—unless you're forced to use it. My advice is to use it if you have to (in those categories where all the other listings employ it), but otherwise not.

Gallery

eBay's gallery option started out as a way to display your items in a separate picture gallery. That gallery still exists, although few buyers use it. Instead, the gallery option today displays a photo next to your item listing on all browsing category pages, as shown in Figure 21.2. This is particularly important if you're selling a highly visual item, such as a painting or collectible. It's also important in those categories where a majority of other sellers use the option—which is an increasing number of categories, these days.

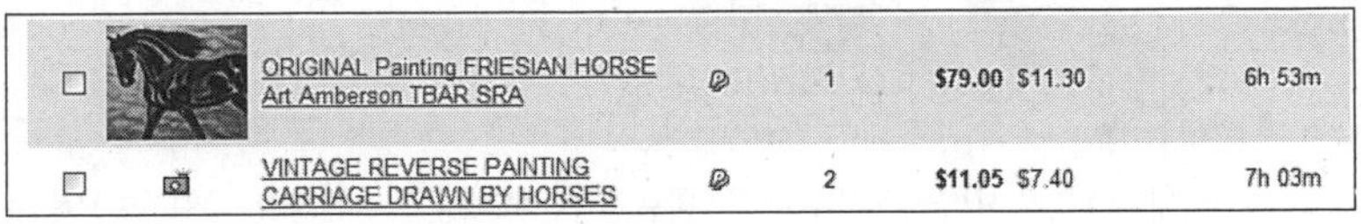

FIGURE 21.2

Two listings—
one with a
gallery picture,
one without.

At just $0.35, this is one of the few listing enhancements that I recommend.

Gallery Featured

eBay also offers a second gallery option, called Gallery Featured. When you pay for this option, your item will periodically show up in the special Featured section above the general gallery.

Pricing for the Gallery Featured option is $19.95. It's a fairly expensive enhancement, and I'm not sure it gets you much; most buyers look beyond the first listings on a page.

Gallery Plus

eBay's newest listing option is Gallery Plus. Not to be confused with Gallery Featured, Gallery Plus puts an Enlarge icon below your gallery image on search results pages. Users who click the icon, or just hover over the icon with their mouse, display a larger (up to 400 x 400) version of your gallery picture.

You pay an extra $0.75 for the Gallery Plus option—although this fee also gives you the standard $0.35 Gallery option, so it's really just 40 cents extra on top of the regular Gallery, if you think of it that way. While Gallery Plus is too new for me an offer an informed opinion as to effectiveness, it smacks somewhat of opportunism on eBay's part and seems a little pricy for what you get. I'd wait until other users render judgment before embracing this feature.

Bold

How do you make your item stand out on a page full of listings? How about displaying the listing title in boldface? This option, which costs $1.00, displays your item title in bold in any category or search results listings. A boldfaced item listing is shown in Figure 21.3.

> **note** To use Gallery Plus, you must have your pictures hosted by eBay Picture Services.

| | | 8x10 Art Print S/3 FRoG.DuCK.TuRTLe more in ebay stor | | *Buy It Now* | $18.50 $3.50 | Jul-16 15:47 |
| | | RIBBON~FRAME~WOOD WALL LETTERS~NURSERY BABY DECOR~KIDS NEW**CHOOSE OWN DESIGN**MANY TO CHOOSE FROM** | | *Buy It Now* | $15.95 $4.50 | Jul-15 21:17 |

Because of the high price and minimal visual impact of this enhancement, I
can't recommend you use it.

Border

Want something a little more attention-getting than a bold title? How about
putting a frame around your listing?

The Border option puts a dark border around your listing on every search
results page, as shown in Figure 21.4. This option is more expensive than the
bold option, costing you $3.00. I don't think it's worth the money.

| | | *CUSTOM Canvas Letters*Name*N ursery*Kids*Baby*Wall*Art! *BY ERICA* Match your decor~ANY design! 8x10 R 5x7's | | *Buy It Now* | $13.00 $4.95 | Jul-11 15:55 |

Highlight

If you want to spend even more money, how about creating a *shaded* item
listing?

When you select the Highlight option, your listing (on any category or search
results page) is displayed with a colored shade, as shown in Figure 21.5. This
little bit of color will cost you $5.00—and, as with the bold option, I find it too
high-priced to recommend.

| | | Brand New Video Apple iPod 30GB 30 GB Free Case USA POWERSELLER Black Silicone Case Overnight Shipping | | *Buy It Now* | $289.00 $16.00 | 5d 15h 21m |
| | | APPLE IPOD 30GB VIDEO WHITE-FAST SHIPPING. SALE!! | | *Buy It Now* | $214.99 $19.99 | 5d 23h 50m |

Featured Plus!

The Featured Plus! option displays your item in the Featured Items section on the appropriate major category page, as well as in the Featured Items section at the top of any search results page, as shown in Figure 21.6. This option will set you back a whopping $19.95, and I can't recommend it; it puts your "featured" listing at the bottom of the page, which is hardly a prominent position!

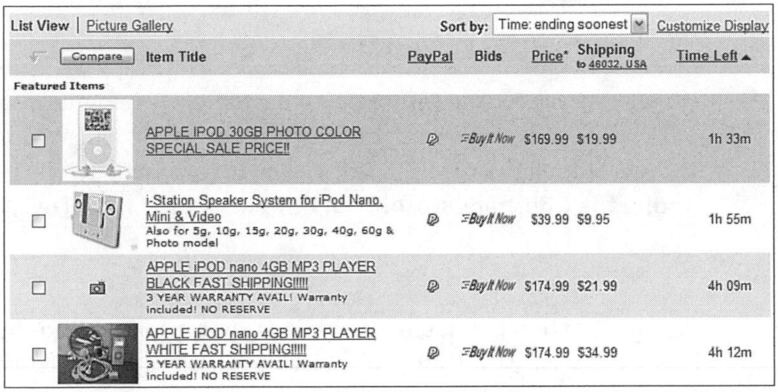

FIGURE 21.6

The Featured Items section at the top of a search results page.

Home Page Featured

Ever wonder how much it costs to have your item featured on the eBay home page? Here's the answer: $39.95. (And this option doesn't even guarantee how often your item will pop up. What a deal—*not*.) All you have to do is select the Home Page Featured option, and your item will *periodically* be displayed on the home page, as shown in Figure 21.7. (And for the same low price, your item also gets displayed in the Featured Items section of normal category and search results pages.) This is another option that I can't recommend, unless you're selling something really special.

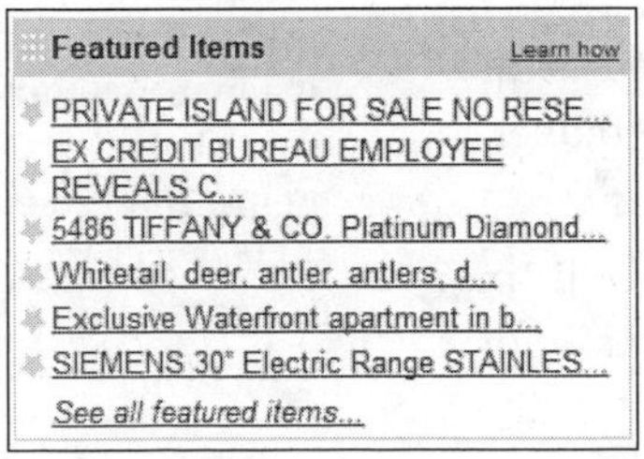

FIGURE 21.7

The Featured Items section in the middle of eBay's home page.

Gift Services

Think your item would make a great gift for a specific occasion? Then pony up $0.25 to add a Gift Services icon beside your item's listing, as shown in Figure 21.8.

FIGURE 21.8

An item enhanced with a Gift icon.

When you pay for the Gift option, you can also choose to promote any extra gift-related services you might offer—in particular, Gift Wrap/Gift Card, Express Shipping, or Ship to Gift Recipient. It's an okay option for some sellers during the Christmas season, but otherwise fairly ineffective.

Counter

This next option available is a free one—a hit counter that appears at the bottom of your item listing, as shown in Figure 21.9. When you opt to include a counter in your listing, you and (in most cases) potential bidders can see how many other users have visited the page. The more page visitors, the more likely you'll receive a substantial number of bids.

FIGURE 21.9

A hit counter at the bottom of an eBay listing page.

`01234`

You can choose from three different types of counters: a basic gray-on-black "odometer"-type counter; a green-on-black "retro-computer" style; and a "hidden" counter that is invisible to bidders but visible to you, the seller.

Should you add a counter to your listing? If you think you're going to get a lot of traffic to your item listing page, by all means display a counter. (It's free, after all.) A high number on a counter will

> **tip** eBay also offers two specially priced packages of listing enhancements that you may want to consider, if you want all the individual enhancements. The Value Pack offers the subtitle, gallery, and Listing Designer options for $0.65. The Pro Pack offers the bold, border, highlight, Gallery Featured, and Featured Plus! options for $29.95.

make bidders think they have to bid *now* to get in on the action. If, on the other hand, you don't want to tip your hand as to how many potential bidders you might have, go with the hidden counter. After all, it doesn't matter if you have 2 or 200 visitors, as long as you have one really good bid!

Skype Real-Time Communication

One of eBay's recent acquisitions was Skype, a company that offers Internet phone service—that is, the ability to make phone calls from your PC, over the Internet. Many people wondered just what Internet phone service had to do with online commerce, but here's what eBay had in mind.

Sellers now have the option, in many product categories, of including a Chat or Voice button in their listings. This lets potential buyers contact you in real time, using the Skype service, to ask any questions they might have about your listing. This option is free, if you choose to use it.

Should you offer live chat or voice contact for your buyers? This is one feature that most sellers are not supportive of, for the simple reason that offering live customer service costs money—even if the technology itself is free. To offer this real-time support, you have to be available to answer the live questions. That means putting yourself (or an employee) in front of your computer for hours on end, just in case somebody asks a question. That's a huge time expenditure.

One of the appealing things about an online business, for many sellers, is that they don't have to have constant one-on-one interaction with customers. That's what makes online retailing more cost-effective than a bricks-and-mortar retail store. Do you really want to take live calls from customers? Most sellers I know don't.

Even if you're a large seller, eBay's customer support option might not make sense. If you're large enough to have your own customer support department, you don't need eBay to offer this service for you. You can simply put your own toll-free number or email address in your auction listings, and answer customers questions through the normal channels. Tying into eBay's Skype-based support simply isn't necessary.

Does it sound like I have a strong opinion about eBay's real-time customer communication? I admit that I do. This smacks of being nothing more than an ill-guided attempt to justify an overpriced and poorly thought-out acquisition. It offers nothing to sellers except more work, and is unlikely to be embraced by many buyers. Avoid it.

e Right Pricing Option

learned way back in Chapter 1, "So You Want to Start an eBay Business...," when you have an item to sell, you can choose to sell it in one of several different ways. While the most traditional way to sell is via eBay's standard online auction process, you can also choose various auction and fixed-price options. Which of these options is best for you? Table 21.1 takes you through the basics.

Table 21.1   eBay Pricing Options

Pricing Option	Pros	Cons
Traditional online auction	Good for items where you're not sure of marketplace upside, and for rare and collectible items; familiar to all experienced eBay buyers	Bad for commodity items; never sure of final price or results; makes you wait seven days to make the sale
Reserve price auction	Good for high-priced items; good if you have a minimum price in mind but you don't want to publicize the price	Confusing to some buyers; could reduce the number of bids on an item
Dutch auction	Good if you have a large quantity of the same item that you believe has upside potential	Confusing to many buyers; if you simply want to sell a bunch of items at a given price, use a fixed-price listing instead
Auction with Buy It Now option	Good if you think you can sell an item at a given price, while still maintaining the familiarity of the auction process; good for commodity items	Reduces the upside of unrestrained bidding
Fixed-price listing (for a fixed listing period)	Good for commodity items; good if you have quantities of a single item	Reduces the upside of unrestrained bidding; might turn off some buyers who prefer the traditional auction process
Fixed-price listing in an eBay Store	Good for commodity items; good if you have quantities of a single item; a good way to "park" items between auctions	Items are not as visible as they are on the main eBay site; no pricing upside

In years past, I would have never advised sellers to run anything but a traditional auction or an auction with the Buy It Now option. Today, however, an increasing number of transactions on the eBay site are of the fixed-price variety; more and more sellers are going the fixed-price route, and more and more buyers are buying fixed-price or Buy It Now items that they can receive faster than they can if they bid on an item listed for a seven-day auction. (Plus, there's no guarantee that they'll win the auction; when they buy a fixed-price or Buy It Now item, they're placing an actual order.)

note There are even more pricing options you can choose from, beyond those discussed here. For example, eBay offers the Best Offer option, which lets potential buyers make you an offer below your listed price; there's also eBay's Want It Now feature, which lets you hook up with interested buyers who've made a request for a specific item. While it pays to check out these other options, the basic choice of auction versus fixed-price remains the most important decision to make.

Should you go the auction route or the fixed-price route? It all depends on the type of product you're selling, the type of competition you face (both on and off eBay), and your own business expectations. For many sellers, running a traditional auction with the Buy It Now option is a good compromise, the best of both worlds, as it were. But that's not the only way to go, or necessarily always the best. You have to make this choice for yourself.

Creating More Successful Auction Listings

In the preceding two chapters we discussed various ways to improve your auction sell-through and selling price. The factor that many users neglect, however, is the auction listing itself. Create a better auction listing, and you'll close more sales—at higher prices.

To make a more powerful auction listing, you need to pay attention to both content and style. That is, the words you write and the way you present those words (and pictures) on the page. You want to write more powerful words and present those words in an appealing fashion. Do so, and you'll notice the results.

Writing an Effective Item Listing

You can't neglect the basics. It's a fact that the better written and more effective your listing title and description, the more successful your auction will be. It's just like advertising copy: Great copy produces the best results.

Write a Title That SELLS!

Let's start right at the top, with the title of your item listing. You can use up to 55 letters, numbers, characters, and spaces, and you need to accomplish two things:

- You have to include the appropriate information so that anyone searching for a similar item will find your item in his or her search results.

- You have to make your title stand out from all the other titles on those long search results pages.

Let's tackle the first point first. Most bidders find the items they want by using eBay's search feature, so you have to construct your title so that it includes the words that people will be searching for.

To do this, you have to think like the people who will be looking for your item. Imagine how you would search for this specific item, and then include the right keywords into your item title to make your item pop up on as many search results pages as possible.

What words should you include in your title? Well, if your item has a model number or series name, that's definitely something to use. As an example, you might be selling a **1956 Gibson ES-175 Red Jazz Guitar**. This title gets in the year (1956), the manufacturer (Gibson), the model number (ES-175), the color (Red), and a brief description of what it is (a jazz guitar)—which pretty much covers all the bases.

Beyond including as many relevant facts as possible in your title, how do you make your title POP off the page and STAND OUT from all the other boring listings? Obviously, one technique is to employ the judicious use of CAPITAL LETTERS. The operative word here is *judicious*; titles with ALL capital letters step over the line into overkill.

Thinking like an advertising copywriter also pays off. What words almost always stop consumers in their tracks? Use attention-getting words such as **FREE** and **NEW** and **BONUS** and **EXTRA** and **DELUXE** and **RARE**—as long as these words truly describe the item you're selling and don't mislead the potential bidder. (And don't bump more important search words for these fluffier marketing terms—that won't help your item show up in bidder searches.)

You also need to make sure that your title "searches" well. That means adopting a few tricks that play to the way eBay's search engine works. For example, when describing an item in your title, you should use the full phrase or title

for the item. Leave out a word—even if it's the word "and"—and
won't come up as a hit on the search. For example, if you're selling a copy or
Robert Browning's *The Ring and the Book*, enter the entire book title in the title
field; if you enter only **Ring and Book**, you'll be excluded from the results of
anyone searching for the exact phrase "**The Ring and the Book**".

In short, use your title to both inform and attract attention—and include as
many potential search keywords as possible.

Write the Right Description

If the listing title is the headline of your ad, the listing description is your ad's
body copy. This means it's time to put on your copywriter's hat and get down
to the nitty-gritty details.

What makes for good copy? Remember, you have all the space you need
(there's no character limit, as there is with the item title), so say as much as
you need to say. You don't have to scrimp on words or leave anything out. If
you can describe your item adequately in a sentence, great; if it takes three
paragraphs, that's okay, too. (Just make sure you break your info into easily
digestible chunks; three short paragraphs are better than a single overly long
one!)

When you're writing the description for your ad, make sure you mention anything and everything that a potential bidder might need to know. Users expect
to see certain key data points in your item description; they include

- Name (or title)
- Condition (new, used, mint, and so on)
- Age (if it's a used item)
- Original use (if it's a used item)
- Value (if you know it)
- Important measurements, contents, colors, materials, and so on
- Any included accessories
- Any known defects or damage
- Warranty or guarantee (if you offer one)

When you're writing the item description, you need to put the most important
and motivating information in your initial paragraph, since a lot of folks
won't read any further than that. Think of your first paragraph like a lead
paragraph in a newspaper story: Grab 'em with something catchy, give them
the gist of the story, and lead them into reading the next paragraph and the
one after that.

Stress Benefits, Not Features

Although you need to be descriptive (and in some collectibles categories, you need to be *obsessively* so), it doesn't hurt to employ a little marketing savvy and salesmanship. Yes, you should talk about the features of your item, but it's even better if you can talk about your product's *benefits* to the potential buyer.

note If you use an abbreviation in the item title, you might want to spell out the entire term in the description—for the benefit of less knowledgeable bidders.

Let's say you're selling a used cordless phone, and the phone has a 50-number memory. Saying "50-number memory" is stating a feature; saying instead that the phone "lets you recall your 50 most-called phone numbers at the press of a button" is describing a benefit. Remember, a *feature* is something your item has; a *benefit* is something your item does for the user.

Use the Right Abbreviations

When dealing with some types of items, collectibles especially, you can use abbreviations and acronyms to describe the product's condition. This helps to conserve valuable space, especially in the listing's title.

For example, if you're describing an item that is in mint condition and still in its original box, you might use the abbreviation MIB, for "mint in box." If you're describing a new (not used) item of clothing that is missing its original tags, you might use the description NWOT, for "new without tags."

There are literally dozens of these common abbreviations you can use in your listing titles. See Appendix B, "Listing Abbreviations," for a complete list of these useful abbreviations.

Don't Reinvent the Wheel—Reuse Item Listings That Work

Here's another good reason to standardize the types of items you sell on eBay. Once you create the perfect item title and description, *reuse it*. That's right; there's no reason to write a new listing every time you put another item up for auction. Use the old cut and paste to recycle your winning title and description text. That's not to say you shouldn't tweak your copy over time, but once you come up with a winner, why change it? High-volume sellers use the same copy over and over—just as real-world advertisers do—for a simple reason. It works!

note One easy way to reuse an item listing is to use eBay's Sell Similar option, which lets you create a new listing based on an older one.

Creating Better-Looking Item Listings

Now it's time for the fun stuff—making your item listings look more attractive. Yes, we're talking style over substance, but style draws the eyeballs. So let's look at the various ways you can make your listings stand out from eBay's standard plain-text listings.

note The single most effective way to improve your item listings is to include a photograph of the item for sale. This is such an important step that I've devoted an entire chapter to the process. Turn to Chapter 23, "Displaying More Powerful Photographs," to learn more.

eBay's Listing Designer

We'll start with the listing templates that are available with eBay's Listing Designer. As you can see in Figure 22.1, Listing Designer is available to all users from the basic listing creation form—providing you pay the extra $0.10 per listing to use it.

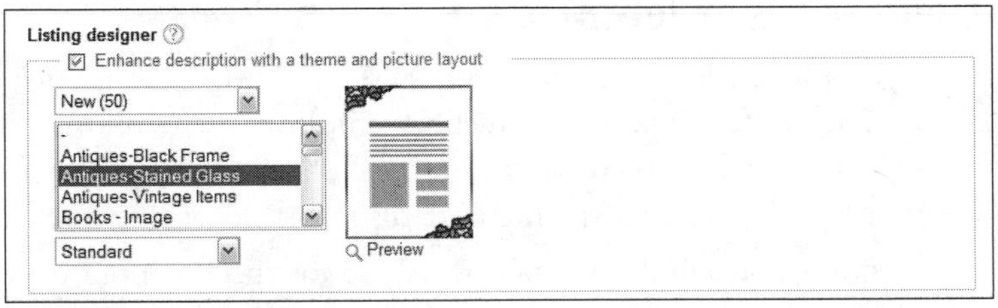

FIGURE 22.1

Any seller can use eBay's Listing Designer to choose a template for an item listing.

Listing Designer provides several hundred predesigned templates, which eBay calls *themes*. You choose a theme from the list and then choose a related picture layout. Listing Designer is easy to use and requires no additional software or ongoing subscription.

eBay Turbo Lister

The same themes that are available in Listing Designer are also available in eBay's Turbo Lister bulk listing software (pages.ebay.com/turbo_lister/). You choose your template on the Design Your Listing screen, shown in Figure 22.2. As you learned in Chapter 19, "Automating Auction Management," Turbo Lister is available free of charge—making it the listing creation software of choice for cost-conscious sellers.

FIGURE 22.2

Apply a theme to all your bulk listings with eBay Turbo Lister.

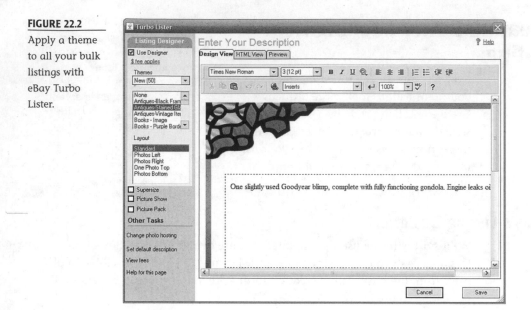

Downloadable Listing Templates

If you place a lot of listings, eBay's $0.10 Listing Designer fee can start to add up. Fortunately, lots of free auction templates are available for use; it's always good when you can cut your auction costs. (There are also several sites that offer templates for sale, which are also worth checking out.)

Most of these templates work by asking for specific input and then let you choose from a number of colors and designs. This generates a batch of HTML code, which you copy from the template site into eBay's standard listing creation form (using the Enter Your Own HTML tab). Other sites have pre-designed template code you can download to your own computer. The results are similar.

Here are some of the most popular of these auction template sites:

- Alou Web Design (www.alouwebdesign.ca/free-ebay-templates.htm)
- Antique-Central eZ Auction Template (www.antique-central.com/eztemplate.html)
- Auction AD Creator (www.auctionlotwatch.co.uk/auctionadcreator.html)
- Auction Insights (www.auctioninsights.info/templates/)
- Auction Riches Free Auction Ad Creator (www.auctionriches.com/freead/create.pl)

- Auction Template Central (www.auctiontemplatecentral.com)
- Bay Dream Design (www.bay-dream.com)
- Auction Writer (www.auctionwriter.com)
- AuctionFlash (www.auctionflash.com)
- AuctionSpice (www.auctionspice.com)
- AuctionSupplies.com Free Auction Templates (auctionsupplies.com/templates/)
- BiggerBids (www.biggerbids.com)
- Birddogs Garage (www.birddogsgarage.com)
- DeadZoom (www.deadzoom.com/auction-template/)
- DeSa C.S. (www.desacs.com)
- Free Auction Help (www.freeauctionhelp.com/free_auction_template.htm)
- K&D Web Page Design (www.kdwebpagedesign.com)
- ListTailor (www.listtailor.com/quickstart.html)
- Nucite Auction Templates (members.nucite.com)
- RobsHelp.com FreeForm Builer (www.robshelp.com)
- SaverSites (www.saversites.com/services_ebay_auction_templates.htm)
- Two Wizards Designs (www.2wiz.net/dtemplates1.shtml)
- The Ultimate eBay Resource (www.sellingonebay.info/templates.html)
- Wizard's Free Auction Template Creation Form (www.ambassadorboard.net/hosting/free-form.php)
- Xample.net Auction Templates (www.xample.net/templates.htm)
- Woo Woo Designs (www.woowoodesigns.com)

Third-Party Listing Tools

Back in Chapter 19, we talked about third-party bulk listing tools. Most of these third-party tools also help you create fancy-looking listings, using a variety of predesigned templates.

Most of these tools work in a similar fashion. You go to a particular web page or program screen, select a template from a list, choose available layout options, and then enter your normal listing title and description. You'll see a preview of what your listing will look like; if you like the way it looks, click a button to post the listing on the eBay site and start your auction.

Here are some of the most popular of these third-party listing-creation tools:

- Ándale Lister (www.andale.com)
- Auction Hawk (www.auctionhawk.com)
- Auction Lizard (www.auction-lizard.com)
- Auction Wizard 2000 (www.auctionwizard2000.com)
- AuctionSage (www.auctionsage.com)
- AuctionTamer (www.auctiontamer.com)
- Auctiva (www.auctiva.com)
- ChannelAdvisor Pro (www.channeladvisor.com)
- eBay Blackthorne Basic (pages.ebay.com/blackthorne/basic.html)
- eBay Blackthorne Pro (pages.ebay.com/blackthorne/pro.html)
- eBay Turbo Lister (pages.ebay.com/turbo_lister/)
- inkFrog (www.inkfrog.com)
- Vendio (www.vendio.com)

note Want to learn more about creating your own auction templates? Then check out my companion book, *eBay Auction Template Starter Kit* (Que, 2006), which offers advice and instruction for choosing third-party listing templates or building your own templates from scratch, using HTML. The book even comes with a free CD chock-full of free auction templates, that you can use in your own eBay auctions.

Using HTML in Your Listings

Here's a secret known to successful sellers: eBay lets you use HTML to spruce up your item listings. While this isn't a task for the faint of heart, writing your own code lets you create highly individualized item listings—much fancier than you can do with a template-driven listing creator.

How HTML Works

HTML coding might sound difficult, but it's really pretty easy. HTML is really nothing more than a series of hidden codes that tell web browsers how to display different types of text and graphics. The codes are embedded in a document, so you can't see them; they're visible only to your web browser.

These codes are distinguished from normal text by the fact that they're enclosed within angle brackets. Each particular code turns on or off a particular attribute, such as boldface or italic text. Most codes are in sets of "on/off" pairs. You turn "on" the code before the text you want to affect and then turn "off" the code after the text.

For example, the code <h1> turns specified type into a level-one headline; the code </h1> turns off the headline type. The code <i> is used to italicize text; </i> turns off the italics. (As you can see, an "off" code is merely the "on" code with a slash before it.)

Entering HTML Codes

You enter HTML codes while you're creating your item listing. Just go to the Describe Your Item page, scroll down to the Description box, and click the HTML Mode option. When the box changes to the HTML editor view, as shown in Figure 22.3, enter your code in the box. You can switch back to normal text editing mode to view the results of your code.

FIGURE 22.3

Enter your own HTML code when creating your eBay auction listing.

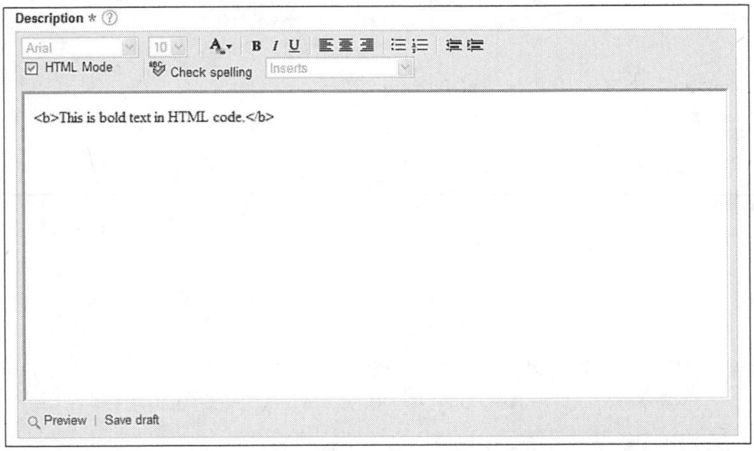

Description * (?)

Arial   10   A▾ B I U   ☰ ☰ ☰ ☰ ☰ ☰ ☰
☑ HTML Mode   ✓ Check spelling   Inserts

This is bold text in HTML code.

Q Preview | Save draft

While most users enter HTML code directly into the listing creation form, you can create your code in another application and then cut and paste it into the Description box. The only thing you have to remember is that the pasted code must be in plain-text format—you can't paste a Word document into the box.

For example, I typically use Windows Notepad to create short amounts of HTML code. I'll actually save some boilerplate code in a Notepad file and then edit it for my individual ads. It's very easy to cut from Notepad and then paste into the

note If all you want to do is add some bold or color text to your listing, you don't have to learn HTML or use fancy listing-creation tools. eBay's standard text editor is available when you create your item listing with the Sell Your Item form. It lets you add HTML effects in a WYSIWYG environment, much the same way you add boldface and italics in your word processor. Just highlight the text you want to format and then click the appropriate formatting button. No manual coding necessary.

Description box. And I can save the code I use in a Notepad file, so it can be reused in multiple auction listings.

Codes to Format Your Text

We'll start off with some of the most common HTML codes—those used to format your text. Table 22.1 shows some of these text-formatting codes you can use in your item description.

Table 22.1   HTML Codes to Format Text

Effect	On Code	Off Code
Bold	\<b\>	\</b\>
Strong (bold)	\<strong\>	\</strong\>
Italic	\<i\>	\</i\>
Emphasis (italic)	\<em\>	\</em\>
Underline	\<u\>	\</u\>
Center	\<center\>	\</center\>
First-level headline	\<h1\>	\</h1\>
Second-level headline	\<h2\>	\</h2\>
Third-level headline	\<h3\>	\</h3\>

Just surround the text you want to format with the appropriate on and off codes, and you're ready to go. For example, to format a piece of text as bold, you'd write something that looks like this:

`<b>this text is bold</b>`

Codes for Font Type, Size, and Color

You can also use HTML to specify a particular font type or size, using the \<font\> code.

To specify a font type for selected text, use the \<font\> code with the `face` attribute, like this:

`<font face="xxxx">text</font>`

Replace the *xxxx* with the specific font, such as Arial or Times Roman—in quotation marks.

Another common use of the `<font>` code is to specify type size. You use the `size` attribute, and the code looks like this:

`<font size="xx">`text**`</font>`**

Replace the *xx* with the size you want, from –6 to +6, with –6 being the smallest, +6 being the biggest, and 0 (or no size specified) being "normal" size type.

You can also use the `<font>` code to designate a specific text color. In this instance, you use the `color` attribute, like this:

`<font color="#xxxxxx">`text**`</font>`**

Replace the *xxxxxx* with the code for a specific color. Table 22.2 lists some basic color codes.

Table 22.2   Common HTML Color Codes

Color	Code
Black	000000
White	FFFFFF
Gray	808080
Silver	C0C0C0
Yellow	FFFF00
Orange	FFA500
Brown	A52A2A
Red	FF0000
Maroon	800000
Olive	808000
Fuchsia	FF00FF
Chartreuse	7FFF00
Green	008000
Lime	00FF00
Teal	008080
Aqua	00FFFF
Navy	000080
Blue	0000FF
Purple	800080
Violet	EE88EE

If you don't want to bother with learning hexadecimal color codes, you also have the option of simply entering the actual name of the color (still within quotation marks, of course). While this limits you to a handful of primary colors, it's easier than remembering all the detailed codes. For example, to rewrite our previous red text example, you use the following simplified code:

note By the way, the twenty colors listed in Table 22.2 are just a fraction of the available colors you can use in your auction listings. To view all available colors, consult one of the many web-based HTML color charts, such as the ones at `www.immigration-usa.com/html_colors.html` and `www.html-color-codes.com`.

`<font color="red">red text</font>`

Codes for Paragraphs, Line Breaks, and Rules

Some of the simplest HTML codes let you break your text into separate lines and paragraphs—and add horizontal rules between paragraphs. These codes are inserted into your text just once; there are no matching ending codes.

Table 22.3 lists these "on-only" codes.

Table 22.3   HTML Codes for Lines and Paragraphs

Action	Code
Line break	` `
New paragraph	`<p>`
Horizontal rule (line)	`<hr>`

Codes for Graphics

Adding pictures to your item listings really brings some excitement to the normally plain-text world of eBay. While you can add pictures the eBay way (via the Sell Your Item page), you can also add pictures in the middle of your item description, using HTML.

Before you can insert a graphic into your listing, you need to know the address of that graphic (in the form of a web page URL). Then you use the following code:

`<img src="URL">`

No off code is required for inserted graphics. Note that the location is enclosed in quotation marks—and that you have to insert the `http://` part of the URL.

> **note** eBay allows links to pages that provide additional information about the item listed, additional photos of the item, and your other eBay auctions. eBay prohibits links to pages that attempt to sell merchandise outside eBay. Link at your own risk.

Codes for Links

You can use HTML to add links to your own personal web pages (a great idea if you have additional images of this specific item) or to related sites. Many sellers also like to provide a direct email link in case potential bidders have questions they need answered.

To insert a link to another web page in your item listing, you use the following HTML code:

```
<a href="URL">this is the link</a>
```

The text between the on and off codes will appear onscreen as a typical underlined hyperlink; when users click that text, they'll be linked to the URL you specified in the code. Note that the URL is enclosed in quotation marks and that you have to include the `http://` part of the address.

You can also create a mail-to link in your listing; users will be able to send email to you by simply clicking the link. Here's the code for a mail-to link:

```
<a href="mailto:yourname@domain.com">click here to email me</a>
```

Codes for Tables

Believe it or not, tables are key to creating some of the more interesting auction listing effects. You create a table and then format the cells within the table however you like—and put whatever you like within each cell. Used correctly, a table creates an invisible (or visible, if you like) grid that lets you align multiple text and graphic items within your listing.

You start by enclosing your table with `<table>` and `</table>` codes. Then you enclose each individual row in the table with `<tr>` and `</tr>` codes and each cell in each row with `<td>` and `</td>` codes.

A basic table with two rows and two columns (four cells total) is coded like this:

```
<table>
<tr>
<td>row 1 cell 1</td>
<td>row 1 cell 2</td>
</tr>
<tr>
<td>row 2 cell 1</td>
<td>row 2 cell 2</td>
</tr>
</table>
```

Within any individual cell in your table, you can insert any type of item—plain text, formatted text, bulleted lists, background shading, and even graphics. Figure 22.4 shows what this simple table looks like (with borders separating the cells—as described next).

FIGURE 22.4

A simple two-column, two-row table.

row 1 cell 1	row 1 cell 2
row 2 cell 1	row 2 cell 2

You can also use HTML to format both a table as a whole and the cells within the table, to some degree:

- To dictate the width of the table border, use the `<table border="`*xx*`">` code, where *xx* is in pixels. (A border value of "1" is common.)

- To specify the border color, use the `<table bordercolor="`*xxxxxx*`">` code, where *xxxxxx* is the color hex code.

- To shade the background of an individual cell, use the `<td bgcolor="#`*xxxxxx*`">` code, where *xxxxxx* is the color hex code.

note I've shown just a handful of the huge number of HTML codes available to you. If you want to learn more about these and other HTML codes, I recommend that you go to the HTML Goodies (www.htmlgoodies.com/tutors/) website. You can also pick up a copy of *Sams Teach Yourself HTML and CSS in 24 Hours, 7th Edition*, by Dick Oliver and Michael Morrison (Sams, 2005), available wherever good books are sold; this book is a great primer for creating your own web pages with HTML. And Nicholas Case's *Easy HTML for eBay* (Que, 2004) offers a variety of eBay-specific code you can use in all your auction listings.

■ To dictate the width of a cell, use the `<td width="xx%">` code, where *xx* is a percentage of the total table width; for example, `<td width="50%">` specifies a cell that is 50% of the total table width. You can also specify an exact width, in pixels, like this: `<td width=xxx`, where *xxx* is the number of pixels wide.

Ready-to-Use HTML Templates

Let's look at two examples of graphically appealing ads created with simple HTML codes. You can use these codes exactly as printed in your own listings. Just copy the code—character for character—into the Enter Your Own HTML tab in the Description box in the Sell Your Item page, and insert your own description in place of my generic sample text.

Second-Column Details

The first example, shown in Figure 22.5, is an all-text listing that uses a simple two-column, single-row table. The left column is designed to hold the ad's headline and the bulk of the descriptive copy; the thinner right column holds a bulleted list of item details and features.

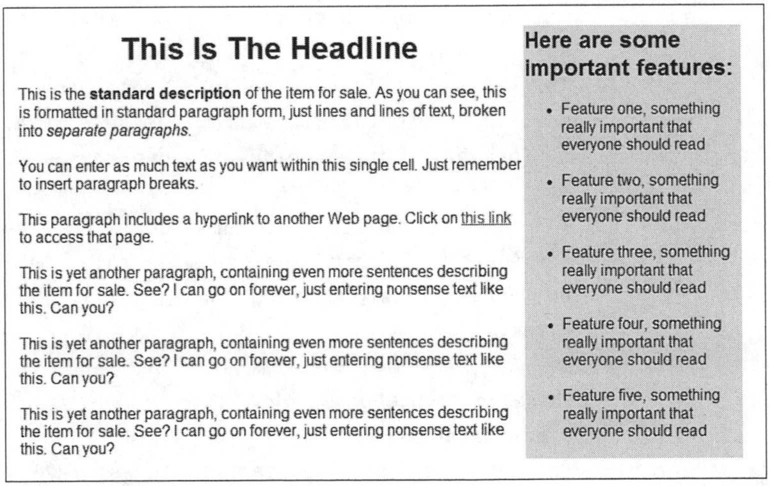

FIGURE 22.5

A two-column listing, with bulleted copy in the subsidiary shaded column.

This Is The Headline

This is the **standard description** of the item for sale. As you can see, this is formatted in standard paragraph form, just lines and lines of text, broken into *separate paragraphs*.

You can enter as much text as you want within this single cell. Just remember to insert paragraph breaks.

This paragraph includes a hyperlink to another Web page. Click on this link to access that page.

This is yet another paragraph, containing even more sentences describing the item for sale. See? I can go on forever, just entering nonsense text like this. Can you?

This is yet another paragraph, containing even more sentences describing the item for sale. See? I can go on forever, just entering nonsense text like this. Can you?

This is yet another paragraph, containing even more sentences describing the item for sale. See? I can go on forever, just entering nonsense text like this. Can you?

Here are some important features:

• Feature one, something really important that everyone should read

• Feature two, something really important that everyone should read

• Feature three, something really important that everyone should read

• Feature four, something really important that everyone should read

• Feature five, something really important that everyone should read

Here's the code you use to create that ad:

```
<table border="0">
    <tr>
        <td width="70%">
            <font face="Arial">
            <center><h1>This Is The Headline</h1></center>
            <p>
            This is the <b>standard description</b> of the item
            for sale. As you can see, this is formatted in
            standard paragraph form, just lines and lines of
            text, broken into <i>separate paragraphs</i>.
            <p>
            You can enter as much text as you want within this
            single cell. Just remember to insert paragraph breaks.
            <p>
            This paragraph includes a hyperlink to another Web page.
            Click on <a href="http://www.molehillgroup.com">this
            link</a> to access that page.
            <p>
            This is yet another paragraph, containing even more
            sentences describing the item for sale. See? I can go
            on forever, just entering nonsense text like this. Can you?
            <p>
            This is yet another paragraph, containing even more
            sentences describing the item for sale. See? I can go
            on forever, just entering nonsense text like this. Can you?
            <p>
            This is yet another paragraph, containing even more
            sentences describing the item for sale. See? I can go
            on forever, just entering nonsense text like this. Can you?
            </font>
        </td>
        <td bgcolor="#DDDDDD" width="30%">
            <font face="Arial">
            <h2>Here are some important features:</h2>
            <p>
            <ul>
                <li>Feature one, something really important that
                everyone should read</li>
```

```
<p>
<li>Feature two, something really important that
  everyone should read</li>
<p>
<li>Feature three, something really important that
  everyone should read</li>
<p>
<li>Feature four, something really important that
  everyone should read</li>
<p>
<li>Feature five, something really important that
  everyone should read</li>
        </ul>
        </font>
      </td>
    </tr>
</table>
</font>
```

You can add a picture to this listing by inserting the appropriate <img> code in either the left or right cell of the table.

Big Picture, Colored Background

The next example is even easier than the first. You create another two-column, one-row table. This time, though, don't bother to set the column widths. This way, the columns size naturally, based on their contents.

The contents in this ad are pretty simple. The left column contains a picture of your item, and the right column contains a brief description (in large text). The table background is all blue, and you reverse the text out of the background by coloring the text white.

The whole thing is preceded by a large colored headline above the table. The completed ad looks like Figure 22.6.

Here's the code you use to create that ad:

```
<h1><center><font color="#FF0000">This Is The Headline
<br>
On Two Lines, In Color!</font></center></h1>
<p>
<center>
```

```
<table bgcolor="#0000FF">
   <tr>
      <td>
         <img src="http://www.webserver.com/picture.jpg">
      </td>
      <td>
         <center><h2><font color="#FFFFFF">Look at this item!
         <p>
         It's really cool!
         <p>
         You should buy it!
         <p>
         Send me all your money <i>now!</i></font></center></h2>
      </td>
   </tr>
</table>
</center>
```

FIGURE 22.6

Another table ad, with the picture on the left and the description on the right.

Obviously, you can add as much text as you want in the right-hand cell—or additional pictures on the left.

note Use these examples as basic templates, and then add your own codes to see what results.

Displaying More Powerful Photographs

Showing a picture of your product in your item listing greatly increases your chances of success. It also helps to increase the average selling price of your item.

Managing product photos is an important part of any successful eBay business. You need to learn how to take good photos of your products and how to insert those photos into your item listings. It isn't hard, once you get it figured out—but it does require some small degree of photographic skill and mastery of a photo editing software program. So clean off your camera lens and get ready to shoot—it's time to learn all about photography for eBay!

Taking Effective Photos

Taking an effective product photo takes a bit of effort; it's not quite as easy as snapping off a quick Polaroid. To take quality photos of the items you intend to sell, you'll need a decent digital camera and a variety of photographic accessories, including

- Digital camera
- Tripod
- Lighting
- Clean space with plain black or white background
- Photo editing software

Let's take a detailed look at what's involved.

Shopping for a Digital Camera

Although you can take pictures with a normal film camera, develop the film, and have a film processing lab transfer your photos to graphics files on a photo CD, that's a lot of work. Much better to start with digital photos at the source by using a digital camera to take all your product photos. You can pick up a low-end digital camera as little as $100 these days, and going direct from camera to computer to eBay is a lot easier than any other method.

What type of digital camera should you buy? The good news is that you don't need a really high-end model. In fact, if you buy a super-expensive camera with multi-megapixel resolution, you'll just be wasting a lot of the camera's picture-taking power. When it comes to putting pictures on eBay, you actually need to take relatively low-resolution pictures, so all those megapixels are pretty much photographic overkill.

That doesn't mean you can get by with the cheapest camera available, however. To take good product photos, you want a camera with a quality lens, preferably with at least 3X optical zoom, and with a macro mode. (You use the macro mode to take close-up photos of those very small items you have for sale.) Make sure you can easily configure the camera for low-resolution mode and that there's a quick and simple way to get your photographs from your camera to your computer's hard disk.

Don't Forget the Accessories

When you're spending $200 or more for a decent digital camera, keep a few bucks back for those accessories that will help you take better photos every time. In particular, you'll want to invest in a tripod and auxiliary lighting.

note A good lighting kit to consider is the KT500 from Smith-Victor (www.smithvictor.com). It includes two 250-watt lamps with 10-inch reflectors and stands, for about $135—good enough for most eBay product photography.

A tripod is invaluable for steadying your camera when you're taking photographs. A tripod will help you avoid camera shake and corresponding blurry pictures. It's also useful in low-light situations, where you need to hold your camera especially still for long exposures. And it's not expensive; you can pick up a decent tripod for less than $20.

Of course, you can avoid the low-light problem by using auxiliary lighting. While you might think you have enough natural light to take good photos, you probably don't. A set of low-cost photo floodlights will provide the lighting necessary to take the ultra-sharp photos your customers expect. You can find two-piece lighting kits for under $150.

While we're talking about lights, consider investing a few more bucks for diffuser screens. You get better results when your subject is lit by diffused lighting; direct lighting is a little harsh and can cause glare. Look for a diffuser you can attach directly to your light reflectors.

And if you sell a lot of smaller items, you may want to consider some sort of light box. These are small enclosures into which you place the item to be photographed; the enclosure includes internal lighting or diffusion, and you take your photo from an opening on the side or top of the box. You can purchase these light boxes from Cloud Dome (www.clouddome.com), Cubelite (www.cubelite.com), Litesate (www.litestage.com), and similar companies.

Finally, think about where you'll be taking your photos. You'll need some sort of flat surface, and some sort of simple background—either flat black or white. That might necessitate buying a small table and an appropriate expanse of colored cardboard or cloth. Even better, although a bit more expensive, is a roll of colored photographic background paper, which provides a professional-looking seamless background.

How to Take a Good Photograph

Once you have the proper equipment, taking a good product photo is as simple as following these steps:

1. Prepare the photo area. Clear off a good-sized flat surface, and cover the surface and background with a plain white, black, or gray material. (Use a light background for dark objects and a dark background for lighter objects.)

2. Position the product in the middle of the photo area, at an angle that best shows off the product's visual attributes.

3. Position your floodlights to the sides and slightly in front of the item, as shown in Figure 23.1. (If you have a third light, position it to the back and below the object, to provide a slight amount of backlighting.)

FIGURE 23.1

Position auxiliary lighting to best effect.

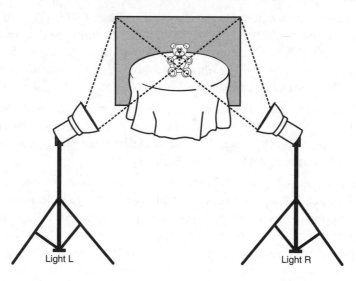

Light L   Light R

4. Mount your camera to the tripod, and position it directly in front of the object to be photographed.

5. Start shooting!

The result should be a focused, well-lit, centered photograph, like the one in Figure 23.2.

FIGURE 23.2
FIGURE 23.2
A good product
photo—it's easy
to see what
you're selling.

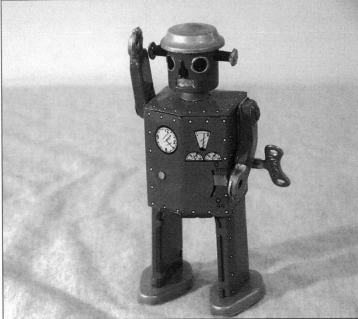

It's important that you don't just snap off a quick picture and move on. You need to shoot your item from several different angles and distances. And remember to get a close-up of any important area of the item, such as a serial number or a damaged area. You may want to include multiple photos in your listing, or just have a good selection of photos to choose from for that one best picture. Remember, it's always good to have a backup photo, just in case you messed up the first one!

Five Types of Pictures *Not* to Take

Okay, you're saying. You know how to take a good picture. Let's just get on with it!

Not so fast, pal. I've seen enough eBay listings to realize that most people who say they know how to take good photos don't. Let's look at five cardinal sins of product photography and how you can avoid them.

Blurry Picture

See the photo in Figure 23.3? See how blurry it is? That's because the picture was taken *without a tripod*. The camera wasn't held steady, and it moved slightly while the photograph was being taken. The result is a blurry photograph where it's hard to see what the product is—let alone make out fine details.

FIGURE 23.3

A blurry picture—the result of moving the camera when shooting.

A better approach is to mount your camera to a tripod. The results will be clear and crisp—just what you want for your item listing.

By the way, blurry photos can also result from not focusing the camera lens properly. If your camera has autofocus, make sure that it is aimed at the product, and not at the background or another object. If you're focusing manually, do a better job!

Picture Too Dark

Another common mistake amateur photographers make is to shoot the picture without enough light. Figure 23.4 shows the result of inadequate lighting. See how the picture is just too dark, with the details almost completely obscured?

FIGURE 23.4

The picture's too dark—you didn't use enough lighting!

How can you ensure that you have enough light for your picture? Here are your options:

- Buy a set of auxiliary lights. One light helps but can still result in unwanted shadows. Two lights are better because they'll fill out any unlit areas.

- Shoot outdoors. This is the poor man's lighting solution, but it works. Try to shoot in early morning or late afternoon, when you get a softer, less severe light; avoid shooting in the harsh overhead light of midday. Even better—shoot in the shade by the side of a building.

- Use a flash. Most cameras include a built-in flash, which can shine a ton of light directly onto the front surface of the item being photographed. Watch out for glare and washout, however—as discussed in the next section.

Too Much Flash

Casual photographers are tempted to use the flash whenever they shoot indoors. Used properly, flash can be a good thing. Too much flash, however, can cause the object to wash out. Flash is also bad when

note Inadequate lighting—or shooting under fluorescent lights—can also affect the color of your photos. More light generally results in more accurate colors.

you're shooting a glossy object or a product that's encased in plastic or shrink wrap. Figure 23.5 shows the type of glare you can get from a flash photo.

FIGURE 23.5

Flash photography can produce glare on shrink-wrapped products.

Subject Too Small

Look at the object in Figure 23.6. It's so far away it seems as if the photographer was afraid to get any closer! You need to get that product up front and center, close enough to the camera so that your customers can see what you're selling. You want the object to fill up the entire picture. That means getting close with your camera, using your camera's zoom lens, or cropping the photo in the editing process.

Subject Doesn't Stand Out

You'd think you'd know better. Shooting your object against a busy background, as shown in Figure 23.7, detracts from the main point of the photograph. The background competes with the object you're trying to sell, which is less than ideal.

FIGURE 23.6
Bad composition—the object's way too small!

FIGURE 23.7
There's too much happening here. What are you trying to sell?

It's far better to remove all competing objects from the picture and hang a white or black sheet (or T-shirt) behind the item. This makes the main object stand out better—and increases the sex appeal of your product.

Scanning Instead of Shooting

You don't always have to photograph the items you want to sell. If you're selling relatively flat items (books, comics, CDs, DVDs, and so on), you might be better off with a scanner than a camera. Just lay the object on a flatbed scanner, and scan the item into a digital file on your computer. Scanning something like a book or a DVD case is actually easier than taking a picture of it. You don't have to worry about lighting, or focus, or any of that. And when you're scanning compact discs, take the CD booklet out of the jewel case to scan, instead of scanning the jewel case itself.

Here's something else: Since your scanner operates just like a camera, you can scan practically anything you can fit on the glass. The item at hand doesn't even have to be perfectly flat. Just about any item in a box can be easily scanned, as can many other small objects. When in doubt, test it.

Editing Your Photos—Digitally

When you're taking a digital photo or making a scan, you want to save your images in the JPG file format. This is the default file format for most digital cameras and scanners, although some devices give you a choice of other formats (GIF, TIF, and so on). The JPG format is the de facto standard for web images and what eBay expects for your item listings. Given the choice, choose JPG.

With your photos in JPG format, you can easily touch them up with digital photo editing software. What kind of touch-up are we talking about? Here's a list of the most common photo editing operations:

- Lighten up photos shot in low light
- Correct the color in poorly shot photos
- Crop the picture to focus only on the subject at hand
- Resize the image to fit better in your eBay listings
- Decrease the resolution or color count to produce a smaller-sized file

If you're a perfect photographer, you may never need to touch up the pictures you take. But since most of us are far from perfect, it's great to be able to

"punch up" the photos we take—and make them as per
eBay listings.

Choosing Image Editing Software

To edit your photos, you need a software program designed to edit digital photographs. There are a lot of programs out there, some free and some tremen-
dously expensive. (Adobe Photoshop, used by many professional
photographers, falls into the latter category.) You want something in the middle—a low-cost program that's easy to use and includes all the image editing
features you need to create quality product photos.

There are a number of easy-to-use, low-cost programs available. The most
popular among eBay users include

- Adobe Photoshop Elements (www.adobe.com)
- IrfanView (www.irfanview.com)
- Paint Shop Pro (www.corel.com)
- Picasa (picasa.google.com)
- Microsoft Digital Image (www.microsoft.com/products/imaging/)
- Roxio PhotoSuite (www.roxio.com)

Most of these programs cost less than $100 and have similar features. (And
Picasa and IrfanView are free!) I personally use Photoshop Elements, but any
of these programs should do the job for you.

Resizing Your Pictures for Best Effect

While you're editing, you'll probably need to resize your photographs to best
fit within your eBay listings. Most pictures you take with a digital camera will
come out too big to fit on a web page without scrolling. Even the smallest digital photos are typically sized at 640 × 480—that's 640 pixels wide, which is
too wide to fit comfortably on most computer screens.

eBay recommends that you size your image to no more than 400 pixels high
by 400 pixels wide—unless you're using the Supersize option, which can
accept photos up to 800 × 800. This is particularly important if you use eBay
Picture Services, which will compress any larger pictures to these dimensions.
The results of this compression are yucky-looking pictures, so either resize to
fit or use a different picture-hosting service—which we'll discuss in a moment.

Personally, I find the 400 pixels-wide requirement okay in most instances, but
will sometimes go up to 500 or even 600 pixels wide, depending on the item

photographed and the importance of viewing item detail. I won't go over 600 pixels, however.

While you're considering the physical size of the photograph, you should also consider the size of the file that holds the photograph. The bigger the file, the longer it takes to download from the Internet. Create too big a file, and users won't want to wait to view your item listing.

The right file size is something less than 50KB—and less is better. Holding the files under the 50KB level keeps the loading time for each photo down to a reasonable level.

Your photo editing software should include settings that let you reduce both the physical size and the file size for your photographs. And, of course, the two go hand in hand: Reduce the physical size, and you'll also reduce the file size.

Adding Photos to Your Item Listings

When you have your photos properly edited, it's time to add photos to your item listings. The easiest way to add a photo to an item listing is to use eBay's picture management services and choose the appropriate options when you're creating your item listings. You also have the option of using third-party image management services; we'll look at both options.

Using eBay Picture Services

When you have eBay host your photos, you have some choices to make. If you want to show only one picture, eBay's built-in picture management is a good choice. It's free (for a single picture), and you can use the Listing Designer (discussed in Chapter 22, "Creating More Successful Auction Listings") to choose the right position for your photo.

If you want to include more than one photo in your ad, you'll have to pay for it. Here's how eBay's fee structure works:

- First photo: Free
- Each additional picture (up to six, total): $0.15 each
- Picture Show (multiple pictures in a slideshow format): Free
- Supersize pictures (allow users to click a photo to display at a larger size): $0.75
- Picture pack (up to six pictures, supersized, with Gallery display): $1.00—or $1.50 for from seven to twelve photos

You can see how the costs start to add up. Let's say you have two pictures of your item (front and back, perhaps) that you want to display large. You'll pay $0.90 for this privilege ($0.15 for the second picture, plus $0.75 for supersizing). As you can see, if you have more than one photo in your listing, finding another site to host your pictures might be cheaper, which we'll talk about in the next section.

If you choose to use eBay to manage your photos, you do so from the Pictures section of the listing creation form. Click the Add Pictures button and when the Add Pictures window appears, select the Enhance tab, shown in Figure 23.8. Now you should click the Add Pictures button in the first (top left) box. An Open dialog box now appears on your computer desktop; use this dialog box to locate and select the photo you want to use. Click the Open button when done; the photo you selected now appears in the Add Pictures window.

FIGURE 23.8

Using eBay Picture Services to insert photos in your item listing.

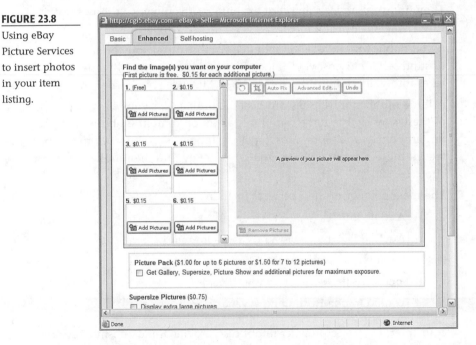

To insert an additional picture (for $0.15 extra), click the Add Picture button in the second box and repeat the previous instructions. To insert even more pictures, click the Add Picture button(s) in the next box(es) and repeat the instructions again.

When you're done adding pictures, you'll need to select which picture options you want—Standard, Supersize Pictures, Picture Show, or Picture Pack. This done, click the Upload Pictures button to upload the selected photos from your computer to eBay.

note If you choose to use eBay's Listing Designer, return to the listing creation page, scroll to the Listing Designer section, and select a position for your photo(s) from the layout list.

That's it. eBay will automatically upload the pictures from your hard disk to its picture hosting server and automatically insert those pictures into your item listing.

Using Third-Party Image Management Services

Many experienced sellers choose not to use eBay's picture hosting service. They find this service somewhat expensive (if you want to show a lot of pictures) and somewhat limited.

If you don't want to let eBay manage your pictures, you can use another web hosting service to host your image files and then manually insert these pictures into your item listings using the HTML code you learned in Chapter 22.

A large number of websites will host picture files for your eBay auctions. Most of these sites charge some sort of fee, either on a monthly basis for a certain amount of storage space or on a per-picture basis. You'll want to compare the fees at these sites with what you'll pay at eBay and then make the smart choice.

The most popular of these services include

- Ándale Images (www.andale.com)
- Auction Pix Image Hosting (www.auctionpix.com)
- Photobucket (www.photobucket.com)
- PictureTrail (www.picturetrail.com)
- Vendio Image Hosting (www.vendio.com)

Your Internet service provider might also provide image hosting services, often for free. Many ISPs give their users a few megabytes of file storage space as part of their monthly service; you may be able to upload your photos to your ISP's server and then link to that server in your eBay item listings.

Inserting a Single Photo—the Easy Way

After you have your pictures uploaded, you can then add them to your new item listing. If you're adding a single photo, you can do so when you're creating your item listing. You do this from the Pictures section of the listing creation form. After you click the Add Pictures button to display the Add Pictures window, select the Self-Hosting tab, shown in Figure 23.9. Now you should enter the full web address of your photo into the Picture URL box. If you have multiple photos, check the Picture Show option and follow the onscreen instructions to add additional URLs; otherwise, click the Upload Pictures button and continue with the rest of the listing creation process, as normal.

FIGURE 23.9

Pointing to a picture file uploaded to another hosting service.

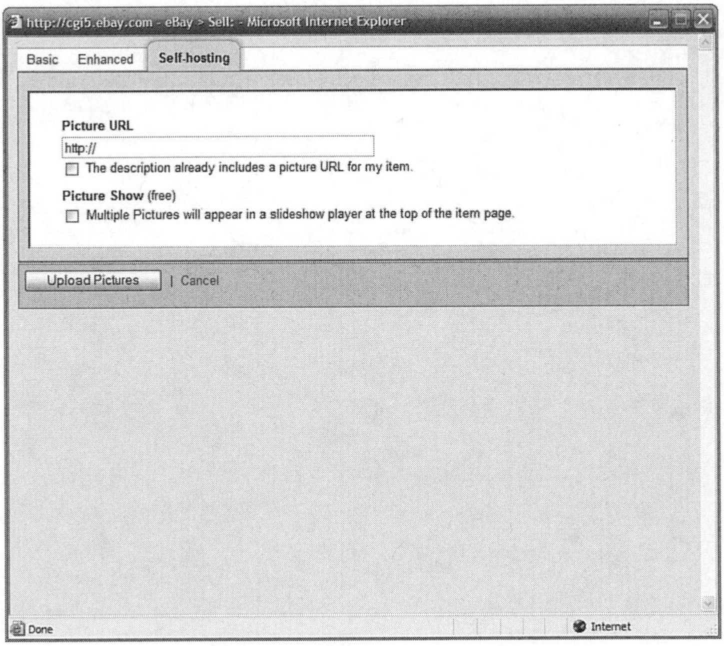

That's it. Your completed listing will now include the photograph you linked to. Simple as that.

Inserting Photos via HTML

As you learned in Chapter 22, you can include HTML code in your item descriptions—and you can use this code to link to pictures you've already uploaded to an image hosting service. This process isn't as hard as it sounds, assuming you've already found a hosting service, uploaded your picture file, and obtained the full URL for the uploaded picture. All you have to do is insert the following HTML code into your item description, where you want the picture to appear:

```
<img src="http://www.webserver.com/picture.jpg">
```

Just replace *www.webserver.com/picture.jpg* with the correct URL for your picture. And remember, when you use this method, you can include as many photos in your listing as you want.

Promoting Your eBay Auctions

If you've followed all the instructions and advice throughout this book, you should now have your eBay business up and running and generating a steady stream of sales. But no matter how much revenue you're generating, you always want more—which is what this chapter is about. A sure-fire way to make your auctions more successful is to promote them, and there are lots of ways to do that. We'll look at some of the more efficient ways to promote your auctions and hopefully help you increase your traffic—and your selling prices.

Cross-Promoting All Your Auctions

The most obvious place to promote your eBay auctions is on eBay itself. Once you have potential customers interested in one thing you're selling, why not show them what else you have for sale? You'd be surprised how many customers can turn into purchasers of multiple items—and those extra sales are especially profitable.

Linking to Your Other Auctions

eBay helps you cross-sell in this fashion by including a View Seller's Other Auctions link at the top of all item listing pages, as shown in Figure 24.1. It links to a page that lists all your current auctions.

FIGURE 24.1

Every item list-
ing page
includes a link
to your other
eBay auctions.

Meet the seller

Seller: (349 ☆)
Feedback: **99.7% Positive**
Member: since Oct-08-02 in United States
 ▪ Read feedback comments
 ▪ Ask seller a question
 ▪ Add to Favorite Sellers
 ▪ **View seller's other items**

Unfortunately, many buyers tend to overlook this link, so you might want to emphasize your other auctions by including another, more prominent link to this page in your item listings. You can create this link by adding the following line of HTML code to your item description:

```
<a
href="http://cgi6.ebay.com/ws/eBayISAPI.dll?ViewSellersOtherItems&amp
;userid=USERID&amp;include=0&amp;since=-
1&amp;sort=3&amp;rows=50&amp;sspageName=DB:OtherItems" target=_blank>
Check out my other items!
</a>
```

Naturally, you should replace *USERID* with your own eBay user ID. You can also replace the Check out my other items! text with any text of your choosing.

Linking to Your About Me Page

You can also create a separate link to your About Me page, which includes a list of all your current eBay auctions. This is an easier way to provide a constant link to all your auctions in progress, and it can be inserted into any web page—not just your item listings.

You create a link to your About Me page by adding the following HTML code:

note Of course, another way to promote your auctions on the eBay site is to employ eBay's extra-cost listing enhancements, such as bold and highlight. Learn more about these features in Chapter 21, "Choosing the Most Effective Listing Options."

```
<a href="http://members.ebay.com/aboutme/USERID/">text</a>
```

Again, replace *USERID* with your own eBay user ID and *text* with the text you want for the link.

Linking from Other Sites to Your eBay Auctions

One of the best ways to promote your eBay auctions is to include links to your auctions on as many other websites as you can. For example, if you have a separate web storefront, you should use that site to promote all the auctions you're running on eBay. You can also promote your auctions on any personal web pages you or your family might have.

The question is, how do you promote individual auctions—particularly when those auctions have an extremely short life? If you include a link to a specific item listing page, that link will be good only for seven days (or whatever the length of the auction is). If you're okay with constantly editing and linking URLs, that's fine. For the rest of us, however, it would be nice to have a permanent URL to link to.

Linking to Your About Me Page

The good news is that you have such a permanent URL. It's called your eBay About Me page. As we just covered, your About Me page includes a list of all your current auctions, which makes it a perfect page to link to from other sites. Just add text that mentions "My eBay Auctions" or some such, and link that text to your About Me URL, using the code previously discussed. The URL never changes, even though your About Me page is constantly updated with the auctions you're running.

Adding an eBay Button to Your Web Page

You can also add a "Shop eBay with Me" button, like the one shown in Figure 24.2, to your business or personal web pages. When visitors click this button, they'll be taken to your Items for Sale page, which lists all your current auctions.

FIGURE 24.2

Add a Shop eBay with Me button to any web page.

To add this button to a web page, go to the Link Your Site to eBay page, located at `pages.ebay.com/services/buyandsell/link-buttons.html`. Check the box next to the My Listings on eBay button, enter the URL of the page where you want to display the button, scroll to the bottom of the page, and click the I Agree button. When the next page appears, copy the generated HTML code, and paste it into the code for your web page.

Cross-Promoting with Other Sellers

eBay's Cross-Promotion Connection lets you team with other eBay sellers to market your auctions at the bottom of each other's item listings. You can work with friendly sellers you know, or request to work with other sellers whose auctions you like.

The cross-promoted items from other sellers appear at the bottom of all your active items, just like your own cross-promoted items from your eBay Store. Your own cross-promoted items will be displayed first, followed by items from connected sellers.

To form a cross-promotion connection with another seller, go to the My Account page in My eBay, click the Marketing Tools link, and then click the Cross-Promotion > Connections link. When the next page appears, click the Request New Connection button, and then enter the user ID or eBay Store name of the seller with which you want to cross-promote. If the seller accepts your request, the cross-promoting begins.

Promoting with eBay Keywords

Another way to promote your auction listings or eBay Store is to use the eBay Keywords program. This program, administered by adMarketplace, lets you purchase specific eBay keywords. When buyers enter these keywords into eBay's search function, they're greeted with a banner ad that drives them to your listings or eBay Store. This is exactly how keyword advertising works on Google and the big search engine sites, with the exception that eBay Keywords is limited to eBay searches only. You bid on how much you want to pay (per click) for a specific keyword; a minimum bid is $0.10 per click. Find out more at the eBay Keywords website (`ebay.admarketplace.net`), shown in Figure 24.3.

FIGURE 24.3

Use the eBay Keywords program to promote your eBay listings.

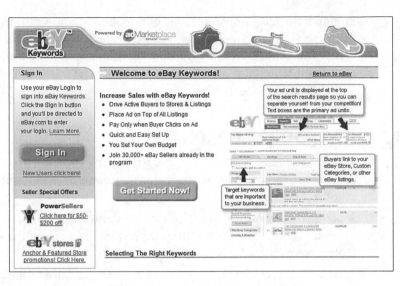

Other Ways to Advertise Your Auctions

Where else can you advertise the items you have for auction on eBay? Here are some ideas you might want to explore:

- Send emails to previous customers when you have new items for auction that they might be interested in. (Know, however, that eBay frowns against spamming other users, so take care when making this type of email solicitation.)

- When you're sending out end-of-auction emails to your high bidders, include a link to your About Me page—or even a list of other items you have for sale or plan to have for sale in the near future.

- Post messages on Internet message boards and Usenet newsgroups that are dedicated to the types of items you have for auction.

- Barter with other website owners to include links to your auctions or About Me page on their sites, in return for links to their sites on your site.

- Include your About Me URL or eBay Store URL as a signature in all your personal and business email messages.

- Include your About Me or eBay Store URL on your business cards and stationery.

Probably the most important type of promotion, however, is word of mouth—based on your good reputation. You want to encourage repeat bidders and drive buyers into your other auctions or online store (if you have one) for additional sales. That means treating your buyers fairly and with respect and going the extra mile to ensure their satisfaction.

Using eBay's Seller Resources

When it comes to promoting your auctions, the eBay site itself offers a lot of resources for sellers. Most of this help is informational in nature, and almost all of it is free.

A good place to start is eBay's Guide to Seller Resources (`pages.ebay.com/help/sell/services.html`). This page includes links to all the seller-related tools services offered by eBay, from seller education to global trading advice.

Another good resource is eBay's Seller Central Advanced Selling page (`pages.ebay.com/sellercentral/techniques.html`). Here is where you'll find links to selling tools of particular interest to eBay businesses—inventory sourcing, promotional opportunities, data and research, you name it.

Finally, there's the topic of seller education, in the form of eBay's online workshops. Check out the Workshop Calendar (`pages.ebay.com/community/workshopcalendar/current.html`) to see what workshops are available in the near future; eBay usually offers three or four different workshops a week, many of them targeted at the professional seller community.

In other words, there's a lot of free advice available directly from eBay on how to improve your online sales—and smart sellers always take advantage of free advice.

Part 5

Growing Your Online Business

Becoming an eBay PowerSeller

One of the steps to running your own eBay business—although not a requirement, by any means—is to become an eBay PowerSeller. eBay's 600,000 or so PowerSellers generate enough business to warrant special attention from eBay, in the form of dedicated customer support, premier tools, and the occasional special offer. Plus, they get to display that cool PowerSeller logo in all their auction listings.

Should you be aiming for PowerSeller status? Read on and find out what's involved—and whether it's worth the effort.

What Is a PowerSeller?

PowerSellers are the most profitable sellers on the eBay site; that is, they generate the most profits *for eBay*. They don't necessarily sell the most merchandise; instead, they generate the most revenue, which is how eBay generates its fees. Still, an eBay PowerSeller does a fair amount of business, however you measure it.

You can't choose to be a PowerSeller—eBay chooses you, based on your past sales performance. If you're chosen, you don't have to pay for the privilege; membership in the PowerSellers program is free.

When you become a PowerSeller, a special logo (shown in Figure 25.1) is displayed next to your user ID in all your eBay auctions, and you automatically qualify for the rewards appropriate to your level.

note Just because you qualify as a PowerSeller doesn't mean you have to display the logo in your item listings. Some PowerSellers prefer to forgo the logo in an attempt to seem more like normal folks and less like ruthless business types.

FIGURE 25.1

The sign of an eBay PowerSeller.

Do You Qualify?

To become a PowerSeller, you must meet the following requirements:

- Average a minimum of $1,000 in sales per month, for three consecutive months
- Maintain a minimum of four average monthly total item listings for three straight months
- Have been an active eBay seller for at least 90 days
- Achieve and maintain a minimum feedback rating of 100, 98% positive
- Not have violated any eBay policies in the past 60 days
- Be an eBay member in good standing, and uphold eBay's "community values"—including honesty, timeliness, and mutual respect

The most important point is the first, because it's the most quantifiable. There are five levels in the PowerSeller program; qualification for each level is based on average gross monthly sales, calculated over the past three months of selling activity. Table 25.1 shows the qualifying requirements for each level.

note To keep your PowerSeller status, you have to *maintain* this sales rate. If your sales drop below these levels, eBay will give you 30 days to bring your account back into compliance. If you don't, your membership in the program will be revoked. (You're free to requalify at a later date, however.)

Table 25.1   PowerSeller Requirements, by Level

Level	Requirement (Average Monthly Sales)
Bronze	$1,000
Silver	$3,000
Gold	$10,000
Platinum	$25,000
Titanium	$150,000

That's right, some eBay sellers average $150,000 or more in sales every month. That's almost $2 million a year in revenues from eBay auctions—no slight accomplishment!

Should you become a PowerSeller? As you'll soon see, the choice isn't yours to make; you'll either qualify for the program (based on your current eBay sales rate) or you won't.

PowerSeller Benefits

There are reasons to become a PowerSeller, beyond the obvious one of making lots of money. eBay offers PowerSellers better support, more information, and a few other decent perks. In fact, each level in the PowerSeller program comes with its own collection of rewards—the bigger you are, the more you get.

Priority Customer Support

Chief among the benefits of PowerSeller status is priority customer support, as detailed in Table 25.2. Having the extra handholding from eBay is great—especially the ability to talk with an actual live eBay employee, which is darned near impossible for us regular sellers to do.

Table 25.2   PowerSeller Priority Customer Support

Level	Fast 24/7 Email Support	Toll-Free Phone Support	Dedicated Account Manager
Bronze	Yes	No	No
Silver	Yes	Yes	No
Gold	Yes	Yes	Yes
Platinum	Yes	Yes	Yes
Titanium	Yes	Yes	Yes

Other Official Benefits

Other benefits offered to members of the PowerSeller program include

- Free eBay Keyword banner ads—up to $200 per quarter
- Health insurance for PowerSellers and their employees
- Access to the PowerSeller discussion board
- Monthly *PowerUp!* email newsletter—and quarterly printed newsletters
- Invitations and VIP admission to special eBay events, including the yearly eBay Live convention
- Ability to purchase unique PowerSeller logo merchandise
- Ability to display the PowerSeller logo in all item listings and About Me pages

note In addition to eBay's PowerSeller discussion board, check out The Powerseller Report (www.tprweb.com), an independent site that caters to eBay's top sellers. PowerSellers can also join the Professional eBay Sellers Alliance (www.gopesa.org), a nonprofit trade organization for eBay's highest-volume sellers.

Psychological Benefits

As you can see, the concrete benefits that accrue from PowerSeller status are less than awe-inspiring. (Fast responses to your emails—boy, is that impressive or what?) No, the real benefits of being a PowerSeller are psychological.

Some buyers see a listing that features the PowerSeller logo and assume that they're dealing with a trustworthy and presumably savvy seller. If, to potential buyers, the PowerSeller logo inspires a greater degree of confidence, then membership in the program is beneficial. On the other hand, some users view the PowerSeller logo as the sign of a big business. If these users prefer dealing with individuals, displaying the PowerSeller logo can actually be detrimental.

Bottom line, being a PowerSeller is probably a wash. If you qualify, great. If not, no big deal—although a lot of users really like the status that goes with the qualification. It's a badge of honor that signifies how successful you are on eBay.

How to Become a PowerSeller

The main eBay PowerSellers page (pages.ebay.com/services/buyandsell/welcome.html) offers more information about the PowerSellers program. This is also where you go if want to become a PowerSeller.

But the thing is, you can't become a PowerSeller just by asking. In fact, there's really no way to request membership at all; the program operates by invitation only. Each month eBay sends out invitations to sellers who meet the PowerSeller criteria. You become a member by (1) meeting the criteria, (2) receiving an invitation, and (3) responding positively to the invitation.

Know, however, that it's not a big deal if you don't qualify for PowerSeller status. The benefits offered aren't all that great, and I've been unable to quantify any sales increases that accrue from displaying the PowerSeller logo. Better to concentrate on improving the profitability of your eBay business than on reaching some artificial PowerSeller level!

Ten Tips for Achieving PowerSeller Status—or Just Increasing Your Day-to-Day Sales

The key to becoming a PowerSeller is to increase the number of auctions you close—and to increase your final selling prices. To that end, anything you can do to make your auctions more effective will improve your chances of achieving PowerSeller status.

What can you do to improve the success of your eBay auctions? Here are 10 tips that will benefit *any* eBay seller, PowerSeller or not:

Tip #1: Focus your sales activity. Occasional sellers can get by selling onesies and twosies that they pick up here and there. High-volume sellers focus on a specific type of merchandise—and sell lots of it. By focusing your activities, you can be much more efficient in your packing and shipping, as well as have a better feel for the category you're working with.

Tip #2: Buy low, sell high. It goes without saying—you want to make as much money as possible on each item you sell. That means obtaining your inventory at the lowest possible prices. Some sellers try to double or triple their cost when they sell an item. You may not be able to achieve this type of profit margin, but you should definitely be aiming to reduce your product costs however possible.

Tip #3: List in volume. You won't become a PowerSeller by selling one or two items a week. You need to list in volume to sell in volume. That means running multiple listings simultaneously, having listings close daily, and utilizing the Dutch auction feature when you have multiple quantities to sell.

Tip #4: Be organized. When you're closing a large number of auctions every week, you have to get the process down to a science. That means being more efficient every step of the way—from creating your listings to shipping out the merchandise. Wasted time and energy cost you money.

Tip #5: Create professional-looking listings. The better-looking your item listings, the more auctions you'll close—at higher prices. For best results, invest in a good-quality digital camera (for crisp product photos), and utilize a professional auction creation and listing service.

Tip #6: Write powerful headlines and descriptive listings. Pack as much useful information as you can into the item list's headline. Avoid fluff words, and focus on words and phrases that are "search-friendly." In the body of your listing, be as descriptive as possible. Include all the information a buyer might need to make an intelligent purchasing decision.

Tip #7: Use auction management tools. Running dozens—or hundreds—of auctions a week can task even the best-organized sellers. Utilize one of the many auction management programs or services to help you track every step of your auction activity—including the crucial post-auction communication and shipping processes.

Tip #8: Accept credit card payments. A large number of your potential customers want the convenience of paying via credit card. Don't turn away business; at the very least, sign up as a PayPal merchant so you can accept payment by plastic. Make it as easy as possible for your customers to pay.

Tip #9: Provide stellar customer service—and fast shipping. Remember, the customer is king. Bend over backward to satisfy your auction customers—which includes shipping your merchandise promptly and securely.

Tip #10: Take your business seriously. To run a successful eBay business, you have to be serious about it. For most PowerSellers, it's a full-time activity. Treat it like a business—*not* a hobby or occasional pastime. Be professional in everything you do, and you'll reap the rewards.

Selling Fixed-Price Items on eBay Express and Half.com

If you're tired of the auction grind—and sell items that are more suitable to the fixed-price format—consider selling at a site that specializes in this type of merchandise. eBay runs two such sites: eBay Express and Half.com. Should you list on these sites? Maybe, maybe not. Read on to learn more.

Obtaining Additional Exposure with eBay Express

eBay Express (express.ebay.com) is an odd bird. As you can see in Figure 26.1, eBay Express is eBay's attempt to provide a fixed-priced marketplace for buyers intimidated or otherwise put off by the online auction process. eBay Express offers consumers the ability to shop from multiple sellers yet pay via a single shopping cart and checkout. Buyer peace of mind is enhanced by a special Buyer Protection Policy; payment is via PayPal.

FIGURE 26.1

eBay's new fixed-price mar-ketplace—eBay Express.

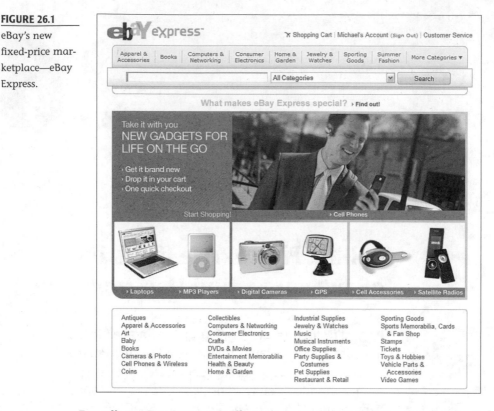

For sellers, eBay Express really isn't a separate thing. That is, you don't explic-itly list items for sale on the eBay Express site. Instead, any fixed-price item or auction item with the Buy It Now option that you have listed on the general eBay site or in an eBay Store is automatically made available to eBay Express shoppers. When a customer makes a purchase via the eBay Express checkout system, you're notified the same way you would be if it were an eBay or eBay Stores purchase.

Listing Requirements

That's not to say that you don't have to meet some listing criteria. After all, eBay Express is intended to be a "safer" marketplace than the wild and wooly world represented by eBay auctions; they don't want a lot of riff-raff clogging the virtual aisles with shoddy merchandise. To that end, if you want your mer-chandise listed on eBay Express, you as a seller have to meet the following requirements:

- You must be a registered U.S. seller (or a Canadian seller shipping from the U.S.).
- You must have a minimum feedback score of 100, with at least a 98% positive rating.
- Your feedback profile must be public.
- You must have a PayPal Premiere or Business account. (All eBay Express payments are via PayPal.)
- Your PayPal settings must be set to allow shipping to unconfirmed addresses.

In addition, the merchandise you sell must meet these requirements:

- It must be listed on the eBay.com site, and it must be located in the United States.
- It must be listed in fixed-price, auction with Buy It Now option, or eBay Stores inventory format.
- The Item Condition field (New, Used, or Refurbished) must be filled in.
- You must use prefilled information when available.
- All shipping costs (either flat or calculated) must be spelled out in advance, and the appropriate listing fields must be completed.
- The item listing must include a photo.
- The selling preferences for this item must allow shoppers to pay by a single combined payment for their purchases.
- Post-sale, purchasing must be routed via eBay's checkout system or a registered third-party service.
- The price of the item must not exceed $10,000.

Assuming you fill in the right fields, most items you sell should meet these criteria.

Listing on eBay Express

As I said, you don't have to do anything to have your item listed on eBay Express. If an item meets the requirements, and if you meet the seller requirements, the item will automatically be listed on eBay Express.

You can check to see if your items are listed on eBay Express by going to search.express.ebay.com/merchant/*USERID*. Replace *USERID* with your own user ID, of course; the resulting page, like the one in Figure 26.2, will list all your items that appear on the eBay Express site.

FIGURE 26.2

Viewing your items that are listed on eBay Express.

Shopping at eBay Express

An eBay Express item listing looks a tad different from the same listing on the eBay auction site. As you can see in Figure 26.3, there's a lot more information at the top of the listing, including item condition, quantity available, and shipping costs and information. Your standard item description appears at the bottom of the listing; the customer makes a purchase by clicking the Add to Cart button.

FIGURE 26.3

A typical eBay Express product listing.

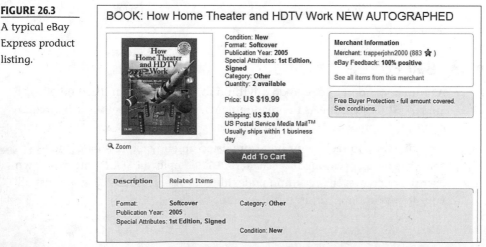

The purchase isn't complete, however, until the customer checks out. All purchases (from multiple sellers) are stored in the eBay Express shopping cart, shown in Figure 26.4. When the customer clicks the Checkout button, all items currently in the cart are officially purchased; the buyer's credit card is charged, and the sellers of each item are notified of the respective sales.

FIGURE 26.4

The eBay Express shopping cart.

Michael's Shopping Cart (Sign Out)

Quantities on these great deals vary. eBay Express can keep items in your cart, but they may be sold to other buyers before you check out.

| Back to Home | | Update Cart | Checkout |

Items in Shopping Cart	Shipping Options for 46032 Change ZIP	Quantity	Price
(8641 ☆)			
Titanic: The Complete Book of the Musical : Story and B ID: 4601944942 Price: US $28.57	Standard Flat Rate Shipping Service: US $3.99	1	US $28.57
Save for later Remove			
(1346 ☆)			
The Pampered Chef : The Story Behind the Creation of On ID: 130003781059 Price: US $19.96	Standard Flat Rate Shipping Service: US $5.25	1	US $19.96
Save for later Remove			

Applicable sales tax and shipping charges will be added to your total during Checkout.   **Item Subtotal:**   US $48.53

| Back to Home | | Update Cart | Checkout |

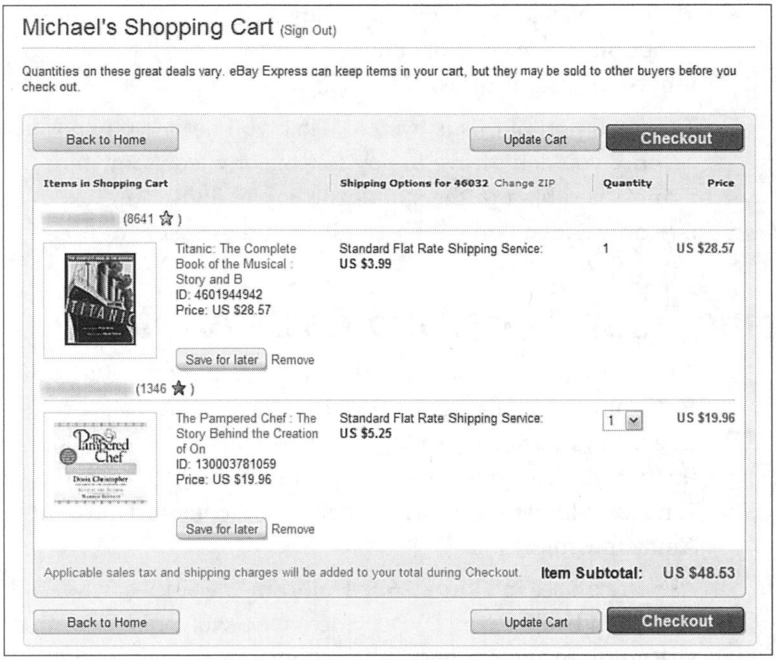

Is eBay Express for You?

Here's the thing about eBay Express: If you're selling fixed-price or Buy It Now items on eBay or in an eBay Store, you don't have any choice as to whether those items appear on eBay Express. As long as you meet the minimal seller and product requirements, your items will appear on both the original site and eBay Express.

In other words, if you want to sell on eBay Express, all you have to do is create a fixed-price eBay listing or an auction with the Buy It Now option, or enter that item

note eBay Express isn't available for all product categories. To be specific, eBay Express doesn't include categories not covered by PayPal Buyer Protection (such as eBay Motors), those that don't have Item Condition values, or those where eBay's Category Managers have not yet worked out all the necessary details. For a list of non-Express (eBay-only) categories, see pages.ebay.com/ sell/itemcondition/list/.

as fixed-price inventory in your eBay
Store. You can't *not* list on eBay Express;
as long as you're selling fixed-price or Buy
It Now items, you're a member of the
eBay Express retailer collective. (That's not
entirely true; you can edit your general
selling preferences on your My eBay page
to opt out completely of eBay Express selling for all your listings.)

> **caution**
>
> eBay Express search results return
> new products only. So if you sell
> used merchandise, you'll be at
> somewhat of a disadvantage
> against other merchants selling the
> same item new.

The good part of this is twofold. First, you get more exposure for your items.
Second, you don't have to pay for this privilege; any item listed on eBay
Express is subject to the standard eBay or eBay Stores listing and final value
fees only. Not a bad deal, overall—more exposure at no extra cost.

Offering Books, CDs, and DVDs on Half.com

As if there weren't enough selling options already, eBay also owns a site called
Half.com (`half.ebay.com`). Half.com lets anyone sell certain types of merchan-
dise in a fixed-price format. List your items for sale, wait for someone to buy
them, and then collect the money. In this respect Half.com works a lot like the
Amazon Marketplace—which belies Half.com's original intent to become an
Amazon competitor.

As you can see in Figure 26.5, Half.com specializes in specific types of merchandise: books, CDs, DVDs, videotapes, video games, and game systems.
Listing these items is easy; all you have to do is enter the item's UPC or ISBN
codes and then describe the item's condition. eBay groups all like items
together, with available sellers listed for the buyer to choose from.

Listing on Half.com

Unlike eBay Express, you have to explicitly list your items on Half.com;
they're not automatically plucked from the eBay fixed-price listing database.
To sell on Half.com, click the Sell Your Stuff link at the top of the page. When
the Sell Your Items on Half.com page appears, as shown in Figure 26.6, you
can click a category link for your item or enter the item's UPC, ISBN, or model
number in the Quick Sell box and click the Continue button. When you've
entered the appropriate identifying information, Half.com then inserts prefilled item information from a massive product database. (It's the same database that feeds eBay's prefilled information in the same categories.)

FIGURE 26.5

A fixed-price marketplace for books, CDs, DVDs, and other media— Half.com.

FIGURE 26.6

Preparing an item for sale on Half.com.

Half.com doesn't charge any listing fees, but you do have to pay the site a commission when an item sells. Table 26.1 lists the current Half.com commission rates.

Table 26.1   Half.com Commission Rates

Selling Price	Commission
<$50.00	15%
$50.01-$100.00	12.5%
$100.01-$250.00	10%
$250.01-$500.00	7.5%
>$500.00	5%

Instead of a buyer paying you directly, Half.com collects the payment as part of the checkout process. The site sends you your payment every two weeks, typically via direct deposit to your bank account.

Shopping at Half.com

When a customer searches for a specific item on Half.com, the site returns a list of all the sellers who have that item for sale, like the one in Figure 26.7. The list is sorted into new and used items, with the used items further sorted by condition—like new, very good, good, acceptable, and so on. To make a purchase, the customer simply clicks the Buy button.

As with eBay Express, Half.com buyers can purchase items from multiple sellers and have all their purchases consolidated into a single shopping cart and checkout, as shown in Figure 26.8. The buyer makes a single payment to complete the checkout; individual sellers are then notified of their respective sales.

Is Half.com for You?

If you sell the types of media-related items that Half.com specializes in, you should give the site a spin. Many sellers like to use Half.com for those products that have market demand but won't necessarily sell in the normal seven-day auction period. Just remember, you have to list your inventory separately for Half.com—unlike with the eBay, eBay Stores, or eBay Express sites.

FIGURE 26.7
Searching for
items for sale on
Half.com.

FIGURE 26.8
Items from mul-
tiple sellers end
up in the same
Half.com shop-
ping cart.

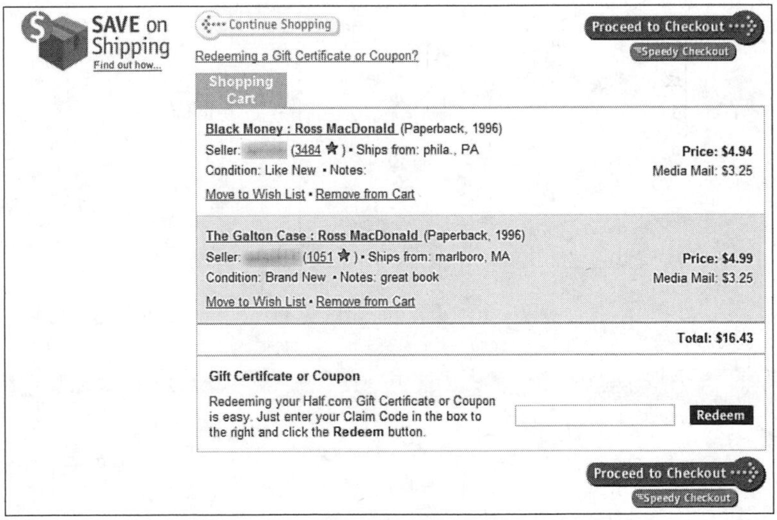

Opening an eBay Store

Another important step in your creation of a successful eBay business is to set up your own online storefront. This is surprisingly easy to do, thanks to a service called eBay Stores.

Running an eBay Store is the way for a heavy seller to provide the facsimile of a retail storefront within the eBay environment. If you're thinking of making the move into real honest-to-goodness retailing, an eBay Store is a relatively painless way to start.

What Is an eBay Store?

An eBay Store, like the one shown in Figure 27.1, is a web page where you can sell fixed-price items that are not currently up for auction on eBay. Your eBay Store also contains all the items you currently have listed for regular auction on eBay. The non-auction items in your eBay Store appear only in your eBay Store—not in the eBay auction listings.

FIGURE 27.1

The author's
Molehill Group
eBay Store.

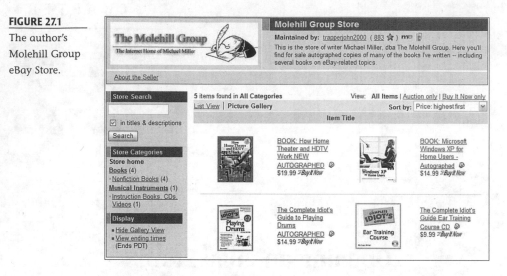

As you can see in Figure 27.2, merchants on the eBay Stores home page (`stores.ebay.com`) are organized by the same categories as the eBay auction site: Antiques, Art, Books, and so on. Buyers can also search for a specific store or a store selling a certain type of item, or view an alphabetical list of all stores.

FIGURE 27.2

The home page
for eBay Stores.

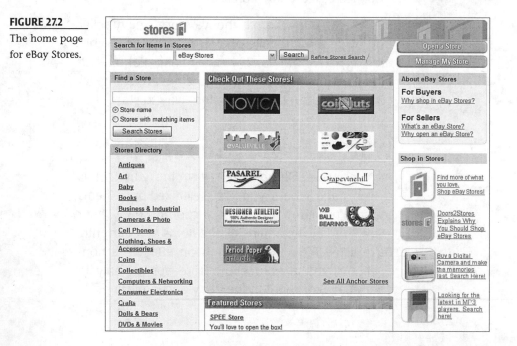

The items offered by eBay Stores merchants are a combination of items currently for auction on eBay and additional fixed-price inventory. When buyers access a particular eBay Store retailer, they have access to this entire collection of merchandise. If they tried searching on eBay proper, they wouldn't find the non-auction items the retailer might have for sale.

For a buyer, purchasing an item from an eBay Store retailer is a little like buying from any other online merchant, and a little like winning an item in an eBay auction. On the one hand, it's buying from an actual merchant at a fixed price, and the buyer can always pay by credit card. On the other hand, eBay Stores offer all the niceties found on eBay, including the ability to check the merchant's feedback rating. Checkout is handled from within the store.

Benefits of Opening Your Own eBay Store

Why would you want to open your own eBay Store? Well, it certainly isn't for casual sellers; you have to set up your own web page and keep the store filled with merchandise, both of which take time and energy. It's also a little expensive, especially after eBay's mid-2006 rate increase.

But if you're a high-volume seller who specializes in a single category (or even a handful of categories), there are benefits to opening your own store. They include being able to sell more merchandise (through your store) than you can otherwise list in auctions, being able to offer more merchandise for sale at a lower cost (due to dramatically lower listing fees), being able to display a special eBay Stores icon next to all of your auction lists, and being able to generate repeat business from future sales to current purchasers.

Opening an eBay Store is an especially good idea if you have a lot of fixed-price merchandise to sell. You can put items in your eBay Store before you offer them for auction, and thus have more merchandise for sale than you might otherwise. An eBay Store is also a good place to "park" merchandise that hasn't sold at auction, before you choose to relist.

In addition, if you do your job right, you can use your eBay Store to sell more merchandise to your existing customers. And, since eBay Store insertion fees are lower than auction listing fees, you'll be decreasing your costs by selling direct rather than through an auction—assuming you have an acceptable sales rate, of course.

All this is made feasible—and more profitable—due to the lower costs associated with eBay Store listings. As you'll learn in the "The Costs of Running an eBay Store" section, later in this chapter, listing fees for eBay Store items are substantially lower than eBay's normal auction listing fees. These lower fees makes it affordable to offer more merchandise for sale—and more profitable when you sell it.

Another benefit of selling merchandise in an eBay Store is that eBay will automatically advertise items from your store on the Bid Confirmation and Checkout Confirmation pages it displays to bidders in your regular auctions. These "merchandising placements" help you cross-sell additional merchandise to your auction customers.

> **note** Accounting Assistant is a software program that enables you to export eBay and PayPal data directly into the QuickBooks accounting program. The program is free to download and use, although to generate the necessary data you also need a subscription to either eBay Stores, Selling Manager (Basic or Pro), or Seller's Assistant (Basic or Pro). Find out more at pages.ebay.com/help/sell/accounting-assistant-ov.html.

In addition, eBay sends all eBay Store owners a monthly Sales Report Plus report. This report provides a variety of data to help you track your Store activity, including total sales; average sales price; buyer counts; and metrics by category, format, and ending day or time.

You'll also receive live Traffic Reports that show the number of page views for each of your listings and Store pages, as well as a list of keywords used by buyers to find your listings. Featured and Anchor Stores also receive an additional path analysis that shows how buyers navigate within your store, and bid/BIN tracking. And all eBay Store owners can export their Store data to QuickBooks, using eBay's Accounting Assistant program, for your personal financial management.

Finally, all eBay Store owners get a free subscription to eBay Selling Manager or Selling Manager Pro. If you'd planned on using one of these tools anyway, getting them free helps to defray the costs of running your eBay Store.

Of course, it isn't all milk and honey in the land of eBay Stores. According to eBay, items listed in eBay Stores take 14 times longer to sell than do items listed in normal eBay auctions, on average—and, in some media categories (books, CDs, DVDs, and so on) up to *forty times* longer. And, while eBay Stores merchandise accounts for 83% of all listings across the eBay empire, they only contribute 9% of

> **note** If you're serious about selling merchandise outside the eBay environment, you may want to create a more full-featured e-commerce presence than available with eBay Stores. See Chapter 28, "Launching a Full-Featured Merchant Website," for more information.

eBay's total gross merchandise value. In other words, there's a lot of stuff parked in eBay Stores that just isn't selling.

This is one reason that eBay raised signficantly its eBay Stores fees in August, 2006—more than doubling insertion fees, as well as adding a couple of points to the base final value fees. These fee increases make an eBay Store less attractive than it was before; you can't just stuff a store with merchandise that may or may not sell. At the new rates (which we'll discuss in a moment), you really only want to put items in your store that you know have viable sales potential.

Do You Qualify?

Just about any seller can open his or her own eBay Store. All you have to do is meet the following criteria:

- Be a registered eBay seller, with credit card on file
- Have a feedback rating of 20 or more, or be ID verified, or have a PayPal account
- Accept credit cards for all fixed-price sales

Given that accepting credit cards can mean using PayPal, you can see that you don't actually have to be a big traditional retailer in order to open an eBay Store. Any individual meeting the requirements can also open an eBay Store, thus making eBay Stores a great way for entrepreneurial types to get started in retailing.

The Costs of Running an eBay Store

Naturally, opening an eBay Store costs money. (eBay isn't in this for the betterment of mankind, after all.) You pay a monthly fee to be an eBay Store merchant, choosing from three subscription levels, as shown in Table 27.1.

Table 27.1   eBay Stores Subscription Levels

Level	Fee	Features
Basic	$15.95/month	Store listed in every category directory where you have items listed; position based on number of items listed; receive monthly store reports; send 100 emails a month to buyers; create five customizable pages; free subscription to eBay Selling Manager

Table 27.1   Continued

Level	Fee	Features
Featured	$49.95/month	All features of Basic, plus Store rotated through a special featured section on the eBay Stores home page; Store receives priority placement in Related Stores section of search and listings pages; Store featured within the top-level category pages where you have items listed; cross-sell products on view item pages; receive more detailed monthly reports; create 10 customizable pages; send 1,000 emails a month to buyers; and you get a free subscription to Selling Manager Pro and $30/month to spend on the eBay Keywords program
Anchor	$499.95/month	All features of Featured, plus premium placement in Related Stores section of search and listings pages; your store logo rotates through category directory pages (1 million impressions); send 4,000 emails a month to buyers; create 15 customizable pages; and you get dedicated 24-hour live customer support and $100/month to spend on the eBay Keywords program

You also have to pay eBay for each item you list and each item you sell—just as in a normal auction. The difference is you're not listing for a (relatively short) auction; you're listing for longer-term inventory.

The insertion fees associated with an eBay Store are relatively simple. You pay 5 cents per month for items priced from $0.01 to $24.99, and 10 cents per month for items priced over $25.00. That's not as cheap as it used to be (the old listing fee was 2 cents per month across the board), but it's still not bad, compared to listings on the main eBay site.

In addition, for every item you sell in your eBay Store, eBay charges a final value fee. Table 27.2 lists these selling charges.

Table 27.2   eBay Stores Final Value Fees

Closing Value	Fee
$0.01–$25.00	10%
$25.01–$100.00	10% of the initial $25, plus 7% of the remaining balance
$100.01–$1,000.00	10% on the first $25 *plus* 7% on the part between $25 and $100, *plus* 5% on the remaining balance
Over $1,000.01	10% on the first $25 *plus* 7% on the part between $25 and $100, *plus* 5% on the part between $100 and $1,000 *plus* 3% on the remaining balance

eBay Stores also offers a full assortment of listing upgrades, just like the ones you can use in regular eBay auctions. These enhancements—Gallery, bold, highlight, and so on—are priced according to the length of your listing. You can also offer multiples of the same item in Dutch auction format.

How to Set Up an eBay Store

Opening your own eBay Store is as easy as clicking through eBay's setup pages. There's nothing overly complex involved; you'll need to create your store, customize your pages (otherwise known as your *virtual storefront*), and list the items you want to sell. Just follow the onscreen instructions, and you'll have your own Store up and running in just a few minutes.

Creating Your Store

To open your Store, start at the eBay Stores main page (`stores.ebay.com`), and click the Open a Store button. When you accept the user agreement, the store creation process begins. You'll start by choosing a name for your Store then, on the subsequent Quick Store Setup page (shown in Figure 27.3), you'll get to choose a Store design, select a color and theme, enter your Store description, select your item layout, insert promotion boxes, and select various marketing options. Click the Apply Settings button to launch your newly created Store. It's that simple!

FIGURE 27.3

Setting up your eBay Store.

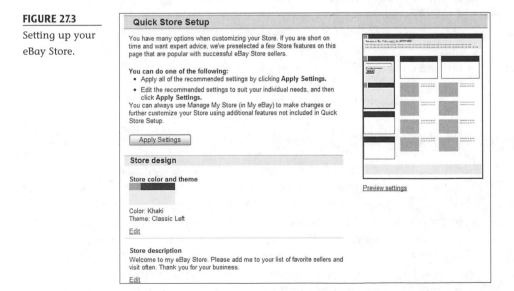

Listing Merchandise for Sale

Now that you've created your eBay Store, you need to add some merchandise. You do this by clicking the Sell link at the top of any eBay listing page; the normal Sell page now includes an option for Store Inventory, which is what you want to select. Go through the normal Sell Your Item listing creation process, and your new listing will be added to your eBay Store. That's one of the nice things about having an eBay Store; it's well integrated with your other eBay activities.

Customizing and Managing Your Store

eBay lets you customize, to some degree, the pages in your eBay Store. You do this by clicking the Seller Manage Store link at the bottom of your Store's home page. This takes you to the Manage My Store page, shown in Figure 27.4. From here, you can

- Customize individual pages in your Store
- Manage your Store subscription
- Put your Store on "hold" while you go on vacation
- Specify which Store items you want to cross-promote in your auction listings
- Add promotional boxes to pages in your Store
- Buy eBay Keywords (as described in Chapter 24, "Promoting Your eBay Auctions")
- Send promotional emails to your customers
- Register your domain name
- Cancel Good 'Til Cancelled listings
- Access your eBay Store reports

Just click the appropriate link for the action you want to perform.

For example, you may want to create a page in your Store to detail your store policies, or to list promotional items, or to showcase specific merchandise. Go to the Manage Your Store page, and select the Custom Pages link. When the next page appears, click the Create New Page link. This displays the Create Custom Page: Select Layout page, shown in Figure 27.5. As you can see, you can create many different kinds of pages. Select the layout you want, and click the Continue button. This displays the Create Custom Page: Provide Content page, where you essentially fill in the blanks with your new page's content—text and pictures. Continue on to preview the new page and load it into your Store.

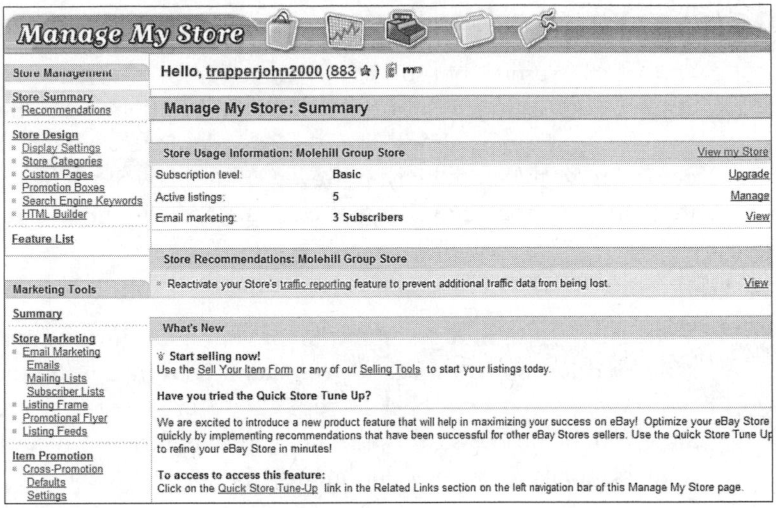

FIGURE 27.4

Managing your eBay Store.

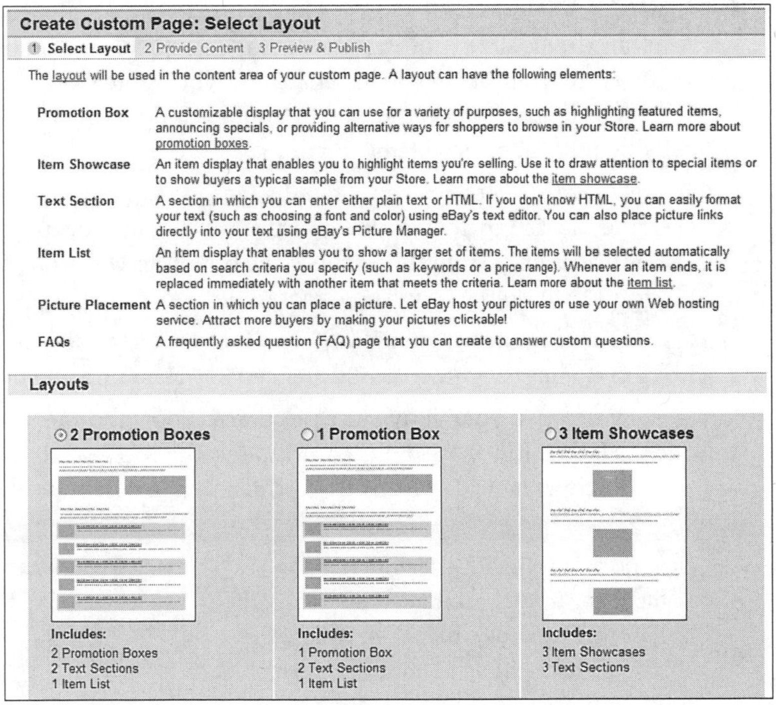

FIGURE 27.5

Adding a new page to your eBay Store.

Promoting Your eBay Store

One of the reasons that sales rates are lower for eBay Stores than they are for regular eBay listings is that many Store owners don't promote their stores—they use their Stores almost like a parking lot for excess merchandise. It doesn't have to be that way, however; smart eBay Stores sellers know to promote their Store listings separate from their regular eBay listings.

Use the URL

Naturally, you should post the URL for your eBay Store as many places as possible, to drive more business to your Store. That means driving sales from any other website you have back to your eBay Store, as well as promoting the Store URL on business cards, local advertisements, and such. Your eBay Store address should be on every promotional item you deliver.

Create a Listing Feed

Another way to drive traffic to your eBay Store is to create an RSS listing feed. This feed lists all the new items you list in your store. You can then syndicate or distribute this feed, so that anyone subscribing to the feed will automatically be notified of new items in your eBay Store.

To create an RSS feed for your Store listings, go to your My eBay page and click the Marketing Tools link. From the Marketing Tools page, click the Listing Feeds link. From there, check the option to Distribute Your Listings via RSS, and then click Apply. That creates the feed.

Once you've created the feed, you now have to distribute it. One of the best ways to do this is via the FeedBurner service. Here's how to do this.

Start by going to your eBay Store page. Scroll down to the bottom of the page and click the orange RSS box. This displays the RSS feed for your site. Write down or copy the URL for this feed, which appears in your browser's Address box.

Now go to the FeedBurner site (www. feedburner.com). You'll need to create an account (no charge), and then follow the onscreen instructions to "burn" a feed. You'll enter the URL that you copied for your eBay Store RSS feed, and continue following instructions to save and distribute the feed. Feedburner will then make sure your feed is syndicated across the Web.

tip Since updates to your feed go out only when you add new items to your store, you want to list something new in your store every few days. There's no need to add a lot of items at a time, the key is a constant addition of merchandise, so that subscribers are receiving almost-daily updates.

Whenever you add a new item to your eBay Store, your RSS feed will be updated, and any subscribers to the feed will be notified. It's a great way to attract repeat business to your Store.

Export Your Listings to Search Engines and Shopping Sites

There's another promotional opportunity available on the Listing Feeds page. eBay lets you export your Store listings to third-party search engines and price comparison sites.

When you check the Make a File of Your Store Inventory Listings Available option, eBay creates a special file of your store listings, and posts that file to a web page. This is an XML-format file that contains the following information for each item listed in your store:

- Item title
- Item description
- URL of the item page
- Whether the item is orderable
- Current price
- Availability
- Item number
- Shipping cost (if specified ahead of time)
- Gallery picture (if available)
- Quantity
- Currency

You can then submit the URL for this file to your favorite search engines (Google, Yahoo!, MSN Search, and so on), as well as to various price comparison sites (Shopping.com, Yahoo! Shopping, NexTag, and the like). While eBay creates the file for you (and keeps it updated with your latest listings), it's your responsibility to submit the file's URL to whatever sites you choose. Naturally, you should follow the submission instructions for each particular site.

When you submit your eBay Store listings to a web search engine, your listings will appear in the search engine's search results. When you submit your Store listings to a price comparison site, your Store will appear as an option whenever someone is price-shopping for a particular item. It takes a little work on your part, but the result is much wider exposure—and wider exposure means more sales.

Earn Referral Fees

There's an added incentive for spreading your eBay Store URL around to as many websites as possible. That's because you earn eBay credit when you refer people from other sites to your eBay Store.

Earning credit is as simple as adding a referrer code to every link you post to your eBay Store. When someone clicks on the link + referrer code and ends up buying something, eBay gives you a 75% credit on the item's final value fee. Learn more about these referrer codes at `pages.ebay.com/help/` `specialtysites/referral-credit-faq.html`.

Launching a Full-Featured Merchant Website

In Chapter 27, "Opening an eBay Store," we looked at eBay Stores, where you can sell additional fixed-price merchandise to your auction customers. An eBay Store, however, is a rather limited online storefront. If you want to move full-force into online retailing, you need something more fully featured.

Fortunately, setting up your own online storefront isn't nearly as involved as you might think. Numerous services, including eBay itself, provide prepackaged storefront solutions; all you have to do is point and click (and pay some money) to get your store online. Or, if you want something really fancy, you can design your own store on your own website, complete with your own proprietary web domain.

However you do it, opening a dedicated web storefront lets you sell your merchandise 24 hours a day, 365 days of the year. You don't have to wait for an auction to end to sell an item and collect your money; you're open for business anytime your customers want to buy.

If you have dreams of turning your online auction business into the next Amazon.com, read on—and learn how to become a bona fide Internet e-tailer.

Utilizing a Prepackaged Storefront

The easiest way to create an online storefront is to let somebody else do it for you.

Several of the big auction services' sites offer prepackaged web storefronts you can use to sell both auction and nonauction merchandise. The advantage of using a prepackaged storefront is that all the hard work is done for you: You put your storefront together by filling out the appropriate forms. The disadvantage of a prepackaged storefront is that, in many cases, it's not really *your* storefront; there aren't a lot of customization options, and you have to settle for a somewhat generic look and feel (which means that your store is going to look like every other store managed by the same service—not necessarily a good thing).

Still, if you want to launch a storefront without a lot of fuss and muss—and get it up and running in record time—then a prepackaged storefront service might be for you. We'll look at some of the most popular services next.

Ándale Stores

Ándale (www.andale.com) lets you build your own storefront on its service. As you can see in Figure 28.1, an Ándale Store is similar to an eBay Store, but maybe a bit nicer looking and somewhat more functional. An Ándale Store can be fully customized with your own personal color scheme and graphics.

Pricing to open an Ándale Store is $9.95 per month, cheaper than the $15.95 fee for an eBay Store. You also have to pay Ándale 5% of all your online sales. These fees cover everything you need to run your storefront; as with all these third-party services, Ándale provides all the web hosting and storage space you need for your store.

Ándale also does a little marketing for you. When you open an Ándale Store, your items are listed on the Froogle, Shopzilla, and Shopping.com comparison shopping sites—in addition to Ándale's own Ándale Plaza shopping destination site. It's good exposure, something you don't get with many other e-commerce services.

FIGURE 28.1

The
AstroGadgets.
com Ándale
Store (www.
astrogadgets.
com).

ChannelAdvisor

The ChannelAdvisor Stores service (www.channeladvisor.com), which is part of the ChannelAdvisor Merchant package, helps you incorporate a full-service storefront into your eBay About Me page or create a more full-featured online storefront, including integrated checkout and payment services. (Figure 28.2 shows an About Me–type store page.) You'll need to contact the service personally to get a price quote for your particular needs.

eBay ProStores

I guess eBay got tired of losing business to third-party storefront services, because in 2005 it launched its own prepackaged storefront service, dubbed eBay ProStores (www.prostores.com). eBay ProStores offers much the same types of services that you find at the third-party sites, including domain hosting, real-time credit card processing, and an e-commerce shopping cart. Figure 28.3 shows a typical ProStores merchant site.

FIGURE 28.2

A ChannelAdvisor
storefront on an
About Me page—
Sophia's Style
Boutique
(members.ebay.
com/ws/
eBayISAPI.dll?
ViewUserPage&
userid=sophias*
style).

FIGURE 28.3

The Travelled
Home's ProStores
site (www.
thetravelled
home.com).

ProStores offers four different packages for different-sized businesses. These are detailed in Table 28.1.

Table 28.1   eBay ProStores Packages

	ProStores Express	ProStores Business	ProStores Advanced	ProStores Enterprise
Target	Individual sellers	Small businesses	Medium-sized businesses	Enterprise-sized businesses
Price	$6.95/month	$29.95/month	$74.95/month	$249.95/month
Transaction fees	1.5%	0.5%	0.5%	0.5%
Web hosting	Yes	Yes	Yes	Yes
Personalized domain name	Optional	Yes	Yes	Yes
Web storage space	NA	5 GB	10 GB	20 GB
Data transfer limits	NA	50 GB/month	200 GB/month	400 GB/month
Customizable design templates	Yes	Yes	Yes	Yes
Number of products allowed	10	Unlimited	Unlimited	Unlimited
Shopping cart with SSL checkout	No	Yes	Yes	Yes
PayPal payments accepted	Yes	Yes	Yes	Yes
Real-time credit card processing	No	Yes	Yes	Yes
Inventory management	No	Yes	Yes	Yes
Drop-shipment management	No	No	No	Yes
Daily submission to shopping comparison sites	No	Yes	Yes	Yes
Accounting integration with QuickBooks	No	Yes	Yes	Yes
Shipping integration with FedEx, UPS, USPS, and Canada Post	No	Yes	Yes	Yes
Integrated with eBay and eBay Stores	Yes	Yes	Yes	Yes

The chief advantage to eBay ProStores over competing services is the seamless integration with regular eBay auctions and eBay Stores. You can copy your eBay listings directly to your ProStores product catalog, transfer items from your ProStores inventory to an eBay auction or eBay Stores listing, display your eBay listings in your ProStores store, and manage all your eBay listings from your ProStores store. No other e-commerce service offers this level of eBay integration.

Homestead Storefront

Homestead Storefront (`storefront.homestead.com`), which is powered by the same technology that powers eBay ProStores, offers an easy-to-setup solution, especially for smaller sellers. You get your choice of packages, priced from $6.99/month to $59.99/month, depending on how many items you want to merchandise and how much storage space and data transfer you need.

Storefront sites can look quite professional, as you can see in Figure 28.4. Getting started is as easy as working through a few wizards.

FIGURE 28.4

The Homestead Storefront of Worldwide Child (www.world widechild.com).

Infopia

Infopia (`www.infopia.com`) is one of those companies that cloaks what it does in a suffocating blanket of business-to-business buzzwords. According to its website, the Infopia Marketplace Manager "is an all inclusive multi-channel e-commerce platform." In plain English, that translates into web storefronts that link to your eBay auctions, like the one in Figure 28.5. (For what it's worth, Infopia drives many of the big consignment drop-off chains, including Auction Mills and iSold It.)

A full list of features includes auction-listing creation, automated communication and feedback, image hosting, email marketing, tracking and reporting, inventory and order management, and a "smart" shopping cart and checkout. To determine pricing, you have to contact Infopia for a "no-obligation assessment" of your needs.

NetStores

NetStores (www.netstores.com) offers a variety of online storefront services, from shopping-cart integration into your existing website to complete storefront design. Figure 28.6 shows one of its online storefronts.

In addition to the shopping cart, you get sales and traffic reporting, bulk product uploading, web hosting, customizable layouts, real-time credit card authorization, and a secure checkout system. Prices start at $19.95 per month.

FIGURE 28.6

The NetStores-
driven website
of V i X (www.
vixswimwear.
com).

Vendio

Vendio (www.vendio.com) offers web storefronts as part of its Vendio Stores
service. Stores, such as the one in Figure 28.7, include a free gallery, mailing-
list management, and a fully customizable look and feel. Vendio also pro-
motes your store items on the Dealio, Froogle, and Shopzilla comparison
shopping sites.

FIGURE 28.7

The Rare
Performance
DVDs store
(shop.vendio.
com/RareDVDs),
driven by
Vendio Stores.

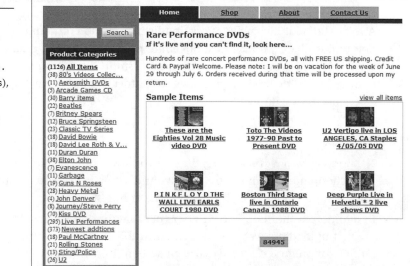

Vendio offers three different pricing plans, as detailed in Table 28.2. All plans let you list an unlimited number of items in your store.

Table 28.2   Vendio Stores packages

Plan	Monthly Fee	Final Value Fee
Bronze	$4.95	1% of selling price ($4.95 max per item)
Silver	$9.95	$0.20 per item sold
Gold	$14.95	$0.10 per item sold

Yahoo! Small Business

That's right, along with all its search-related services, Yahoo! offers small business website hosting, too. Yahoo! Small Business is actually one of the largest hosts for small online retailers, offering all-in-one e-commerce solutions that link back to the Yahoo! Shopping marketplace.

Yahoo!'s merchant solutions start at $39.95/month for the Starter plan, and go up to $299.95 for the Professional level. You get all the usual features, including integrated shopping cart, credit card processing (via PayPal), automated shipment processing, easy-to-use site setup wizards, and the like. Figure 28.8 shows a typical Yahoo!-powered online store.

FIGURE 28.8

Trains4tots (www.trains4tots.com), powered by Yahoo! Small Business.

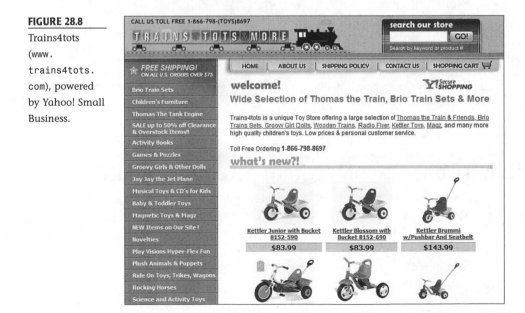

Zoovy

Zoovy (www.zoovy.com) offers its Zoovy Storefront service for online merchants. Figure 28.9 shows a typical Zoovy merchant.

With Zoovy you get order and inventory management, integration with shipping and payment providers, hundreds of predesigned store layouts, and the ability to sell your items on eBay and other online marketplaces. Zoovy also pipes your store inventory for listing on the Froogle, NexTag, PriceGrabber, and Shopping.com comparison shopping sites. As with several others of these services, you have to contact the site to get a custom quote.

FIGURE 28.9

The Zoovy storefront of Perfect PJs (www.perfectpjs.com).

Building Your Own Merchant Site from Scratch

Prepackaged storefronts are fine, but if you want a truly full-featured web storefront, independent of stock layouts and generic checkout systems, you'll need to build your own e-commerce website from scratch. This is a lot of work and will cost a lot of money, so it's not for novice or hesitant sellers. But if you're really serious about making a lot of money on the Internet, building your own e-commerce site is the only way to go.

Finding a Web Host

You can't build a complex e-commerce website on Yahoo! GeoCities or other typical home page communities. These sites are designed to host individual web pages, not complete sites; you certainly don't want your professional site to be burdened with a URL that begins www.geocities.com/*yourname/*.

Instead, you need to find a professional web-hosting service, a master site that will provide hundreds of megabytes of disk space, robust site-management tools, and the ability to use your own unique domain name. (And with your own domain name, your site's URL will read www.*yourname*.com—just like the big sites do!)

A professional web-hosting service, at the most basic level, provides large amounts of reliable storage space for your website—normally for a monthly or yearly fee. Most hosting services also provide other types of services, and many offer e-commerce-specific tools.

All of these services will cost you, of course; that's part and parcel of going pro. A good web-hosting service can run as little as $10 a month—or a lot more, depending on the storage space and tools you need.

Literally hundreds of site-hosting services exist on the Web. The best way, then, to look for a web-hosting service is to use a site that performs the search for you.

Several sites on the Internet offer directories of web-hosting services. Most of these sites let you look for hosts by various parameters, including monthly cost, disk space provided, programming and platforms supported, and extra features offered (such as e-commerce hosting, control panels, and so on). Many also offer lists of the "best" or most popular hosting services, measured in one or another fashion.

Among the best of these host search sites are the following:

- HostIndex.com (www.hostindex.com)
- HostSearch (www.hostsearch.com)
- TopHosts.com (www.tophosts.com)
- Web Hosters (www.webhosters.com)

Obtaining a Domain Name

A professional e-commerce website needs its own unique URL, in the form of a dedicated domain name. Reserving a domain name is just part of the process, however. Once you have a name, that name needs to be listed with the

Internet's domain name system (DNS) so that users entering your URL are connected to the appropriate IP address where your site is actually hosted. Most website-hosting services will provide DNS services if you provide a unique domain name; some will even handle the registration process for you. You can also go directly to the Network Solutions website (www.networksolutions.com) to register your web address.

Creating Your Website

Once you have a host for your storefront and a domain name registered, it's time for the really hard work—creating your site. If you're handy with HTML and Cascading Style Sheets and have a lot of free time, you can choose to do this work yourself. Or you can bite the bullet and hire a firm that specializes in designing e-commerce websites and pay it to produce the kind of site you want.

If you opt to build your site yourself, you'll need to invest in a powerful website-creation tool. You don't build a complex website using Microsoft Notepad or a freeware HTML editing utility. You need to use a fully featured program, such as

- Adobe Creative Suite (www.adobe.com)
- Macromedia Dreamweaver (www.adobe.com)
- Microsoft FrontPage or its successor programs, Microsoft Expression Web Designer and Microsoft Office SharePoint Designer (www.microsoft.com)
- NetObjects Fusion (www.netobjects.com)

Incorporating E-commerce Software

To power your new storefront, you'll need to incorporate special e-commerce software. This software will enable you to build web pages based on your current inventory, generate customer shopping carts, funnel buyers to a checkout page, and handle all customer transactions. Here are some of the most popular:

- AbleCommerce (www.ablecommerce.com)
- BazaarBuilder (www.bazaarbuilder.com)
- Miva Merchant (www.miva.com)
- Nexternal (www.nexternal.com)
- X-Cart (www.x-cart.com)

note You'll also need your new storefront to be able to handle customer payments via credit card. Learn more about enabling credit card processing in Chapter 16, "Managing Customer Payments."

Web Design Firms

If you're not an experienced web page designer, you may be better off hiring someone who is to build your new storefront site. Tons of web design firms are out there, most of them small and local. When it's time to go professional, use the following directories to find a professional web page designer that's right for your needs:

- AAADesignList.com (www.aaadesignlist.com)
- The Firm List (www.firmlist.com)
- The List of Web Designers (webdesign.thelist.com)

Putting It All Together

At the end of the day, what you want is a site that showcases all the products you have to sell, is easy for potential buyers to navigate, provides enough information (including product photos) for buyers to be comfortable ordering sight unseen, offers a shopping-cart system with secure checkout, and lets you collect credit card payments online. Ideally, the site should also link back to your current eBay auctions and eBay Store listings so that everything you have for sale is listed all in one place.

Then, once your perfect e-commerce site is launched, you need to keep it up and running—and monitor it constantly for current sales. You want as much of the operation as possible (including payment and postsales operations) to be automated so that you don't have to do a whole lot of work by hand. And you want the whole thing to be relatively easy to maintain and not cost you an arm and a leg. (Let's face it: As your business gets bigger, you probably don't want to be paying a big cut of your sales to whichever service is hosting or managing your site.)

Sound like a lot to ask? Not really; you should be able to find an e-commerce service that delivers what you need at a reasonable price—or, if your business is big enough, you can just build it yourself. The key is to make sure the site is easy for customers to use and conveys your business's branding in its overall look and design. Once the site is up and running, you can go about the business of promoting it and driving sales through your checkout system.

Other Places to Sell Online

You don't have to open up a sophisticated e-commerce website to supplement your eBay business with other online sales. Read on to learn about the *other* places to sell online.

Other Online Auction Sites

While eBay is far and away the largest online auction site today, it's not the only one. You can use several other online auctions, many of which feature lower fees than you pay to eBay. (Some even let you list for free!)

Know, however, that these sites have a lot—and I mean a *lot*—fewer members than does eBay. Fewer members means fewer potential buyers, and fewer potential buyers typically means fewer sales and lower selling prices. That might not be the case in all categories, of course, and a lower sales rate might be offset by a lower fee structure. You'll need to evaluate the potential of these sites personally, to see if they offer anything for you.

Amazon.com Auctions

Amazon.com Auctions (`auctions.amazon.com`) is just one component of the massive Amazon retailing megasite. You know Amazon as a great site to buy stuff; the fact that it also runs an online auction site might come as a bit of a surprise. But auctions it does run, as you can see in Figure 29.1.

FIGURE 29.1

Amazon.com Auctions.

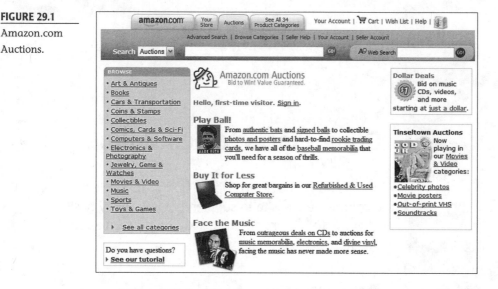

Amazon's auction fees are quite affordable. You pay just a dime to list an item, no matter what the starting bid price. (eBay listing fees start at $0.20 and go up to $4.80, depending on the starting price.) Naturally, Amazon also offers a number of listing enhancements at additional cost, such as boldface and featured placement, but they're easily skipped.

Final value fees (what Amazon calls *payment fees*) are also more affordable than eBay's. You pay 25 cents per listing plus 5% of the final price. This fee includes the payment transaction through the Amazon Payments system, which means the 5% fee is the same as eBay's 5.25% final value fee *plus* the 2.9% PayPal fee. Do the math, and you see that Amazon is significantly lower priced for sellers than eBay is—even if Amazon's 5% fee is on the selling price *plus* shipping and handling fees.

ArtByUs

If you sell original artwork, you probably want to check out ArtByUs (`www.artbyus.com`), an online auction site specifically for artists. As you can see in

Figure 29.2, ArtByUs is like an eBay auction that specializes exclusively in original artwork. It's still relatively new, so it may or may not work for you, but many artists have achieved good initial results.

FIGURE 29.2

ArtByUs art auctions.

ArtByUs charges no listing fees and no final value fees. It does charge for listing enhancements, such as Featured and Bold. Obviously, the volume isn't near as large as eBay's; on any given day, only a few thousand items were listed. (Of course, that makes your item stand out even more!)

Bidville

Bidville (www.bidville.com) is another eBay-like online auction site. As you can see in Figure 29.3, it offers merchandise in many of the same categories as offered on the eBay site. On a recent day, close to a million items were listed—75% of which were in the Sports & Memorabilia category.

You can list any item on Bidville free of charge; this site doesn't charge any listing fees. Final value fees (what Bidville calls *final success fees*—a nice positive attitude, that) run 5% for items up to $25.00. For items between $25.01 and $1,000.00, you pay $1.25 plus 2.5% of the amount over $25.00. For items over $1,000.00, you pay $25.63 plus 1% of the amount over $1,000.00.

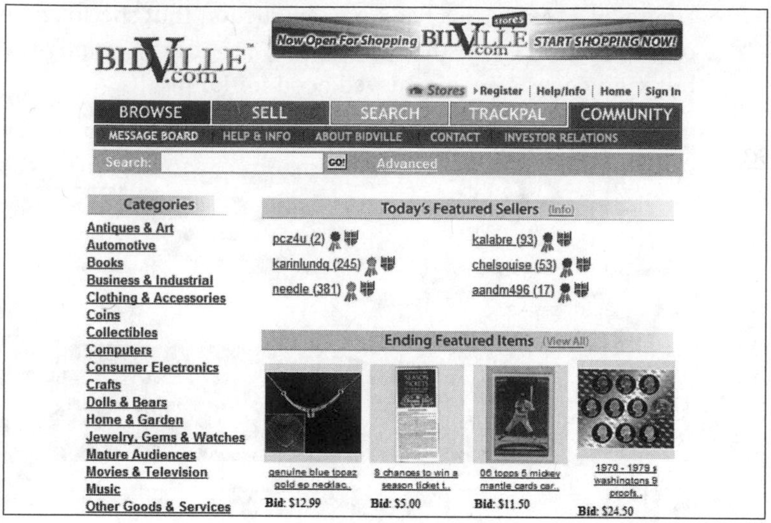

FIGURE 29.3

Bidville auc-
tions—no listing
fees!

iOffer

iOffer (www.ioffer.com) is an auction site that isn't an auction site. Unlike the traditional online auction format, iOffer (shown in Figure 29.4) is based on the principles of negotiation. That is, you list an item for sale, a buyer makes you an offer, and you decide to accept or decline the offer. You can go back and forth with a potential buyer until you find an agreeable selling price.

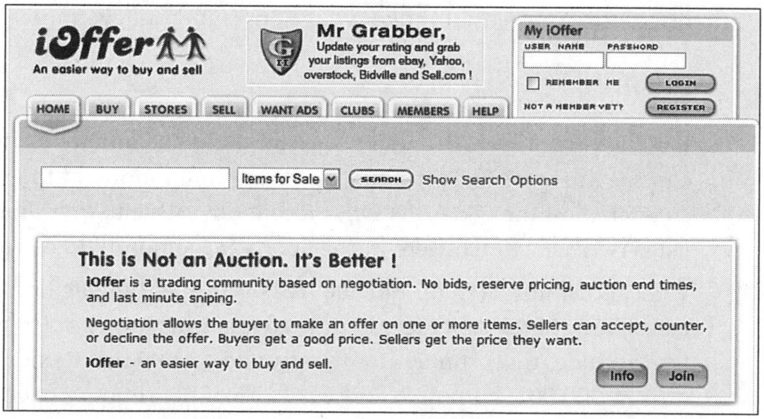

FIGURE 29.4

Make an offer
at iOffer.

The site doesn't charge any listing fees. Final value fees range from $0.50 (for items under $4.99) to 5% (items priced from $25.00–$99.99), with lower rates for higher-priced items. On a recent day iOffer had almost a half-million items listed for sale.

whaBAM!

The newest competitor in the online auction space is whaBAM! (www.whabam.com), shown in Figure 29.5. This site doesn't charge any listing fees; instead, you pay 1% of your final selling price, or a maximum of $25. If you're a heavy seller, you can opt for the Fee Buster service, which charges a single monthly $49.99 fee for an unlimited number of transactions. So far, whaBAM! doesn't seem to have generated much traction, with the number of items listed hovering below 25,000.

FIGURE 29.5

The newest online auction site, whaBAM!

Yahoo! Shopping Auctions

The auction site that's number two (to eBay's number one) is Yahoo! Shopping Auctions (auctions.yahoo.com). As shown in Figure 29.6, Yahoo! Shopping Auctions looks and feels a lot like eBay, and its auctions work pretty much the same way, too—but without listing or final value fees. That's right, Yahoo! Shopping Auctions, which started out by charging lower-than-eBay fees, is now completely free to buyers and sellers. (It still costs to accept PayPal payments, however.) Pretty tempting—even if the volume level is several orders of magnitude below what you're used to with eBay.

FIGURE 29.6

An affordable
alternative to
eBay—Yahoo!
Shopping
Auctions.

Other Selling Sites

If you want to skip the auction format, there are a few sites let you sell your
merchandise at a fixed price—kind of like selling an item with a Buy It Now
price or in an eBay Store.

Amazon Marketplace

If you're tired of the auction grind—and sell items that are more suitable to
the fixed-price format—consider selling at the Amazon Marketplace. This is a
subset of the Amazon.com site that lets individuals and small businesses sell
all manner of new and used items; it's particularly well suited to selling used
books, CDs, videotapes, DVDs, and other fixed-priced items.

Marketplace items are listed as options on normal Amazon product listing
pages (to the right of the main listing) and show up when customers search
for specific products. Figure 29.7 shows a typical listing of Marketplace items
for sale.

One nice thing about selling in the Amazon Marketplace is that customers
can integrate their orders and payments with other Amazon merchandise.
Customers place their orders with and pay Amazon; then Amazon informs
you of the sale and transfers payment (less its fees and plus a reimbursement
for shipping costs) to you. You ship the item to the customer.

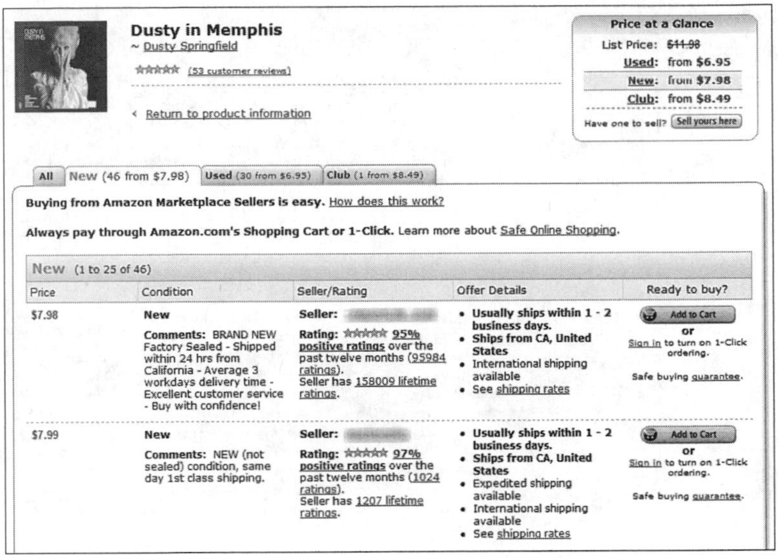

FIGURE 29.7

Amazon
Marketplace
items for sale.

You pay $0.99 to list an item in the Marketplace (although the fee isn't charged until the item sells) and then pay Amazon a percent of the final selling price. You pay a 6% fee for computers, 8% for electronics and cameras, 10% for office products, 12% for musical instruments, and 15% for all other items. Each listing lasts for 60 days. To learn more or place a listing, click the Marketplace link on the bottom-left side of the Amazon home page (www. amazon.com), in the Making Money section.

Craigslist

The dominant online classified advertising site on the Web is the venerable Craigslist. As you can see in Figure 29.8, Craiglist has local sites for all major cities and states, from Atlanta to Washington (DC). Posting a classified ad is completely free; there are no listing fees or sales commissions involved. And, in many categories, Craigslist is a major force, equal to eBay in terms of number of listings and sales. It's worth checking out—especially if you're selling something big or difficult to ship across the country.

Google Base

An up-and-coming competitor to Craigslist is Google Base (base.google.com), from the good folks at Google. As you can see in Figure 29.9, Google Base is a big database of product listings. Items you sell can be paid for via Google Checkout, which is Google's payment service that competes directly with PayPal.

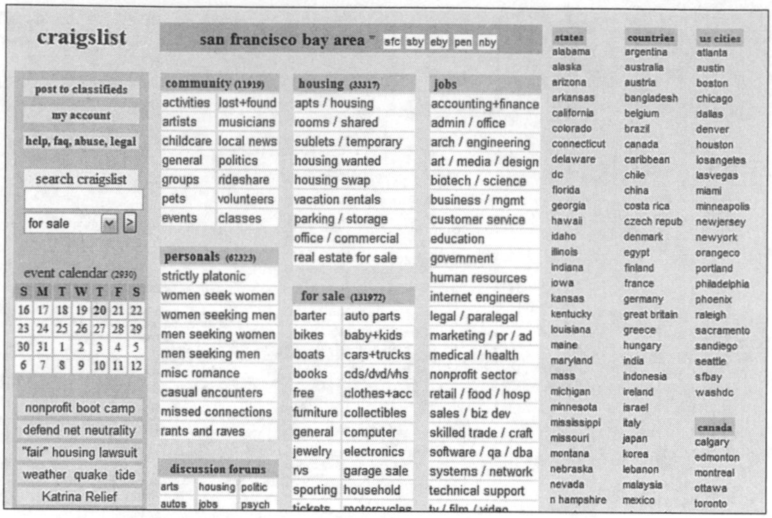

FIGURE 29.8

The place to sell items locally—Craigslist.

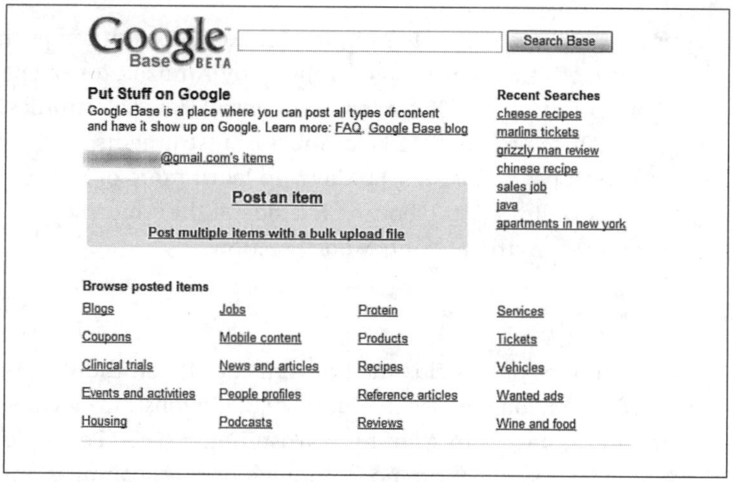

FIGURE 29.9

Google Base—a competitor to either Craigslist or eBay, or maybe both.

The nice thing about Google Base is that it's a totally free service, for both buyers and sellers. Not only can you post items for sale, you can also choose how—or, more precisely, *where*—you sell or distribute your items. If you want to use Google Base as a classified advertising services to sell items for local pickup or delivery, you can. If you want to offer items online for shipment anywhere in the country (or the world), you can. It's your choice.

While Google Base is starting small, it never pays to underestimate Google. It's possible that Google Base could become a true competitor to eBay—or, at the very least, a viable alternative to Craigslist. Only time will tell.

LiveDeal.com

If you're interested in selling your goods locally, consider LiveDeal.com (www.livedeal.com) . As you can see in Figure 29.10, this site lets you market goods locally or regionally, on a fixed-price basis. LiveDeal.com was founded by one of the original members of the eBay development team, so it works and feels quite a bit like the eBay site—but without the auction process. The site doesn't charge any listing or final value fees; the only charges are for various listing enhancements and for the use of PayPal. It's worth checking out if you have large or heavy items that would be difficult to ship nationwide, or if you want to supplement your eBay business with more local sales.

FIGURE 29.10

Sell locally at LiveDeal.com.

Managing Growth

If you're successful with your eBay business, you'll see the sales start to grow from month to month. That's what you want, after all; the bigger your business, the more money you make.

Managing your business growth, however, can be a challenge. It's one thing to move from $50 to $500 of sales every month; it's quite another to advance to the $5,000/month—or even $50,000/month!—level. As your business grows, everything gets bigger. You have more auctions to manage, more photos to take, more emails to send, more items to pack and ship. The prospect of all this extra work can be daunting, but all in all, it's a good problem to have.

This final chapter will help you prepare for and deal with the various issues that result from business success. Are you ready to play with the big boys?

Analyzing Your Business

As your eBay business grows, it's increasingly important for you to analyze your business's performance. That's because lots of sales don't always translate into lots of profits.

Let's take the example of a businessperson I know who had grown his eBay business to the $2,500/month level. Do the math, and you see that this person was on a pace to generate $30,000 a year in sales. That sounds good, but the seller couldn't figure out why he couldn't quit his regular job and rely on his eBay business for full-time employment.

The answer, if you remember my advice from Chapter 3, "Creating a Business Plan," is that revenues aren't the same as profits. Yes, this seller was going to sell $30,000 of merchandise over the course of a year, but after subtracting the costs of that merchandise, along with all relevant eBay fees, the money left over—his profit—was less than $10,000. That $10,000 profit—*not* the $30,000 in revenues—is the seller's salary. And you can't live on $10,000 a year. This person would have to triple his sales rate to generate a minimal net income to live on.

I've seen even worse situations. What about the seller who was moving $2,000/month worth of merchandise and never built up any money in her bank account? She was selling collectible cards for a buck or two a piece, but selling a lot of them to achieve those sales figures. The problem is that she wasn't making any money on it. Yeah, she was able to generate revenues of a buck or so a card, but eBay's listing and final value fees (along with PayPal's credit card fees) ate up every bit of that buck, and sometimes more. Almost every sale this person made cost her a few pennies, and you simply can't sell at a loss and make it up in volume. This seller needed to reevaluate her entire business model and consider charging more for what she sold—or move into higher-priced products.

The takeaway from both these stories is that you not only have to run your eBay business on a day-to-day basis, you have to analyze it, as well. That's why establishing a solid recordkeeping system is important so that you can generate the financial reports necessary to determine just how much profit you're really generating. Only after you're sure that you're truly making money—and enough of it to matter—can you think about increasing your sales and growing your business.

note Learn more about accounting and financial analysis in Chapter 6, "Setting Up a Recordkeeping System," and Appendix A, "Accounting Basics."

Locating More Merchandise to Sell

As you grow your business, you have to feed more merchandise into the pipeline. That means somehow obtaining more inventory to sell; you don't want to be constrained by product availability.

How do you beef up your product inventory? Here are some suggestions:

- If you resell used items you find at garage sales and thrift stores, consider hiring someone to scrounge for you full-time. Also consider buying large assortments at estate sales and live auctions.

- If you're a collector, consider purchasing large collections for resale, or expanding your selection to include related merchandise and accessories.

- If you purchase closeout or liquidated merchandise, consider purchasing larger lots or entire pallets.

- If you purchase merchandise from a manufacturer or authorized distributor, consider upping your orders or expanding your selection.

- If you're an artist, consider selling prints in addition to original paintings. Also consider reselling works by other artists you know.

- If you create your own crafts to sell, consider hiring someone to help you create a larger volume of items.

- If you're a manufacturer, consider increasing your production output.

- If you're a Trading Assistant, consider increasing your advertising and promotion for new clients, or opening a drop-off location.

In short, you need to start thinking more about your purchasing, in addition to your selling. And remember to buy smart. Shaving a few pennies off the price of each item can result in huge profits as you increase your sales volume.

Finding More Space

Naturally, the more inventory you buy, the more space you need to store it. If you're running your eBay business out of your house, there will come a time when you simply run out of room. Short of kicking out your kids (and that may not be a bad thing, for various reasons...), there are only so many empty rooms you can use to store your merchandise. When the walls start to bulge, you need to think about finding additional warehouse space.

This extra space can come in many forms. For many eBay businesses, you may be able to make do with rented storage space in one of those "u-store-it" places. If you're getting really big—or selling really big items—then you may need to look at more professional warehousing solutions.

The challenge in all this, of course, is the cost. When you get big enough to require paid warehousing, you have to figure that monthly rent into your business costs. The first month you have a rent bill will be a big shock, trust me.

And you may need more than just warehousing space. Consider how much space you need for your packing operation and for general office work. As your business grows, all your space needs grow, as well—and space costs money.

Hiring Additional Employees

Space isn't the last of your problems. The more items you sell, the more physical work you have to do. As your weekly sales increase from 10 items to 100 to 1,000, how do you handle all the listing and packing and shipping and such?

The answer is that when you reach a certain point, you won't be able to do it all yourself. When the work becomes too overwhelming, you'll need to bring in someone to help you with it. That's right, I'm talking about hiring employees.

When I say "employee," I'm not talking about the neighbor kid you pay a few bucks to run some boxes down to the post office. I'm talking about honest-to-goodness employees, part-time or full-time, that you write a paycheck to at the end of every week. The kind of employees who call you "boss"—which you now are.

Hiring employees is a challenge, a subject worthy of an entire book; I don't have the space to go into all the ins and outs here. Suffice to say you first have to find your potential employees (via help wanted ads and other venues), interview them, figure out how much to pay them, set their work schedules, and then train and manage them. Yes, being a boss is a lot of work; you'll have to devote some portion of your day to employee-related issues, including basic management.

What Should Your Employees Do?

Before you hire an employee, you need to be clear about what it is that you want that employee to do. At its most basic, you want an employee to handle some of your auction-related activities—to lighten your workload. The question is, *which* activities do you want your employee to do?

Most eBay sellers hire an employee to do those activities that they either don't like to do, don't do well, or don't add any value by doing themselves. In many (but not all) instances, this translates into letting your employee handle your "back end" activities—packing and shipping. That's because, when you evaluate what it is you do, you'll probably find that your talents are better suited to purchasing merchandise and creating and managing your eBay listings. It's easier, in most instances, to train someone to pack boxes and drive to the post office than it is to train him or her to create effective item listings.

You should, of course, make your own decision about what you want from your employees. I know some sellers who hire people to go to garage sales, yard sales, and the like, while they stay in the office and manage the other auction activities. Other sellers hire people to take photos and write HTML code for their listings. Deciding what you want your employees to do depends on what you need done—and what you like doing.

Don't Forget the Details

Obviously, a certain degree of recordkeeping needs to be done when your business has employees. You'll have to add your employees to your accounting system, start paying employment taxes, and do all the associated paperwork.

There's not enough space here to go into all the details, but here are some specific things to keep in mind:

- You'll need to have each employee provide you with his or her full name and Social Security number, which you then enter on a W-2 form.
- You must verify that each new employee is legally eligible to work in the U.S., by having him or her fill out the Employment Eligibility Verification form I-9.
- You'll also need each new employee to fill out an Employee's Withholding Allowance Certificate form W-4.
- You'll have to withhold the proper amount of income tax from each of your employee's paychecks, which is tied to the W-4 form. Obviously, you don't get to keep the money you withhold; you have to pass it on to the government, according to a predetermined schedule.

■ Speaking of paying taxes, you're also responsible for paying various federal, state, and local employment taxes, including Social Security and Medicare taxes.

note Learn more about your tax responsibilities as an employer from the IRS Employer's Tax Guide, at `www.irs.gov/publications/p15/index.html`.

■ At the end of each calendar year, you'll need to prepare and provide W-2 forms to each employee; you also need to send copies to the Social Security Administration.

Sound complicated and potentially messy? It is, which is why now is definitely the time to schedule a meeting with your accountant. And if you don't yet have an accountant, get one.

Another thing to think about is what sorts of benefits you want to offer your employees. These benefits might include paid vacations, health care, and the like. Again, your accountant is a good person to consult about these issues.

Managing Your Time

The whole point of hiring employees is to help you better manage your personal time. What's the point of making a lot of money from an eBay business if you have to work 20 hours a day to do so? It's okay for your eBay business to be a full-time job, but you don't want it to be more than that. You have to learn to manage your time in an efficient manner—and offloading some work to others is just part of that process.

A large component of time management is developing processes and a schedule. You can't run a big business if you treat every sale as a special event. You need to plan your time so that you handle things in batches. Maybe you handle all financial transactions in the evening, or all your packing on a certain day, or make just one trip to the post office a week. You have to strive for efficiency, or else you'll become overwhelmed by everything you need to do. And don't forget to offload some of that workload to your employees—that's why they're there!

How Big Is Too Big?

As you can see, it costs more (in both time and money) to run a bigger business than it does to run a smaller one. At some point you'll need to ask yourself just how big you want your business to grow. Do you want to run a

$50,000/year business that takes 80 hours a week of your time, or limit yourself to a $30,000/year business that you can manage in an eight-hour day? Is growing your sales worth the hassle of hiring an employee or two or renting warehouse space, or can you be happy with a smaller home-based single-person business?

Running a bigger business is a lot different than running a smaller one. When you have a small business, you're truly working for yourself. As your business grows, you're now working as part of a machine—even though you're supposedly running that machine. There is much stress associated with managing employees, making sure you have money in the bank to pay for rent, and so forth. Many people prefer to keep their businesses small and their stress levels low; others like the challenge of running and growing a thriving enterprise.

Bottom line, you can control just how big your eBay business becomes. If you want to keep it small, keep it small; there's nothing that says it has to grow beyond a certain point. If you want to run a bigger business, go for it. (Although there's no guarantee that will happen, of course.) The point is, it's your choice to make. That's one of the benefits of running your own business, after all; you have total control over the form that business takes.

With an eBay business, you control the size by controlling the number of auctions you run. You grow your business by running more auctions; you limit its size by running fewer auctions. That's one of the things I really like about an eBay business—your future is fully in your own hands.

Part 6

Appendixes

Accounting Basics

For those of you who slept through your college accounting classes, this appendix will help you brush up on just enough basic accounting to help you manage your burgeoning eBay business.

What follows are the key financial concepts that describe how a business is doing, money-wise.

Revenues, Expenses, and Profits

Three related concepts are key to the running of any business:

- **Revenues**. Revenues (also called *sales*) are the dollars you generate by selling your products. There are two types of revenues: gross revenues and net revenues. *Gross revenues* are the straight sales dollars you record; *net revenues* are your sales dollars less any returned or discounted sales. Revenues never have any costs or expenses deducted. They're pure sales; nothing else is included.

■ **Expenses**. Expenses are your costs, the money you have to pay for various goods and services. There are several different types of expenses. *Cost of goods sold* (COGS) are product costs directly associated with the manufacture or purchase of the goods that contribute to your revenues. *Operating expenses* are those nonproduct costs that reflect the day-to-day operations of your business—supplies, salaries, rent, and so on. COGS and operating expenses are typically reported in different parts of your income statement.

note Costs can be either *fixed* or *variable*. Fixed costs are typically those operating expenses that you have to pay no matter how many (or how few) products you sell; your monthly Internet bill is a good example of a fixed cost. Variable costs are those costs that vary depending on your revenues; eBay final value fees are variable expenses.

■ **Profits**. If revenues reflect how much money you take in and expenses reflect how much money you pay out, profits reflect how much money you have left after the two previous activities. (Profit is often referred to as *income* or *earnings*.)

Don't get these concepts confused. It's easy to slip and think of your revenues as "earnings" (since you "earned" that money!), but the word "earnings" actually refers to profits. Same with income—income is profit, not revenue. If in doubt, refer to Table A.1 for some quick guidance.

Table A.1   Basic Financial Terms

Proper Names for ...

What You Sell	What You Spend	What You Get to Keep
Revenues	Expenses	Profits
Sales	Costs	Earnings
		Income
		Bottom line

The way it works is simple. You generate your revenues from selling items on eBay. You subtract your expenses (cost of goods sold, daily operating expenses), and that leaves you with your profit. (Hopefully.) Here's what the equation looks like:

Profit Equation

REVENUES − EXPENSES = PROFITS

If you subtract expenses from revenues and get a negative number, that means you've generated a loss; that is, you've spent more than you earned. Not a good thing.

Let's work through a short example. Let's say that in a given month you generate $1,000 in eBay sales. The items you sold cost you $500 to purchase, and you spent another $300 on miscellaneous day-to-day expenses—shipping boxes, labels, Internet access, and the like. Add the $500 to the $300 to get your total expenses, and then subtract that number ($800) from your $1,000 of revenues. You end up with $200 left over—which is your profit for the month.

Assets and Liabilities

Revenues, expenses, and profits are used to describe what your business does; assets and liabilities describe what your business *owns* and *owes*. Here's how they're defined:

- **Assets**. Assets are those items that you own. Assets can be in the form of physical things (land, buildings, equipment, fixtures), cash or cash equivalents, or accounts receivable. In short, anything you own or that is owed to you is counted as an asset.

- **Liabilities**. Liabilities are the opposite of assets; they're things that someone else owns and for which you owe. Liabilities are typically in the form of loans, expenses, or taxes due.

If you take everything you own and subtract everything you owe, the balance represents your *net worth* in your business—also known as your *equity*. This equation is the core concept behind that financial statement called a *balance sheet*.

Equity Equation

ASSETS − LIABILITIES = NET WORTH

Again, a short example. Let's say that you have $300 in inventory sitting in your garage, another $100 in unused shipping boxes, plus you're owed $100 for closed auctions that the buyer hasn't paid yet. You also happen to have a whole $100 sitting in your business bank account. Add it all together, and that $600 total represents your assets.

Now let's look at what you owe. Rummaging through your "bills to pay" file, you see that you have a $100 bill due to pay for those shipping boxes, plus another $220 due for various other expenses—utilities, Internet service, and the like. That $320 total represents your liabilities.

Subtract the $320 in liabilities from the $600 in assets, and you end up with a net worth of $280. That's your current equity in your business.

The Difference Between Profits and Cash

Let's return for a moment to your income statement, and your business's revenues, expenses, and profits. You might think that the profits you make would feed the cash component of your assets. In theory, this could be the case—especially if you run a relatively small, relatively simple business. However, two factors can make these two numbers get out of whack.

First, you probably don't pay all your bills on the day you receive them. When a bill is due but you haven't paid it yet, you have created a liability, which will change your asset position. Let's use an example in which you start with zero assets and zero liabilities. You sell an item for $5 and, after subtracting $2 cost of goods sold, generate a $3 gross profit. That $3 in your pocket is both cash and asset—until you receive a bill from eBay for $1 worth of fees. Now you have a $1 liability—and a $1 expense. Even though you haven't paid the bill yet, you still have to figure the expense, which reduces your *net* profit to $2. You still have $3 in cash, but your profit is now just $2. So, for the time being, your cash doesn't equal your profit. (This will be rectified as soon as you write a check for $1 to eBay, of course.)

The second way in which cash and profits differ is if you accept payment on credit. Let's say you sold that $5 item (which generated a $3 gross profit) to Mr. Smith, who signed the invoice and promised to pay within 30 days. Now you have a $3 profit but zero dollars in cash—and you won't have the cash until Mr. Smith sends you a check later this month.

This is all to demonstrate why you must look at your cash situation as being separate from your profits—as tempting as it might be to think that your monthly profits would equate to real cash on hand.

note The $5 due from Mr. Smith becomes an asset on your books, in the form of an *accounts receivable*.

Just because you have a certain amount of cash in the bank doesn't mean that all that cash is yours. Some of it may have to be used to pay future bills.

Financial Statements

You measure all your financial activity via a series of numerical reports that we call, in general, *financial statements*. There are two key financial statements for any business: the income statement and the balance sheet.

Income Statement

An income statement is a financial statement that details your business's revenues, expenses, and profit (or loss). As you can see in Figure A.1, it acts kind of like a giant equation. You start at the top with your revenues; then you subtract the cost of goods sold and the operating expenses. What you have left, at the bottom of the statement, is your net profit (or loss).

FIGURE A.1

A typical income statement.

Income Statement

Gross Sales (Gross Revenues)	$53,697
Returns	$767
Net Sales (Net Revenues)	$52,930
Cost of Goods Sold (COGS)	$12,642
Gross Profit	$40,288
Gross Profit Margin (Gross Margin)	76.1%
Operating Expenses	
Salaries (Wages)	$14,672
Marketing	$1,200
Selling	$5,463
General & Administrative	$1,767
Utilities	$650
Automobile	$1,165
Travel & Entertainment	$542
Dues/Subscriptions	$273
Loan Payments	$1,750
Total Operating Expenses	$27,482
Net Profit (Loss)	$12,806
Net Margin	24.2%

Operating expenses are typically broken out into multiple line items. In addition, you'll see the gross profit and net profit described as percentages of net revenues. (When shown this way, they're called *gross margin* and *net margin*.)

Here's a brief explanation of the most important line items on the income statement:

- **Gross Revenues**. This line (also called *Gross Sales*) reflects all of your dollar sales for the period, not counting any damaged or returned goods.

- **Returns**. Sometimes called *Returns and Allowances*, this line reflects the cost of any returned or damaged merchandise, as well as any allowances and markdowns.

- **Net Revenues**. Net Revenues (also called *Net Sales*) reflect your Gross Revenues less your Returns and Allowances.

> **note** Not all income statements include the Gross Revenues and Returns lines. Many income statements start with the Net Revenues number as the first line, assuming the necessary gross-minus-returns calculation.

- **Cost of Goods Sold**. This line (also called *COGS* or *Cost of Sales*) reflects the direct costs of the products you sold for the period.

- **Gross Profit**. This line reflects the direct profit you made from sales during this period. It is calculated by subtracting the Cost of Goods Sold from Net Revenues.

- **Gross Margin**. This line (also called *Gross Profit Margin*) describes your Gross Profit as a percent of your Net Revenues. You calculate this number by dividing Gross Profit by Net Revenues.

- **Operating Expenses**. This line reflects all the indirect costs of your business. Typical line items within this overall category include Salaries, Advertising, Marketing, Selling, Office, Office Supplies, Rent, Leases, Utilities, Automobile, Travel and Entertainment (T&E), General and Administrative (G&A), Dues and Subscriptions, Licenses and Permits, and Training. *Not* included in this section are direct product costs (which should be reflected in the Cost of Goods Sold), loan payments, interest on loans, taxes, depreciation, and amortization.

- **Net Profit (Loss)**. This line (also called *Net Earnings* or *Net Income*; the words "income," "earnings," and "profit" are synonymous) reflects your reported profit or loss. You calculate this number by subtracting Operating Expenses from Gross Profit; a loss is notated within parentheses.

> **note** In all financial statements, a loss is typically noted by inserting the number in parentheses. So, if you see ($200), you note a loss of $200. An alternative, although less accepted, method is to put a negative sign in front of any losses. If you're printing in color, you would use red (in addition to the parentheses) to notate all losses.

- **Net Margin**. This line describes your Net Profit as a percentage of your Net Sales. You calculate this number by dividing Net Profit by Net Sales.

Balance Sheet

The balance sheet is a companion record to the income statement. As you can see in Figure A.2, it lists your business's assets (on the left side) and your liabilities (on the right). The total value of your assets should be equal to the total value of your liabilities; the basic concept is that what you're worth balances with what you owe.

Balance Sheet

Assets			Liabilities		
Current Assets			Current Liabilities		
	Cash	$12,453		Accounts Payable	$1,647
	Accounts Receivable	$894		Interest Payable	$128
	Inventories	$1,275	Total Current Liabilities		$1,775
Total Current Assets		$14,622			
			Long-Term Liabilities		
Long-Term Assets				Long-Term Notes Payable	$3,375
	Equipment	$4,975		Taxes Payable	$563
Total Long-Term Assets		$4,975	Total Long-Term Liabilities		$3,938
			Equity (Net Worth)		$13,884
Total Assets		$19,597	Total Liabilities and Net Worth		$19,597

Here's a brief explanation of the most important asset items on the balance sheet:

- **Current Assets**. This category includes those items that can be converted into cash within the next 12 months. Typical line items would include Cash, Accounts Receivable, Inventories, and Short-Term Investments.

- **Fixed Assets**. This category (sometimes called *Long-Term Assets*) includes assets that are *not* easily converted into cash, including Land, Buildings, Accumulated Depreciation (as a negative number), Improvements, Equipment, Furniture, and Vehicles.

- **Long-Term Investments**. This category includes any longer-term investments your business has made.

- **Total Assets**. This line reflects the value of everything your company owns. You calculate this number by adding together Current Assets and Fixed Assets.

The following are the key line items on the liabilities side of the balance sheet:

- **Current Liabilities**. This category includes any debts or monetary obligations payable within the next 12 months. Typical line items include Accounts Payable, Notes Payable, Interest Payable, and Taxes Payable.

■ **Long-Term Liabilities**. This category includes debts and obligations that are due to be paid over a period exceeding 12 months. Typical line items include Long-Term Notes Payable and Deferred Taxes.

note To make your balance sheet actually balance, the Total Liabilities and Net Worth number must equal the number for Total Assets.

■ **Equity**. This line (sometimes called *Net Worth*) reflects the owners' investment in the business. Depending on the type of ownership, this line may be broken into separate lines reflecting the individual equity positions of multiple partners or the company's capital stock and retained earnings.

■ **Total Liabilities and Net Worth**. This line (sometimes called *Total Liabilities and Equity*) reflects the total amount of money due plus the owners' value. You calculate this number by adding Current Liabilities, Long-Term Liabilities, and Equity.

Listing Abbreviations

The following table presents the most common abbreviations you can use in your item listings. These abbreviations can be used to describe the condition of the items you're selling.

Abbreviation	Description
1E	First edition. The first edition of a book or similar item. Don't confuse with first *printing*, which is the initial print run of a given edition.
1st	Same as 1E.
2E	Second edition. The second edition of a book or similar item.
2nd	Same as 2E.
ABM	Automatic bottle machine (bottles prior to 1910).
ACC	Accumulation (stamps).
ACL	Applied color label (bottles).
ADV	Adventure (books/movies).
AE	American Express.
AG	About Good (coins).
AIR	Air mail (stamps).
AMEX	American Express.
ANTH	Anthology (books).
AO	All original.
ARC	Advanced readers copy. A prepublication version of a book manuscript, typically released to reviewers and bookstores for publicity purposes.
AU	About Uncirculated (coins)
AUTO	Autographed. An item that has been autographed by the artist or other celebrity.
BA	Bronze Age.
BB	BB-sized hole. A small hole drilled through a record label. (Can also be an abbreviation for Beanie Baby.)
BC	Blister card. The display card packaging for many retail items. (Can also be an abbreviation for *back cover*.)
BCE	Book club edition. A special edition of a book sold exclusively through book clubs.
BIM	Blown in mold (bottles prior to 1910).
BIN	Buy It Now.
BIO	Biography.
BJ	Ball jointed body (dolls).
BK	Bent knee (dolls).
BKL	Booklet (stamps).

Abbreviation	Description
BLB	Big Little Book.
BLK	Block (stamps).
BOMC	Book of the Month Club edition. A special edition of a book published exclusively for the Book of the Month Club.
BP	Blister pack. (Can also be an abbreviation for *booklet pane*, which is a type of display case for collectible stamps.)
BTAS	*Batman: the Animated Series.*
BU	Built up. For models and other to-be-assembled items, indicates that the item has already been assembled. (Can also be an abbreviation for *brilliant uncirculated*, a condition for collectible coins.)
BW	Black and white (photos, illustrations, drawings).
C & S	Creamer & sugar; can also be an abbreviation for *cup and saucer*.
C	Cover (stamps). (Can also be an abbreviation for *cartridge only* when referring to videogames—no instructions included.)
CART	Cartridge (videogame).
CB	Club book (stamps).
CC	Cut corner. Some closeout items are marked by a notch on the corner of the package. (Can also be an abbreviation for *carbon copy, credit card*, and—when referring to collectible stamps—*commemorative cover*.)
CCA	Comics Code Authority.
CCG	Collectable card game.
CDF	Customs declaration form (stamps).
CF	Centerfold (magazines).
CFO	Center fold out (magazines).
CI	Cartridge and instructions (videogames, computer equipment).
CIB	Cartridge/instructions/box (videogames, computer equipment).
CIBO	Cartridge/instructions/box/overlay (videogames, computer equipment).
CLA	Cleaned, lubricated, adjusted. For cameras, notes standard pre-sale maintenance.
CM	Customized.
CO	Cut out; closeout item.
COA	Certificate of authenticity. Document that vouches for the authenticity of the item; often found with autographed or rare collectible items.
COC	Cutout corner. Same as CC (cut corner).
COH	Cut out hole. Some closeout items are marked by a small hole punched somewhere on the package.

Abbreviation	Description
COL	Collection.
CONUS	Continental United States (ship-to destination).
CPN	Coupon.
CPP	Colored picture postcard.
CS	Creamer & sugar. (Can also refer to *cup & saucer*.)
CTB	Coffee table book.
CU	Crisp uncirculated. For currency, a description of condition.
D	Denver mint (coins).
DB	Divided back (postcards).
DBL	Double; 2-in-1 (paperback books).
DG	Depression glass.
DJ	Dust jacket included with many hardcover books. (Can be an abbreviation for *disk jockey copy*, when referring to promotional records or CDs distributed to DJs and radio stations.)
DOA	Dead on arrival (item in nonworking order when received).
DUTCH	Dutch auction (multiple quantities available).
EAPC	Early American Prescut (a type of Anchor Hocking glass c. 1960+).
EAPG	Early American pattern glass.
EC	Excellent condition.
EF	Extra Fine condition.
EG	Elegant glass (Depression-era).
EP	Extended Play (records, videotapes).
ERR	Error.
EX	Excellent (condition), extra, or except.
EXLIB	Ex-library. A book that was obtained from a public or school library.
EXT	Extended
F/E	First edition (books).
FC	Fine condition. (Can also be an abbreviation for the *front cover* of a book or magazine.)
FDC	First day cover (stamps).
FE	First edition (books).
FFC	First flight cover (stamps),
FFEP	Free front end page/paper. This refers to the first blank page of a book, usually an extension of the part pasted down on the inside front cover.

Abbreviation	Description
FFL	Federally licensed firearms (dealer).
FN	Fine condition.
FOR	Forgery
FPLP	Fisher Price Little People.
FS	Factory sealed. Still in the original manufacturer's packaging.
FT	Flat top (beer cans).
FVF	Final value fee; the fee charged by eBay based on the final price of auction.
G	Good condition.
GA	Golden Age.
GD	Good condition.
GF	Gold filled.
GGA	Good girl art (paperback book covers).
GP	Gold plate. Item is gold plated. (Can also refer to *gutter pair* in the world of stamp collecting.)
GSP	Gold sterling plate.
GU	Gently used.
GW	Gently worn. Used clothing with little wear.
HB	Hardback or hardcover book.
HB/DJ	Hardback with dust jacket. Hardcover book complete with original dust jacket.
HC	Hardcover (as opposed to softcover, or paperback) books. (Can also refer to *hand colored* maps or engravings.)
HE	Heavy gold electroplated. Item has heavy gold plating.
HIC	Hole in cover. A book with a hole stamped through the cover.
HIL	Hole in label. Same as HIC, but for any type of merchandise label.
HIST	Historical (books).
HM	Happy Meal (McDonald's).
HOF	Hall of Famer (baseball memorabilia/autograph/trading cards).
HP	Hard plastic; a particular type of doll. (Can also refer to any *hand painted* item, or to products from the *Hewlett-Packard* company.)
HS	Hand stamp (stamps).
HTF	Hard to find. Item isn't in widespread circulation.
IBC	Inside back cover.
IFC	Inside front cover.

Abbreviation	Description
ILLO	Illustration.
ILLUS	Illustration or illustrated.
INIT	Initial, initials, or initial issue.
IRAN	Inspect and repair as decessary.
ISH	Issue.
JUVIE	Juvenile delinquency theme.
L	Large.
LBBP	Large bean bag plush (Disney).
LBC	Lower back cover.
LE	Limited edition. Item was produced in limited quantities.
LFC	Lower front cover.
LFT	Left.
LLBC	Lower left of back cover.
LLFC	Lower left of front cover.
LP	Little People (Fisher Price toys) or long-playing record.
LRBC	Lower right on back cover.
LRFC	Lower right on front cover.
LSE	Loose
LSW	Label shows wear. Item's label shows normal usage for its age.
LTBX	Letterbox (video that re-creates a widescreen image).
LTD	Limited edition.
LWOL	Lot of writing on label (records).
M	Medium, mint, or mono (records).
MA	Madame Alexander (dolls).
MAP	Map back (paperback books).
MC	Miscut.
MCU	Might clean up. Might show a higher grade if cleaned or otherwise restored.
MEDIC	Medical genre (paperbacks).
MIB	Mint in box. Item in perfect condition, still in the original box—although the box itself might not be in mint condition.
MIBP	Mint in blister pack. Item in perfect condition, still on the original blister packaging.
MIJ	Made in Japan.

Abbreviation	Description
MIMB	Mint in mint box. Item in perfect condition, still in the original box—which itself is in perfect condition.
MIMP	Mint in mint package. Item in perfect condition, still in the original package—which itself is in perfect condition.
MIOJ	Made in occupied Japan.
MIOP	Mint in opened package. Item in perfect condition, although the package itself has been opened.
MIP	Mint in package. Item in perfect condition, still in the original package.
MISB	Mint in sealed box. Item in perfect condition, still in the original box with the original seal.
MIU	Made in USA.
MM	Merry Miniatures (Hallmark). (Can also stand for *mounted mint* collectible stamps.)
MMA	Metropolitan Museum of Art.
MNB	Mint, no box. Mint-condition item but without the original package.
MNH	Mint never hinged (stamps)
MOC	Mint on card. For action figures and similar items, an item in perfect condition still in its original carded package.
MOMA	Museum of Modern Art.
MOMC	Mint on mint card. Item in perfect condition, still on its original carded package—which is also in mint condition.
MONMC	Mint on near-mint card. Same as MOMC, but with the card in less-than-perfect condition.
MONO	Monophonic (sound recordings and equipment).
MOP	Mother of pearl.
MOTU	*Masters of the Universe*.
MP	Military post (stamps).
MS	Mint state (coins), usually followed by a number from 62 to 70, such as "MS62" or "MS-62." (Can also stand for *miniature sheet* when referring to collectible stamps, or *Microsoft* when referring to computer software.)
MWBMT	Mint with both mint tags. For stuffed animals that typically have both a hang tag and a tush (sewn-on) tag, indicates both tags are in perfect condition.
MWBT	Mint with both tags. Same as MWBMT, but with the tags in less-than-mint condition.

Abbreviation	Description
MWBTM	Mint with both tags mint; same as MWBMT.
MWMT	Mint with mint tag. Mint-condition item with its original tag, in mint condition.
MYS	Mystery (books/movies).
N/R	No reserve.
NAP	Not affected play. Refers to scratches and other blemishes on a vinyl record that doesn't affect the playback of the recording.
NARU	Not a registered user.
NASB	Nancy Ann story book.
NBW	Never been worn (clothes).
NC	No cover. A used book or magazine that is missing its original cover.
ND	No date or no dog (when referring to RCA record labels).
NDSR	No dents, scratches, or rust. A well-preserved tin can or similar item.
NIB	New in box. Brand-new item, still in its original box.
NIP	New in package. Brand-new item, still in its original packaging.
NL	Number line. Refers to a means of telling the edition of a book; occurs on the copyright page and reads "1234567890." (The lowest number indicates the edition.)
NM	Near mint. An item that is in almost perfect condition.
NORES	No reserve.
NOS	New old stock. Old, discontinued parts in original, unused condition.
NP	Not packaged or no package.
NR	No reserve. Indicates that you're selling an item with no reserve price.
NRFB	Never removed from box. An item bought but never used or played with.
NRFSB	Never removed from sealed box.
NRMNT	Near mint.
NW	Never worn. Clothing that has never been worn.
NWOT	New without tags. Item, unused, but without its original tags.
NWT	New with tags. Item, unused, that still has its original hanging tags.
O	New Orleans mint.
O/C	On canvas (paintings).
OB	Original box. An item that comes with its original packaging.
OC	Off center, off cut, or on canvas.
OEM	Original equipment manufacturer.

Abbreviation	Description
OF	Original finish.
OJ	Occupied Japan.
OOAK	One of a kind.
OOP	Out of print/production. Item is no longer being manufactured. (Can also be an abbreviation for *out of package*.)
OP	Out of print.
OS	Operating system (computers).
OST	Original soundtrack.
P	Poor condition. (Can also refer to *Philadelphia mint* coins.)
P/O	Punched out. Same as CC (cut corner).
P/S	Picture sleeve (records).
PB	Paperback or paperbound. A softcover book.
PBO	Paperback original.
PC	Picture postcard or poor condition.
PD	Picture disk (a record with a photo or image on it).
PF	Proof coin.
PIC	Picture.
PM	Post mark (postcards; first day covers), postal markings (postcards; first day covers), or Priority Mail.
POC	Pencil on cover. A book with slight pencil markings on the cover.
POPS	Promo only picture sleeve.
POTF	Power of the Force (*Star Wars*).
PP	Parcel Post or PayPal.
PPD	Post paid.
PR	Poor condition. (Can also refer to *proof* coins.)
PROOF	Proof coin.
PS	Power supply (electronics equipment) or picture sleeve (records).
R	Reprint
RBC	Right side of back cover.
RC	Reader copy. A book that is in good condition but with no true investment value.
RET	Retired.
RETRD	Retired.
RFC	Right side of front cover.

Abbreviation	Description
RFDO	Removed for display only.
RI	Reissue (records).
RMA	Return merchandise authorization number.
ROM	Romantic (books).
RP	Real photo postcard.
RPPC	Real photo postcard; same as RP.
RR	Re-release. Not the original issue, but rather a reissue (typically done for the collector's market).
RRH	Remade/repainted/haired (dolls).
RS	Rubber stamped on label (records). (Can also be an abbreviation for *rhinestone*.)
RSP	Rhodium sterling plate.
RT	Right.
S	Small, stereo (records), or San Francisco mint (coins).
S/H	Shipping and handling.
S/H/I	Shipping/handling/insurance.
S/O	Sold out.
S/P	Salt and pepper (shakers) or silverplate (flatware or hollowware).
S/S	Still sealed or single sheet (stamps).
SA	Silver Age.
SB	Soft bound or soft back (referring to soft large bound books).
SC	Slight crease. A hang tag, book, or magazine that has been folded or creased. (Can also be an abbreviation for *softcover* books.)
SCI	Science (books).
SCR	Scratch.
SCU	Scuff (records).
SD	Shaded dog (RCA record labels).
SF	Science fiction.
SFBC	Science Fiction Book Club (sometimes the true first edition).
SH	Shipping and handling.
SHI	Shipping/handling/insurance.
SIG	Signature.
SLD	Sealed.
SLT	Slight.
SLW	Straight Leg Walker (dolls).

Abbreviation	Description
SO	Sold out.
SOL	Sticker on label. A record that has a pricing or similar sticker on the record label.
SP	Sticker pull. Refers to the discoloration or actual removal of cover color on a book, caused by pulling off a sticker price. (Can also be an abbreviation for *silverplate* flatware or hollowware.)
SR	Shrink wrapped or light ring wear.
SS	Still sealed in the original package; stainless steel; or store stamp (a stamp on the endpaper or edge of a book that displays a store name/address).
ST	Soundtrack (records, CDs), *Star Trek*, or sterling.
STCCG	*Star Trek* collectable card game.
STER	Sterling.
STNG	*Star Trek: The Next Generation*.
SUSP	Suspended or suspense (books).
SW	Slight wear, shrink wrapped, or *Star Wars*.
SWCCG	*Star Wars* collectable card game.
SWCS	*Star Wars* collector series (toys).
TBB	Teenie Beanie Babies.
TC	True crime (books).
TE	Trade edition books. The standard edition of a book, often smaller than the first edition.
TM	Trademark.
TMOL	Tape mark on label (records).
TNG	*The Next Generation (Star Trek)*.
TOBC	Top of back cover.
TOFC	Top of front cover.
TOL	Tear on label. A record with a torn record label.
TOS	Tape on spine, terms of service, or The Original Series (*Star Trek*).
TOUGH	Tough guy genre (paperbacks).
TRPQ	Tall, round, pyroglaze quart (milk bottles).
U	Used (stamps).
UB	Undivided back (postcards).
UDV	Undivided back (postcards); same as UB.
ULBC	Upper left back cover (books, magazines).

Abbreviation	Description
ULRC	Upper right back cover (books, magazines).
UNC	Uncirculated. A coin that has not been released into general circulation.
URFC	Upper right front cover (books, magazines).
V/M/D	Visa/MasterCard/Discover.
VERM	Vermeil. A type of gold plating on sterling silver, bronze, or copper.
VF	Very fine condition.
VFD	Vacuum flourescent display.
VFU	Very fine, used (stamps).
VG	Very good condition.
VHTF	Very hard to find.
W	West Point mint/depository (coins).
W/C	Watercolor (paintings, maps).
WB	White border (post cards).
WC	Watercolor (paintings, maps).
WD	White dog (RCA record labels).
WLP	White label promo.
WOB	Writing on back
WOC	Writing on cover.
WOF	Writing on front.
WOR	Writing on record.
WRP	Warp (records).
WS	Widescreen (same as letterbox).
WSOL	Water stain on label (records).
XL	Extra large.

Index

J - K - L

P

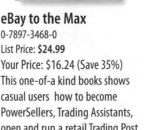

THIS BOOK IS SAFARI ENABLED

INCLUDES FREE 45-DAY ACCESS TO THE ONLINE EDITION

The Safari® Enabled icon on the cover of your favorite technology book means the book is available through Safari Bookshelf. When you buy this book, you get free access to the online edition for 45 days.

Safari Bookshelf is an electronic reference library that lets you easily search thousands of technical books, find code samples, download chapters, and access technical information whenever and wherever you need it.

TO GAIN 45-DAY SAFARI ENABLED ACCESS TO THIS BOOK:

- Go to **http://www.quepublishing.com/safarienabled**

- Complete the brief registration form

- Enter the coupon code found in the front of this book on the "Copyright" page

If you have difficulty registering on Safari Bookshelf or accessing the online edition, please e-mail customer-service@safaribooksonline.com.